EUROPEAN CIVILIZATION

BASIC HISTORICAL DOCUMENTS

by

PAUL L. HUGHES AND ROBERT F. FRIES

The 214 significant works included in this volume were carefully selected in relation to three primary objectives:

1. The expression contained in the document in relation to the meaning and direction of the overall historical development.
2. The exact contribution of the expression to contemporaneous and succeeding circumstances and developments.
3. The clarity and preciseness of the documentary expression.

Also, a majority of the documents have been closely edited so as to present to the student a short, concise reading which yet contains the full meaning and value of the original statement. Wherever necessary to clarity of meaning and ease of assimilation, new translations have been made, and obsolete words and phrases rejected in favor of those having more acute meaning to today's students.

Originally published as
Readings in Western Civilization

EUROPEAN CIVILIZATION

Basic Historical Documents

by

PAUL L. HUGHES
Professor of History
De Paul University

and

ROBERT F. FRIES
Professor of History
De Paul University

Originally published as
Readings in Western Civilization

1972

LITTLEFIELD, ADAMS & CO.
Totowa, New Jersey

First Edition, 1956

Reprinted 1960, 1962, 1964, 1966, 1972

Library of Congress Catalog Card No. 56-14228

Printed in the United States of America

FOREWORD

The use of documents and significant readings in the classroom is by no means a newly discovered method in the teaching and study of the intricate subject matter of history. Every student of history matriculating in the four-year program directed at the attainment of the B.A. degree is subjected sometime in that period, with greater or lesser intensity, to a painful process euphemistically termed "research" wherein the student is sent, hopefully, by the instructor to the endless array of volumes containing an equally endless number of official state papers, important treaties, and significant cultural, economic, political, and sociological expressions. The fruit of such effort all too often is the matching of the student's ultimate boredom by the instructor's frustration; for the very often tenuously stated, but highly significant, meaning of any document is completely obscured to the student by lack of acute personal direction and explanation. Even where the better-than-average student is motivated by more than average desire to gather, in a usable way, data for interpretation, analysis, and discussion, there remains the almost insurmountable barrier of the student's lack of editorial experience and ability. Few students are able to lift out of the context of overly verbose translations of medieval documents or legalistically worded Parliamentary Bills the exact implication of the document or the true intent of the legislator. Thus the bountiful abstractions which constitute the primary essence of the history of western civilization are the very elements which become repugnant to the student.

This volume is dedicated to an attempt to overcome such inherent problems in the study of European history from the period of the Roman Imperial expression to the modern period by first and second year college students, the group normally receiving classroom instruction in any of the various historical survey courses falling under the general heading of Western Civilization.

Nor is this approach of presenting abbreviated documents in mass quantity in European history to such students a new departure in methodology. The basic principles were worked out and pioneered in application with great success by Professor

George L. Mosse* at the University of Iowa a number of years ago, and reapplied with certain modifications more recently at De Paul University with equally pleasing results. In both cases it was believed that students and documents could be brought into juxtaposition in such a way as to cause beneficial intellectual combustion.

With reference to the present volume each of the works included has been carefully considered in relation to three primary objectives;

1. The expression contained in the document in relation to the meaning and direction of the over-all historical development.
2. The exact contribution of the expression to contemporaneous and succeeding circumstances and developments.
3. The clarity and preciseness of the documentary expression.

Also, a majority of the documents have been closely edited so as to present to the student a short, concise reading which yet contains the full meaning and value of the original statement. Wherever necessary to clarity of meaning and ease of assimilation, new translations have been made, and obsolete words and phrases rejected in favor of those having more acute meaning to today's students.

The editors wish to express great appreciation to Professor Margaret Neville for her editorial labors and suggestions, without which this work might well have languished incomplete. The editors retain full claim to all shortcomings.

Paul Hughes
Robert Fries

* See: G. L. Mosse, "Freshman History: Reality or Metaphysics?" *The Social Studies* (March 1949), pp. 1–5.

TABLE OF CONTENTS

PAGE

UNIT 5. THE REFORMATION AND NEW POLITICAL CONCEPTS *(continued)*

UNIT 6. THE CONSEQUENCES OF THE DEVELOPMENT OF THE COMMERCIAL MIDDLE CLASS: MERCANTILISM AND ABSOLUTISM

EUROPEAN CIVILIZATION
BASIC HISTORICAL DOCUMENTS

UNIT 1

Roman Empire

The failure of the political and social institutions of the Roman Empire was cumulative and progressive rather than abrupt or sudden. Devastating as the catastrophe of any particular barbarian invasion might have been, none, nor all in combination, was sufficient alone to destroy the cultural heritage that Imperial Rome was to pass on to later European civilization. This was in great part true because of the new concepts and the fresh patterns of human values that were being formed and polished by other, newer, and more volatile institutions which had been fostered and protected within the confines of the Empire.

Christianity and the German culture, each on the defensive against enemies peculiar to itself, were to become the primary transmitters of the Roman way to ourselves. And, in the process of retaining that which was essentially Roman, both *Germania* and the Christian Church added each its own particular flavor to the fund of human knowledge and experience which it passed on to more modern times.

However, the immediate problem for students of this period of history is primarily concerned with the answer to the question: *Why* did the Roman Empire fall?

As in the case of all historical questions of significance, the answer lies in the realm of possibilities. Many partial and conflicting answers have been offered; and each contains within itself perhaps part of the truth. Both contemporaneous and historical causes are apparent. The preponderance of evidence, though, leads to the inevitable conclusion that the historical factors played a dominant role in the destruction of Roman civilization. If this is true, it is logical to accept the further fact that the so-called "fall" of the Roman Empire was merely a symptom of a broader and more inclusive historic development which was, while destructive in the case of Rome, constructive in terms of the cultural gains which would accrue to future peoples.

If it is true that Rome served as a transmitter of culture from the ancient to modern peoples, and that the Christian Church and the German barbarian were to catch up and modify the ideas and concepts as they fell from the Roman grasp, then, indeed, we are fortunate. Within easy reach are many of the records and documents relating to those historic phenomena. The writings of the Roman observer, Tacitus, give us a contemporary view of the Christians and the German barbarians, both within a century of the birth of Christ. Also, we may gain fresh insight into the social problems precipitated by the existence of the Christians, who did not accept the pagan theology of Emperor-worship from such documents as Trajan's letter to Pliny the Younger.

Later, in the early 5th century, when the Roman people, beset by the unrest which foreshadowed the great invasions from the North, turned on the Christians as having been responsible for their difficulties, Augustine, the defender of early Christianity, turned the bitter scorn of a mind trained in the law and dialectics on them; and for the first time in the modern world set down the precept that Rome's history, not her immediate circumstances, was productive of her difficulties. Nor did Augustine stand alone in his indictment of Rome's loss of ancient principles and traditional precepts. Salvian, a few years later in a candid—and even brutal—appraisal set the Romans down as inferior in every cultural way to the peoples of the Rhine and Danube valleys against whom they would soon be in contention for control of the West. And already, while the debate raged in the capital, the shadow of a more terrifying problem was beginning to spread over northern Europe. From the Baltic region and the bleak Scandinavian peninsula the Vikings were beginning the first of a series of raids that would, by the 9th century, result in the near annihilation of the culture of central Europe.

However, institutions which develop only after many centuries of human effort are not easily eradicated; and even though beset by internal and external problems and suffering the cumulative and stultifying effects of immediate and historic defects, the Roman Empire, dominated by the beginning of the 6th century by its eastern component, was still sufficiently strong to make one last violent attempt at regaining its lost status. Emperor Justinian of Constantinople was able, at terrible cost in treasure and human misery, to bring the two portions of the Empire into homogeneous relationship. Yet this reconquest served only to prove that an empire which reached from Spain to Persia was as much a mistake in the 6th century as it had been in the time of the Caesarian dismemberment. Even while Justinian was failing in his quest for political unity a new movement was making ready to guarantee a different kind of agreement among the parts; for the 6th century in western Europe was to produce the Monastic movement. Also, this same period which produced the brilliant codification of the Roman law by Justinian and Tribonian in the eastern capital gave us the earliest record of another rival system of law in the West—the common law of the early English peoples. The *Anglo-Saxon Chronicle,* though not primarily intended as a code of law, includes the "dooms," or customary law, of the German tribes who conquered the island and laid the groundwork of the English nation.

Caesar's Description of German Tribal Life
(Julius Caesar, *Gallic Wars,* 57 B.C.)

The customs of the Germans differ much from those of the Gauls in that they do not have Druids to preside over religious services, nor do they care much for sacrifices. They hold as gods only things which they cannot see or examine closely, and yet whose benevolent influence is plainly observable, such as the sun and the moon. They seem never to have heard even of any other gods. Their whole life consists of war and hunting, and from childhood they are taught hard labor and to endure cruel conditions of every sort. Those who remain longest in celibacy are held in the highest esteem, and they believe that one's physical stature is increased by it, and that it adds strength and muscles to the body. Indeed, to have had intercourse with a woman prior to the age of 20 is a thing of great disgrace, and one could not possibly conceal such an act because they bathe together naked in the rivers and cover the body ordinarily only scantily with the hides of small animals so that much of the body is bare.

They are not much given to planting and reaping, living mostly on milk, cheese, and flesh, and none claims any specific piece of land as his own possession. Every year the tribal leaders parcel out the land to the clans and to bands of blood relatives who use it for one season and are then forced to take a different piece for another year. They extend many reasons for this; so that they will not lose their appetite for war by continually cultivating the soil to the exclusion of all else, or that they might not grow overly interested in acquiring large possessions, and that they may not come to such attachment for wealth that the strong drive the weak from their land, that they never come to build so well against cold and heat that they become unfit for the rigors of war. For these reasons they try to see that each man's wealth is equal to that of any other man.

It is a matter of great pride to the tribes to lay waste the borders of their territory as great a distance as possible and to make them thus unfit for habitation. They consider it a tribute to their strength when neighboring tribes are forced to retire from their lands and when none dares enter there. Also, they hold that such makes them more secure as it removes the fear of sudden attack or invasion. When a tribe is either repelling an invasion or attacking an enemy, magistrates are chosen to lead them in war. Each magistrate so chosen has full power of life and death. Yet in time when there is no war they have no magistrate except the chiefs of the areas which see to the division of land and minister justice and settle disputes. Robbery, if done outside the borders of the tribe, carries with it no ill repute for it is done with the intent of exercising the youth and thus preventing idleness. When any of the chiefs has stated in a tribal assembly that he is going to be the leader of a foray or attack against an enemy and invites any who would go to accompany him to go along, they who approve the raid hold up their hands and promise their assistance and are given great applause by the people. Those who do not follow him are considered traitors and cowards and after that no one will place any faith in them.

To violate the rights of hospitality they hold to be a crime; whoever comes to them for any reason whatever, they protect from injury, holding them sacred. Everyone's domicile is free to such and they are furnished what they need so long as they remain.

Tacitus Describes the Persecution of the Christians by Nero (Tacitus, *Writings,* A.D. 97)

Therefore, to check the rumor that he was responsible for the burning of the City, those who were called Christians by the mob and hated for their moral enormities, were substituted in his place as culprits by Nero and afflicted with the most exquisite punishments. Christ, from whom the name was given, was put to death during the reign of Tiberius, by the procurator Pontius Pilate. Although checked for the time, this pernicious superstition broke out again not only in Judea, where the evil originated, but throughout the City, in which the atrocities and shame from all parts of the world center and flourish. Therefore those who confessed were first seized; then on their information a great multitude were convicted, not so much of the crime of incendiarism, as of hatred of the human race. The victims who perished also suffered insults, for some were covered with the skins of wild beasts and torn to pieces by dogs, while others were fixed to crosses and burnt to light the night when daylight had failed. Nero had offered his gardens for the spectacle and was giving a circus, mingling with the people in the dress of a driver, or speeding about in a chariot. Although they were criminals who deserved the most severe punishment, yet a feeling of pity arose since they were put to death not for the public good but to satisfy the rage of an individual.

The Earliest Evidence of the Growth of the Comitatus (Personal Dependence) (Tacitus, *Germania,* A.D. 98)

They will do no undertaking unless they be armed, even public or private. Yet no man may assume armaments till the Tribe shall have seen him in them and recognized that he be most able to use them. Only then some chief or perhaps his father, in full council, put the arms on him, that is, shield and spear. This is similar to the taking of the toga by Roman Youths as their beginning honor. Heretofore the boy was no more than a member of a household; now he is a member of the tribe. Great rank or the better services of their ancestors secures for even mere boys the title and rank of Chief. They attach themselves to older chiefs who are of valor, and are looked upon, with respect, as belonging to the older man. It is great honor and a way of strength to secure a large group thus, and he who has the many bravest followers is most honored; for they beautify in peace and are great aid in war. Such a strongly followed chief is courted by foreign agents and given by all many gifts for he often is able in his great renown to decide issues and wars.

When in battle it is dishonor for the Leader to be outdone or matched in deeds of courage; and for the followers not to match the showing of their chief, and for any of the followers to survive his Chief and come from the battle alive is infamy and reproach. They most sacredly swear allegiance to him, to defend and protect him. The Leader fights for victory, they for him. If the tribe loses its cause for war, or taste for it, the youths at once seek other tribes that are more warlike. A life of peace is bothersome to the Germans, and a large following cannot be provided except by violence and struggle. To the Chief they look for their horse and spear. Food is their mere pay; the way for their bounty and riches is provided through war and conquest. Too, they could not be made to cultivate soil. No! They think it foolish and dull to get by their sweat what they can get instead with their blood.

Edict of the Emperor Galerius Granting Religious Toleration to the Christians of the Empire

(Lactantius, *De Mortibus Persecutorum,* 311)

Amongst our other measures for the advantage of the Empire, we have hitherto endeavored to bring all things into conformity with the ancient laws and public order of the Romans. We have especially been anxious that even the Christians, who have abandoned the religion of their ancestors, should return to reason. For they have fallen, we know not how, into such perversity and folly that, instead of adhering to those ancient institutions which were possibly established by their own forefathers, they have arbitrarily made laws of their own and collected together various peoples from various quarters.

After publication, on our part, of a decree commanding the Christians to return to the observance of the Ancient Custom, many of them, it is true, submitted in view of the danger, while many others suffered death. Nevertheless, since many of them have continued to persist in their opinions and we see that in the present situation they neither duly adore and venerate the gods nor yet worship the god of the Christians, we, with our wonted clemency, have judged it wise to extend a pardon even to these men and permit them once more to become Christians and re-establish their places of meeting; in such manner, however, that they shall in no way offend against good public order. . . .

Wherefore it should be the duty of the Christians, in view of our clemency, to pray to their god for our welfare, and for that of the Empire . . . so that the Empire may remain intact in all its parts, and that they themselves may live safely in their habitations.

St. Augustine on the Incapacity of the Pagan Gods, and in Defense of the Christian Religion (Augustine, *City of God,* 426)

In the foregoing book, having begun to speak of the city of God, to which I have resolved, Heaven helping me, to consecrate the whole of this work, it was my first endeavor to reply to those who attribute the wars by which the world is being devastated, and specially the recent sack of Rome by the barbarians, to the religion of Christ, which prohibits the offering of . . . sacrifices to devils. I have shown . . . that for His sake the barbarians, in contravention of all custom and laws of war, threw open as sanctuaries the largest churches, and in many instances showed such reverence to Christ . . . that His servants, and even those who . . . feigned to be so, were exempted from all those hardships which by the custom of war may lawfully be inflicted. . . .

Let them then, along with us, call to mind with what various and repeated disasters the prosperity of Rome was blighted, before ever Christ had come in the flesh, and before His name had been blazoned among the nations with that glory which they vainly grudge. Let them, if they can, defend their gods . . . since they maintain that they worship them in order to be preserved from these disasters, which they now impute to us if they suffer in the least degree. For why did these gods permit the disasters I am to speak of to fall on their worshippers before the preaching of Christ's name offended them, and put an end to their sacrifices?

Moreover, if the Romans had been able to receive a rule of life (Law) from their gods, they would not have borrowed Solon's laws from the Athenians, as they did some years after Rome was founded. . . . Among these regulations were many pertaining to religious observances . . . yet . . . none with respect . . . to moral evils, evils of life and conduct—evils which are so mighty . . . that by them states are ruined—their gods made not the smallest provision for preserving their worshippers from these evils, but, on the contrary, took special pains to increase them, as we have proven. . . .

Now this ruin they did not impute to their own gods, though they impute to our Christ the evils of this life, which cannot ruin good men, be they alive or dead. And this they do, though our Christ has issued so many precepts inculcating virtue and restraining vice; while their own gods have done nothing whatever to preserve that republic that served them, and to restrain it from ruin by such precepts, but have rather hastened its destruction, by corrupting its morality through their pestilent example. No one, I fancy, will now be bold enough to say that the republic was then ruined because of the departure of the pagan gods "from each sacred shrine" . . . had they indeed departed, the Romans would never . . . have been so far transported by their own passions as they were by the instigations of these gods. . . .

Rome never was a Republic, because true justice had never a place in it . . . the fact is, true justice has no existence save in that Republic whose founder and ruler is Christ. . . .

Salvian Compares the Barbaric Culture with the Failing Roman Way of Life (Salvian, *Of God's Government,* 440)

In what respect can our customs be preferred to those of the Goths and Vandals, or even compared with them? To speak of affection and charity, almost all barbarians, at least those who are of one race and kin, love each other, while the Romans persecute each other. For what citizen does not envy his fellow citizen? What citizen shows to his neighbor full love and charity? And it is even worse than that; for the many are mistreated by the few, who regard public exactions as their own peculiar right, who carry on private traffic under the guise of collecting the taxes. And this is done not only by nobles, but by the judges and their subordinates. For where in the Empire is the city—or even the town or village—which has not as many tyrants as it has curiales? What place is there, therefore, where the substance of widows and orphans, or even saints, is not devoured by the chief citizens?

Even those in a position to protest against the iniquity which they see about them dare not speak lest they make matters worse than before. So the poor are despoiled, the widows sigh, the orphans are oppressed, until many of them, born of Roman families, and educated, flee to our enemies that they may no longer suffer the oppression of public persecution. They doubtless seek Roman humanity among the barbarians because they cannot bear barbarian inhumanity among the Romans.

So they migrate to the Goths, or to the Burgundians, or to some other tribe of barbarians who are ruling everywhere, and do not regret their exile. For they would rather live *free* under an appearance of slavery than live as captives under an appearance of liberty. The name of Roman citizen, once so highly esteemed and so dearly bought, is now a thing that men repudiate and flee from.

A Fifth Century Description of the Norsemen (Apollinaris Sidonius, *Epistulae,* 480)

Everyone of them is a great pirate; with such wonderful cohesion, all together obey, command, teach, and learn their chosen work, brigandage. . . .

Our enemy is the most vicious of enemies. He attacks without warning, destroys those who block his path or who are not on guard; he always cuts off the escape of his enemy, while never failing to escape himself. Too, to these men shipwreck is merely an exercise—never a terror. The danger of the seas is not counted as a mere acquaintance but as an intimate friend, since it is that a storm of winds slackens the defences of the invaded and prevents the invader from being seen from a distance. They hail with great joy the clashing of waves on rocks since it gives them chance to escape enemies.

The Institutes of the Emperor Justinian (*Corpus Juris Civilis,* 529)

The Law of Nature is that which she has taught all animals, a law not peculiar to the human race. . . . Hence comes the union of male and female, which we call marriage or matrimony, the procreation of children, the rearing of children. . . .

The Civil Law of Rome, and the law of all nations differ from each other therein. . . . Those rules which a state enacts for its own members are peculiar to itself and are called Civil Law; those rules prescribed by natural reason for all men are called the laws of nations . . . these are then also Laws of Nature. . . .

By the law of nature all men from the beginning were born free, (yet) when the Roman people had been so increased that it was difficult to assemble together for the purpose of enacting statutes, it seemed right that the Senate should be consulted instead of the whole people. Again, what the Emperor determines has the force of law, the people having conferred on him all their authority and power by the *lex regia*. . . .

Consequently, whatever the Emperor settles by rescript, or decides . . . or ordains by edict, is clearly a statute; and these are called constitutions. . . .

The whole of the law relates either to persons, or to things, or to actions. And first let us speak of persons; for it is useless to know the law without knowing the persons for whose sake it was established.

Concerning Pater Potestas (Paterfamilia). Roman citizens are joined together in lawful wedlock when they are united according to law, the man having reached the age of puberty and the woman of marriageable age. . . . They must have the consent of the parents in whose power they are. . . .

Not only natural children are subject to paternal power but also adoptive children.

The power which we have over our children is peculiar to the citizens of Rome; for no other people have a power over their children such as we have over ours.

The child born to you and your wife is in your power. And so is the child born to your son by his wife, that is your grandson or granddaughter, and all other descendants. But a child born to your daughter is not in your power but in the power of its own father.

Concerning Property and Ownership. Things become private property in many ways; for the titles by which we acquire ownership in them are . . . titles of natural law. . . .

Some things are corporeal, and others incorporeal. Those are corporeal, which in their own nature are tangible, such as land, clothing, gold, silver, and others innumerable. Things incorporeal are such as are intangible, rights, for instance, such as inheritance, usufruct, and obligations, however acquired. (These are immutable).

The Monastic Rule of St. Benedict (Migne, *Patrologia Latina,* 550)*

The eighth degree of humility is for a monk to do nothing except what the common rule of the monastery or the example of his seniors impel him to do. The ninth degree of humility is for a monk to restrain his tongue from speaking, and, keeping silence, not to speak until he is spoken to. The tenth degree of humility is for him not to be ready and easily inclined to laugh. . . . The eleventh degree of humility is for a monk, when he speaks, to do so slowly and without laughter, humbly and seriously, using few and only reasonable words, and for him not

* Translated by George L. Mosse, in *History of Western Civilization,* 1950. Used with the permission of the translator.

to be loud of voice. . . . The twelfth degree of humility is for a monk, not only in his heart but with his whole body, to show humility to all who see him, that is to say, when at work, or at prayer, in the monastery, in the garden, on the road or in the fields. Everywhere, sitting or walking or standing, let him always have his head bowed, his looks fixed upon the earth, remembering every hour that he is guilty of his sins. . . . Let him think that he is already being brought before the dread Judgment of God, saying always to himself within his heart what the publican in the Gospel, his eyes fixed upon the ground, said, "Lord, I am not worthy, being a sinner, so much as to lift up mine eyes unto Heaven". . . .

The monk should possess absolutely nothing, neither book, nor tablets, nor pen, nothing at all. For, indeed, monks are not allowed to have their own bodies or wills under their own control. But they must look to the Abbot for everything they need . . . . Everything should be common to them all. . . .

Idleness is the enemy of the soul. Therefore, at certain fixed times the brethren ought to be engaged in manual toil; and at other times in reading sacred books. . . . So that from Easter until the Calends of October, going out early, from the first to about the fourth hour they shall do whatever work has to be done. From the fourth hour until about the sixth, they shall be free to read. After rising from their meal taken at the sixth hour, they shall rest upon their beds in complete silence; though, perhaps, one who wishes to read may read to himself in such a way that he does not disturb the others. The second meal shall be gone through more moderately about the beginning of the eighth hour; and then they shall again work at whatever is to be done until Vespers. . . .

Although at all times the monk's life should be as if Lent were being observed, nevertheless, since few have such virtue, on those said days of Lent he shall keep his life in complete purity, and wipe out, during those holy days, the failings of other times. This is properly done if we refrain from all evil-doing, if we devote ourselves to prayer with weeping, to reading, to repentance of heart, and to abstinence. Therefore, in such days let us add on our own account something extra to the customary amount of our service; special prayers, abstinence from food and drink; so that everyone, over and above the amount allotted to him, shall offer something to God on his own initiative, with rejoicing of the Holy Spirit. . . . But each shall report to the Abbot the offering that he makes, so that it may be done with his prayers and by his will. For what is done without the assent of the spiritual father shall be ascribed to presumption and vain-glory, and not to a monk's credit.

The Early Laws of England, Anglo-Saxon Period
(*Anglo-Saxon Chronicle,* 601–901)

Dooms of Aethelbert (601–04)

These are the dooms of King Aethelbert established in the days of Augustine.

One who steals the property of God and the Church shall pay twelvefold compensation; the property of a bishop, elevenfold; the property of a priest, ninefold; he who breaks the peace . . . of a public assembly, doublefold.

If the King is drinking in a man's house, and if anyone commits any kind of misdeed there, he shall pay double compensation to the householder.

If a man slays another in a villa of the king, he shall pay 50s compensation to the king.

If a man slays another, he shall pay as compensation to the kindred the ordinary *wergeld* of 100s.

Dooms of Hlothaere and Eadric (685–86)

If someone's servant slays a man of noble birth, one whose *wergeld* is 300s, his master shall give up the slayer to the kindred and also pay them the value of three ordinary men.

If, where men are drinking, one draws his weapon but inflicts no injury with it, he shall pay ls to the householder and 12s to the king.

If the house is bloodied, he shall pay the *mundbyrd* (fee) to the householder, and to the king a fine of 50s.

Dooms of Wihtraed (695–96)

The word of a bishop or of the king shall be incontestable even without an oath.

A priest shall clear himself by his own affirmation; dressed in his sacred garments, he shall declare before the altar, *Veritatem dico in Christo; non mentior* (Before Christ I speak the truth;

I do not lie).

An ordinary freeman shall clear himself at the altar with three oath-helpers of his own rank. . . .

If anyone slays a man in the act of theft, let him lie without *wergeld.*

If a man coming from afar, or a stranger, leaves the highway and neither calls out nor blows a horn, he shall be considered a thief, to be slain. . . .

Dooms of Ine (688–95)

I, Ine, . . . King . . . with the *Witan* in counsel . . . ordain. . . .

If anyone wreaks vengeance on his enemy before demanding justice in court, he shall give back anything he has seized together with as much again, and shall pay 30s to the King.

If a nobleman holding land neglects army service, he shall pay 120s and forfeit his land; one who holds not land shall pay 60s. . . .

Dooms of Alfred (871–901)

I, King Alfred, have collected these dooms and ordered them to be written down. . . . I . . . have shown these dooms to all my *Witan,* who have declared it is the will of all that they be observed. . . .

If anyone plots against the king's life . . . he shall forfeit his life. . . .

If anyone fights or draws his weapon in the King's hall . . . he may be put to death. . . .

If anyone at court brings an accusation for theft . . . let him make his proof . . . if he cannot, he shall pay a fine. . . .

We . . . ordain that anyone who has land left him by his kinsmen is not to give it outside his kindred if there be written or oral evidence that to do so was forbidden by the man who originally . . . gave it to him.

Anglo-Saxon Chronicle (552–605)

A.D. 552. This Cynric fought with the Britons at the place which is called Old Sarum, and he put the Britons to flight. Cerdic was Cynric's father, Cerdic was the son of Elesa, Elesa of Esla, Esla of Gewis, Gewis of Wig, Wig of Freawin, Freawin of Frithogar, Frithogar of Brond, Brond of Beldeg, Beldeg of

Woden.

A.D. 555. In this year Aethelbert, the son of Ermenric, was born, who on the two and thirtieth year of his reign, received the rite of baptism, the first of all the kings of Britain. . . .

In this year Aethelbert succeeded to the kingdom of the Kentish people, and held it fifty-three winters. In his days the holy pope Gregory sent us baptism; that was in the two and thirtieth year of his reign. And Columba the mass-priest came to the Picts and converted them to the faith of Christ. They are dwellers by the northern mountains; and their king gave him the island which is named Ii (Iona), where there are five hides, from what men say. There Columba built a monastery; and he was abbot there thirty-two winters, and there died when he was seventy-seven winters; his inheritors yet have the place. The south Picts had been baptized long before; to them bishop Nina, who had been taught at Rome, preached baptism, whose church and his monastery are at Whiterne, hallowed in the name of St. Martin; there he rests with many holy men.

A.D. 596. In this year pope Gregory sent Augustine to Britain with a great many monks, who preached the word of God to the Angles.

A.D. 605. In this year pope Gregory died, ten years after he had sent us baptism. His father was called Gordian, and his mother Silvia. And in this year Ethelfrith led his army to Chester, and there slew innumerable Welsh; and so was fulfilled the prophecy of Augustine, which he uttered: "If the Welsh refuse peace with us, they shall perish at the hands of the Saxons." There were also slain two hundred priests who came thither that they might pray for the army of the Welsh. Their chief was called Brocmail, who escaped thence with some fifty.

A Contemporary Account of the Early English Christian Church (Bede, *Ecclesiastical History: The Council of Whitby,* 664)

Then Wilfrid, being ordered by the king to speak, delivered himself thus: "The Easter which we observe, we saw celebrated by all at Rome, where the blessed apostles, Peter and Paul, lived, taught, suffered, and were buried; we saw the same done in Italy and in France, when we traveled through those countries for pilgrimage and prayer. We found the same practised in Africa, Asia, Egypt, Greece, and all the world, wherever the Church of Christ is spread abroad, through several nations and tongues, at one and the same time: except only these and their accomplices in obstinacy, I mean the Picts and the Britons, who foolishly, in these two remote islands of the world, and only in part even of them, oppose all the rest of the universe. . . ."

To this Colman rejoined: "Did Anatolius, a holy man, and much commended in Church History, act contrary to the law and the Gospel, when he wrote, that Easter was to be celebrated from the fourteenth to the twentieth? Is it to be believed that our most reverend Father Columba and his successors, men beloved by God, who kept Easter after the same manner, thought or acted contrary to the Divine writings? . . . .

" It is evident", said Wilfrid, ". . . concerning your Father Columba and his followers, whose sanctity you say you imitate . . . It is much more just to believe what is good, than what is evil, of persons whom one does not know. . . . Nor do I think that such keeping of Easter was very prejudicial to them, as long as none came to show them a more perfect rule. . . .

"But as for you and your companions, you certainly sin, if, having heard the decrees of the Apostolic See, and of the universal Church, and that the same is confirmed by Holy Writ, you refuse to follow them. For though your Fathers were holy, do you think that their small number, in a corner of the remotest island, is to be preferred before the universal Church of Christ throughout the world? And if that Columba of yours (and, I may say, ours also, if he was Christ's servant), was a holy man and powerful in miracles, yet could he be preferred before the most blessed Prince of the Apostles, to whom our Lord said, 'Thou art Peter, and upon this rock I will build my Church, and the gates of hell shall not prevail against it; and to thee I will give the keys of the kingdom of heaven. . . . ?' "

This disputation happened in the year of our Lord's incarnation 664, which was the twenty-second year of the reign of King Oswy.

UNIT 2

The Development and Expansion of Feudal Institutions and Ideas

It is apparent that at the beginning of the 6th century Rome was no longer able to offer political or intellectual leadership to the peoples of the West; and more, that the administrative machinery, so efficient during the Republican and early Imperial periods, was incapable of serving further the variant needs of the newly developing civilization of that area. And yet, this seeming breach of historic continuity did not create a cultural—or even a political—vacuum, for, as need became the stimulant, a hardy and dynamic people, the Franks, facing the problems of existence, took up the position of control and direction vacated by Rome.

The Merovingian dynasty of the Saline Franks was the first to impose effective political and military unity on the people of Gaul. Successful for a century and a half, the Merovingians gave way to the Carolingians, a dynasty which was to produce Charlemagne and the institution of the Holy Roman Empire.

While Merovingian and Carolingian, and Frank and German struggled for supremacy and security against each other and against other non-European invaders and against the Vikings, the Christian Church was being further integrated into its contemporaneous surroundings, and becoming more articulate as a directing force in the political, social, and economic, as well as the purely spiritual life of the people. Nor was this development inconsistent with the historic pattern. Since no other universal institution of equal moral or intellectual capacity existed to extend the necessary directive force, the Church came to be accepted as both a valid and positive influence. This growing realization of unity of Church and State is well exemplified by Pippin's appeal to the Church for the title of King of the Franks, and by such acts as the imposition of peaces and truces of God, in the appointment of Bishops (who were political spokesmen as well as spiritual leaders), and finally in the Pope's crowning of Charles the Great as the Emperor of the Romans in the year 800.

This apparent leadership, or the partnership between the temporal and spiritual arms, was never more clearly demonstrated than it was by Pope Urban II in his speech at Clermont, France, when in 1095 he marked the beginning of a new era in European history by inaugurating the Crusading movement against a non-European people. However, this vast and spirited demonstration of zeal and human greed was also rooted in Europe's past. Since the loss of Roman leadership, Europe, torn by internal disorder and under constant attack by external enemies, had been on the defensive. By the 11th century many of those problems had been solved and Europe was beginning to assume an offensive posture against her tormentors. Urban's speech, which appealed to the religious fervor, the pride, and the cupidity of the West, was the triggering force, not the cause of the Crusades against the Moslem civilization of the East.

It is worth while to point out that the cultural attainment of the Arabic world at the time of the Crusades should not be underestimated. Mohammed, born in Arabia within a decade of Justinian's death, had founded not only a political empire but a whole way of life and culture. While Charlemagne was attempting to construct a simple system of grammar schools in the Courts and Monasteries of his domain, the Moslem universities were applying and studying many of the demonstrable laws of mathematics, chemistry, and physics. Their teachers were transcribing and absorbing the philosophical works of the ancient Greeks, and their merchants were reaching into the far corners of a world as yet unknown to the primitive map makers of the West. Spain had fallen to the followers of Gebel-Tarik as early as the first half of the eighth century, and the military strength of the Eastern Empire was already before Constantinople, the easternmost defense bastion of Christianity. This tremendous cultural expression was in some part possible because Mohammed, the simple camel boy, gave to the Arabian people the two elements vitally necessary to a renaissance: a personal and dynamic concept of the worth of the individual, and a written guide around which to center activity—the *Koran.*

The Failure of the Merovingian Dynasty in 650 (Einhard, *Vita Karoli Magni,* 801)

In ancient times they of the Frank confederation always elected their kings from the Merovingian clan. It is now said that the Merovingian family is ended with Childress III who was cast from the dignity by the instruction of Stephen, the Roman Pope, who had his hair cropped and was sent into a Monastery. This is only partly true—for if the title of King passed from Childress it was only a title, since for many years this family had no power or dignity except the name of King.

This situation had grown from this: The Major Domo, or the Mayor of the Palace had always grown great in power usurped from the King until finally it was he who was supreme and the King had nothing and must rest satisfied with his title, his beard, and his long locks. Yet, without power, he was still seated on a throne and seemed to carry on the tasks of state and receive and send missions. This was not of his own authority, but on that of the Mayor who really commanded.

The only thing other than the meaningless title of King he had was his small income which the Mayor gave him from time to time and his plot of ground where he had a few servants. When he must move from the land to the castle for his empty services he went in an ox-cart which was led by a field worker, but he had no more than this and no real power in the state.

The Social Teachings of Mohammedanism (The *Koran*, c. 650)

O ye who do believe! eat of the good things wherewith we have provided you, and give thanks unto God if it be Him ye serve. He has only forbidden for you what is dead, and blood, and flesh of swine . . . and with filth polluted and contaminated. . . .

Thus . . . have their gods made seemly to many of the idolators the killing of their children, to destroy them . . . but to please God they would not have done it. . . .

When the sun is folded up,
And when the stars do fall,
And when the mountains are moved,
And when souls shall be paired with bodies,
. . . the child who was buried alive shall be asked
for what sin she was slain.

Those who devour by usury shall not rise again, save as he riseth whom Satan hath paralyzed with a touch; and that is because they say "selling is only like usury", but God has made selling lawful and usury unlawful . . . for . . . God shall blot out usury. . . .

O ye who believe! approach not prayer while ye are drunk, until ye well know what ye say; nor yet while filthy . . . until ye have washed yourselves. . . . But if ye are sick, or on a journey, or one of you from the privy . . . and ye cannot find water, then use good surface (dirt or sand) and wipe your faces and your hands therewith. . . .

O ye who believe! if ye engage to one another in a debt for a stated time, then write it down . . . and let him who owes dictate and let the scribe write it down faithfully as God taught him . . . but if he who owes be a fool, or weak, or cannot dictate himself, then let his agent dictate faithfully, and let them call two witnesses. That is more just in the sight of God. . . .

On Religion

God has made the Kaabah, the sacred House, to be a station for men. . . .

Fight in God's way with those who fight with you . . . God loves not those who do transgress.

Kill them wherever ye do find them, and drive them out from whence they drive you out; for sedition is worse than slaughter; but fight them not by the Sacred Mosque until they fight you there; then kill them, for such is the recompense of those that disbelieve. . . .

But fight them that there be no sedition and that the religion may be God's. . . .

When your Lord inspired the angels—"Verily, I am with you; make ye firm then those who believe; I will cast dread into the hearts of those who misbelieve—strike off their necks then, and strike off from them every finger tip."

That is, because they went into opposition against God and His Apostle . . . O ye who believe! when ye meet those who misbelieve in swarms, turn not from them. . . . Ye did not slay them, but it was God . . . nor didst thou shoot . . . but God did.

An Early Example of Papal Authority and Influence in the Choice of Kings in 752
(Einhard, *Annals,* 789)

In the year as stated Pippin sent ambassadors to Pope Zacharias to ask his opinion in the matter of the kings of the Franks, who, though of the royal line, and called kings, enjoyed in truth no power in the realm except that official documents were issued in their name. Otherwise they were destitute of power, and did only what the mayor of the palace told them.

Pope Zacharias, therefore, in virtue of apostolic authority, told the ambassadors that he judged it better and more expedient that he should be king and be called king who had the power rather than he who was falsely called king.

The said pope accordingly enjoined the king and the people of the Franks that Pippin, who already exercised the regal power, should be called king and raised to the throne.

And this was done by St. Boniface, the archbishop, who anointed him king in the city of Soissons. And so it came to pass that Pippin was called king, while Childress was shaven and sent to the monastery.

In the next year Pope Stephen came to King Pippin in the town which is called Kiers, to ask protection for himself and the Roman Church from the attacks of the Lombard peoples.

And in that year, but one added, after King Pippin had assured him that he would defend the Roman church, Stephen consecrated him to the honor of the royal dignity, and with him also his two sons, Karl and Carloman. . . .

Charlemagne Commands that the Local Church Authorities Establish Schools
(Einhard, *Annals,* 789)

Although it is better to do the right than know it, nevertheless knowledge should precede action. Therefore, each one ought to study what he would accomplish, so that the mind may better know what ought to be done of right. Therefore, we exhort you not to neglect the study of letters.

And further, let the ministers of the altar of God adorn their ministry by good manners, and likewise the other orders who observe a rule, and the congregation of monks. We implore them to lead a just and fitting life, just as God himself commanded in the gospel.

Let them join and associate to themselves not only children of servile condition, but also sons of freemen. And let schools be established in which boys may learn to read. Correct carefully the Psalms, the signs in writing, the songs, the calendar, the grammar, in each monastery or bishopric, and the Catholic book; because often men desire to pray to God properly, but they pray badly because of the incorrect books. And do not permit mere boys to corrupt them in reading or writing. If there is need of writing the Gospel, Psalter, and Missal, let men of mature age do the writing with all diligence.

Charlemagne Establishes the Institution of the *Missi Dominici* (Einhard, *Annals,* 801)

The most serene and most Christian lord Emperor Charles has chosen from his nobles the wisest and most prudent men, archbishops, and some other bishops also, together with venerable abbots and educated laymen and men of the law, and has sent them throughout his whole kingdom; through them he would have all the various classes of persons live strictly in accord with the law.

Moreover, where anything which is not right and just has been enacted in the law, he has ordered them to inquire into this most closely and to inform him of it that it might be made right again.

And let these *missi dominici* themselves make diligent investigation whenever any man claims that an injustice has been done to him by any one, just as they desire to deserve the grace of God and to keep their fidelity, so that in all cases, everywhere in the realm, they shall, in accordance with the will of God, administer the law fully and justly; and especially in cases pertaining to the poor, wards and widows, and of the lower orders of the people. And if there shall be anything of such a nature that they, together with the provincial counts, are not able to correct, they shall, without any reservations, refer this, with their reports, to the Emperor. And they must take good care that justice be not impeded by any one on account of flattery or gifts, or on account of any relationship, or from fear of the powerful.

Concerning Proof by the Process of the Ordeal (*Anglo-Saxon Records and Chancells,* c. 900)

And with regard to the ordeal, according to the commands of God and of the archbishop and of all the bishops, we order that, as soon as the fire has been brought to heat the iron or water for the ordeal, no one shall come into the church except the priest and the man to be tried. And if the ordeal is by iron, nine feet, according to the feet of the man to be tried, shall be measured from the starting post to the final mark. If, on the other hand, it is to be ordeal by water, that shall be heated until it becomes boiling hot, whether the kettle is of iron or of brass, or of lead, or of clay. And if the process is "single" the hand shall be plunged in for the stone up to the wrist; if it is "threefold," up to the elbow. And when the water for the ordeal is ready, two men from each party shall go in and they shall agree that it is as hot as we have ordered.

Then an equal number of men from both parties shall go in and stand along the church on each side of the ordeal, and all of them shall be fasting and shall have held themselves from their wives during the previous night. And the priest shall sprinkle them all with holy water; and he shall give them the Book to kiss and make over them the sign of Christ's cross.

. . . then shall the iron be laid on the starting post. And nothing else shall be said inside the church except a prayer to God Almighty that He disclose the fullness of truth. And after the man has undergone the ordeal, his hand shall be bound up and sealed; and after the third day it shall be inspected to see whether, within the sealed wrapping, it is foul or clean. And if any one breaks these provisions, the ordeal shall be counted a failure for him, and he shall pay a fine of 120s to the King.

Customary Feudal Oaths, c. 1000

Oath of a Man to His Lord

By the Lord before whom this holy thing is holy, I will to (name of Lord) be faithful and true, loving all that he loves and shunning all that he shuns, according to the law of God and the custom of the world; and never by will or by force, in word or in deed, will I do anything that is hateful to him; on condition that he will hold me as I deserve and will furnish all that was agreed between us when I bowed myself before him and submitted to his will.

Oath of an Accuser Before a Court of Law

By the Lord before whom this holy thing is holy, I thus bring my charge with full folkright, without deceit and without malice, and without any guile whatsoever, that stolen from me was this property (description), which I claim I was in possession of.

Oath in Reply to Such Accusation

By the Lord before whom this holy thing is holy, I am guiltless, both in thought and in deed of the accusation made against me by (the accuser).

Oath of an Oath-Helper

By the Lord before whom this holy thing is holy, the oath which (name of swearer), has sworn is clean and without falsehood.

Form of a Feudal Contract Concerning Land and Services

To my great lord, (lord's name), I, (vassal's name):

Since, as was well-known, I had not wherewith to feed and clothe myself, I came unto you and told you my wish, to commend myself to you and to put myself under your protection. I have now done so, on the condition that you shall supply me with food and clothing as far as I shall merit by my services, and that as long as I live I shall perform such services for you as are becoming to a freeman, and never have the right to withdraw from your power and protection, but shall remain under them all the days of my life. It is agreed that if either of us shall try to break this contract he shall pay (a specified amount), and the compact shall still hold. It is also agreed that two copies of this letter shall be made and signed by us, which also has been done.

Charter of Subinfeudation (1121–22)

William Peverel of Dover to Hamund Peverel, his brother, and to William Peverel, his nephew, and to all his faithful men, French and English, as well as to all his friends, both present and future, greetings.

Know that, for his service, I have given to Thurstan, my steward, and to all his heirs Gidding and Daywell, to be held of me and my heirs in fee and inheritance, with *sac* and *soc, toll* and *team,* in wood and in plain, in vill and in street, in fields and in meadows, in waters and in all other places, in return for the service of half a knight. Witnesses:———

The Activities of the Church as a Social Institution (*The Truce of God:* Diocese of Cologne, 1083)

Inasmuch as in our times the Church has been greatly afflicted by tribulations and difficulties, so that tranquility and peace were wholly despaired of, we have endeavored by God's help to aid it. And we have provided this remedy, so that we might to some extent re-establish, on certain days at least, the peace which, because of our sins, we could not make enduring.

Accordingly we have enacted and set forth the following:

Namely, that from the first day of the Advent of Our Lord through Epiphany, and from the beginning of Septuagesima to the 8th day after Pentecost, and throughout the year on every Sunday, Saturday, and Friday, and on the days of Feast for the four Seasons, and on the eve and the day of all Apostles, and on all other days set aside for feast or fast, this decree of truce shall be obeyed; so that both those who travel and those who remain at home may enjoy security and full peace, so that no one may commit murder, arson, robbery or assault, no one may injure another with sword, club, or any kind of weapon, and so that no one be irritated into any wrong in this period none may carry arms, shield, sword, lance, or body armor.

If it be necessary for anyone to travel from here to another place where the Peace is not maintained in any forbidden period it shall be reasonable for him to be armed.

If it shall happen that any castle or house is besieged during the days which are included in the peace, the besiegers shall cease from attack unless they are set upon by the besieged rallying out and are thus compelled to beat the latter back.

And in order that this statute of peace should not be violated by any one rashly or with impunity, a penalty is fixed by common consent; if a freeman or noble violate it—that is—commits murder or wound on anyone, he shall be expelled from our territory and his heirs shall take all his property. His fiefs shall escheat. If his heirs aid him his properties shall be given to the king.

If an unfree man kills a man, he shall be beheaded. If he wounds a man he shall lose a hand. But each may clear himself if accused in the ordeal of cold water. If he flees without trial he shall be permanently excommunicated.

In the case of boys over twelve years breaking the peace—they shall lose one hand by cutting at the wrist. But it is not an infringement of the peace if the Lord King orders an expedition to attack the enemies of the Kingdom.

Wherefore, we exhort all in Christ to guard this necessary contracted peace. Yet in the Church honor and reverence must always be paid to God, so that if a robber or criminal flees there he is not to be seized or killed but is to remain there until by hunger driven out.

The Rule and Way of William the Conqueror in England, a Contemporaneous Account (*Anglo-Saxon Chronicle,* 1087)

A.D. 1087. . . . If any person desires to know what kind of man he was, or what worship he had, or of how many lands he was lord, then will we write about him so as we understood him, who have often looked upon him, and at another time sojourned in his court. The King William about whom we speak was a very wise man, and very powerful, more dignified and strong than any of his predecessors were. He was mild to the good men who loved God, and over all measure severe to the men that gainsayed his will. On that same stead where God granted him that he might subdue England, he reared a noble monastery, and there placed monks, and well endowed it. In his days was the noble monastery in Canterbury built, and also very many others over all England. This land was also plentifully supplied with monks, and they lived their lives after the rule of St. Benedict. . . .

So also was he a very rigid and cruel man, so that no one durst do anything against his will. He had earls in his bonds, who had acted against his will; bishops he cast from their bishoprics, and abbots from their abbacies, and thanes into prison; and at last he spared not his own brother Odo. . . .

Amongst other things is not to be forgotten the good peace that he made in this land; so that a man who had any confidence in himself might go over his realm, with his bosom full of gold unhurt. Nor durst any man slay another man, had he done ever so great evil to the other. And if any common man lay with a woman against her will, he forthwith lost the members that he had sinned with. He truly reigned over England, and by his capacity so thoroughly surveyed it, that there was not a hide of land within England that he knew not who had it, or what it was worth, and afterwards set it down in his Writ. . . .

Certainly in his time men had great hardship, and very many injuries. Castles caused he to be made, poor men to be greatly oppressed. The king was so very rigid, and took from his subjects many a mark of gold, and more hundred pounds of silver, which he took by right and with great unright from his people, for little need. He had fallen into covetousness, and altogether loved greediness. . . . Alas! that any man should be so proud, to so raise himself up, and account himself above all men. May the Almighty God show mercy to his soul, and grant him forgiveness of his sins! These things we have written concerning him, both good and evil, that good men may imitate their goodness, and wholly flee from the evil, and go in the way that leads us to the kingdom of heaven.

The Height of Papal Claims
(*Dictatus Papae,* c. 1090)*

The Roman Church was established by God alone.

The Roman Pontiff alone is rightly called universal.

He alone has the power to depose and reinstate bishops.

His Legate, even if he be of lower ecclesiastical rank, presides over bishops in council, and has the power to give sentence of deposition against them.

He alone has the right, according to the necessity of the occasion, to make new laws, to create new bishoprics, to make a monastery of a chapter of canons, and *vice versa,* and either to divide a rich bishopric or to unite several poor ones.

He alone may use the imperial insignia.

He has the power to depose Emperors.

No general synod may be called without his order.

No action of a synod and no book shall be regarded as canonical without his authority.

His decrees can be annulled by no one, and he can annul the decress of anyone.

He can be judged by no one.

The Roman Church has been and is infallible, according to the testimony of the Holy Scriptures.

By his command or permission subjects may accuse their rulers.

No one can be regarded as Catholic who does not agree with the Roman Church.

He has the power to absolve subjects from their oath of fidelity to wicked rulers.

Pope Urban's Speech at Clermont Concerning the Crusades Against the Moslems
(Robert the Monk, *Urban's Speech,* 1095)

Oh, Franks, race set apart and blessed by God, set apart from all other races by the situation of your country, as well as by your faith, we wish you to know what a grievous cause has led us to your country, and what peril threatens you and all the faithful.

---

* *Bibliotheca rerum Germanicarum* (Trans. by G. L. Mosse, in *Western Civilization,* 1950. Used with the permission of the translator.)

From Jerusalem and the city of Constantinople a terrible tale has come to us, namely, that a race from the kingdom of the Persians, an accursed race, a race alienated from God, has invaded the lands of those Christians and has depopulated the Holy Land by the sword, rapine, and fire; it has led away a part of the captives into slavery and a part it has destroyed by inhuman tortures; it has destroyed the churches of God or taken them for the rites of its own religion. They destroy the altars, after having defiled them. They circumcise the Christians and the blood of the circumcision they either spread on the altars or pour into the baptismal font. When they wish to torture people by a base death, they perforate their navels, and dragging forth their intestines, bind them to a stake; then with whipping they force the victim to walk until the viscera runs forth and the Christian dies. Others they compel to extend their necks, bared, and compete to see which can cut through the neck with a single blow. On whom therefore is the labor of avenging these wrongs if not on you? You, upon whom above other nations God has conferred remarkable glory in arms, courage, and strength to humble those who resist you.

But if you are hindered by love of children, parents and wife, remember what the Lord says in the Gospel, "He that loveth father or mother more than me, is not worthy of me."

Jerusalem is the navel of the world; the land is fruitful above all others, like another paradise of delights. While your land is shut in on all sides by the seas and surrounded by the mountains and is too narrow for your large population; nor does it abound in wealth. Therefore, enter upon the road to the Holy Sepulchre; wrest that land from the wicked race, and subject it to yourselves.

When Pope Urban had said these and other things he so influenced to one purpose the desires of all who were present that they cried out, "It is the will of God! It is the will of God!"

And Urban, lifting his eyes to heaven said, "Unless the Lord God had been present in your spirits, all of you would not have uttered the same cry, therefore, let that be your motto and battle word, "It is the will of God."

Moreover, therefore, whoever shall determine upon this holy work shall make his vow to God as a living sacrifice, and shall wear the sign of the cross of the Lord on his forehead or on his breast. When having fulfilled his vow he returns to his own domain let him place the cross on his back between his shoulders.

UNIT 3

The Crystallization of Medieval Social, Political, and Economic Institutions

By the beginning of the 13th century crusading had become almost a habit with the people of the West. One historian refers to the crusading ideal as a "psychosis." And, indeed, as the Moslem resistance grew in scope, it became ever clearer to the West that the Crusades must fail, if their objectives were to be considered only in terms of territorial conquest. However, the spirit of unrest which pervaded the times in conjunction with man's weakness for use of force in settling disputes was instrumental in giving the Crusades a new purpose.

In the year 1248 a Crusade was declared against the Holy Roman Emperor. Already the heretics of the Albegension sect had suffered at the hands of a superior force because of their political and theological deviation. However, the passion for enforced uniformity which beguiled Europe into turning its weapons on itself could not be maintained at such a pitch. Other problems, organizational, administrative, and economic, presented themselves for solution as Feudal naiveté gave way to greater knowledge and awareness. It is very clear that by the last quarter of the 13th century more modern concepts were beginning to shape and pattern the medieval world. St. Thomas Aquinas, aware of the economic implications of these forces attempted to hold them back by applying the concept of the "just price" to those groups engaged in unbridled pursuit of profit. And it was St. Thomas, too, who reminded man that all authority and truth stemmed from God, and that while men were bound to obey the legitimate authority of monarchs, monarchs, too, were bound to obey the all-pervading authority of God. This was to remain for all time the clearest statement of medieval limitations on political power.

However, if the complex political and moral philosophy of St. Thomas Aquinas is proof that man was making great strides forward in this period, there is evidence of equal weight to make a sound case for his desire to preserve the *status quo*. In the same year that St. Thomas wrote of the "just price" Albertus Magnus set forth a list of recommended medications and cures for illness. Albertus's concept of medicine was as primitive as had been that of his tribal ancestors; in fact most of the cures listed by him in 1260 were those having been in constant use in Europe for at least 1000 years.

While the continental peoples were attempting solutions to the problems engendered by conflicting ideals, the Normans and Saxons and Celts in Britain were, by the 12th century, since they existed in semi-isolated independence of Europe, able to turn a great portion of their energies into constitutional and political channels and with results of extreme significance.

All English monarchs since Alfred the Great had been limited in political expression by the several other components of the Constitution—the Church, the Law, the Nobility, and by their inherent inability to gain control over the rights of private property. The 12th, 13th, and 14th centuries were to emphasize the validity of these limitations, and to expand them within the framework of the common law. The reality of limitations, though, did not serve to maintain the elements of the constitution in unchanging position relative to each other in this period. The aggressiveness of the second estate and the weakness of individual kings sometimes led to an imbalance of forces. Some Kings, according to the strength of their right to the throne, were dominant in the political scene. Some, like Edward II, were forced to give weak charters in order to win and consolidate sufficient public support to maintain the throne. Between 1200 and 1215 the English aristocracy made its strongest bid for attention. Dedicated to the purpose of making monarchy functionable within the feudal frame of references and limitations, but with no intention of destroying its prerogatives, the barons, in 1215, forced a weak but resilient king to sign and accept the *Great Charter*. However, by 1295, when Edward called the "Model Parliament," a new institution was beginning to mature which would one day absorb all prerogative—that of the king as well as that of the aristocracy. By the beginning of the 14th century, Parliament, having displaced the barons of Runnymede, was able to prove its strength by bargaining with the King, and refusing to give supplies unless certain rights were guaranteed in return.

However, it must be remembered, England, like the countries of Europe, was still in the Feudal Age. In 1329 Edward III must still make legal homage to the French king, and in 1350 the medieval guilds were still in essential control of the regulatory processes of English economic production and distribution.

One of the First Attempts at Taxation in England (*Ordinance of the Saladin Tithe,* 1188)

Every one shall give in alms for this year's aid to the land of Jerusalem a tenth of his rents and movables, except the arms, horses, and clothes of knights, and except likewise the horses, books, clothes, vestments, and all sacred furnishings of clergymen, and except the precious stones of both clergymen and laymen.

Moreover, this money is to be collected within each parish in the presence of the parish priest and the archpriest . . . after excommunication has been proclaimed by the . . . bishops . . . of every man who will not lawfully give the aforesaid tenth. . . .

Clergy and knights who have taken the cross, however, shall give nothing toward the said tenth except from their own property and demesnes. . . .

A Papal Attempt to Enforce Church Law on the King of France (*Papal Bull Placing France under Interdict.* Innocent III, 1200)

Let the Churches be closed, and no one be admitted except to baptize infants; let them not be opened except for the purpose of lighting the lamps, or when the priest shall come for the Sacrament for the sick. It is permitted to celebrate the mass one time the week, on Friday, early in the morning, for the purpose of consecration of the Host for the use of the sick, but only one clerk is to be admitted to aid the priest. Let the clergy preach on Sunday in the vestibules of the churches, and in place of the mass let them disseminate the word of God. Let them recite the Hours outside the Churches, where the people do not hear them; if they recite an epistle or a gospel let them beware lest the laity hear them; and let them not permit the dead to be buried, nor let their bodies be placed unburied in the cemeteries. Let them, moreover, say to the laity that they sin and err greatly by burying bodies in the earth, even in unconsecrated ground for in so doing they take to themselves an office pertaining to others. Let them forbid their parishioners to enter churches that may be open in the King's territory and let them not bless the purses of the pilgrims except outside the churches. Let them not celebrate the offices in Passion week, but refrain even till Easter day, and then let them celebrate in private, no one being admitted except the priest; let no one communicate even at Easter, except he be sick to the point of death. During the same week, or on Palm Sunday, let them announce to their parishioners that they may assemble on Easter morning before the Church and there have permission to eat flesh and consecrated bread. Women are expressly forbidden to be admitted into the churches for purification, but are to be warned to gather their neighbors together on the day of the purification and pray outside the church, nor may the women who are to be purified enter even to raise their children to the font until they are admitted by the priest after the expiration of the interdict. Let the priest confess all who desire it in the entrance of the church . . . and not otherwise. . . . Let no vessels of holy water be placed outside the church, nor shall the priests carry them anywhere, for all the sacraments of the church . . . beyond those two which were reserved are absolutely prohibited. Extreme unction . . . may not be given.

The First Charter of English Liberties (*Magna Carta*, 1215)

John, by the grace of God, king of England, etc. . . .

1. We have in the first place granted to God and by this our present charter have confirmed, for us and our heirs forever, that the English Church shall be free and shall have its rights entire and its liberties inviolate. And how we wish that freedom to be observed appears from this, that of our own pure and free will, before the conflict that arose between us and our barons, we granted and by our charter confirmed the liberty of election that is considered of prime importance for the English Church, and we obtained confirmation of it from the lord pope Innocent III. . . .

2. If any one of our earls or barons or other men holding of us in chief dies, and if when he dies his heir is of full age and owes relief, he shall have his inheritance for the ancient relief; namely: (here the ancient and customary price is stated for heirs of barons, earls, knights.)

3. If, however, the heir of any such person is under age and is in wardship, he shall, when he comes of age, have his inheritance without relief and without fine. . . .

4. The guardian of the land of such an heir who is under age shall not take from the land of the heir more than reasonable issues and reasonable customs and reasonable services, and this

without destruction and waste of men or things. . . .

8. No widow shall be forced to marry so long as she wishes to live without a husband; yet so that she shall give security against marrying without our consent if she holds of us, or without the consent of her lord if she holds of another.

9. Neither we nor our bailiffs will seize any land or revenue for any debt, so long as the chattels of the debtor are sufficient to repay the debt. . . .

12. Scutage or aid shall be levied in our kingdom only by the common counsel of our kingdom, except for ransoming our body, for knighting our eldest son, and for once marrying our eldest daughter. . . .

14. And in order to have the common counsel of the kingdom for assessing aid other than in the three cases aforesaid, or for assessing scutage, we will cause the archbishops, bishops, abbots, earls, and greater barons to be summoned by our letters individually; and besides we will . . . summon . . . all those who hold of us in chief—for a certain day. . . .

17. Common pleas shall not follow our court, but shall be held in some definite place.

21. Earls and barons shall be amerced only by their peers, and only according to the degree of the misdeed.

25. All counties, hundreds, wapentakes, and trithings shall remain at the ancient farms (feudal dues) without any increment. . . .

32. We will hold the lands of those convicted of felony only for a year and a day, and the lands shall then be given to the lords of the fiefs concerned.

39. No freeman shall be captured or imprisoned or disseised or outlawed or exiled or in any way destroyed, nor will we go against him or send against him, except by the lawful judgment of his peers or by the law of the land.

50. We will utterly remove from their offices the relatives of Gerard d'Athee, Engelard de Cigogne, Peter and Guy and Andrew de Chanceaux, Guy de Cigogne, Geoffrey de Martigny and his brothers, Philip Marc and his brothers and his nephew Geoffrey, together with all their adherents. . . .

61. Since moreover for the love of God, for the improvement of our kingdom, and for the better allayment of the conflict that has arisen between us and our barons, we have granted all these liberties aforesaid, wishing them to enjoy those liberties by full and firm establishment forever, we have made and granted them

the following security: namely, that the barons shall elect twenty-five barons of the kingdom, whomsoever they please, who to the best of their ability shall observe, hold, and cause to be observed the peace and liberties that we have granted to them and have confirmed by this our present charter; so that, specifically, if we or our justiciar or our bailiffs or any of our ministers are in any respect delinquent toward any one or transgress any article of the peace or the security, and if the delinquency is shown to four barons of the aforesaid twenty-five barons, those four barons shall come to us . . . to explain to us the wrong. . . . And if within a period of forty days, counted from the time that notification is made to us . . . we do not redress the wrong . . . the four barons . . . shall refer that case to the twenty-five barons, and those twenty-five barons, together with the community of the entire country, shall distress and injure us in all ways possible, namely, by capturing our castles, lands, and possessions and in all ways that they can . . . saving our person and the person of our queen and the persons of our children. . . . Moreover, in all the matters entrusted to those twenty-five barons for execution, if perchance the same twenty-five are present and disagree among themselves in some respect, or if certain of those summoned are unwilling or unable to be present, that which the majority of those present may provide or command shall be held as settled and established, just as if all twenty-five had agreed to it. . . .

63. . . . . By the witness of the aforesaid men and many others. Given by our hand in the meadow that is called Runnymede between Windsor and Staines, June 15, in the seventeenth year of our Reign.

John, *Rex*

Monarchial Writs Summoning a Medieval English Parliament (*Writs of Summons,* Edward I, 1295)

The King to the Sheriff of Northampton, greeting.

Whereas we wish to have a conference and discussion with the earls, barons, and other nobles of our realm concerning the provision of remedies for the dangers that in these days threaten the same kingdom—on which account we have ordered them to come to us at Westminster on the Sunday next after the feast of St. Martin in the coming winter, there to consider, ordain, and do whatever the avoidance of such dangers may demand—we command and firmly enjoin you that without delay you cause two knights, of the more discreet and more capable of labour, to be elected from the aforesaid county, and two citizens from each city of the aforesaid county, and two burgesses from each borough, and that you have them come to us on the day and at the place aforesaid; so that the said knights shall then and there have full and sufficient authority on behalf of themselves and the community of the county aforesaid, to do whatever in the aforesaid matters may be ordained, by common counsel; and so that, through default of such authority, the aforesaid business shall by no means remain unfinished. And you are there to have the names of the knights, citizens and burgesses, together with this writ.

Edward, by the Grace of God, King of England, to the venerable father in Christ, Robert, by the same Grace Archbishop of Canterbury and primate of all England, greeting.

Whereas, with regard to certain arduous affairs touching us and our kingdom, as well as you and the other prelates of the same kingdom, which we are unwilling to settle without your presence and theirs, we wish to hold our parliament and to have a conference and discussion with you concerning these matters, we command and firmly enjoin you, in the fealty and love by which you are bound to us, to come to us at Westminster on the first day of the month of August next, or in any case within the third day following at the latest, in order with us to consider the said affairs and to give us your counsel.

The King to his beloved and faithful kinsman, Edmund, earl of Cornwall, greeting.

Whereas we wish to have a conference and discussion with you and with the other magnates of our kingdom to provide ways to meet the dangers that in these days threaten our entire kingdom, we command and firmly enjoin you, in the faith and love by which you are bound to us, to be present in person at Westminster on Sunday next after the feast of St. Martin in the coming winter, in order to consider, ordain, and decide, together with us, the prelates, and the rest of the magnates, and with other inhabitants of our kingdom, how such dangers are to be obviated.

A Norman Charter of Manumission About the Middle of the *Thirteenth Century*
(Usual Form of *Manumission Charter,* c. 1250)

Be it know by these presents, to all who shall come by these writings that Fulbert, by Divine Providence, heir to, and legally seized and holden of Faiure Crossing and the lands and manors thereto pertaining, sends greetings in the Lord.

Item. Further be it known that for certain values and services we have freed from all further servitude and have manumitted Robert, son of Robert of Faiure, whom we held prior as born bondman. From all hold and tenure and servitude we have further freed his children and chattels, so that none after us, in the name of this present bond-hold be able to demand or cause to be exacted any right or claim in the said Robert, his progeny, or properties. But that he remain free and fully quit without any claim of us or of our successors forever.

Item. Further be it known that he and his heirs shall have and hold, fully seized, rents, lands, and fields fallow and in furrow, in Faiure, which were had of our ancestors by his; by giving as did they, merchet fine for the marriage of each of his female children, and usual tallage each year at our demand—and that he further pay to us 30 pence silver for all other exaction, service, and demand; yet this payment being understood to be beyond usual attendance at our Court the year twenty times, Wardship, and the Ordinary Aids.

Item. Further be it known that should Robert, or any of his heirs seized, die without heir legal, the land, buildings, rents and fields fallow and in furrow shall escheat, fully and rightfully, to us and our heirs.

Item. Nor will it be rightful of the seized or his heirs to give, sell, alienate, or mortgage or encumber any possession here named —and such shall void this deed and what is encumbered or alienated shall escheat from then.

Done in the presence of God in the Churchyard before the Priest.

The English Parliament, in Bargaining with the King, Threatens to Withhold Tax Payment Unless Its Desires Are Fulfilled by the King (The *Parliamentary Bill* of 1301)

Bill of the Primates and nobles delivered to our lord King on behalf of the whole community in the Parliament of Lincoln in the year aforesaid;

. . . Thus the said community is of the opinion that, if it please our lord the King, the two charters, of liberties and of the forest, shall henceforth be entirely observed in all particulars.

(King's Response) It expressly pleases the King.

And statutes contrary to the said charters shall be annulled and voided.

(King's Response) It expressly pleases.

And offences and trespasses committed by the King's ministers against the tenor of the said charters and prises extortionately taken without consent or payment, against the form of the lord King's statute made at Westminster during Lent just past, shall henceforth cease.

(King's Response) It expressly pleases.

And henceforth sheriffs shall be answerable for their revenues according to the customary practice . . . which revenues have been and are now to the great improverishment of the people. And sheriffs shall not be placed under increased charges.

(King's Response) It pleases the lord King that in this respect a fit remedy shall be provided by common counsel as quickly as is well possible.

On condition that the aforesaid matters are carried out and firmly established and accomplished, the people of the realm grant him a fifteenth in place of the twentieth recently granted—yet so that all the matters aforesaid are carried out between now and Michaelmas next; otherwise nothing is to be taken.

(King's Response) It expressly pleases.

Edward III, King of England Renders Homage to Philip V, King of France

(Discussion and Form of the *Contract of Homage,* 1329)

The King of England was honorably received by the King of France, and they, with many knights and Peers held at Amiens a half-month and together had several meetings and discussions and builded many statutes.

Yet, I do recall that the King of England swore homage only by his word and did not place his hands in those of the French King or any agent appointed by the French King or Prince of the Church.

Further than that he would not proceed concerning his fealty; since the French King demanded Liege Homage. Indeed, he set upon returning to his realm to seek in the ancient charters how it had been done by his predecessors; and thus in what manner and way he must render Service to the French King.

And the King of France said to he of England,

Kinsman, we would not mislead you in this, but shall wait

until you have returned to your fief and have found in the records of your Fathers what be the manner proper for your Oath.

And the King of England sailed with his Knights to England again.

And King Edward III, having made investigation of the true form of the ancient homage as set for him by use; and as had been demanded of his predecessors for Aquitaine, with the advice of his Curia Regis wrote a letter patented under the Great Seal admitting therein the Services and Homage, and the forms of them, he must by usage do to the King of France. The parchment was carried to the King of France by the special envoys.

The letter stated as follows:

Edward, by the Grace of God, King of England, Lord of Ireland, and Duke of Aquitaine, Greetings.

Be it known that when we Swore at Amiens to the King of France, our Kinsman, he did of us demand full promise of fealty and obedience in liege. We refused because we were unaware of the full way of ancient ways in these matters—and instead we made promise only of Homage in General; stating that we entered such contract in the same manner as our Fathers. Yet, now that we are fully known of the ancient and rightful way we admit by these statements that the Homage we swore to in the court of Amiens to the French King was liege-homage, and that we do justly owe him our full loyalty and fealty. And, in order that there shall never be further misunderstanding about this oath we make full troth for our successors, and hold that that Oath be made in this manner:

The King of England, Duke of Aquitaine shall extend his hands between those of the King of France, and swear,

"I am here become true liege-man to the King, my Lord, as Peer of France."

The French King shall then accept the King of England as the Duke of Guienne and Aquitaine by mouth and hand.

Parliament's Attempt to Overcome the Scarcity of Labor Due to the Plague
(*Statute of Laborers*, 1349)

Whereas late against the malice of servants, which were idle and not willing to serve after the pestilence without taking excessive wages due to their scarcity, it was ordained by our Lord the King, and by the assent of the Prelates and others of his Council, that such manner of servants, as well men as women, shall be bound to serve, receiving salary and wage as accustomed in the twentieth year of the reign of the King; and that the same servants refusing to so serve in such manner shall be punished by imprisonment. Therefore it is ordained and established:

That Carters, Ploughmen, Shepherds and other servants take liveries and wages accustomed in the twentieth year of our reign. And that each serve a whole year, and not by the day.

That none take for the threshing of a quarter of wheat or rye over two pence. Those who refuse to perform shall be put in the stocks by the Lords, Bailiffs, and Constables for three days or more, or sent to the jail until they justify themselves. And if any servant shall run away from his service he shall be put in jail.

That carpenters, masons, and tillers shall not take by the day for their work but in the manner as they were wont to take in times prior.

That cordwainers and shoemakers shall not sell boots nor shoes in any other manner than in the said year 20th. And goldsmiths, saddlers, tanners, tawers, and all artificers be sworn before a Justice to use their offices and crafts as they did in the year 20. And all artisans and sellers shall also sell at a reasonable price.

That the Stewards, Bailiffs, and Constables of the Towns be sworn before the same Justices to inquire diligently of all that come under this ordinance so that all who rebel may be attacked in their person and commanded to prison. And for each refusal to abide by the regulation after the first each so offending shall suffer double pain.

If the Lords of the Towns or Manors presume in any way to come against this ordinance then pursuit shall be made against them, and if any has covenanted before this Ordinance with any to serve for more wages he shall not be bound to pay, nor upon pain shall he presume to pay more.

Since many beggars sound of limb, refuse to work if they can abide on alms, and are holden to sin and vice and robbery and crime, none may for pieties sake alm them; so they are forced into honest labor to get what they need.

Rules for the Leather-Tanning Guild Drawn Up by the Guild Masters of London
(*Guild Charter and Rules,* 1350)

In honor of God, of Our Lady, and of All Saints, and for the growth of peace among the good folks, the leather tanners, we have, by assent of the Mayor, and the Aldermen, ordained the following points:

In first part, the tanners together will find a wax candle, to burn before our Lady in the church of Allhallows, near the City wall.

Also, each person of the trade shall put in the box of the guild such sum as he shall think fit, in aid of maintaining the said candle.

Also, if by any chance anyone of the said trade shall fall into poverty, because of old age or because he cannot work, and have nothing with which to keep himself, he shall have every week from the said box 7 pence, for his support, and after his decease, if he have a wife, she shall weekly for her support also 7 pence so long as she remain unmarried.

And that no stranger shall work in the said trade, or keep house for the same in the city, if he be not an apprentice.

And that no one shall take the apprentice of another to work with him, during his term, unless it be with the permission of his master.

And if anyone of the said guild shall have work in his house that he cannot complete, or if for want of assistance such work shall be in danger of being lost, those of the said trade shall aid him, that so the said work be not lost.

And if anyone of the said guild shall depart this life, and have not wherewithal to be buried, he shall be buried at the expense of their common box. And when anyone of the said trade shall die, all those of the said trade shall go to the vigil, and make offering then.

And that the folks of the guild shall once in the year be assembled in a certain place, convenient thereto, there to choose two men of the most loyal and benefitting of the said trade, to be overseers of work and all things touching the trade for that year.

Also, that all leather skins falsely and deceitfully wrought in their trade which the said overseers shall find on sale in the hands of any person, citizen, or foreigner, within the franchise shall be forfeited and the worker of them shall be fined.

Also, that no one who has not been an apprentice, and has not finished his term of apprenticeship in the said trade, shall be made free of the same trade; unless it be attested by the overseers for the time being that such person is able and skilled to be made free of the same.

Also, that no one shall take for working in the said trade more than is the usual and just price, on the pain of being fined; that is to say, for ten Scotch stag leathers, half mark; for ten Irish stag skins, half mark; for a hundred goat skins, 20 shillings; for a hundred skins of young deer, 8 shillings; and for a hundred skins of young kids, 8 shillings.

Privileges Granted for a Crusade Against Frederick II, Holy Roman Emperor
(Letter: *Innocent IV to The Bishops,* 1248)

Wherefore we advise that publicly in Rome, Campania, and Maratima, you preach a Crusade against the aforesaid Frederick and that you also cause suitable men to preach the Crusade frequently and solemnly. And by your authority grant the remission of sins, which was granted in the General Council to those who went to the succor of the Holy Land, to all those who with fervent zeal choose to undertake a Crusade against the same Frederick in order to aid the Church in rooting out, from the aforesaid Kingdom, the perfidy which flows from its diseased head to the adjacent members, and in restoring there the Faith formerly cherished. And also publish solemnly, and cause others to publish, that the same Frederick and all who aid him by council, succor or favor, in person or property, openly or secretly, are excommunicated by us; and also that the whole Kingdom . . . is placed under an ecclesiastical interdict, as long as it shall adhere to him.

Privileges Granted for a Crusade Against the Heretics in Languedoc, France (Albeginsians)
(Letter: *Innocent III to the Princes of France,* 1207)

Since those who fight for liberty of the Church ought to be fostered by the protection of the Church, we, by our Apostolic authority, have decided that our beloved, who in obedience to Christ are signed—or are about to be signed—against the provincial heretics, from the time that they, according to the ordinance of our legates, place on their breasts the sign of the quickening Cross, to fight against the heretics, shall be under the protection of the Apostolic seal and of ourselves, with their persons and lands, their possessions and men, and also all of their other property; and until full proof is obtained of their return or death all the above shall remain as they were, free and undisturbed.

St. Thomas Aquinas on the "Just Price"
(Thomas Aquinas, *Summa Theologiae,* 1260)

We should consider the sins which have to do with buying and selling in voluntary exchange: first, fraud committed in buying and selling; second, usury taken on loans. . . .In the case of other forms of voluntary exchange no kind of sin is noted which is to be distinguished from rapine or theft. . . .

The value of a thing which is put to human use is measured by the price given; and for this purpose money was invented, as is explained in (Aristotle's) *Ethics.* Hence, whether the price exceeds the value of a thing or conversely, the equality required by justice is lacking. Consequently, to sell dearer or to buy cheaper than a thing is worth is in itself unjust and unlawful.

We speak of buying and selling in another sense, also; namely, the case where it accidently turns out to the advantage of one and to the injury of the other; for example, when a man greatly needs something, and another man is greatly injured if he is deprived of it; in such a case the just price will be one which takes both sides into consideration. And thus a thing may lawfully be sold for more than it is ordinarily worth to its possessor. However, if a man is greatly profited by something he has obtained moderately from another, and the seller does not suffer any loss from doing without it, he ought not to charge more than a usual price for it, since the advantage which accrued to the first man is not due to the seller but to the condition of the buyer. He, however, who derives great benefit from something received from another, may of his own accord pay the seller something in addition to the original price. This is a matter of a man's good honor. . . .

It is the function of traders to devote themselves to exchanging goods. But as the Philosopher says there are two kinds of exchange. One may be called natural and necessary, by means of which one thing is exchanged for another, or things for money to meet the needs of life, and this kind of trading is not the function of traders, but rather of household managers or of statesmen, who have to provide a family or a state with the necessaries of life. The other kind of exchange is that of money for money or of things for money, not to meet the needs of life, but to acquire gain; and this kind of trading seems to be the function of traders, according to the Philosopher. Now the first kind of exchange is praiseworthy, because it serves natural ends, but the second is justly condemned, because, in itself, it serves the desire of material gain. . . .

Usury for money lent is, in itself, unjust, since it is a sale of what does not exist; whereby inequality obviously results, which is contrary to all justice. . . .

Money . . . was devised . . . for the purpose of effecting exchanges; and so the proper and principal use of money is the consumption or alienation of it, whereby it is expended in making purchases. Therefore, in itself, it is unlawful to receive a price for the use of money lent, which is called usury. . . .

The Political Theory of St. Thomas Aquinas
(Thomas Aquinas, *Concerning the Rule of Princes,* 1266)

If it is natural to man to live in a numerous society it is necessary that there should be provision for ruling such a society. Where there are many men and each seeks that which is agreeable to himself, the group will soon fall apart, unless there be some one who cares for those things which concern the good of the aggregate. . . . Moreover, the interests of different people are diverse. It is, therefore, right that in addition to that which works to the private advantage of each there should be something which acts for the common good of the many. . . .

In some pursuits directed toward an end it is possible to proceed rightly or wrongly. There is a right and a wrong way in the government of a multitude. Anything is rightly directed when it is brought to its proper goal, and wrongly when it is guided to an unfitting end. . . . If the government is directed not to the common good, but to the private good of the ruler, then it is unjust and perverted. . . . If an unjust government should be established by one man who in governing seeks his own benefit, and not that of the multitude committed to him, such a ruler is called a tyrant . . . because he coerces with force, instead of ruling with justice. . . .

If just power belongs to one alone, he is properly called King. . . . Thus it is clearly manifest that from the nature of a king he is one who is set above, and that he should be a shepherd seeking the common good of the multitude and not his own.

Since it is fitting for man to live in a multitude because he is not sufficient unto himself with regard to the necessaries of life, the society of the multitude ought to be as much more perfect than life in isolation as it is in itself more sufficient in the necessaries of life. . . .

The aim of any ruler ought to be to secure the safety of that which he has undertaken to rule. . . . It is for this, therefore, that the ruler of a multitude ought especially to strive, that he may obtain the unity of peace. . . . The more efficacious is the government in preserving the unity of peace, the more useful will it be. For we regard that as more useful which leads more directly to a proposed end. And it is clear that unity can be more readily created by that which is one in itself than by a multiple agent. . . . Therefore, the rule of one is more beneficial than the rule of many. . . .

Furthermore, those things which follow nature are best, for in every instance nature operates best. But all natural government is by one. Among the numerous members of the human body, there is one member, the heart, which controls all the others; and in the parts of the soul, one force rules supreme, namely, the reason. There is one king among bees; in the universe there is one God, the creator and ruler of all things. And this is reasonable. For every multitude is derived from one. Wherefore, if things of art imitate things of nature, and a work of art is by so much the better as it achieves similitude to what is in nature, then necessarily a human multitude is best governed by one. . . . Experience proves the same thing. Those provinces . . . which are not ruled by one are beset with dissension and . . . are without any peace. . . . On the other hand, the provinces and states which are ruled by one king enjoy peace, are strong in justice, and rejoice in affluence. Wherefore, the Lord, through His prophets, promised His people, as a great reward, that He would place over them one head, and that there should be one Prince among them. . . .

Medical Cures Recommended by Albertus Magnus
(Albertus Magnus, *Medicines,* c. 1260)*

Epilepsy:

Take some part of the hind leg of a calf, also part of a bone of a human body, from a graveyard; pulverize both, mix the mass well, and give the patient three points of a knife-full. . . .

Colds, an especially approved powder:

Burn the blood and skin of a hare in a new earthen jug;

* Albertus Magnus, *Medicines.* Edited by the de Laurence Publishing Company, Chicago, 1919. (Used with the permission of the de Laurence Publishing Co.)

dissolve the ashes in warm water. Let him take a spoonful before breakfast. It is astonishing what a powerful effect this powder exercises!

Fever, a remedy:

Cut the ear of a cat; let three large drops of blood fall in some brandy; add pepper thereto, and give it to the patient to drink.

Violent toothaches:

Take a new nail; pick the tooth with this till it bleeds; then take this nail and insert it in a place where neither sun nor moon ever shines. At the first stroke upon the nail speak,

"Toothache, fly away;" by the second stroke, "toothache, cease, pain allay."

How to be able to see at night:

Grease the eyes with the blood of a bat.

To ascertain whether a sick person will become well again:

Cut a piece of bread, rub the patient's teeth with it, and throw it before a dog. If he eats it, the patient will recover, if not the disease is dangerous.

Gout:

Take the skull of a corpse, scrape some bone-dust off the cranium with your knife and strew it in the wounds.

To wean a tippler from drinking:

Take an apple, put it in the hand of a dying man, and let the apple remain there till the person dies. If you desire the tippler to drink only half the quantity he usually does, give him only half the apple—but if you wish him to abstain in full give him the full apple. Only let him know nothing about it.

A cure for love:

When you are infatuated and bewitched by a woman so that you may not love another, take blood from a buck and grease your head and soon you will be all right again.

UNIT 4

The Beginning of the Renaissance

The 15th and the 16th centuries presented western civilization with additional problems, for in this period three new historical forces combined to complicate further the already disordered complex of ideas, institutions and customs with which man had to live.

Of the three new factors, the rise of the new nation-states under the national monarchs was perhaps the least significant and the most painful in the immediate sense. In this period a monarch claiming the full loyalty of a whole people was not essentially incompatible with the needs and desires of the rising, commercial middle class, which had few roots in the past and no love for the feudal system of division of rights and responsibilities which placed the middle class in an inferior position and rationalized this repression on grounds that the order to which the individual had been born necessarily decided the degree of his rights and burdens, and that, since the system was inspired by Divine ordination it would be treason against civil society and presumption against God to desire change. "Thou shalt not covet" was the most important of the commandments to the upper orders of medieval society.

However, as the 15th century drew to a close, certain of the states of Europe began to show signs that the ancient bonds were beginning to lose their binding force, and national kings began to emerge from the confusion of claims to power by the many vested interests. France produced its Louis XI; Spain, Isabella and Ferdinand; and England, Henry VII. Thus, in the later middle ages the national ideal was destroying the theoretical unity of western Christendom, while on the other hand the disunited political fragments were being fused into homogenous states under the national kings.

In its early search for freedom of expression the new middle class, dedicated to profit, and accepting the philosophy of materialism, was not the only factor in the production of nationalism and monarchy. Wealth itself gave new time for leisure, and leisure stimulated intellectual pursuits. Such men as Frederick of Urbino led the way in searching out the ancient manuscripts and volumes, the works of the classical scholars, and the Church fathers, and in the humanistic study of the Greek and Hebrew languages so that more knowledge might be added to that already available.

This renaissance of interest and effort was in turn to bring into being an additional, and more ominous area for endeavor. While Vittorino and Castiglione were working out the program for the training of the completely secular gentleman of the Renaissance, Niccolo Machiavelli was in the process of clarifying and applying the amoral philosophy of relativism to political life—a philosophy and an application which would become the basis for national policies in many of the states of western civilization in the next two centuries.

Despite the apparent strides being made in the fields of political organization and in the developments of art and literature, many of the old ideas lived on in Europe. The 15th century came to represent the high point of witch hunting and burning, and the period, too, saw the greatest expression of religious intolerance and the use of the Inquisition as a political weapon by civil governments. It was a century of war and of pestilence, as well as one of intellectual and artistic expansion. In many ways the 16th century was a century of reactionism as had been its predecessor. In 1509 the English political philosopher Edmund Dudley wrote his famous *Tree of Commonwealth,* and in 1500 the Turkish Prince Suleiman the Magnificent wrote his most unflattering but nevertheless presumably true, account of the Christians wherein he termed them liars and cheats and cowards. In this work Suleiman stated that "Everyone of them takes care of himself only"—an extremely interesting observation in the light of the later tendency in the West toward social irresponsibility.

A Contemporary Discussion of the Reformer, Savonarola (1494)
(Philip Commines, *Memoirs of Philip Commines*)

I had almost forgotten to mention that while I was at Florence, on my way to join the king, I went to pay a visit to a certain Dominican, named Friar Jerome, who, by all reports, was a very holy man, and had lived in a reformed convent fifteen years. There went along with me one Jean Francois, a prudent person, and steward of the king's household. The occasion of my going to visit Friar Jerome was that he had always preached much in our king's favor, and his words had served to keep the Florentines from turning against us; for never had any preacher enjoyed so much authority in a city.

In spite of what has been said or written to the contrary, he always affirmed that our king would come into Italy, saying that he was sent by God to chastise the tyranny of princes, and that none would be able to oppose him. He foretold likewise that he would come to Pisa and enter it, and that the state of Florence would be dissolved on that day. And so it fell out; for Piero de' Medici was driven out that very day.

Many other things he presaged long before they came to pass, as, for instance, the death of Lorenzo de' Medici; and he openly declared that he knew it by revelation; as likewise he predicted that the Church would be reformed by the sword. This is not yet accomplished; but it must be said that it very nearly occurred, and he still maintains that it will come to pass.

Many persons blamed him for pretending to receive divine revelations, but others believed him; for my part, I think him a good man.

I asked him whether our king would return safe into France, considering the great preparations that the Venetians were making against him, of which he gave a better account than I could, though I had lately come from Venice. He told me he would meet with difficulties by the way, but that he would overcome them all with honor, though he had but a hundred men in his company; for God, who had conducted him thither, would securely guard him on his way back again.

But because he had not applied himself as he ought to the reformation of the Church, and because he had permitted his soldiers to rob and plunder the poor people—those who had freely opened their gates to him as well as the enemy who had opposed him—therefore God had pronounced judgment against him, and in a short time he would receive chastisement.

However, he bade me tell the king that if he would have compassion on the people, and command his soldiers to do them no wrong, and punish them when they did, as it was his office to do, God would then mitigate, if not revoke, his sentence; but that it would not be sufficient for him to plead that he did the people no wrong himself. And he declared that he would meet the king when he came, and tell him so from his own mouth; and so he did, and pressed hard for the restitution of the Florentine towns.

Medieval Directions for Torturing a Witch (Witch-Hammer, a Handbook for the Treatment of Witches Drawn Up by the German Inquisition. c. 1486)

The method of beginning an examination by torture is as follows:

First the jailers prepare the implements of torture; then they strip the prisoner. This stripping is lest some means of witchcraft may have been sewed into the clothing—such as often, taught by the devil, they prepare from the bodies of unbaptized infants, murdered that they may forfeit salvation. And when the implements of torture have been prepared, the judge, both in person and through other good men, zealous in the faith, tries to persuade the prisoner to confess the truth freely; but if he will not confess, he bids the attendants make the prisoner fast to the strappado or some other implement of torture. The attendants obey forthwith, yet with pretended sorrow.

Then at the plea of some of those present, the prisoner is loosed again and taken aside and once more persuaded to confess, being led to believe that if he does so he will not be put to death.

Here it may be asked whether the judge, in the case of a prisoner much defamed, convicted both by witnesses and by proofs, nothing being lacking but his own confession, can properly lead him to hope that his life will be spared—when, even if he confess his crime, he will be punished with death.

. . . some hold that such a witch may be assured her life, and instead condemned to perpetual imprisonment on bread and water, in case she give convincing testimony against other witches; yet this penalty must not be announced to her—but only that her life will be spared and that she will be punished by exile. . . .

Another holds, as to this point, that for a time the promise made to the witch . . . be kept, but after a time she is to be burnt. . . .

A third way is, that the judge may safely promise witches to spare their lives, if only he will later excuse himself from the trial and let another condemn her to fire in his stead. . . .

The judge shall see to it, moreover, that during intervals between tortures guards are constantly with the prisoner, so that she may not be left alone; because she will be visited by the devil and tempted to suicide.

On the Divine Ordination of Medieval Order and Degree (Edmund Dudley, *The Tree of Commonwealth,* 1509)

And now to speak of the Tree of Commonwealth. It is a thing for which all true Englishmen have great need to pray to God that our Lord and King will have a singular regard and favour thereon, for . . . God hath ordained him to be our King; and thereto is every King bound, for it is his charge; for as subjects are bound to their Prince, so be bound all Kings to their subjects by the commandment of God . . . for though the people be subjects to the King yet are they the people of God, and God hath ordained their Prince to protect them and they to obey their Prince. The commonwealth of this realm . . . may be resembled to a fair and mighty tree. . . .

The principal and chief root of this tree . . . must be the love of God. . . . The Bishops and they of the spirituality have special charge of this root. . . . The Bishops and others of the spirituality (are) to be the . . . Lanterns of Light and to show good examples to the temporality. . . .

Besides this principal root, the tree surely, to be borne up, must have four other roots, that is to say, *justice, truth, concord,* and *peace.* . . . Justice must needs come of our Sovereign Lord himself, for the whole authority thereof is given to him by God. . . .

This tree shall bear four fruits corresponding to the four other roots . . . the first . . . honorable dignity . . . the second, wordly prosperity; . . . the third, tranquility . . . the fourth, good example. . . .

But how shall these four fruits be bestowed amongst our sovereign Lord and his subjects? Shall every man take of these fruits as . . . he lusteth, having no regard to the state. . . .? Nay . . . this fruit must be taken discreetly . . . else they will do more harm than good. . . .

And as touching the first fruit, which is Honorable Dignity there may none presume to take one piece of this fruit by his own power or authority, but must have it . . . of his Sovereign. . . . The whole of this fruit is ordained and reserved for him . . . and where he pleases to dispose it. . . .

As to the second fruit, which is Worldly Prosperity, this fruit serveth most properly for the Nobility of this realm, which be Dukes, Earls, Barons, Knights, and so forth. They may take right plenteously of this fruit (so long as) one of them do not usurp or take the part belonging to his superior . . . *every man must be content of the fruit of his own property. . . .*

As for the third fruit of this tree, which is Tranquility . . . it is most . . . necessary for the . . . Common People of this realm. . . . There are two manner of fruits of Tranquility; the one in ease and pleasure, *but of this fruit I do not mean for the Common People to meddle with,* but utterly to refuse it as they would . . . poison. . . .

What are the parings of the fruit of worldly prosperity which ye the Nobility have? . . . to defend the poor . . . to defend your Prince, the Church and the realm. . . .

As for the fruit of Tranquility . . . to what person shall they (the Commoners who become wealthy through hard work) distribute their (wealth)? To none other but to their own children and servants. . . .

Humanistic Activity in Italy. Concerning the Library of Duke Frederick of Urbino (*Vite di Vomini Illustri del Secolo XV,* 1450)*

. . . and consider the very great love in which the Duke held the old Latin and Greek scholars, ecclesiastical, and lay, too. And he had the hope to do what none for a millenium had done: to build the finest library since olden times. And in this he hesitated not at cost or hardship in obtaining volumes. These fourteen years past he has maintained about forty scribes in his work. In this he took the best way to creating such a library: first the Latin poets, then the orators, and the works of Tully and the other Latin writers and grammarians. . . . He sought for, too, all the possible works on History, and likewise the Histories in the Greek tongue. Also the Greek and Latin writers on morals and philosophy.

Of the works of the Church Fathers in Latin, he had the Four . . . bought without regard to cost. After the Four he was desirous of the works of St. Bernard, Tertullian, Hilarius Remigius, Hugh of St. Victor, Isidore, Anselm, Rabanus, and the others. Then came the Greek works done into Latin: Dionysius the Areopagite, Basil, Cyril, Gregory, Nazianzen, John of Damascus, John Chrysostom, Gregory of Nicea, the works of Eusebius, Ephrem the monk. . . . Coming to the Latin Doctors of Philosophy and Theology, the writings of Thomas Aquinas, Albertus Magnus, Alexander of Alexandor, Scotus, Bonaventura . . . of the Arch-

* *Problems in Medieval History,* edited by T. Mendenhall, B. Henning, and A. Foord. Holt and Co., 1950. Used with the permission of the publisher.

bishop of Antoninus. . . . Likewise the writers of astrology, geometry, arithmetic, architecture, and military affairs; works on painting, carving, music, canon law. . . . In medicine, the works of Avicenna, Hippocrates, Galen . . . and the complete product of Averroes in logic and natural philosophy, a volume of the Councils held since olden times, and the works of logic and philosophy of Boethius

There were all the books of many modern men . . . of Petrarch and Dante in Latin and vulgar tongues . . . also the complete works of Aristotle and Plato; of Homer, the Iliad, the Odyssey, Sophocles, Pindar, and Menander . . . Plutarch's Lives . . . the Cosmography of Ptolemy . . . and the works of Herodotus, Thucydides, Polybius, Demosthenes . . . and Plotinus.

All the Greek Commentaries, Hippocrates, Galen, Xenophon, St. Basil, St. John Chrysostom . . . St. Gregory, Dionysius . . . Aeneas the Sophist . . . and a great book in Hebrew, Latin, and Greek on geometry and astrology. . . .

Having completed this task at the cost of 30,000 ducats of gold the Duke bound each in scarlet and silver, all beautifully written by hand and illuminated on parchment . . . and included all writers, sacred and secular.

A Sixteenth Century Expression of Discontent with Social Organization
(Sir Thomas More, *Utopia,* 1516)

Thus I have described to you, as particularly as I could, the constitution of that commonwealth, which I do not only think the best in the world, but indeed the only commonwealth that truly deserves that name. In all other places it is visible, that while people talk of a commonwealth, every man seeks only his own wealth; but there, where no man has any property, all men zealously pursue the good of the public; and, indeed, it is no wonder to see men act so differently; for in other commonwealths, every man knows that unless he provides for himself, how flourishing soever the commonwealth may be, he must die of hunger; so that he sees the necessity of preferring his own concerns to the public; but in Utopia, where every man has a right to everything, they all know that if care is taken to keep the public stores full, no private man can want anything; for among them there is no unequal distribution, so that no man is poor, none in necessity; and though no man has anything, yet they are all rich; for what can make a man so rich as to lead a serene and cheerful life, free from anxieties; neither apprehending want himself, nor vexed with the endless complaints of his wife? He is not afraid of the misery of his children, nor is he contriving how to raise a portion for his daughters, but is secure in this, that both he and his wife, his children and grandchildren, to as many generations as he can fancy, will all live both plentifully and happily; since among them there is no less care taken of those who were once engaged in labor, but grow afterwards unable to follow it, then there is elsewhere of these that continue still employed. I would gladly hear any man compare the justice that is among them with that of all other nations; among whom, may I perish, if I see anything that looks either like justice or equity; for what justice is there in this, that a nobleman, a goldsmith, a banker, or any other man, that either does nothing at all, or at best is employed in things that are of no use to the public, should live in great luxury and splendor, upon what is so ill acquired; and a mean man, a carter, a smith, or a plowman that works harder even than the beasts themselves, and is employed in labors so necessary, that no commonwealth could hold out a year without them, can only earn so poor a livelihood, and must be led so miserable a life, that the condition of the beasts is much better than theirs? For as the beasts do not work constantly, so they feed almost as well, and with more pleasure; and have no anxiety about what is to come, whilst these men are depressed by a barren and fruitless employment, and tormented with the apprehensions of want in their old age; since that which they get by their daily labor does but maintain them at present, and is consumed as fast as it comes in, there is no overplus left to lay up for old age.

Is not that government both unjust and ungrateful, that is so prodigal of its favors to those that are called gentlemen, or goldsmiths, or such others who are idle, or live either by flattery, or by contriving the arts of vain pleasure, and on the other hand, takes no care of those of a meaner sort, such as plowmen, colliers, and smiths, without whom it could not subsist? But after the public has reaped all the advantage of their service, and they come to be oppressed with age, sickness, and want, all their labors and the good they have done is forgotten; and all the recompense given them is that they are left to die in great misery. The richer sort are often endeavoring to bring the hire of laborers lower, not only by their fraudulent practices, but by the laws which they procure to be made to that effect; so that though it is a thing most unjust in itself, to give such small rewards to those who deserve so well of the public, yet they have given those hardships the name and color of justice, by procuring laws to be made for regulating them.

Therefore, I must say that, as I hope for mercy, I can have no other notion of all the other governments that I see or know, than that they are a conspiracy of the rich, who on pretence of managing the public only pursue their private ends, and devise all the ways and arts they can find out; first, that they may, without danger, preserve all that they have so ill acquired, and then that they may engage the poor to toil and labor for them at as low rates as possible, and oppress them as much as they please. And if they can but prevail to get these contrivances established by the show of public authority, which is considered as the representative of the whole people, then they have accounted laws. Yet these wicked men after they have, by a most insatiable covetousness, divided that among themselves with which all the rest might have been well supplied, are far from that happiness that is enjoyed among the Utopians; for the use as well as the desire of money being extinguished, much anxiety and great occasions of mischief is cut off with it.

And who does not see that the frauds, thefts, robberies, quarrels, tumults, contentions, seditions, murders, treacheries, and witchcrafts, which are indeed rather punished than restrained by the severities of law, would all fall off, if money were not any more valued by the world? Men's fears, solicitudes, cares, labors, and watchings, would all perish in the same moment with the value of money: even poverty itself, for the relief of which money seems most necessary, would fall.

Concerning the Evil Social Results of Land Enclosures (Edward VI: *Royal Proclamation,* 1548)[1]

Forasmuch as the King's majesty . . . hath been advertised and put in remembrance, as well by divers supplications and pitiful complaints of his majesty's poor subjects . . . that of late by the enclosing of lands and arable grounds in divers and sundry

[1] This royally issued edict, and those found on pages 53, 55, 57, 58, 72, 78, 79, 102, 103, 107, 109, are rendered in full in Paul L Hughes and Frank J. Larkin, C.S.V., *Tudor Royal Proclamations, Vol. I, The Early Tudors, 1485-1553,* and *Vol. II, The Later Tudors, 1553-1603,* Yale University Press, 1964. Used here with the permission of Yale University Press.

[2] Other English counties, boroughs, towns, and villages.

places of this realm many have been driven to extreme poverty and compelled to leave the places where they were born and to seek them livings in other countries[2], with great misery and poverty; insomuch that whereas in time past, 10, 20, yea, in some places 100 or 200 Christian people hath been inhabiting and kept household to the bringing forth and nourishing of youth and to the replenishing and fulfilling of his majesty's realms with faithful subjects who might serve both Almighty God and the King's majesty to the defense of this realm, now there is nothing kept but sheep or bullocks; all that land which heretofore was tilled and occupied with so many men, and did bring forth not only divers families in work and labor, but also capons, hens, chickens, pigs, and other such furniture of the markets, is now gotten, by insatiable greediness of mind into one or two men's hands and scarcely dwelled upon with one poor shepherd, so that the realm thereby is brought to a marvelous desolation, houses decayed, parishes diminished, the force of the realm weakened, and Christian people, by the greedy covetousness of some men, eaten up and devoured of brute beasts and driven from their houses by sheep and bullocks; and that although of the same thing many and sundry complaints and lamentations hath been heretofore made, and . . . divers and sundry laws . . . hath been made for the remedy thereof, yet the insatiable covetousness of men doth not cease daily to encroach hereupon and more and more to waste the realm, after this sort bringing arable grounds into pastures, and letting houses, whole families, and copyholds to fall down, decay, and be waste:

. . . And further [his majesty] is advertised that by the ungodly and uncharitable means aforesaid the said sheep and oxen, being brought into a few men's hands . . . who . . . hold them dear and carry their advantage of the market;

. . . And therefore [his majesty] hath appointed . . . a view and inquiry to be made of all such as contrary to the said acts and godly ordinances hath made enclosures and pastures of that which was arable ground, or let any house, tenament, or mese decay and fall down, or otherwise committed or done anything to the contrary of the good and wholesome articles contained in the said acts; and therefore willeth and commandeth all his loving subjects who knoweth any such defaults and offenses . . . to insinuate and give information of the offense to the King's majesty's commissioners . . . that a speedy reformation might be made herein . . .

Royal Censorship of Drama and Plays
(Edward VI: *Royal Proclamation,* 1549)

Forasmuch as a great number of those that be common players of interludes and plays, as well within the city of London as elsewhere within the realm, do for the most part play such interludes as contain matter tending to sedition, and contemning of sundry good orders and laws; whereupon are grown, and are daily like to grow and ensue much disquiet, division, tumults, and uproars in this realm:

The King's majesty, by the advice and consent of his dearest uncle Edward, Duke of Somerset, governor of his person and protector of his realms, dominions, and subjects, and the rest of his highness' Privy Council, straightly chargeth and commandeth all and every his majesty's subjects, of whatsoever state, order, or degree they be, that from the ninth day of this present month of August until the Feast of All Saints next coming, they nor any of them openly or secretly play in the English tongue any kind of interlude, play, dialogue, or other matter set forth in form of play, in any place, public or private, within this realm; upon pain that whosoever shall play in English any such play, interlude, dialogue, or other matter, shall suffer imprisonment and further punishment at the pleasure of his majesty.

For the better execution whereof, his majesty, by the said advice and consent, straightly chargeth and commandeth all and singular mayors, sheriffs, bailiffs, constables, headboroughs, tithing men, justices of peace, and all other his majesty's head officers, in all the parts throughout the realm, to give order and special heed that this proclamation be in all behalves well and truly kept and observed.

The Classic Statement of Moral and Political Relativism
(Niccolo Machiavelli, *The Prince,* 1514)

A Prince should have no other thought or study but war, and the arts and disciplines of it. He never, then, ought to stop his thoughts from the exercises of war . . . a thing . . . which can be done in two ways, by the application of the body, and the mind. As to his bodily applications, or matter of action, besides that he is bound to keep his armies in training and exercise, he ought to harden his own body by sports and exercises against hardships and hunger and fatigue. As to the exercises of the mind, a Prince can do that by study in History, and sound consideration of the actions of the most excelling warriors; by considering how they used themselves in war. . . .

There is no better remedy against flattery than to let everyone realize that you are not angered by the truth; yet if you allow every person to tell the truth, you injure yourself and lessen your self-respect. Thus a wise Prince should go a third road, and choose out of the state certain dependable men to whom only he should commit the liberty of speaking truth to him, and then only when de demands they speak and of what matters. Nothing else. However, a wise Prince will inquire of all things, hear the permitted truth, and afterwards act as he sees fit. Yet, too, the Prince should consider well before he reaches a conclusion; but once having decided a course of action nothing should alter it.

And there arises a new question, whether it is best to be loved or feared by the people. To be both loved and feared would be the best, but that is difficult to attain. Therefore, it is better and much safer to be feared than loved; for in general men are inclined to ingratitude, inconstancy, hypocrisy; they fear danger and are greedy for material gain. . . . Love is fastened only by ties of esteem and obligation; which the base nature of mankind will disrupt whenever opportunity will lead to his own gain, but fear depends upon the distaste for punishment, which will never be disrupted or forgotten.

There are two ways of war; by law and by force. The first is the way of men, the other is the way of animals; but because many times the first is not sufficient one must often resort to the second. A Prince, therefore, must understand both; when to make use of the rational, and when the brutal way. . . . So he must be a fox to elude the traps and a lion to keep away the wolves, but he who keeps wholly to the way of the lion has no true notion of himself. A Prince that is wise cannot, nor ought to have any desire, to keep his word or treaty; particularly when the keeping of it is not to his advantage, or when the causes for which he promised are removed or the goals attained. Were all men virtuous this doctrine would not be taught, but men are wicked, and not likely to be honest with you, so you are not bound to any honesty with them. It is always easy to find lawful cause to justify a breach of faith.

A Prince is not obliged to really have all the good qualities mentioned before, but it is necessary that he appear to have them. Let him do all he can to preserve his supremacy; the means which he uses will be thought honourable and he will be congratulated by everyone.

Papal Recognition of a Royal Right
(Henry VII: *Royal Proclamation Summarizing the Papal Bull Recognizing His Claim to the English Throne,* 1486)

Our Holy Father the [Pope,][1] Innocent VIII, to the perpetual memory of this [event] to be had, by his proper motion, without procurement of our sovereign lord the King or [of any] other person, for conservation of the universal peace and eschewing of slanders an[d to en]gender the contrary of the same, understanding of the long and grievous variance, dissensions, and debates that hath been in this realm of England between the house of the Duchy of Lancaster [on the] o[n]e part and [the] house of the Duchy of York on the other part, willing all such divisions [therefrom] following to be p[ut a] part:

By the counsel and consent of his college of Cardinals, approveth, confi[rmeth,] and establisheth the mat[ri]mony and conjunction made between our sovereign lord, King Henry VII of t[he house] of Lancaster of that one party and the noble Princess Elizabeth of the house of York of that other [party,] with all their issue lawfully born between the same.

And in likewise His Holiness confirmeth, establisheth, and approveth the right and title to the crown of E[ngland] of the said our sovereign lord Henry VII, and the heirs of his body lawfully begotten to him [as ap]pertaining, as well by reason of his nighest and undoubted title of succession as by the right of his most noble [victory], and by election of the lords spiritual and temporal and other nobles of his realm, and by the [ordi]-nance and authority of parliament made by the three estates of this land.

Furthermore he approveth, confirmeth, and declareth that if it please God that the said Eli[zabeth,] which God forbid should decease without issue between our sovereign lord and her of their bodies bor[n and had], then such issue as between him and her whom after that God shall join him to shall be had and born [shall be] heritors to the same crown and realm of England. . . .

Over this, the same our Holy Father giveth his blessing to all princes, nobles, and other inhab[itants] of this realm, or outward, that favoreth, aideth, and assisteth the said our soverign lord and his heirs a[gainst his] or their rebels, giving them that die in his and their quarrel full and plenary pardon an[d remissi]on of all their sins.

Finally he commandeth all metropolitans and bishops, upon the pain of interdict of [all men of] the church, abbots, priors, archdeacons, parish priests, wardens of the friars an[d other] men of the church, exempt and not exempt, upon the pain of his great curse which they falleth in [if they do it] not to denounce and declare, or cause to be denounced and declared, all such contrary doers and rebels a[t every] such time as they to the same in the name of the said our sovereign lord shall be required.

Prohibiting the Arming of Private Armies by the Nobility (Henry VII: *Royal Proclamation,* 1502)

The King our sovereign lord Henry, by the grace of God King of England and of France and lord of Ireland, for the tender zeal and inward affection that he naturally beareth to his loving subjects within his county of Kent, reserved from the beginning of his reign the retainer to himself of all his subjects within his said county, in avoiding the divisions, enormities, and inconveniences that else percase might have ensued amongst them, to have inquietations and subversion of all good policies. And whereas it is come to the perfect knowledge of our said sovereign lord that retainers within his said county, as well by liveries, tokens, cognizances, promises, and badges, as otherwise, have now late been used and given there, and daily increase, contrary to his mind and laudable statutes in such case provided; by the sufferance of which enormities, dissensions, debates, and other inconveniences be not unlike to ensue, to the universal annoyance, hurt, and damage of his subjects, without speedy provision of convenable remedy be provided in this part:

His highness, having tender respect to the said governance of all his said subjects and intending his said statutes to be inviolably observed, chargeth therefore and expressly commandeth that none of his subjects within his said county presume or take upon them to use any retainers, or to be retained by livery, wages, cognizance, or promise; but to reserve them wholly to his person and to be ready to serve him like as they shall be commanded and appointed . . . and that not to fail to obey and fully execute this his solemn proclamation and pleasure, upon the penalties in his said statutes . . . and in avoiding his high displeasure.

Castiglione on the Complete Man of the Renaissance
(Baldisare Castiglione, *The Courtier,* 1517)

I will have this our Courtier therefore to be a Gentleman born and of good house. For it is a great deal easier for him that is not born a gentleman to fail in the acts of virtue than for a gentleman. If he swerve from the steps of his ancestors, he stains the name of his family, and does not only not get, but loses that which may have been already gotten. For nobleness of birth is a clear lamp that shows forth and brings into light, works both good and bad, and inflames and provokes unto virtue, as well with the fear of slander, as also with the hope of praise.

To come therefore to the quality of the person, I say it is well, if he be neither of the least, nor of the greatest size. For both the one and the other have with it a certain spiteful wonder, and such men are marveled at, almost, as much as men marvel to behold monstrous things. Yet if there must needs be a default in one of the two extremes, it shall be less hurtful to be somewhat of the least size, than to exceed the common stature in height. For men so shut up of body, besides that many times they are of a dull wit, they are also unapt for all exercises of nimbleness, which I much desire to have in the Courtier.

You know in great matters and adventures in wars, the true provocation is glory: and who for money's sake or for any other consideration takes it in hand deserves not the name of gentleman, but is a most vile merchant. And every man may conceive it to be the true glory, that is stored up in the holy treasure of letters, except such unlucky creatures as have had no taste thereof. What mind is so faint, so bashful and of so base a courage, that in reading the acts and greatness of Caesar, Alexander, Scipio, Hannibal, and so many others, is not incensed with a most fervent longing to be like them: and does not prefer the getting of that perpetual fame, before this rotten life that lasts so short a time?

Therefore, to return again to our Courtier, whom in letters I will have to be more than indifferently well taught, at least in those studies which they call Humanities, and to have not only the understanding of the Latin tongue, but also of the Greek, because of the many and sundry things that with great excellency are written in it. Let him much exercise himself in poets, and no less in Orators and Historiographers, and also in writing both rhyme and prose, and especially in the vulgar tongue. For beside the contentment that he shall receive thereby himself, he shall by this means never want pleasant entertainments with women which ordinarily love such matters. And if by reason either of his other business beside, or of his slender study, he shall not attain unto that perfection that his writings may be worth much commendation, let him be circumspect in keeping them close, lest he make other men laugh at him.

Therefore, the Courtier must do well many things:

He must be well born.

He must be of average structure, rather with the sleight than large.

He must not be feminine in manner or speech.

He must not praise himself unshamefully.

He must perform his best feats casually as though they were natural, and always when there is noble rather than common audience.

He must not be stubborn nor always at contention.

He must be able to draw well and paint.

He must dance nimbly, yet with dignity.

To sing well.

To play the violin and other instruments and the lute.

He may not be overly affable and never humiliate any man.

He must play well at tennis and other games with ladies.

And he must know the hawk and the hunt,

And to swim, and dart, and throw the javelin, and run and jump.

He must never ask his Lord for any special favor for himself.

And he should not love too greatly office; nor plead for it.

In his conversation with women he must be guileless, sober, mild, and pleasing; not crude or suggestive.

All his appetites must be in proportion to good taste, and they should be ruled by reason.

The Condemnation of Galileo
(*Sentence of the Court of Inquisition,* 1632)

We, . . . cardinals of the Holy Roman Church, Inquisitors General . . . specially deputed against heretical depravity throughout the whole Christian Republic. . . .

Whereas you, Galileo . . . were in the year 1615 denounced to this Holy Office for holding as true the false doctrine taught by many that the sun is the center of the world and immovable, and that the earth moves, and also with a diurnal motion. . . .

The proposition that the sun is the center of the world and does not move from its place is absurd and false philosophically and formally heretical because it is expressly contrary to the Holy Scripture. . . .

. . . Therefore, having seen and maturely considered the merits of this your cause . . . we have arrived at the underwritten final sentence against you:

. . . We say, pronounce, sentence, declare, that you, the said Galileo . . . have rendered yourself in the judgment of this Holy Office vehemently suspected of heresy . . . and that consequently you have incurred all the censures and penalties imposed and promulgated in the sacred canons and other constitutions . . . against such delinquents. From which we are content that you be absolved; provided first, with a sincere heart and unfeigned faith, you abjure, curse, and detest the aforesaid errors and heresies, and every other error and heresy contrary to the Catholic and Apostolic Roman Church in the form prescribed by us.

And in order that this your grave and pernicious error and transgression may not remain altogether unpunished, and that you may be more cautious for the future, and as an example to others, that they may abstain from similar delinquencies—we ordain that the book of the *Dialogues of Galileo Galilei* be prohibited by public edict.

We condemn you to the formal prison of the Holy Office during our pleasure and by way of salutory penance we enjoin that for three years to come you repeat once a week the seven penitential psalms. . . .

UNIT 5

The Reformation and New Political Concepts

One of the chief problems of the 16th and 17th centuries was that of resistance to authority, with the additional problem of placing resistance on a moral basis. In the light of the long tradition of medieval obedience the solution to this problem would not be one easy to find or one quick in application, for, as in every age, disobedience to law or disregard of custom would beget in turn an even narrower intolerance. Yet, this was the age of Luther and Calvin, of Robert Parsons and Cardinal Bellarmine, of Puritanism and religious radicalism, and the problems of toleration and resistance followed almost naturally in the wake of historic events.

The first real breach in the spiritual universality of the West was that of Martin Luther in 1517, and the reaction to Luther's preachment was immediate. In the Edict of Worms the Emperor Charles V pledged the full might of the empire to the struggle against freedom of religious expression. Determined to maintain political sovereignty and freedom of conscience, the Lutheran princes of northern Germany defended themselves with such vigor and unity that the Emperor was willing to accede to their demands for uninhibited liberty at the peace negotiations at Augsburg in 1555. Almost a century later the *Treaty of Westphalia* extended the same right to Calvinist worshippers at the end of the Thirty Years War. However, the treaties and agreements which brought an end to the religious wars in Europe were applicable only in geographic terms: acceptance of the principle "whose territory, his religion" brought an end to hostilities between states but tended toward the increase of religious frictions and tensions within states where both Catholics and Protestants were each seeking political means for imposing their respective form of worship on the others.

Yet, in time, each state and each people was able to work out the problem of religious differentiation in light of the circumstances and historical conditions peculiar to itself. In 1534 Henry VIII of England broke with the Church of Rome when Nationalism and Protestantism became allied in the popular conception against Spanish dominated political universalism and Catholicism. In the next century the French monarch promulgated the *Edict of the Liberties of the Gallican Church,* which limited papal political authority in France but in no way attacked the spiritual headship of the Pontiff. These solutions, however, were seldom peaceably applied. The Puritans and the Anglicans were locked in deadly struggle for over three-quarters of a century in England after the death of Elizabeth, and the *Revocation of the Edict of Nantes* was the direct result of the *Liberties of the Gallican Church* in France. There is no method for measuring the depth or breadth of human misery, but it is both interesting and significant to note that Frederick, the Great Elector of Brandenburg, progenitor of the Hohenzollern Kings of Prussia, enriched his Prussian domain by inviting the Huguenot refugees from France after the *Revocation* to settle with the aid of state subsidies in his realm, and, whereas France lost a large portion of her economically productive middle class, Prussia benefited in inverse ratio from the continued capability of that class.

In England the Reformation begun by Henry VIII went through many developmental stages before it was brought to a conclusion in 1688. This was so because the English people never accepted the Reformation as a purely religious movement, but rather as an opening in the medieval barriers against change through which might erupt spasmodically the new forces of reform in every field of social activity.

Thus the English Reformation was concerned with political and economic as well as religious liberty. The first expression of contempt by Henry VIII for traditionally superior power would have far-reaching effect on the development of English and American political institutions, for in the end the representative ideal which was inspired and stimulated by Henry's use of Parliament in crystalizing the Reformation would attack and destroy the very prerogatives upon which monarchy was erected.

In the continuing struggle for liberty in England the year 1688 was of more than passing significance. Its successful conclusion not only brought to a close the claim to unlimited monarchial power, but stimulated the English Parliamentarians to reiterate in the *Bill of Rights* the old claim first made by any

Parliament in Elizabeth's day that English rights rested on "ancient usage." John Locke, the apologist for the Glorious Revolution, dissatisfied with a rationale he considered ineffectual and dangerous chose to base English liberty on the Law of Nature.

An Early Criticism of the Clergy
(John Wycliff, *How the Office of Curates is Ordained of God,* c.1377)

The office of curate is ordained of God; few do it well and many full evil, therefore test we their defaults. . . .

They are more busy about worldly goods than virtues and good keeping of men's souls. For he that can best get riches of this world together, and have a great household, and worldly array, is held to be a worthy man of holy church, though he know not the best point of the gospel. Such a one is praised and borne up by the bishops. . . . But the curate that gives himself to study holy writ and teach his parishioners to save their souls . . . is held to be a fool and destroyer of holy church. . . .

The second default is, that they run fast, by land and by water, in great peril of body and soul, to get rich benefices; but they will not knowingly go a mile to preach the gospel, though . . . men are running to hell for want of knowing and keeping of God's law. . . .

Since they so much love worldly riches . . . and labor so little for God's worship and the saving of Christian souls, who can excuse these covetous clerks from simony and heresy? Neither God's law, nor man's law, nor reason, nor good conscience. And let the King and his council inquire how much gold goes out of our land, for purchase of benefices, into aliens' hands. . . .

The third default of evil curates is, that they are angels of Satan to lead men to hell; for, instead of truly teaching Christ's gospel, they are dumb, or else tell men's traditions. Instead of example of good life, they hurt their parishioners in many ways —by example of pride, envy, covetousness, and unreasonable vengeance—cruelly cursing for tithes. . . . They teach idleness, gluttony, drunkenness, and lechery. . . .

The fourth error is, that they think more of statutes of sinful men than the most reasonable law of Almighty God. For they dread the pope's law, and statutes made by bishops and other officers, more than the noble law of the gospel. Therefore they have many great and costly books of man's law . . . but few curates have the bible and expositions of the gospel, they study them but little and do them less. . . .

The fifth default is, that they practice strife and plea [law] and gather envy and hate from laymen for tithes, and summon men to account, and by force take their goods, or else curse them . . . and afterwards draw men to prison as though they were kings and emperors of men's bodies and goods. . . .

The seventh error is, that they teach sinful men to buy hell full dear, and not to come to heaven which is proffered them for little cost. For they teach . . . men to suffer much cold, hunger, and thirst, and much waking and despising to get worldly honor; and a little dirt by false warring. . . .

The eighth default. They shut the kingdom of heaven before men, and neither go in themselves, nor suffer other men to enter, for they shut up holy writ . . . by false new laws, and evil glossing, and evil teaching. For they will neither learn themselves, nor teach holy writ, nor suffer other men to do it, lest their own sin and hypocrisy be known, and their pleasurable life withdrawn. . . .

The ninth error is, that they waste poor men's goods on rich furs and costly clothes, and worldly array, feasts of rich men, and in gluttony, drunkenness, and lechery. . . .

The tenth default is, that they haunt lords' courts, and are occupied in worldly offices. . . .

The eleventh error is, that they attend more to wrongful commandments of sinful men than to the most rightful commandments of God. For if the pope or bishop send a letter to receive a pardoner [seller of Indulgences] to deceive the people by grants of many thousand years of pardon, he shall be dispatched; although if there come a true man to preach the gospel . . . he shall be hindered. . . .

The Beginning of the Reformation
(Martin Luther, *On the Liberty of a Christian Man,** 1520)

Thesis: First, that we may thoroughly understand what a Christian man is . . .

I will set down these two propositions:

A Christian man is a free lord over all things and subject to no one.

* Martin Luther, *Werke,* Vol. VII (Weimar, 1897). Translated by Lenore Rickels.

A Christian man is a dutiful servant of all things and subject to everyone.

. . . .To take up these two contradictory statements concerning freedom and servitude, we must keep in mind that a Christian man is really of two natures, spiritual and corporal. According to the spiritual, he is called a spiritual, new, inner man; according to the corporal, he is called a carnal, old, or outward man. . . .

Let us therefore consider the inward, spiritual man, to see what is necessary to make him a righteous, free, Christian man. It then becomes evident that no outward thing, whatever it may be, makes him free or righteous, since his righteousness and liberty, as well as his unrighteousness and bondage are neither corporal nor outward. What does it profit the soul if the body is free, renewed, and whole; if it eats, drinks, or lives as it wishes? And again, what does it harm the soul, if the body is in bondage, ill, and feeble; if it hungers, thirsts, or suffers, as it would rather not? None of these things affects the soul, either to free it or to enslave it, to make it righteous or unrighteous. . . .

Therefore it does not profit the soul if the body puts on sacred robes, as the priests and clerics do, or if it lives in churches and holy places, or if it is occupied with sacred duties, or if it prays, fasts, makes pilgrimages, or does any good work which could possibly be done, from now to eternity. There must be something beyond this which provides righteousness and liberty for the soul, since all the things mentioned above may also be done by a hypocrite and dissembler; and such works produce only vain hypocrites. . . .

The soul requires nothing else, either in heaven or earth, wherein it exists righteous, free, and Christian, than the holy Gospel, the Word of God in Christ . . . the soul can do without all things except the Word of God, and without the Word of God nothing is profitable to it. . . .

Christ came into the world for no other service than to preach the Word of God. All the apostles, bishops, and priests, also, and the whole spiritual estate, are called and established only for the sake of the Word. . . .

If you should ask, "What is this Word, which confers such grace, and how shall I use it?" the answer (is): it is none other than the preaching of Christ, as contained in the Gospel. . . . Which if you rightly believe, being guilty, you will have to despair of yourself, and acknowledge that the word of Hosea is true: "O Israel, there is nothing in thee but thine destruction; in me alone is thine help." That you may be saved from yourself, that is, from your sinfulness, God places before you His dear Son, Jesus Christ, and tells you through His living, comforting Word: Believe in Christ with complete confidence, and trust in Him wholly. For the sake of this faith, all your sins will be forgiven, your unworthiness will be overcome, and you will be truly just, at peace, righteous, meritorious, and free from all condemnation. As St. Paul says, Romans 1, "The just shall live by his faith," and Romans 10, "Christ is the end and fulfillment of all the commandments to those who believe in him." . . . .

Now as Christ possesses the honor and glory of the firstborn (of God) he also shares it with all his Christians, so that through faith they too must all be kings and priests with Him . . . it follows that through faith a Christian man is so highly exalted over all things that he becomes spiritual lord over all, since nothing is injurious to his salvation. In fact, all things must be subject unto him and contribute toward his salvation . . . this is a spiritual dominion, which rules in spite of corporal bondage, which means that I can make all things spiritually profitable to me, so that even suffering and death must serve me and be profitable to salvation. . . .

Enough has been said concerning the inward man, his freedom and his chief righteousness, which requires neither commandments nor good works, yea rather finds them injurious, should anyone use them as a measure for his justification.

Now we come to the second part, to the outward man. . . .

Even though a man inwardly, according to the spirit, is justified sufficiently through his faith, and possesses everything needful (for his salvation), yet this faith and sufficiency must be strengthened throughout this life, since he still exists in this bodily and temporal life, and has to regulate his body and associate with others. Here it is that works enter in: here he must not be idle; here, indeed, he must take care to discipline his body with fastings, watchings, intercessions, and all temperate discipline, so that it becomes obedient to and one with the inner man and with faith, and neither hinders it nor rebels against it, as the tendency of the body is, if it is not controlled. . . .

So it is that a man on behalf of his own body cannot be idle, and must, moreover, practice many good works, so that he masters the body. Yet the works are not the actual good through which he is righteous and just before God, but they are freely done out of pure love, unconstrainedly, to please God, without thought of anything beyond that which pleases God, whose will he gladly does with all his might. . . .

Christ, in Matthew 17, when the tribute money was demanded of his disciples, debated with St. Peter, whether the children of the king were not free from payment of the tribute, and when Peter said "Yes," Christ yet commanded him to go to the sea, and said, "Lest we offend them, go, take up the first fish you see, and in its mouth you will find a piece of money; give that for me and thee." This is a fine illustration of this doctrine: here Christ calls Himself and His disciples free children of the king, who require nothing, and yet submits Himself willingly, is dutiful, and pays the tribute. . . .

St. Paul also commands, Romans 13 and Titus 3, that (Christians) be subject to temporal powers, not because they will thus be made righteous, but to be ready to serve the magistrates and others freely, doing their will out of love and freedom. . . .

Martin Luther Condemned by the Council of the Diet of Worms
(*The Edict of the Diet of Worms,* 1521)

We, Charles V, by Grace Roman emperor, salute and tender our good wishes to each and all of the electors, princes—both spiritual and secular:

Most revered, honorable, and illustrious friends and relatives: as it pertains to our office of Roman emperor, not only to enlarge the bounds of the Holy Roman Empire, which our fathers of the German nation founded for the defense of the Holy Roman and Catholic Church, subduing unbelievers by the sword, with much shedding of blood, but also, adhering to the rule hitherto observed by the Holy Roman Church to take care that no stain of heresy should contaminate our holy faith within the Roman Empire, or, if heresy had already begun, to extirpate it with all necessary diligence, prudence, and discretion, as the case might demand;

Whereas, certain heresies have sprung up in the German nation within the last three years, which were formerly condemned by the holy councils and papal decrees, with the consent of the whole Church, and are now drawn anew from hell.

Since now without doubt it is plain to you all how far these errors and heresies depart from the Christian way, which a certain Martin Luther, of the Augustinian order has sought violently and virulently to introduce and disseminate within the Christian religion and its established order, especially in the German nation, so that unless it is speedily prevented, the whole German nation, and later all other nations, will be infected by this same disorder.

And although, after the delivery of the papal bull and final condemnation of Luther we proclaimed the bull in many places in the German nation, nevertheless he has taken no account of it, nor lessened nor revoked his errors, nor sought absolution from his Papal Holiness, but like a madman plotting the manifest destruction of the holy Church, he daily scatters abroad much worse fruit and effect of his depraved heart and mind through numerous books both in Latin and German.

Therein he destroys, overturns, and abuses the number, arrangement, and use of the seven sacraments, and in ways shamefully pollutes the indissoluble bonds of holy matrimony; and says also that holy unction is a mere invention. And he begins to attack confession. For he teaches a loose, self-willed life, severed from all laws and wholly brutish; and he is a loose, self-willed man, who condemns and rejects all laws.

And now, on account of these things, we have summoned here to Worms the electors, princes, and estates of this our Holy Empire, and carefully examined the aforesaid matters with great diligence, and with unanimous advice and consent of all we decree what follows.

Although one so condemned and persisting in his obstinate perversity, separated from the rites of the Christian Church and a manifest heretic, is denied a hearing under all laws; nevertheless, to prevent all unprofitable dispute we gave him a safe conduct to come hither, in order that he might be questioned in our presence and in that of the electors, princes, and estates of the Empire.

Accordingly, in view of all these considerations and the fact that Martin Luther still persists obstinately and perversely in maintaining his heretical opinions, we have declared and made known that the said Martin Luther shall hereafter be held and esteemed by each and all of us as a limb cut off from the Church of God, an obstinate schismatic and manifest heretic, and we command that immediately after the fourteenth day of May, you shall refuse to give the aforesaid Martin Luther hospitality, food, or drink; nor shall any one give him counsel or help, but in whatever place you meet him, you shall take him prisoner. And in like manner you shall proceed against his friends.

Luther's Condemnation of Social Unrest
(Martin Luther, *Against the Murdering and Robbing Rabble of the Peasants,* 1525)

In my preceding pamphlet I had no occasion to condemn the peasants, because they promised to yield to law and better instruction, as Christ demands. Before I can turn around, they go out and appeal to force, in spite of their promises, and rob and pillage and act like mad dogs. In short, they practice the devil's work, and are led by Munzer who is the arch-devil. Because of this I would instruct those in authority how to conduct themselves in this matter.

First, these peasants have sworn to their true and gracious rulers to be submissive and obedient. But since they have deliberately and sacrilegiously abandoned their obedience, and in addition have dared to oppose their lords, they have thereby forfeited body and soul, as perfidious, perjured, lying, disobedient wretches and scoundrels are wont to do.

Second, they cause uproar and sacrilegiously rob and pillage monasteries and castles that do not belong to them, for which, like public highwaymen and murderers, they deserve the twofold death of body and soul. It is right and lawful to slay at the first opportunity a rebellious person who is known as such, for he is already under God's and emperor's ban. Every man is at once judge and executioner of a public rebel; just as, when a fire starts, he who can extinguish it first is the one to do it. Rebellion is not simply vile murder, but is like a great fire that kindles and devastates a country; it fills the land with murder and bloodshed, makes widows and orphans, and destroys everything, like the greatest calamity.

Therefore, whosoever can, should smite, strangle, and stab, secretly or publicly, and should remember that there is nothing more poisonous, pernicious, and devilish than a rebellious man. Just as one must slay a mad dog, so, if you do not fight the rebels, they will kill you, and the whole country with you.

Henry VIII Breaks with the Church of Rome
(*The Act of Supremacy,* 1534)

Albeit the king's Majesty justly and rightfully is and ought to be the supreme head of the Church of England, and so is recognized by the clergy of this realm in their convocations, yet nevertheless, for corroboration and confirmation thereof, and for increase of virtue in Christ's religion within this realm of England, and to repress and extirpate all errors, heresies, and other enormities and abuses heretofore used in the same, be it enacted, by authority of this present Parliament, that the king, our sovereign lord, his heirs and successors, kings of this realm, shall be taken, accepted and reputed the only supreme head on earth of the Church of England, called *Anglicana Ecclesia;* and shall have and enjoy, annexed and united to the Imperial crown of this realm, as well the title and style thereof, as all honors, dignities, pre-eminences, jurisdictions, privileges, authorities, immunities, profits, and commodities to the said dignity of the supreme head of the same church belonging and appertaining; and that our said sovereign lord, his heirs and successors, kings of this realm, shall have full power and authority from time to time to visit, repress, redress, record, order, correct, restrain, and amend all such errors, heresies, abuses, offenses, contempts, and enormities, whatsoever they be, which by any manner of spiritual authority or jurisdiction ought or may lawfully be reformed, repressed, ordered, redressed, corrected, restrained, or amended, and to the pleasure of Almighty God, the increase of virtue in Christ's religion, and for the conservation of the peace, unity, and tranquility of this realm; any usage, foreign law, foreign authority, prescription, or any other thing or things to the contrary hereof notwithstanding.

The Execution of Sir Thomas More
(*Hall's Chronicles,* 1535)

. . . . the sixth day of July was Sir Thomas More beheaded for the like treason . . . which, as you have heard, was for the denying of the King's Majesty's supremacy (in the Church). This man was also counted learned, and as you have heard before, he was lord chancellor of England, and in that time a great persecutor of such as detested the supremacy of the bishop of Rome, which he himself so highly favored that he stood to it until he was brought to the scaffold on the Tower Hill, where on a block his head was stricken from his shoulders and had no more harm.

I cannot tell whether I should call him a foolish wise man or a wise foolish man, for undoubtedly he, besides his learning, had a great wit, but it was so mingled with taunting and mocking, that it seemed to them that best knew him that he thought nothing to be well spoken except he had ministered some mock in the communication, insomuch as at his coming to the Tower one of the officers demanded his upper garment for his fee, meaning his gown, and he answered he should have it and took him his cap, saying that it was the uppermost garment that he had. Likewise, even going to his death at the Tower gate, a poor woman called unto him and besought him to declare that he had certain evidence of hers in the time that he was in office (which after he was apprehended she could not come by), and that he would entreat she might have them again, or else she was undone. He answered, "Good woman, have patience a little while, for the king is so good unto me that even within this half hour he will discharge me of all business, and help thee himself." Also when he went up the stair on the scaffold he desired one of the sheriff's officers to give him his hand to help him up, and said, "When I come down again let me shift for myself as well as I can."

Also the hangman kneeled down to him asking him forgiveness of his death (as the manner is), to whom he said, "I forgive thee, but I promise thee that thou shalt never have honesty of the striking of my head, my neck is so short." Also even when he should lay down his head on the block he, having a great gray beard, struck out his beard, and said to the hangman, "I pray you let me lay my beard over the block lest ye should cut it." Thus with a mock he ended his life.

Regulating the Reading of Scripture
(Henry VIII: *Royal Proclamation,* 1539)

The King's most royal majesty hath been informed that great murmur, malice, and malignity is risen and sprung amongst divers and sundry of his subjects by diversities of opinions; some of them minding craftily by their preaching and teaching to restore into this realm the old devotion to the usurped power of the Bishop of Rome, the hypocrite religion, superstitious pilgrimages, idolatry, and other evil and naughty ceremonies and dreams justly and lawfully abolished . . .; and some other, taking and gathering divers Holy Scriptures to contrary senses and understanding, do wrest and interpret and so untruly allege the same to subvert and overturn as well the sacraments of Holy Church as the power and authority of princes and magistrates, and in effect generally all laws and common justice . . .; some of them also using the Scripture permitted to them by the King's goodness in the English tongue [*much contrary to his highness' expectation: for his majesty's intent and hope was that they would read the Scripture, would with meekness and wish to accomplish the effect of, read it, and not to maintain erroneous opinions and preach, nor for to use the reading or preaching of it in sundry times and places and after*][1] such fashions and feats as it is not convenient to be suffered. And thus each of them dispute so earnestly [*arrogantly*] against the other of their opinions as well in churches, alehouses, taverns, and other places and congregations, that there is begun and sprung among themselves slander and railing each at other as well by word as writing, one part of them calling the other papist, the other part calling the other heretic; whereby is like to follow sedition [*dissension*] and tumult [*to their own confusions*] and destructions [*not only to their own confusions that teach and use the same, but also to the disturbance and likelihood of destruction of all the rest of the King's true and well-beloved subjects*]. . . .

For remedy whereof his most royal majesty . . . to reduce his people, committed by God to his cure, to unity of opinion . . . intendeth . . . to proceed to a full power [*order*] and resolution to extinct all such diversities of opinions by terrible [*good and just*] laws to be made for the same by authority of his parliament; and yet nevertheless, now in the beginning of his parliament, of his most excellent and virtuous goodness, mindeth by this his [*a*] proclamation set forth by the advice [*his highness with the advice*] of his council, by authority of parliament [*according to an authority of parliament already to his highness, successors, and council granted*] to extirpate and take away some occasions [*as hereafter followeth*] which have moved and bred division among sundry of his subjects. . . .

And over this, his majesty straightly chargeth and commandeth that no person, except . . . such as be or shall be admitted to preach by the King's license, . . . shall teach or preach the Bible or New Testament, nor expound the mysteries thereof to any other; nor that any person or persons shall openly read the Bible or New Testament in the English tongue in any churches or chapels [*or elsewhere*] with any loud or high voices, [*and specially*] during the time of divine service of celebrating and saying of masses. . . .

And also [*Notwithstanding*], his highness is pleased and con-

[1] Bracketed italicized words and phrases represent interlinear modifications and corrections interpolated into the original document in the handwriting of King Henry VIII after the document had been drawn up by the King and his council. As such they constitute an official part of the document.

tented that such as can [*and will*] read in the English tongue shall and may quietly and reverently read the Bible and New Testament [*quietly and with silence*] by themselves [*secretly*] at all times and places convenient for their own instruction and edification, to increase thereby godliness and virtuous living. . . .

Finally his highness signifieth to all and singular his loving and obedient subjects that his majesty was, nor is, compelled by God's word to set forth the Scripture in English to all [*his*] lay subjects, but of his own liberty [*liberality*] and goodness was and is pleased that his said loving subjects should have and read the same in convenient places and times, to the only intent to bring them from their old ignorance and blindness to virtuous living and godliness, to God's glory and honor, and not to make and take occasion of sedition or division [*dissension or tumult*] by reason of the same.

An Excerpt from the *Constitution of the Society of Jesus* (1540)

In this Society, which we wish to call after Jesus, whoever wishes to fight under the sacred banner of the Cross, and to serve God and the Roman Pope, Christ's Vicar on earth, after a solemn vow of perpetual chastity, must keep in mind that he is part of a group, instituted for the purpose of perfecting souls through public preaching, ministering the word of God, works of charity, and especially through the teaching of the young and those ignorant of the Christian faith and for giving comfort to believers in hearing their confessions. Let him be aware first of God, then of the laws of this society, which is the way to God; and let him follow after the goal proposed with all his being.

Let each one know, and not only at the beginning of his profession, but think on it daily as long as he live, that the society as a whole, and each individual, owes obedience to our most Holy Lord, the Pope, and his successors, and to live with faithful obedience to God. And no matter how well he is known in the true faith, let him always profess himself under the Roman Pontiff as leader, and vicar of Jesus Christ on earth. For the greater humility of our society, and toward the complete mortification of the individual and in order to aid in the submersion of our own wills, let each one, besides that common obligation, be true to this especial vow. So that whatever the present or succeeding Roman Pontiffs order in what concerns the saving of souls and the spread of the true faith, and to whatever lands he shall send us, this let us seek to accomplish as far as we are able, without any retreat or fear, whether he shall send us to the Turks, or other infidels, even those in the Indies; or to any heretics or schismatics, or pagans whatever.

So let those that wish to join with us think long and well before they set their shoulders to this task, whether they have sufficient grace to mount this citadel at the command of their superiors. . . .

The Counter-Reformation Activity of the Council of Trent

(*Canones et decreta sacrosancti concilii Tridentini,* 1545)

The Universal Church has always understood that the complete confession of sins was instituted by the Lord, and is of divine right necessary for all who have fallen into sin after baptism. . . .

This holy Council enjoins on all bishops and others who are charged with teaching, that they instruct the faithful diligently concerning the intercession and invocation of the saints, the honor paid to relics, and the legitimate use of images. . . .

If anyone holds that the New Testament does not provide for a distinct, visible priesthood; or that this priesthood has not any power of consecrating and offering up the true body and blood of the Lord . . . let him be anathema. . . .

If anyone holds that in the Catholic Church there is not a hierarchy instituted by divine ordination, consisting of bishops, priests, and ministers; let him be anathema. . . .

In order that the faithful may approach and receive the sacraments with greater reverence and devotion of mind, this holy Council enjoins on all bishops that, not only when they are themselves about to administer them to the people they shall first explain, in a manner suited to the capacity of those who receive them, the efficacy and use of those sacraments, but they shall endeavor that the same be done piously and prudently by every parish priest; and this even in the vulgar tongue, if need be. . . .

It is to be hoped that those who undertake the office of Bishop should understand what their portion is, and comprehend that they are called, not to their own convenience, not to riches or luxury, but to labors and cares, for the glory of God. . . . Wherefore this holy Council, being minded that these things are of the greatest importance towards restoring ecclesiastical discipline, admonishes all bishops that, often meditating thereon, they show themselves conformable to their office by their actual deeds and the actions of their lives . . . that others may thence be able to derive examples of frugality, modesty, continency. . . .

It strictly forbids them to strive to enrich their own kindred or friends out of the revenues of the Church; seeing that even the canons of the apostles forbid them to give to their kindred the property of the Church, which belongs to God. . . . And what has been said of Bishops, the same is to be observed by all who hold ecclesiastical benefices, whether secular or regular, each according to the nature of his rank. . . .

An Agreement Concerning Religious Toleration (*The Treaty of the Peace of Augsburg,* 1555)

We, Ferdinand, by God's Grace King of the Romans, Greetings:

Whereas, at all the diets held during the last generation and more, there have often been negotiations to establish between the estates of the Holy Empire a general, and enduring peace in regard to the contending religions; but in spite of them the estates of the Empire remained continually in bitterness and distrust toward each other. But now, to secure peace and confidence, and to save the German nation, our beloved fatherland from final dissolution and ruin, we have united and agreed in all of this following.

We therefore establish, will and command that from henceforth no one, whatsoever his rank or character, for any cause, or upon any pretense whatsoever, shall engage in feuds, or make war upon, rob, seize, or besiege another. Nor shall he for any reason attack another for religion.

And in order that such peace, which is especially necessary in view of divided religions, as is seen from the causes before mentioned, and is demanded by the sad necessity of the Holy Roman Empire of the German nation may be the better established and made secure and enduring between us, we, the electors, princes, and estates of the Holy Empire will not make war upon any estate of the empire on account of the Augsburg Confession and the doctrine, religion, and faith of the same, nor do injury or violence to those who hold it, nor force them, against their conscience, knowledge, and will, to abandon the religion and ceremonies of the Augsburg Confession, where these have been established, or may hereafter be established in their principalities, lands, and dominions.

On the other hand, the estates that have accepted the Augsburg Confession shall suffer his Imperial Majesty and the electors, princes and other estates of the Holy Empire, adhering to the old religion, to abide in like manner by their religion, faith, church usages, and ceremonies. They shall also leave undisturbed their possessions, lands, people, and governments.

But all others who are not adherents of either of the abovementioned religions are not included in this peace, but shall be altogether excluded.

No estate shall urge another estate, or the subjects of the same, to embrace its religion.

But when our subjects and those of the electors, princes, and estates, adhering to the old religion or to the Augsburg Confession, wish, for the sake of their religion, to go with wife and children to another place in the lands, principalities, and cities of the Holy Empire, and settle there, such going and coming, and the sale of property and goods, shall be everywhere unhindered, permitted and granted.

John Calvin on the Church and the State
(John Calvin, *Institutes of the Christian Religion,* 1534)

. . . civil government is designed, as long as we live in this world, to cherish and support the external worship of God, to preserve the pure doctrine of religion, to defend the constitution of the Church, to regulate our lives in a manner requisite for the society of men, to form our manners to civil justice, to promote our concord with each other, and to establish general peace and tranquility. . . .

If we direct our attention to the word of God, it will carry us even to submit to the government, not only of those princes who discharge their duty to us with becoming integrity and fidelity, but of all who possess the sovereignty, even though they perform none of the duties of their function. For, though the Lord testifies that the magistrate is an eminent gift of his liberality to preserve the safety of men, and prescribes to magistrates themselves the extent of their duty, yet he at the same time declares, that whatever be their characters, they have their government only from him; that those who govern for the public good are true specimens and mirrors of his beneficence; and that those who rule in an unjust and tyrannical manner are raised up by him to punish the iniquity of the people; that all equally possess that sacred majesty with which he has invested legitimate authority. . . .

But in the obedience which we have shown to be due to the authority of governors, it is always necessary to make one exception, and that is entitled to our first attention—that it do not seduce us from obedience to Him, to whose will the desires of all kings ought to be subject, to whose decrees all their commands ought to be subject, to whose decrees all their commands ought to yield, to whose majesty all their sceptres ought to submit. And, indeed, how preposterous it would be for us, with a view to satisfy men, to incur the displeasure of God on whose account we yield obedience to Kings! The Lord, therefore, is the King of Kings; who, when he has opened his sacred mouth, is to be heard alone, above all, for all, and before all; in the next place, we are subject to those men who preside over us; but not otherwise than in Him. If they command anything against Him, it ought not to have the least attention; nor, in this case, ought we to pay any regard to all that dignity attached to magistrates; to which no injury is done when it is subjected to the unrivalled and supreme power of God.

Concerning the Marriage of Queen Mary Tudor and Philip II of Spain
(Queen Mary: *Royal Proclamation,* 1554)

And where it hath pleased Almighty God so to direct our heart that a treaty is of late contracted for a marriage to be solemnized, within this our realm, between our dearest cousin, the Prince of Spain, and us, with such covenants, parts, and agreements for the preservation of the laws, liberty, surety, and honor of our realm as may appear by the articles hereto sent unto you:

We understand that certain ill-disposed persons meaning, under the pretense of misliking this marriage, to rebel against the Catholic religion and divine service restored within this our realm, and to take from us, their sovereign lady and Queen, that liberty which is not denied to the meanest women in the choice of their husbands, cease not to spread many false, vile, and untrue reports of our said cousin and others of that nation, moving and stirring our good and loving subjects, by these and sundry other devilish ways, to rebel and enter a mere commotion to the great peril of our person and utter subversion of the whole realm, if speedy remedy be not provided.

For redress whereof, and to the intent our loving subjects may the better understand this unnatural conspiracy and the falsehood thereof:

Our pleasure is you shall not only cause the said articles herewith sent to be published in all parts of that our county, by sending abroad copies and such other good means as you may think best, but also that you and every of you, taking diligent heed of the preservation of the peace and charge committed unto you, do cause the authors and spreaders of these or any other false bruits and rumors to be apprehended, committed to ward, and otherwise punished as the qualities of their offenses shall merit.

For the better doing whereof our pleasure is you shall assemble together immediately, upon the sight of these our letters, and taking such order for division of yourselves into sundry hundreds and parts, and for the publication of the said articles, admonition of our good subjects, and stay of the rest, as may best tend to the quiet of that our county. Whereby you shall show yourselves our good and obedient subjects, which we will be glad always to consider toward you as any occasion may serve.

Censorship of Books in Counter-reformation England (Philip & Mary: *Royal Proclamation,* 1555)

The King and Queen our soverign lord and lady (most entirely and earnestly tendering the preservation and safety, as well of the souls as of the bodies, lands, and substance of all their good and loving subjects and others, and minding to root out and extinguish all false doctrine and heresies and other occasions of schisms, divisions, and sects that come by the same heresies and false doctrine) straightly charge and command that no person or persons, of what estate, degree, or condition soever he or they be, from henceforth presume to bring or convey or cause to be brought or conveyed into this realm any books, writings, or works hereafter mentioned:

That is to say, any book or books, writings or works made or set forth by or in the name of Martin Luther, or any book or books, writings, or works made or set forth by or in the name of Oecolampadius, Swinglius, John Calvin, Pomeraine, John Alasco, Bullinger, Bucer, Melancthon, Bernardinus Ochinus, Erasmus Sarcerius, Peter Martyr, Hugh Latimer, Robert Barnes, otherwise called Friar Barnes, John Bale, otherwise called Friar Bale, Justus Jonas, John Hooper, Myles Coverdale, William Tyndale, Thomas Cranmer, late archbishop of Canterbury, William Turner, Theodore Basille, otherwise called Thomas Becon, John Frith, Roy, and the book commonly called *Hall's Chronicles,* or any of them, in the Latin tongue, Dutch tongue, English tongue, Italian tongue, or French tongue, or any other like book, paper, writing, or work, made, printed, or set forth by any other person or persons, containing false doctrine contrary and against the Catholic faith and the doctrine of the Catholic church:

And also that no person or persons presume to write, print, utter, sell, read, or keep, or cause to be written, printed, uttered, read, or kept any of the said books, papers, works, or writings, or any book or books written or printed in the Latin or English tongue concerning the common service and ministration set forth in English to be used in the churches of this realm in the time of King Edward VI, commonly called the communion book, or books of common service and ordering of ministers, otherwise called *The Book Set Forth by Authority of Parliament for Common Prayer and Administration of the Sacraments, to be Used in the Mother Tongue, Within the Church of England,* but shall within the space of 15 days next after the publication of this proclamation, bring or deliver or cause the said books, writings, and works and every of them remaining in their custodies and keeping, to be brought and delivered to the ordinary of the diocese where such books, works, or writings be or remain, or to his chancellor or commissaries, . . . to be burnt . . . as by the canons and spiritual laws it is in that case limited and appointed. . . .

And their majesties by this proclamation giveth full power and authority to all bishops and ordinaries, and all justices of peace, mayors, sheriffs, bailiffs, . . . and other head officers within this realm and the dominions thereof, and expressly commandeth . . . every of them [to] search out the said books, writings, and works, and for this purpose enter into the house or houses, closets, and secret places of every person . . . suspected to keep any such book, writing, or works . . . and . . . finding any of the said subjects negligent and faulty in this behalf, shall commit every such offender to ward, there to remain without bail or mainprize. . . .

The King's Refusal to Recognize the Court Established by Commons for his Trial.

(*Speech of King Charles I to the Court of Trial,* 1649)

Having already made my protestations, not only against the illegality of this pretended court, but also that no earthly power can justly call me, who am your king, in question as a delinquent, I would not any more open my mouth upon this occasion more than to refer myself to what I have spoken, were I in this case alone concerned; but the duty I owe to God in the preservation of the true liberty of my people will not suffer me at this time to be silent. For how can any free-born subject of England call life or anything he possesseth his own, if power without right daily make new and abrogate the old fundamental laws of the land—which I now take to be the present case?. . . .

There is no proceeding just against any man but what is warranted either by God's laws or the municipal laws of the country where he lives. Now I am most confident this day's proceeding cannot be warranted by God's laws; for, on the contrary, the authority of obedience unto Kings is clearly warranted and strictly commanded in both the Old and New Testament. . . .

Then for the law of this land, I am no less confident that no learned lawyer will affirm that an impeachment can lie against the king, they all going in his name. And one of their maxims is that the King can do no wrong. . . .

How the house of Commons can erect a court of judicature, which was never one itself (as is well known to all lawyers), I leave to God and the world to judge. And it were full as strange that they should pretend to make laws without King or Lords, to any that have heard speak of the laws of England. And admitting, but not granting, that the people of England's commission could grant your pretended power, I see nothing you can show for that; for certainly you never asked the question of the tenth man in the kingdom; and in this way you manifestly wrong even the poorest ploughman, if you demand not his free consent. . . .

Thus you see that I speak not for my own rights alone . . . but also for the true liberty of all my subjects—which consists, not in the power of government, but in living under such laws, such a government, as may give themselves the best assurance of their lives and property of their goods. . . . Besides all this, the peace of the kingdom is not the least in my thoughts. And what hope of settlement is there so long as power reigns without rule or law, changing the whole frame of that government under which this Kingdom hath flourished for many hundred years? . . . And believe it, the common people of England will not thank you for this; for they will remember how happy they have been of late years under the reigns of Queen Elizabeth, the King my father, and myself, until the beginning of these unhappy troubles, and will have cause to doubt that they shall never be so happy under any new. And by this time it will be too sensibly evident that the arms I took up were only to defend the fundamental laws of this kingdom against those who have supposed my power hath changed the ancient government.

Thus, having showed you briefly the reasons why I cannot submit to your pretended authority without violating the trust which I have from God for the welfare and liberty of my people, I expect from you either clear reasons to convince my judgment . . . or that you will withdraw your proceedings. . . .

Religious-Social Radicalism in Seventeenth Century England (Correspondence Concerning the "Diggers," 1650)

From an Informant to the Council of State. 16 April, 1649.

Informeth that on Sunday last, there was one Everard . . . who termeth himself a prophet (and several followers) all living at Cobham, came to St. George's Hill in Surrey, and began to dig on that side of the hill next to Campe Close, and sowed the ground with parsnips, carrots, and beans. . . . On Friday last they came again, between twenty and thirty, and wrought all day at digging. They did intend to have two or three ploughs at work. . . . They invite all to come in and help them and promise them meat, drink, and clothes. They do threaten to pull down and level all parks and lay open and plant all of them. . . . It is feared they have some design in hand.

Council of State to Lord Fairfax

My Lord—By the narrative enclosed your Lordship will be informed . . . of a disorderly . . . sort of people assembling . . . not far from Oatlands. . . . That conflux of people may be a beginning whence things of a greater and more dangerous consequence may grow. . . . We therefore recommend it to your Lordship's care that some force of horse may be sent . . . to disperse the people. . . .

Captain Gladman to Lord Fairfax

According to your order I marched towards St. George's Hill . . . met with Mr. Winstanley and Mr. Everard (which are the chief men . . .) . . . Everard . . . is no other than a madman. Sir, I intend to go with two or three men . . . this day, and persuade these people to leave this employment if I can. . . . Indeed the business is not worth the writing . . . or taking notice of. . . .

Gerard Winstanley to Lord Fairfax

Now, Sir, the end of our digging and ploughing upon the common land is this, that we and all the impoverished poor in the land may get a comfortable livelihood by our righteous labors thereupon; which we conceive we have a true right unto, by virtue of the conquest over the king, for while he was in power he was the successor of William the Conqueror, and held the land as a conqueror from us, and all Lords of Manors held title to the common lands from him; but seeing the common people of England by joint consent of person and purse, have cast out Charles our Norman oppressor, we have by this victory recovered ourselves from under his Norman yoke, and the land is now to return into the joint hands of those who have conquered, that is the commoners. . . .

We told you that we were not against . . . magistrates and laws to govern, . . . but as for our parts we shall need neither the one nor the other . . . for as our land is common, so our cattle is to be common, and our corn and fruits of the earth common, and are not to be bought and sold among us, but to remain a standing portion of livelihood to us and our children, without that cheating entanglement of buying and selling. . . .

I affirm that the earth was made to be a common treasury of livelihood for all, without respect to persons, and was not made to be bought and sold;. . . . then none ought to be lords or landlords over another, but the earth is free for every son and daughter of mankind to live free upon.

John Knox on Calvinism in Scotland: a Discussion with Queen Mary
(John Knox, *The History of the Reformation in Scotland,* 1560)

. . . . the queen spake with John Knox, and had long reasoning with him . . . the sum of their discussion being this. . . .

"But yet," said she, "ye have taught the people to receive

another religion than their Prince can allow; and how can that doctrine be of God, seeing, that God commands subjects to obey their Prince?"

"Madam," said he, "as that right religion takes neither origin nor authority from worldly princes, but from the eternal God alone, so are not subjects bound to frame their religion according to the appetite of their princes; for oft it is, that princes are the most ignorant of all others in God's true religion, as we may read well in the histories before the death of Christ Jesus, and after . . . and so, Madam, ye may perceive, that subjects are not bound to the religion of their princes, albeit they are commanded to give them obedience."

"Yea," said she, "none of these men raised the sword against their princes."

"Yet madam," said he, "ye cannot deny but that they resisted; for these that obey not the commandments that are given, in some part they resist. . . ."

"Think ye," said she, "that subjects having power may resist their princes?"

"If their princes exceed their bounds," said he, ". . . it is no doubt but they may be resisted, even by power. . . ."

At these words, the queen stood as if amazed, more than quarter of an hour; her countenance altered. . . . At length she said, "Well then, I perceive, that my subjects shall obey you and not me; and shall do what they list, and not what I command; and so must I be subject to them, and not they to me."

". . . kings," (said he) ". . . be, as it were, foster-fathers to His Kirk. . . ."

"Yea," said she, "but ye are not the kirk that I will nurse. I will defend the kirk of Rome, for it is, I think, the true kirk of God."

"Your will," said he, "madam, is no reason; neither doth your thought make that Roman harlot to be the true and immaculate spouse of Jesus Christ. . . ."

" My opinion," said she, "is not so."

"Opinion," said he, "requires knowlege; and I fear that right knowledge you have none."

"Ye interpret the scriptures," said she, "in one manner, and they in another; whom shall I believe, and who shall be judge?"

"You shall believe God," said he, "that plainly speaketh in His Word. . . . The word of God is plain in the self . . . so that there can remain no doubt, but unto such as will remain obstinately ignorant."

Cardinal Richelieu Establishes the Intendancies in France (Letter of Message: *Richelieu to the Parlement of Paris,* 1642)

His Majesty, Louis, King of France, had wished that the established laws, customs, and officers would ever serve full justice to all men; and this so effectively that methods out of the ordinary to this purpose would never be necessary. This policy of generosity and gentleness has not been successful. France requires a system of discipline and law in proportion to her size, greatness, and prosperity. To insure this it falls incumbent on those responsible in the State to place in the Provinces of France and the local areas men especially chosen by the State for their enlightened abilities, justice, and loyalty, to guide and direct and oversee those functions of government stemming from the Monarch.

In addition, it is well to send these councellors of the State also as Intendants of the King into all areas of the Kingdom to proceed in all judicial, taxation, and financial matters—and specifically to find if the taxes taken by the collectors are in the just amount set by the law, and to know if the Nobility does any hurt to the people, and to insure against civil war and tumult. But of greater significance to hold the wealthy and strong from doing hurt to the poor and weak.

Instructions Sent by Oliver Cromwell to Mr. Daniel Goodkin Concerning the Newly Won Island of Jamaica, October 27, 1655 (Letter: *Cromwell to Goodkin*)

I. You shall upon receipt of these instructions, repair aboard the ketch, the *Fraternity,* bound for New England . . . where being arrived;

II. You shall apply yourself to the governors, magistrates, and General Courts of the English Colonies . . . to acquaint them, that it hath pleased God to put the island of Jamaica into the . . . possession of this state. . . .

III. You shall describe unto them, the content, situation, and goodness of the said island, the same as expressed in this paper. . . .

V. You shall assure them, that we shall . . . defend the island against all attempts whatsoever . . . our intention being . . . to have a good fleet always in those seas.

VI. This being the true state of that affair, and the reality of our intentions therein, we have thought it expedient to send you . . . unto the Colonies . . . to explain these things unto them; and to make them an offer of removing themselves . . . into Jamaica, which we have done chiefly upon these ensuing reasons. . . .

1. Our desire is, that this place (if the Lord so please) may be inhabited by people who know the Lord and walk in his fear, that by their light they may enlighten the parts around them,
2. Out of love and affection to themselves, and the feeling we have always had of the difficulties . . . they have been put to contest with, ever since they were driven from the land of their nativity into that desert and barren wilderness for their consciences' sake . . . an opportunity is offered for . . . removing them out of a hard country into a land of plenty.

Puritan Massacre of the Irish Catholics at Drogheda (Oliver Cromwell, *Letter to Parliament,* 1649)

Upon Tuesday the 10th . . . we began the storm, . . . the enemy disputing it very stiffly with us. And indeed, through the advantages of the place . . . our men were forced to retreat quite out of the breach, not without some considerable loss. . . .

. . . Our men . . . made a second attempt, wherein God was pleased to animate them that they got ground of the enemy, and . . . forced him to quit his entrenchments . . . and our men became masters of their retrenchments and the church. . . .

The enemy retreated, divers of them, into the mill-mount; a place very strong and of difficult access, being exceedingly high, . . . and strongly palisadoed. The Governor . . . and divers considerable officers being there, our men getting up to them, were ordered by me to put them all to the sword. And indeed, being in the heat of action, I forbade them to spare any, . . . and, I think that night they put to the sword about 2,000 men, divers of the officers and soldiers being fled over the bridge into the other part of the town, where about 100 of them possessed St. Peter's church steeple, some the west gate, and others a strong round tower next the gate called St. Sunday's. These being summoned to yield to mercy, refused, whereupon I ordered the steeple of St. Peter's church to be fired, where one of them was heard to say in the midst of the flames: "God damn me, God confound me; I burn, I burn."

The next day the others two towers were summoned, in one of which was about six or seven score; but they refused to yield themselves, and we knowing that hunger must compel them, set only good guards to secure them from running away until their stomachs were come down. . . . When they submitted their officers were knocked on the head and every tenth man of the soldiers killed, and the rest shipped for the Barbadoes. The soldiers in the other tower were . . . shipped likewise for the Barbadoes. . . .

And now give me leave to say how it comes to pass that this work is wrought. It was set upon some of our hearts that a great thing should be done, not by power or might, but by the Spirit of God. And is it not so clear? That which caused your men to storm so courageously, it was the Spirit of God who gave your men courage . . . and therewith this happy success. And therefore it is good that God alone have all the glory. . . .

A Parliamentary Act Aimed at Restraining Nonconforming and Catholic Ministers from Performing Religious Rites (*Five Mile Act,* 1665)

An act for restraining non-conformists from inhabiting in corporations. Whereas divers . . . persons in holy orders have not declared their unfeigned assent and consent to the use of all things contained and prescribed in the Book of Common Prayer . . . or have not subscribed the declaration or acknowledgment contained in a certain act of parliament made in the fourteenth year of his majesty's reign . . . or any other subsequent act; and whereas they, or some of them, and divers other person and persons not ordained according to the form of the Church of England, and as have, since the Act of Oblivion, taken upon them to preach in unlawful assemblies, conventicles, or meetings, under colour or pretence of exercise of religion, contrary to the laws and statutes of this kingdom, have settled themselves in divers corporations in England, sometimes three or more of them in a place, thereby taking an opportunity to distill the poisonous principles of schism and rebellion into the hearts of his majesty's subjects, to the great danger of the church and kingdom: be it therefore enacted . . . that the said . . . persons in holy orders or pretended holy orders, or pretending to holy orders, and all . . . persons who have been possessed of any ecclesiastical or spiritual promotion . . . who have not declared their unfeigned assent and consent as aforesaid, and subscribed the declaration aforesaid, and shall not take and subscribe the oath following . . . and all such person and persons as shall take upon them to preach in any unlawful assembly, conventicle, or meeting, under colour or pretence of any exercise of religion, contrary to the laws and statutes of this kingdom, shall not at any time . . . unless only in passing upon the road, come or be within five miles of any city or town corporate or borough that sends burgesses to the parliament, within his majesty's kingdom of England, principality of Wales, or of the town of Berwick-upon-Tweed, or within five miles of any parish, town or place wherein he or they have since the Act of Oblivion been parson, vicar, curate, stipendiary, or lecturer, or taken upon them to preach in any unlawful assembly, conventicle, or meeting . . . upon forfeiture for every such offence the sum of £40 of Lawful English money. . . .

Provided always . . . that it shall not be lawful for any person or persons restrained from coming to any city, town corporate, borough, parish, town, or place, as aforesaid, or for any other person or persons as shall not first take and subscribe the said oath and as shall not frequent divine service established by the laws of this kingdom and carry him or herself reverently, decently, and orderly there, to teach any public or private school, to to take any boarders or tablers that are taught or instructed by him or herself, or any other, upon pain for every such offence to forfeit the sum of £40. . . .

A Parliamentary Act for Disinfranchising Catholics from Political Rights and Civil Office (*First Test Act,* 1673)

An act for preventing dangers which may happen from popish recusants and quieting the minds of his majesty's good subjects: be it enacted . . . that all and every person or persons, as well peers as commoners, that shall bear any office or offices civil or military; or shall receive any pay, salary, fee, or wages by reason of any grant from his majesty; or shall have command or place of trust from or under his majesty or from any of his majesty's predecessors . . . within the realm of England, dominion of Wales, or town of Berwick-upon-Tweed, or in his Majesty's navy, or in the several islands of Jersey and Guernsey; or shall be of the household or in the service or employment of his majesty or of his royal highness the duke of York, who shall inhabit, reside, or be within the city of London or Westminster or within thirty miles distant from the same . . . the said person and persons shall personally appear . . . in his majesty's high court of chancery or in his majesty's court of king's bench, and there in public . . . take the several oaths of supremacy and allegiance. . . . And the said respective officers aforesaid shall also receive the sacrament of the Lord's Supper according to the usage of the Church of England . . . in some parish church upon some . . . Sunday immediately after divine service and sermon. . . .

And be it further enacted . . . that all . . . that do . . . refuse to take the said oaths and sacrament in the said courts and places . . . shall be *ipso facto* adjudged incapable and disabled in law . . . to have . . . the said office or offices. . . . And be it further enacted that all . . . that shall . . . refuse to take the said oaths or the sacrament as aforesaid . . . and yet after such neglect and refusal shall execute any of the said offices or employments after the said times expired . . . and being thereupon lawfully convicted . . . shall be disabled from thenceforth to sue or use any action, bill, plaint, or equity or to be guardian of any child or executor or administrator of any person or capable of any legacy or deed of gift, or to bear any office within this realm of England, dominion of Wales, or town of Berwick-upon-Tweed; and shall forfeit the sum of £500, to be recovered by him that shall sue for the same. . . .

And be it further enacted that, if any person or persons, not bred up by his or their parent or parents from their infancy in the popish religion and professing themselves to be popish recusants, shall breed up, instruct, or educate his or their child or children, or suffer them to be instructed or educated, in the popish religion, every such person, being thereof convicted, shall be thenceforth disabled of bearing any office or place of trust or profit in church or state. . . .

And be it further enacted . . . that at the same time when the persons concerned in this act shall take the aforesaid oaths of supremacy and allegiance, they shall likewise make and subscribe this declaration following, under the same penalties and forfeitures as by this act is appointed: "I, A.B., do declare that I do believe that there is not any transubstantiation in the sacrament of the Lord's Supper, or in the elements of bread and wine, at or after the consecration thereof by any person whatsoever."

Edict Concerning the Liberties of the Gallican Church (*Edict of Louis XIV,* 1683)

Abundant forces seek to deny the laws of the French Church

and to set aside its legitimate and ancient freedom which is rooted in the Holy Canons and in the traditions of the Fathers of the Church. These professors of heresy strive mightily to destroy the state of harmony which exists between the Church, Kings, and subjects.

To check and alleviate these troublesome errors, we, the Primates of the Church Universal, gathered by the Kings decree in Paris here render this further statement:

Peter and his successors, and the institution of the Church, are delegated to Authority in spiritual affairs only. Nothing civil or temporal is theirs; for even Christ said, "My Kingdom is not of this World," and "Render to Caesar what is Caesar's and to God what is God's."

Also, St. Paul said, "There is no power but of God, and the powers that now be are truly ordained by God, and who resists power also resists the law of God."

Rightfully, then Kings are free by God's word of any demand in earthly things by any Church officer; and Kings cannot be deposed by the Spiritual power nor can their subjects be freed from their legal bonds of obedience and loyalty to Kings by any power.

Also, this must be affirmed, that even though the Pope has greater voice in Spiritual matters than any other, and even though all Churches bend in obedience to his voice in these matters, his decree is not sovereign unless it be at the consent of the whole Church.

The Revocation of the Edict of Nantes
(*Edict of Louis XIV,* 1685)

Louis, by the Grace of God, King of France:

Henry the Great, our grandparent, seeking peace against the machinations of the Calvinists gave regulations concerning them at Nantes in 1598, so that he might one day bring them back to union with the true church.

Our parent, King Louis XIII, in 1629 gave yet a new Edict, that of Nimes, to further protect the Kingdom against such unrest —since general European unrest made it impossible for him to do anything by way of fulfilling the hopes of Henry.

God now having given our people peace and repose we may set our whole design at facilitating the attainment to which our ancestors were determined, and which is always before us.

Since all but a small minority of the Calvinists have rejoined the Catholic faith, the whole purpose of the Edict of Nantes and that of Nimes is negated and nullified and it at once becomes our duty to forget the time of troubles and obliterate the evidences of the existence of the heresy, and wholly to rescind the Edict of Nantes and all that since its promulgation was done to aid that profession.

Therefore:

We do by this present statute revoke in full and wholly suppress the Edict of Henry IV given at Nantes, and the Edict later given at Nimes; and we declare them voided and we desire that all the Church's of the Calvinists in our realm be forthwith demolished.

We enjoin all subjects against meeting in any place for this religious practice.

We forbid all noblemen to cause to exist, or to attend, such services on pain of incarceration and escheat.

Priests and officers of the Calvinist group must swear to the true Church or go out of our realm within fourteen days. During that period they may not preach, teach, or publicly pray.

We forbid private institutions of education for children of the Reformed group.

Children newly born to parents of the Reformed group shall be baptized in the true church. Local magistrates are enjoined to guarantee that such children be raised in the Roman faith.

It is forbidden to the Calvinists, their wives and progeny, to leave our realm, or to transport any goods out of the Kingdom.

Frederick, the Great Elector, Welcomes the French Huguenots to His Domain
(*Edict of Frederick of Brandenburg,* 1685)

In view of the sympathy which we ought to, and do feel for our brethren of the reformed evangelical religion in France, who have been driven by persecution to leave their homes and settle in other countries, we, Frederick William, . . . desire by this edict to offer them a free and safe refuge in all our lands and possessions and to specify what rights, privileges, and prerogatives we are graciously minded to grant them.

We particularly specify the towns of Stendal, Werben, Rathenow, Brandenburg, and Frankfurt in the electorate of Brandenburg, Magdeburg, Halle, and Calbe in the duchy of Magdeburg, and Konigsberg in Prussia, as places where living is cheap and opportunities for trade and other means of support abundant;

and we command herewith that when any of the said French people of the reformed evangelical religion make their appearance, they shall be well received in the said towns, and that every opportunity and assistance shall be given them in establishing themselves there. They shall, moreover, be free to establish themselves in any other place in our lands and dominions outside the above-mentioned towns which shall seem to them more convenient for the purposes of their trade or calling.

They shall be permitted to bring with them any furniture, merchandise, or other movable property free of all duties or imposts of any kind whatever.

In towns or other places where there are unoccupied or waste lands or properties, we ordain that these shall be given over to our said French brethren of the reformed evangelical religion, free of all and every incumbrance, to hold and enjoy for themselves and their posterity. We further ordain that the necessary materials for the cultivation of these lands shall be furnished them gratis.

So soon as any of our said French brethren of the reformed evangelical religion shall have settled themselves in any town or village, they shall be invested, without payment of any kind, with all the rights, benefits, and privileges of citizenship enjoyed or exercised by our subjects who live and were born in said town or village.

If any of them shall desire to establish manufactories of cloth, stuffs, hats, or other articles, we will not only bestow on them all the necessary permissions, rights, and privileges, but will further aid them, so far as is in our power, with money and requisite materials.

Those who wish to settle in the country shall be given a certain amount of land to cultivate, shall be furnished with the requisite utensils and materials and encouraged in every way, as has been done in the case of certain families who have come from Switzerland to settle in our country.

In every town where our said French brethren in the faith are established, we will support a special preacher and set apart a proper place where they may hold their services in the French language, and with such usages and ceremonies as are customary in the reformed evangelical churches in France.

As for the members of the French nobility who have placed themselves under our protection and entered our service, they enjoy the same honors, dignities, and prerogatives as our own subjects of noble birth, and several of them have been given some of the most important offices at our court as well as in our army; and we are graciously disposed to show like favor to all such of the French nobility as may in future present themselves to us.

The Guarantee of English Liberties
(The English *Bill of Rights,* 1689)

Whereas the said late King James II having abdicated the government, and the throne being thereby vacant, his Highness the Prince of Orange did by the advice of the Lords spiritual and temporal, and divers principal persons of the Commons cause letters to be written to the Lords spiritual and temporal, being Protestants, and other letters to the several counties, cities, universities, boroughs, and Cinque Ports, for the choosing of such persons to represent them in order that their religion, laws and liberties might not again be in danger of being subverted; upon which letters elections have been accordingly made.

And thereupon the said Lords spiritual and temporal and Commons, pursuant to their respective letters and elections, being now assembled in a full and free representation of this nation, taking into their most serious consideration the best means for attaining the ends aforesaid, do in the first place, as their ancestors in like case have usually done, for the vindication and assertion of their ancient rights and liberties, declare:

1. That the pretended power of suspending laws, or the execution of laws, by regal authority, as it hath been assumed and exercised of late, is illegal.
2. That the pretended power of dispensing with the laws, or the execution of law by regal authority, as it hath been assumed and exercised of late, is illegal.
3. That the commission for erecting the late court of commissions and courts of like nature, are illegal and pernicious.
4. That levying money for or to the use of the crown by pretense of prerogative, without grant of parliament, for longer time or in other manner than the same is or shall be granted, is illegal.
5. That it is the right of the subjects to petition the king, and all commitments and prosecutions for such petitioning are illegal.
6. That the raising or keeping a standing army within the kingdom in time of peace, unless it be with the consent of parliament, is against law.
7. That the subjects which are Protestants may have arms for their defense suitable to their conditions, and as allowed by law.

8. That the freedom of speech, and debates or proceedings in parliament ought not to be impeached or questioned in any court or place out of parliament.

9. That election of members of parliament ought to be free.

10. That excessive bail ought not to be required, nor excessive fines imposed, nor cruel and unusual punishments inflicted.

11. That jurors ought to be duly impaneled and returned, and jurors which pass upon men in trials for high treason ought to be freeholders.

12. That all grants and promises of fines and forfeitures of particular persons before conviction are illegal and void.

13. And that for redress of all grievances, and for the amending, strengthening, and preserving of the laws, parliament ought to be held frequently.

And they do claim, demand, and insist upon all and singular the premises, as their undoubted rights and liberties; and that no declarations, judgments, doings, or proceedings, to the prejudice of the people in any of the said premises, ought in any wise to be drawn hereafter into consequence or example.

To which demand of their rights they are particularly encouraged by the declaration of his Highness the prince of Orange, as being the only means for obtaining a full redress and remedy therein.

Having therefore an entire confidence that his said Highness the Prince of Orange will perfect the deliverance so far advanced by him, and will still preserve them from the violation of their rights, which they have here asserted, and from all other attempt upon their religion, rights, and liberties:

The said Lords spiritual and temporal, and Commons, assembled at Westminster, do resolve that William and Mary, Prince and Princess of Orange, be, and be declared, King and Queen of England, France, Ireland, the dominions thereunto belonging, to hold the crown and royal dignity of the said Kingdoms and dominions to them the said Prince and Princess during their lives, and the life of the survivor of them; and that the sole and full exercise of the regal power be only in, and executed by, the said Prince of Orange, in the names of the said Prince and Princess, during their joint lives; and after their deceases, the said crown and royal dignity of the said Kingdoms and dominions to be to the heirs of the body of the said Princess; and for default of such issue to the Princess Ann of Denmark, and the heirs of her body; and for default of such issue to the heirs of the body of the said Prince of Orange. And the Lords spiritual and temporal, and Commons, do pray the said Prince and Princess to accept the same accordingly.

Upon which their said Majesties did accept the crown and royal dignity of the Kingdoms of England, France, Ireland, and the dominions thereunto belonging, according to the resolution and desire of the said Lords and Commons contained in the said declaration.

John Locke on Political Society and Government (John Locke, *Of Civil Government,* 1690)

If man in the state of Nature be so free as has been said, if he be absolute lord of his own person and possessions, equal to the greatest and subject to nobody, why will he part with his freedom, and subject himself to the domination and control of any other Power? To which it is obvious to answer, that though in the state of Nature he hath such a right, yet the enjoyment of it is very uncertain and constantly exposed to the invasion of others; for all being kings as much as he, every man his equal, and the greater part no strict observers of equity and justice, the enjoyment of the property he has in this state is very unsafe, very insecure. This makes him willing to quit this condition which, however free, is full of fears and continual dangers; and it is not without reason that he seeks out and is willing to join in society with others who are already united, or have a mind to unite for the mutual preservation of their lives, liberties and estates, which I call by the general name—property.

The great and chief end, therefore, of men uniting into commonwealths and putting themselves under government, is the preservation of their property; to which in the state of Nature there are many other things wanting.

Firstly, there wants an established, settled, known law, received and allowed by common consent to be the standard of right and wrong, and the common measure to decide all controversies between them. For though the law of Nature be plain and intelligible to all rational creatures, yet men, being biased by their interest, as well as ignorant for want of study of it, are apt to allow of it as a law binding to them in the application of it to their particular cases.

Secondly, in the state of Nature there wants a known and indifferent judge, with authority to determine all differences according to the established law. For every one in that state being both judge and executioner of the law of Nature, men being partial to themselves, passion and revenge is very apt to carry them too far, and with too much heat in their own cases, as well as negligence and unconcernedness, makes them too remiss in other men's.

Thirdly, in the state of Nature there often wants power to back and support the sentence when right and to give it due execution. They who by an injustice offended will seldom fail where they are able by force to make good their injustice. Such resistance many times makes the punishment dangerous, and frequently destructive to those who attempt it.

Thus mankind, notwithstanding all the privileges of the state of Nature, being but in an ill condition while they remain in it are quickly driven into society. It is this makes them so willingly give up every one his single power of punishing to be exercised by such alone as shall be appointed to it amongst them, and by such rules as the community, or those authorized by them to that purpose, shall agree on. And in this we have the original right and rise of both the legislative and executive power as well as of the governments and societies themselves.

For in the state of Nature to omit the liberty he has of innocent delights, a man has two powers. The first is to do whatsoever he thinks fit for the preservation of himself and others within the permission of the law of Nature; by which law, common to them all, he and all the rest of mankind are one community, make up one society distinct from all other creatures, and were it not for the corruption and viciousness of degenerate men, there would be no need of any other, no necessity that men should separate from this great and natural community, and associate into lesser combinations. The other power a man has in the state of Nature is the power to punish the crimes committed against that law. Both these he gives up when he joins in a particular society, and incorporates into any commonwealth separate from the rest of mankind.

The first power—viz., of doing whatsoever he thought fit for the preservation of himself and the rest of mankind, he gives up to be regulated by laws made by the society, so far forth as the preservation of himself and the rest of that society shall require; which laws of the society in many things confine the liberty he had by the law of Nature.

Secondly, the power of punishing he wholly gives up, and engages his natural force, which he might before employ in the execution of the law of Nature, by his own single authority, as he thought fit, to assist the executive power of the society as the law thereof shall require. For being now in a new state, wherein he is to enjoy many conveniences from the labour, assistance, and society of others in the same community, as well as protection from its whole strength, he is to part also with as much of his natural liberty, in providing for himself, as the good, prosperity, and safety of the society shall require, which is not only necessary but just, since the other members of the society do the like.

But though men when they enter into society give up the equality, liberty, and executive power they had in the state of Nature into the hands of the society, to be so far disposed of by the legislative as the good of the society shall require, yet it being only with an intention in every one the better to preserve himself, his liberty and property (for a rational creature cannot be supposed to change his condition with an intention to be worse), the power of the society or legislative constituted by them can never be supposed to extend farther than the common good, but is obliged to secure every one's property by providing against those three defects above mentioned that made the state of Nature so unsafe and uneasy. And so, whoever has the legislative or supreme power of any commonwealth, is bound to govern by established standing laws, promulgated and known to the people, and not by extemporary decrees, by indifferent and upright judges, who are to decide controversies by those laws; and to employ the force of the community at home only in the execution of such laws, or abroad to prevent or redress foreign injuries and secure the community from inroads and invasion. And all this to be directed to no other end but the peace, safety, and public good of the people.

The Growth of Religious Toleration
(*The Treaty of Westphalia*, 1648)

When the divisions and disorders which began several years ago in the Roman Empire had grown to a point where not only all Germany but some of the neighboring kingdoms as well, especially Sweden and France, found themselves so involved that a long and bitter war resulted, in the first instance between the most serene and powerful prince and lord, Ferdinand II, emperor elect of the Romans, always august, king of Germany, Hungary, Bohemia, Dalmatia, etc., archduke of Austria, duke of Burgundy,

Brabant, etc., of glorious memory, his allies and adherents, on the one part, and the most serene and powerful prince and lord, Gustavus Adolphus, king of Sweden, of the Goths and Vandals, grand prince of Finland, duke of Esthonia, etc., also of glorious memory, together with the kingdom of Sweden, its allies and adherents, on the other part; later, after the decease of these aforementioned, between the most serene and powerful lord, Ferdinand III, emperor elect of the Romans, always august, king of Germany, etc., and the most serene and very powerful princess and lady, Christina, queen of Sweden, of the Goths and Vandals, etc., from which war resulted a great effusion of Christian blood and the desolation of divers provinces, until at last, through the movings of the Divine Goodness, it came about that both parties began to turn their thoughts toward the means of reestablishing peace, and by a mutual agreement made at Hamburg, December 25 of the year 1641, between the parties, the date July 11 was fixed for the meeting of the plenipotentiaries at Osnabruck and at Munster in Westphalia. In accordance with this, the ambassadors plenipotentiary duly appointed by both parties appeared at the said time and places named, to wit. . . .

After invoking the aid of God and exchanging their credentials, copies of which are inserted word for word in the present treaty, they arranged and agreed upon the articles of peace and amity which follow, to the glory of God and for the welfare of the Christian commonwealth; the electors, princes, and estates of the Holy Roman Empire being present and approving.

UNIT 6

The Consequences of the Development of the Commercial Middle Class: Mercantilism and Absolutism

The pace of institutional and philosophical change so apparent in the 15th century was accelerated in the 16th and 17th centuries, and with good reason. New institutions and new concepts were necessitated by continuous and almost violent shifting of the geographic, productive, and consumptive historical factors, each of which demanded immediate modifications of thought as it presented its peculiar problems. The commercial middle class, economically secure by 1500, began to demand status and recognition in keeping with its true value to society. Yet, according to the law of medieval society and the traditional philosophy of order and degree, the desires of this class were ambitious, presumptuous, and even revolutionary. Thus, outside the accepted pattern of society, denied the liberties essential to its well-being, and scorned by the upper estates, the dynamic and versatile bourgeoisie which was dedicated to profit and to eventual dominance, turned for aid to another institution which was in a sense also an outsider, the rising national monarchies. The ensuing alliance between the class which needed law and order, protection, and strongly centralized government, and the financially weak but determined monarchs who needed ready money, bureaucracies, and moral support, was perhaps the most significant single historical development of the period, and one tremendously productive of new institutions, and of far-reaching modifications in the old.

Two new developments which well document the vitality generated by and consequent to this alliance of the two non-medieval institutions were the economic philosophy of mercantilism and the application of monarchial sovereignty.

Mercantilism, as a system for commercial control rested on the erroneous supposition that precious metals were of themselves wealth, and that national security could be ascertained best by hoarding them in bullion form. Colonies and fleets were integral parts of the system, since one produced raw material for the mother country and consumers for the produce of that country, and the other acted as a protective device. The best expression of the administrative aspect of this theory is that of Thomas Mun in his pamphlet *England's Treasure by Foreign Trade,* written prior to 1630, while one of the outstanding arguments in favor of colonization is that written almost a century earlier by Richard Hakluyt. The clearest and most precise statement of the policies of a continental mercantilist government is that of Colbert in 1664, while the *English Navigation Act* of 1651 is one of the best examples of governmental interference with and strict control of the economic life of the nation.

However, mercantilism as a system contained within itself the seeds of its own destruction. First, since its goal was absolute self-sufficiency, it was essentially isolationist—and in combination these aspirations were expressive of the basic premise that war and strife were the inevitable results of man's very existence. This was at best a philosophy of despair, and there could be no place for despair in an age so uncompromisingly optimistic as the 17th century.

Secondly, since mercantilism was dependent on strict governmental regulation, the middle class, which profited most from the system, was in some part responsible for the development of monarchial absolutism, and this early authoritarianism was destructive of human liberties in direct proportion to the benefits it bestowed on the merchant minority. Eventually this favored group came to desire political rights and social status in the state and found that the political superiority of the new national monarchs alone stood as barrier to attainment of its political objective. Thus in the end the new monarch, like the old aristocracy, and the ancient Church, must give way to the middle class and its later representative systems of government.

Looking backward now at the growth of monarchy, it would seem to us a simple change and an easy and logical development. Nothing could be further from the truth. Before the feudal kings, whose position was dependent on land tenure, could become national monarchs, whose power stemmed from the loyalty of a people, whole centuries of sacred traditions and values had to be cast aside, and a completely new social and political fabric constructed and given form and being. This was a tardy and painful process; for what was ancient and trusted was not lightly repudiated by western civilization which was still cognizant of its essentially conservative medieval heritage. So, as the institution of absolutism grew, step by step, in Europe, in the 16th and 17th centuries, it was rationalized and explained by a host of political thinkers who were pragmatists and realists rather than theorists. Of those many early observers who set down their thoughts relative to sovereignty and power and the rightful location of them in political society, Jean Bodin was not only among the first, but among the most precise and rational. Bodin was more interested in defining sovereign power than in locating it in any particular institution of government. And Bodin, still true to the high awareness of God by the medieval world, defined sovereignty as absolute and perpetual—yet, he pointed out, all power derived in society and it must "conform to the laws of God and Nature." This denied arbitrariness and it retained in God's hands, sanctions against immoral kings. By the late 16th century certain English thinkers were beginning to rationalize the superior power of the State over the Church, and in 1610 the English King James I would stand before Parliament and claim a divine right to rule his subjects as God's lieutenant on earth. "Kings," he said at that time, "are called God by God himself." Four decades later, when time had made greater opportunity for spinning out the fine web of political reasoning, Thomas Hobbes in the *Leviathan* was to develop the concept of the State as the great, unopposable, indestructable, political juggernaught, which, because of its mass basis, not only had all right and power, but was bound by no code of law and was subject to no superior authority.

At the same time, in the France of Louis XIV, Bossuet, in glorifying the monarch, was working out a Scriptural approach to sovereignity, both as to definition and as to location. Where Hobbes had constructed a rationale for amoral power, Bossuet warned the French King that although sovereignty did exist in his hands, and although man had no sanctions against kings, each monarch must one day render a strict accounting to God for every act and every political talent.

Hakluyt Desires England to Colonize America (Richard Hakluyt, *Journeys,* 1550)

I marvel not a little that since the first discovery of America (which is not full four score and ten years), after so great conquests and plantings of the Spaniards and Portuguese there, that we in England could never have the grace to set fast footing in such fertile and temperate places as are left as yet unpossessed of them. But again, when I consider that there is a time for all men, and see the Portuguese time to be out of date, and that the nakedness of the Spaniards and their long hidden secrets are now at length espied, whereby they went about to delude the world, I conceive great hope that the time approaches and now is, that we of England may share and partake (if we will ourselves), both with the Spaniard and the Portuguese, in part of America and other regions, as yet undiscovered. And surely if there were in us that desire to advance the honor of our country which ought to be in every good man, we would not all this while have forborne the possessing of those lands, which of equity and right appertain unto us, as by the discourses that follow shall appear most plainly. Yea, if we would behold with the eye of pity how all our prisons are pestered and filled with able men to serve their country, which for small robberies are daily hanged up in great numbers, even twenty at a clap, out of one jail we would hasten and further every man to one of our Colonies, thus ridding us of our superfluous people into those temperate and fertile parts of America, which, being within six weeks sailing of England, are yet unpossessed by any Christians; and seem to offer themselves unto us, stretching nearer unto her Majesty's Dominions than to any other part of Europe. We read that the bees when they grow to be too many in their own hives at home, are wont to be led out by their captains to swarm abroad and seek themselves a new dwelling place. If the examples of the Grecians and Carthaginians of old time and the practice of our own age may not move us, yet let us learn wisdom of these small weak and unreasoning creatures. It chanced very lately that upon occasion I had great conference in matters of Cosmography with an excellent learned man of Portugal most privy to all the discoveries of his nation who wondered that those blessed countries from the point of Florida northward were all this while unplanted by Christians, protesting with great affection and zeal, that if he were now as young as I he would sell all he had, being a man of no small wealth and honor, to furnish a convenient number of ships to sea for the inhabiting of those countries, and reducing those gentle people to Christianity. . . .

Mercantilism: Prohibiting Export of Precious Metals (Henry VIII: *Royal Proclamation,* 1531)

Our sovereign lord the King, considering that notwithstanding the said good and beneficial statute and all other good laws, ordinances, and statutes heretofore made for the preservation and keeping of the treasure of this realm within the same for the commonwealth of all his subjects, yet many persons having intercourse between this realm and other foreign countries, some by occasions and feats of merchandise and some by other occasions . . . have used commonly at many times heretofore to convey, send, and carry out of this realm by many secret means the coins of this realm and of other realms, plate, bullion, jewels, and other mass of gold and silver, whereby the treasure of this realm hath at sundry times been greatly diminished, and were also now like within short time to be much more diminished to the great impoverishment of this realm, if remedy be not therefor speedily provided.

Our said sovereign lord the King therefore . . . straightly chargeth and commandeth that no manner of person, Englishman, stranger, nor denizen, of what estate or degree soever he be, from henceforth in any wise so convey, send, or carry, or cause to be sent, carried, or conveyed out of this realm by any craft, means, or conveyance, any manner of coin of gold or silver of this realm or of any other realm, country, region, or dominion, or any manner of plate, vessel, bullion, jewels, or mass of gold or silver, under pain of forfeitures specified in the said statute.

And furthermore our said sovereign lord the King notifieth and declareth that whatsoever person hereafter by any manner of means espy, perceive, find, or know any person or persons conveying, sending, or bearing, or which shall cause to be conveyed or sent, any gold or silver, plate, bullion, vessels, jewels, or mass of gold or silver out of this realm, contrary to this proclamation, and thereof make seizure or give information to the lords of his most honorable council or before the Treasurer and Barons of his Exchequer . . . shall have the one half of the said gold or silver . . .

Mercantilism: Royal Regulation of Subjects' Clothing (Queen Elizabeth: *Royal Proclamation,* 1574)

The excess of apparel, and the superfluity of unnecessary foreign wares thereto belonging, now of late years is grown by sufferance to such an extremity that the manifest decay not only of a great part of the wealth of the whole realm generally is like to follow (by bringing into the realm such superfluities of silks, cloths of gold, silver, and other most vain devices, of so great cost for the quantity thereof as of necessity the moneys and treasure of the realm is and must be yearly conveyed out of the same to answer the said excess) but also particularly the wasting and undoing of a great number of young gentlemen, and others seeking by show of apparel to be esteemed as gentlemen, who (allured by the vain show of those things) do not only consume themselves, their goods, and lands which their parents have left unto them, but also run into such debts and shifts as they cannot live out of danger of laws, without attempting of unlawful acts, whereby they are not any ways serviceable to their country. . . .

Which great abuses, tending both to so manifest decay of the wealth of the realm and to the ruin of a multitude of serviceable young men . . . the Queen's majesty hath of her own princely wisdom . . . commanded the same to be presently and speedily remedied both in her own court and in all other places of her realm. . . .

Wherefore her majesty willeth and straightly commandeth all manner of persons in all places, within 12 days after the publication of this present proclamation, to reform their apparel according to the tenor of certain articles and clauses taken out of the said statutes and with some moderations annexed to this proclamation. . . .

A brief content of certain clauses of the statutes of King Henry VIII and Queen Mary, with some moderation thereof, to be observed according to her majesty's proclamation above mentioned:

Men's apparel:

None shall wear in his apparel any silk of the color purple, cloth of gold tissued, nor fur of sables, but only the King, Queen, King's mother, children, brethren, and sisters, uncles and aunts; and except dukes, marquises, and earls, who may wear the same in doublets, jerkins, linings of cloaks, gowns, and hose; and those of the [Order of the] Garter, pulple in mantles only;

Cloth of gold, silver, tinseled satin; silk, or cloth mixed or embroidered with any gold or silver: except all degrees above viscounts, and viscounts, barons, and other persons of like degree, in doublets, jerkins, linings of cloaks, gowns, and hose;

Woolen cloth made out of the realm, but in caps only; velvet, crimson or scarlet; furs, black genets, lucerns; embroidery or tailor's work having gold or silver or pearl therein: except dukes, marquises, earls, and their children; viscounts, barons, and knights being companions of the Garter; or any person being of the Privy Council;

Velvet in gowns, coats, or other uttermost garments; fur of leopards; embroidery with any silk: except men of the degrees above mentioned; barons' sons; knights and gentlemen in ordinary office attendant upon her majesty's person; and such as have been employed in embassages to foreign princes;

Caps, hats, hatbands, capbands, garters, boothose, trimmed with gold or silver or pearl; silk netherstocks; enameled chains, buttons, aglets: except men of the degrees above mentioned; the gentlemen attending upon the Queen's person in her highness' privy chamber, or in the office of cupbearer, carver, skewer, esquire for the body; gentlemen ushers; or esquires of the stable;

Satin, damask, silk, camlet, or taffeta, in gown, coat, hose, or uppermost garments; fur whereof the kind groweth not within the Queen's dominions, except foins, gray genets, and bodge: except the degrees and persons above mentioned; and men that may dispend £100 by the year, and so valued in the subsidy book;

None shall wear spurs, swords, rapiers, daggers, skeans, woodknives, or hangers, buckles of girdles, gilt, silvered, or damasked: except knights' and barons' sons, and others of higher degree or place, and gentlemen in ordinary office attendant upon the Queen's majesty's person; which gentlemen so attendant may wear the premises, saving gilt, silvered, or damasked spurs.

None shall wear in their trappings or harness of their horse any studs, buckles, or other garniture gilt, silvered, or damasked; nor stirrups gilt, silvered, or damasked; nor any velvet in saddles or horse trappers: except the persons next before mentioned and others of higher degrees; and gentlemen in ordinary, *ut supra*.

Note that the Lord Chancellor, Treasurer, President of the council, Privy Seal, may wear any velvet, satin, or other silks, except purple; furs except black genets.

These may wear as they have heretofore used, *viz.*, any of the King's council, justices of either bench, Barons of the Exchequer, Master of the Rolls, sergeants at law, Masters of the Chancery, of the Queen's council, apprentices of law, physicians of the King, Queen, and Prince, mayors and other head officers of any towns corporate, Barons of the Five Ports: except velvet, damask, satin, of the color crimson, violet, purple, blue.

Women's apparel:

None shall wear any cloth of gold, tissue, nor fur of sables: except duchesses, marquises, and countesses in their gowns, kirtles, partlets, and sleeves; cloth of gold, silver, tinseled satin, silk, or cloth mixed or embroidered with gold or silver or pearl, saving silk mixed with gold or silver in linings of cowls, partlets, and sleeves: except all degrees above viscountesses; and viscountesses, baronesses, and other personages of like degrees in their kirtles and sleeves;

Velvet (crimson, carnation); furs (black genets, lucerns); embroidery of passement lace of gold or silver: except all degrees above mentioned; the wives of knights of the Garter and of the Privy Council; the ladies and gentlewomen of the privy chamber and bed chamber, and maidens of honor.

None shall wear any velvet in gowns, furs of leopards, embroidery of silk: except the degrees and persons above mentioned; the wives of barons' sons, or of knights;

Cowls, sleeves, partlets, and linings, trimmed with spangles or pearls of gold, silver, or pearl; cowls of gold or silver, or of silk mixed with gold or silver: except the degrees and persons above mentioned: and trimmed with pearl, none under the degree of a baroness or those of like degrees;

Enameled chains, buttons, aglets, borders: except the degrees before mentioned;

Gowns of silk grosgrain, doubled sarcenet, camlet, or taffeta, or kirtles of satin or damask: except the degrees and persons above mentioned; and the wives of the sons and heirs of knights; and the daughters of knights; and of such as may dispend 300 marks by the year so valued *ut supra;* and the wives of those that may dispend £40 by the year.

Gentlewomen attendant upon duchesses, marquises, countesses, may wear, in their liveries given them by their mistresses, as the wives of those that may dispend £100 by the year and are so valued, *ut supra*.

None shall wear any velvet, tufted taffeta, satin, or any gold or silver, in their petticoats: except the wives of barons, knights of the order, or councilors; ladies and gentlewomen of the privy chamber and bed chamber, and the maidens of honor;

Damask, taffeta, or other silk in their petticoats: except knights' daughters and such as be matched with them in the former article, who shall not wear a guard of any silk upon their petticoats;

Damask, taffeta, or other silk in any cloak or safeguard: except knights' wives, and the degrees and persons above mentioned.

Mercantilism: Royal Regulation of Wages
(Queen Elizabeth: *Royal Proclamation,* 1563)

Where in the parliament holden at Westminster the 12th day of January last it was enacted . . . that the justices of peace of every shire . . . should assemble themselves . . . and appoint the wages of artificers, handicraftmen, husbandmen, laborers, servants, and workmen, as by their discretions should be thought meet . . . and the same rates and taxations should certify into the Queen's highness' Court of Chancery before a certain day limited in the said act; whereupon it would be lawful for the Lord Chancellor or Lord Keeper of the Great Seal of England . . . or to the lords and others of her majesty's Privy Council, to cause proclamations to be made into every of the said shires and places containing the several rates appointed by the said justices . . . :

Therefore, the Queen's majesty having received into her said Court of Chancery . . . one certificate from this her county of Rutland, containing the rates for wages hereafter following . . . straightly chargeth and commandeth all manner of person and persons within her said county of Rutland to keep and observe in all points the said rates, taxations, orders, appointments for wages hereafter following and set forth . . . :

A bailiff of husbandry having charge of two plow-lands at the least may have in wages, by the year, 40*s*., and for his livery, 8*s*.

A chief servant for husbandry, of the best sort, which can sow, mow, thresh, . . and can kill and dress a hog, sheep, and calf, may have in wages, by the year, 40*s*., and for his livery, 6*s*.

A mean servant of husbandry which can drive the plow, pitch the cart, and thresh, and cannot expertly sow, mow, . . . may have for his wages, by the year, 24*s*., and for his livery, 5*s*.

A mean child under the age of 16 years may have for his wages, by the year, 16*s*., and for his livery, 4*s*.

A chief woman servant being a cook, and can bake, make white bread and malt, and able to oversee other servants, may have for her wages, by the year, 20*s.*, and for her livery, 6*s.* 8*d.*

A mean or simple woman servant which can do but out-works and drudgery may have for her wages, by the year, 12*s.*, and for her livery, 3*s.*

A woman child under the age of 16 years may have for her wages, by the year, 10*s.*, and for her livery, 4*s.*

A chief miller which can expertly beat, lay, grind, and govern his mill, may have for his wages, by the year, 40*s.*, and for his livery, 6*s.*

A chief shepherd which is skillful in the ordering of his cattle, both winter and summer, may have for his wages, by the year, 20*s.*, and for his livery, 5*s.*

The Wages of Artificers, Laborers, and Servants, from Easter to Michaelmas as followeth:

A mower by the day, with meat, 6*d.*; without meat, 10*d.*

A man reaper by the day, with meat, 4*d.*; without meat, 8*d.*

A woman reaper by the day, with meat, 3*d.*; without meat, 6*d.*

A man haymaker by the day, with meat, 3*d.*; without meat, 6*d.*

A woman haymaker by the day, with meat, 2*d.*; without meat, 5*d.*

A chief joiner's apprentice which hath not served four years, by the day, with meat, 3*d.*; without meat, 7*d.*

A sawyer by the day, with meat, 5*d.*; without meat, 9*d.*

A horsecollar maker by the day, with meat, 5*d.*; without meat, 9*d.*

A freemason which can draw his plat work, and set cunningly, having charge over others, by the day, with meat, 8*d.*; without meat, 13*d.*

A rough mason which taketh charge over others, by the day, with meat, 5*d.*; without meat, 9*d.*

A master carpenter being able to draw his plat, and to be master of works over others, by the day, with meat, 8*d.*; without meat, 12*d.*

A carpenter's apprentice which hath not been apprentice four years, by the day, with meat, 3*d.*; without meat, 7*d.*

A bricklayer by the day, with meat, 5*d.*; without meat, 9*d.*

A tiler or slater by the day, with meat, 5*d.*; without meat, 9*d.*

A plumber by the day, with meat, 6*d.*; without meat, 10*d.*
A glazier by the day, with meat, 6*d.*; without meat, 10*d.*

The Wages of Artificers, Laborers, and Servants from Michaelmas to Easter as followeth:

A chief joiner by the day, with meat, 4*d.*; without meat, 8*d.*
A joiner's apprentice which hath not served four years, by the day with meat, 2*d.*; without meat, 6*d.*
A sawyer by the day, with meat, 4*d.*; without meat, 8*d.*
A plow wright by the day, with meat, 4*d.*; without meat, 8*d.*
A thatcher by the day, with meat, 4*d.*; without meat, 8*d.*
A rough mason which taketh charge over others, by the day, with meat, 4*d.*; without meat, 8*d.*
An expert carpenter by the day, with meat, 4*d.*; without meat, 8*d.*
A carpenter's apprentice which hath not been apprentice four years, by the day, with meat, 2*d.*; without meat, 6*d.*
A bricklayer by the day, with meat, 4*d.*; without meat, 8*d.*
A tiler or slater by the day, with meat, 4*d.*; without meat, 8*d.*
A plumber by the day, with meat, 5*d.*; without meat, 9*d.*
A glazier by the day, with meat, 4*d.*; without meat, 8*d.*
A glazier's apprentice which hath not served four years, by the day, with meat, 2*d.*; without meat, 6*d.*

Debasement of English Coin
(Queen Elizabeth: *Royal Proclamation*, 1562)

Although the Queen's majesty had determined . . . to have foreborne for the ease of her people from the amendment of the value of the . . . moneys for some convenient time . . . yet is her majesty now, upon many and necessary causes newly happened, moved and induced, . . . to alter this her former purpose. . . .

Whereof among other causes, the rashness of a great sort of people showing their wit out of season . . . by spreading through the realm of rumors that from one market day to another the money should be decried . . . [while another] sort, taking hold of the rumors . . . have already universally enhanced the prices of all things to be sold for money; . . . and thereafter the prices of all things so highly enhanced that until the moneys be indeed brought to the value at which they were intended and ought to be, not only the meaner sort of people, as laborers in husbandry, handicraftmen, and such like, but also all servingmen, soldiers, and others living only by portion or wages . . . shall be pitifully oppressed with unreasonable prices and dearth:

Therefore her majesty . . . by the advice of her council and of many other noble, wise, and expert men, doth declare and by this proclamation doth ordain that all manner of moneys now current within this realm shall . . . be valued and current as hereafter followeth. . . :

First, the moneys of gold shall be current as followeth:

Fine gold: the				
sovereign	that was current for	30 *s.*	shall be current for	20 *s.*
royal	"	15 *s.*	"	10 *s.*
angel	"	10 *s.*	"	6 *s.* 8 *d.*
half-angel	"	5 *s.*	"	3 *s.* 4 *d.*
Crown gold: the				
sovereign	"	20 *s.*	"	13 *s.* 4 *d.*
half-sovereign	"	10 *s.*	"	6 *s.* 8 *d.*
crown	"	5 *s.*	"	3 *s.* 4 *d.*
half-crown	"	2 *s.* 6 *d.*	"	20 *d.*
Strong gold: the				
French crown	"	6 *s.*	"	4 *s.*
Burgundian crown	"	6 *s.*	"	4 *s.*

Secondly, the moneys of silver shall be current as followeth:

Fine sterling silver: the				
shilling	that was current for	12 *d.*	shall be current for	8 *d.*
half-shilling	"	6 *d.*	"	4 *d.*
quarter-shilling	"	3 *d.*	"	2 *d.*
three halfpence	"	1½ *d.*	"	1 *d.*
three farthings	"	¾ *d.*	"	½ *d.*

On the Meaning and Nature of Mercantilism
(Thomas Mun, *England's Treasure by Foreign Trade,* 1630)

1. First, although this realm be already exceedingly rich by nature, yet might it be much increased by laying the waste

grounds into such employments to supply ourselves and prevent importations of hemp, flax, cordage, tobacco . . . which now we fetch from strangers, to our great impoverishing.

2. We may likewise diminish our importations if we refrain from excessive consumption of foreign wares in our diet and raiment.

3. In our exortations we must not only regard our own superfluities, but also we must consider our neighbor's necessities, that we may gain so much of the manufacture as we can, and also endeavor to sell them dear.

4. The value of our exportations likewise may be much advanced when we perform them ourselves in our own ships, for then we get not only the price of our wares, but also the merchants' gains, the charge of insurance and the freight.

7. A staple or magazine for foreign corn, indigo, spices, raw-silk, cotton-wool, or any other commodity to be imported, will increase shipping, trade, treasure, and the King's custom by exporting them again where need shall require.

11. It is needful also not to charge the native commodities with too great customs, lest by indearing them by the state it hinder their vent.

12. Also, lastly, in all things we must endeavor to make the most we can of our own.

The Economic and Mercantilistic Policies of Colbert (Colbert, *Letter, Instructions and Memoirs,* 1664)

Considering how advantageous it would be to this realm to reestablish its foreign and domestic commerce, we have resolved to establish a council particularly devoted to commerce, to be held every fortnight in our presence, in which all the interests of merchants and the means conducive to the revival of commerce shall be considered and determined upon, as well as all that which concerns manufactures.

We also inform you that we are setting apart, in the expenses of our state, a million livres each year for the encouragement of manufactures and the increase of navigation, to say nothing of the considerable sums which we cause to be raised to supply the companies of the East and West Indies;

That we are working constantly to abolish all the tolls which are collected on the navigable rivers;

That there has already been expended more than a million

livres for the repair of the public highways, to which we shall also devote our constant attention;

That we will assist by money from our royal treasury all those who wish to reestablish old manufactures or to undertake new ones;

That we are giving orders to all our ambassadors or residents at the courts of the princes, our allies, to make, in our name, all proper efforts to cause justice to be rendered in all cases involving our merchants, and to assure for them entire commercial freedom;

That we will comfortably lodge at our court each and every merchant who has business there during all the time that he shall be obliged to remain there, having given orders to the grand marshal of our palace to indicate a proper place for that purpose, which shall be called the House of Commerce;

That all the merchants and traders by sea who purchase vessels, or who build new ones, for traffic or commerce shall receive from us subsidies for each ton of merchandise which they export or import on the said vessels.

We desire in this present letter, not only to inform you concerning all these things, but to require you, as soon as you have received it, to cause to be assembled all the merchants and traders of your town of Marseilles, and explain to them very particularly our intentions in all matters mentioned above, in order that, being informed of the favorable treatment which we desire to give them, they may be the more desirous of applying themselves to commerce. Let them understand that for everything that concerns the welfare and advantage of the same they are to address themselves to Sieur Colbert.

A Parliamentary Attempt to Control the Trade of England in Accordance with the Doctrine of Mercantilism (Navigation Act, 1651)

For the increase of the shipping and the encouragement of the navigation of this nation, which under the good providence and protection of God is so great a means to the welfare and safety of this commonwealth, be it enacted by this present parliament and the authority thereof that, from and after the first day of December, 1651 . . . , no goods or commodities whatsoever of the growth, production, or manufacture of Asia, Africa, or America, or of any part thereof, or of islands belonging to them

. . . , as well of the English plantations as others, shall be imported or brought into this commonwealth of England, or into Ireland, or any other lands, islands, plantations, or territories to this commonwealth belonging . . . in any other ship or ships . . . but only in such as do belong only to the people of this commonwealth or the plantations thereof . . . and whereof the master and mariners are also for the most part of them of the people of this commonwealth, under the penalty of the forfeiture and loss of all the goods that shall be imported contrary to this act, as also of the ship . . . in which the said goods or commodities shall be so brought in and imported—the one moiety to the use of the commonwealth, and the other moiety to the use and behoof of any person or persons who shall seize the said goods or commodities and shall prosecute the same in any court of record within this commonwealth.

And it is further enacted . . . that no goods or commodities of the growth, production, or manufacture of Europe, or of any part thereof shall after the first day of December, 1651, be imported or brought into this commonwealth of England, or into Ireland, or any other lands, islands, plantations, or territories to this commonwealth belonging or in their possession, in any ship or ships, vessel or vessels whatsoever, but in such as do truly and without fraud belong only to the people of this commonwealth . . . ; and in no other, except only such foreign ships and vessels as do truly and properly belong to the people of that country or place of which the said goods are the growth, production, or manufacture, or to such ports where the said goods can only be or most usually are first shipped for transportation. . . .

Jean Bodin Defines Sovereignty
(Jean Bodin, *The Republic,* 1576)

Sovereignty is the absolute and perpetual power of a republic which the Romans called *majestas* . . . the Republic is a legal government of several families and that which they have in common with sovereignty added. I have said that this sovereign power is perpetual. . . . It is possible to give sovereign power to one or to many for a limited time but such men are nothing better than subjects, and when they are in power they cannot call themselves sovereign princes because they are nothing but administrators and trustees of that power until it pleases the people or the prince to revoke it. . . . The people are continually invested of the power. They can give power and authority to judge or to command for a certain time, or for so long and so much time as pleases them. . . . That is why the law says that the governor of a province . . . after his time has expired, gives the power back to those depositories.

Let us perceive now another part of our definition and see what the words "absolute power" actually mean. The people are the rulers of a Republic. They can give pure and simple perpetual power to someone to dispose of their goods and persons, or of all the state at his pleasure, and to let him do as he likes, just as the property owner can give his goods pure and simple without any other reason than his liberality. That is a true gift which has no strings attached once it has been made and accepted, in contrast with other gifts which have conditions and qualifications and which are not true gifts. . . . So the sovereignty or absolute power. It must be that the conditions imposed in the creation of a prince conform, however, to the laws of God and of Nature. . . .

In this we can recognize the power and majesty of a true sovereign prince; when the estates of the people are assembled, persons request and supplicate to their prince in all humility without, however, having any power to command, disclaim, or to deliberate, or to declare laws, edicts and ordinances unless it pleases the king to consent or to dissent, to command or to defend. And those . . . who have written of the duty of magistrates and others have gone out of their way to argue that the estates of the people are more illustrious than the prince; a thing which revolts true subjects in the obedience which they owe to their sovereign monarch. There is neither reason nor any foundation whatsoever for such an opinion. . . .

The prince is not held to ordinances and edicts unless these edicts and ordinances coincide with natural justice. . . . It is divine and natural law to obey the edicts and ordinances of him to whom God has given the power over us, if these edicts are not directly opposed to the rule of God who is above all princes. . . . The subject owes obedience to his sovereign prince against all, saving the majesty of God who is the absolute ruler of all the princes of the world. From this axiom we can draw a rule of state; that is to know that the sovereign prince is held to the contracts which he has made, be it with his subjects or be it with strangers, because he is the guardian for the subjects of those mutual conventions and obligations which they have made one with another. . . .

There is no crime more detestable in a prince than perjury. . . . Also, it is badly spoken to say that the sovereign prince has the power to steal the goods of anyone and to do evil . . . because that connotes weakness, feebleness, and laxness of heart. Moreover, the sovereign prince does not have the power to infringe the law of nature which God, of whom it is the image, has instituted. He, the prince, cannot, therefore, take the goods of anyone without just and reasonable cause, be it by buying or exchange, or legitimate confiscation, or by making a treaty with the enemy which he cannot conclude otherwise than by taking the goods of particular or private persons for the preservation of the state. . . . For natural law decrees that the public good is above all individuals and that subjects surrender not only their injuries and vengeances, but also their goods for the well being of the Republic. . . . Because there is nothing higher on earth after God than sovereign princes, and as they are established by Him as His lieutenants to command men, it is necessary to be aware of their station, to respect them and to revere their majesty in all obedience, to talk to them with all honor; because he who abuses his sovereign prince abuses God of Whom he is the image on earth. . . . In order that one can recognize him who is . . . the sovereign prince, one has to know his qualities which are not common to other subjects; because if they were common they could not be any part of a sovereign prince. . . .

He who has no earthly sovereign is he who gives law to all his subjects, who makes peace and war, who gives power to all the offices and magistrates of his country, who levies taxes, who enfranchises him who seems worthy, and who gives pardon to him who had deserved death; what more power could one desire in a sovereign prince? These are always the marks of sovereign power. . . . Just as the great sovereign God cannot create a god who is his equal because he is infinite, so we can say that the princes whom we have described as the images of God cannot elevate a subject to his station because then his (the prince's) power would no longer exist. . . .

Because this is so, it follows that the prime mark of sovereignty is not to give justice, because that is common to the prince and to the subjects, just as it is the power to institute or to abolish offices, because the prince and the subject both may share that power—especially as respects the officers serving justice or the police, or war or finance . . . nor is it the prime mark of sovereignty to give rewards to them who have merited them, because that is common to the prince and the magistrates, because the magistrates may receive that power from the prince; also, it is not a prime mark of sovereignty to take counsel of the affairs of a state; because that may be the charge of the privy council or the senate of the Republic. . . . We might say the same thing as regards the law which the magistrates can give to them who are within the power of their jurisdiction, but he, the magistrate, can do nothing against the edicts and ordinances of his sovereign prince and to make this point clearer, we must presuppose that the word of the law signifies the right command of him, or of those who have power over all others without exception of person; and to go further, . . . there is no one but the sovereign prince who can give law to all his subjects without exception, be it in the general or in particular.

The Beginning of the Parliamentary Attack on the Royal Perogative
(Peter Wentworth, *Speech to the House of Commons,* 1587)

Mr. Speaker, forasmuch as such laws as God is to be honoured by, and that also such laws as our noble Sovereign and this worthy realm of England are to be enriched, strengthened, and preserved by from all foreign and domestic enemies and traitors, are to be made by this honourable council, I . . . do earnestly desire, by question, to be satisfied of a few questions to be moved by you, Mr. Speaker, concerning the liberty of this honourable council. Wherefore I pray you, Mr. Speaker, oftsoons to move these few articles, by question, whereby every one of this house may know how far he may proceed in this honourable council, in matters that concern the glory of God and our true and loyal service to our prince and state. For I am fully persuaded, that God cannot be honoured, neither our noble prince or commonweal preserved or maintained, without free speech and consultation of this honourable council both which consist upon the liberties of this honourable council, and the knowledge of them, also. So here are the questions Mr. Speaker: I humbly and heartily beseech you to give them reading, and God grant us true and faithful hearts in answering of them; for the true, faithful and hearty service of our merciful God, our lawful prince, and this whole and worthy realm of England, will much consist hereafter upon the answers unto these questions. . . .

Whether this council be not a place for any member of the same here assembled, freely and without controlment of any person, or danger of laws, by bill or speech, to utter any of the griefs of this commonwealth whatsoever, touching the service of God, the safety of the prince, and this noble realm?—Whether that great honour may be done unto God and benefit and service unto the prince and state without free speech in this council, which may be done with it?—Whether there be any council which can make, add to or diminish from the laws of the realm, but only this council of parliament?—Whether it be not against the orders of this council to make any secret or matter of weight, which is here in hand, known to the prince or any other, concerning the high service of God, prince or state, without the consent of the house?—Whether the Speaker or any other may interrupt any member of this council in his speech used in this House, tending to any of the forenamed high services?—Whether the Speaker may rise when he will, any matter being propounded, without consent of the House, or not?—Whether the Speaker may overrule the House in any matter or cause there in question: or whether he is to be ruled or overruled in any matter, or not?—Whether the prince and state can continue, stand, and be maintained without this council of parliament, not altering the government of the state?

Concerning the Sovereignty of Parliament over the Church (Richard Hooker, *The Laws of Ecclesiastical Polity,* 1593)

There are those which wonder that we should count any statute a law, which the high court of Parliament in England hath established about the matter of church regiment; the prince and court of parliament having, as they suppose, no more lawful means to give order to the Church and clergy in these things, than they have to make laws for the hierarchies of angels in heaven; that the parliament being a mere temporal court, can neither by the law of nature, nor of God, have competent power to define of such matters; that supremacy of power in this kind cannot belong unto kings, as kings, because pagan emperors, whose princely power was notwithstanding true sovereignty, never challenged thus much over the Church. . . .

The Parliament of England together with the convocation annexed thereunto, is what whereupon the *very essence* of all government within this kingdom doth depend; it is even the body of the whole realm; it consisteth of the king, and of all that within the land are subject unto him; for they all are there present, either in person or by such as they voluntarily have derived their very personal right unto. The parliament is a court not so merely temporal as if it might meddle with nothing but only leather and wool. . . .

. . . . The public power of all societies is above every soul contained in the same societies. And the principal use of that power is to give laws unto all that are under it, which laws in such cases we must obey, unless there be reason showed which may necessarily enforce that the law of reason or of God enjoin the contrary. . . .

A Parliamentary Statement Concerning the Source of its Privileges
(*The Apology of Commons of 1604*)

To the King's most excellent majesty; from the house of commons assembled in Parliament. Most gracious sovereign . . . your commons of England, represented now in us their knights, citizens, burgesses, do come with this humble declaration to your highness. . . .

We know, and with great thankfulness to God acknowledge, that He hath given us a king of such understanding and wisdom as is rare to find in any prince in the world. Yet, seeing no human wisdom, how great soever, can pierce into the particularities of the rights and customs of people, or of the sayings and doings of particular persons, but by tract of experience and faithful report of such as know them . . . what grief, what anguish of mind hath it been unto us at some times . . . to hear and see . . . ourselves . . . so greatly wronged by information. . . . We have been constrained as well in duty to your royal majesty . . . as to our dear country, for which we serve in this parliament . . . to disclose unto your majesty the truth of such matters concerning your subjects, the commons, as heretofore by misinformation have been suppressed or perverted. . . .

Now concerning the ancient right of the subjects of this realm, chiefly consisting in the privileges of this house of the Parliament, the misinformation openly delivered to your Majesty hath been in three things: first, that we hold not our privileges of right, but of grace only, renewed every parliament by way of donative upon petition, and so to be limited; secondly, that we are no court of record, . . . and, lastly that . . . the writs for knights and burgesses are without compass. . . . Against which assertions . . . which tend directly and apparently to the utter overthrow of the very fundamental privileges of our house—and therein of the rights and liberties of the commons of your realm of England, which they and their ancestors from time immemorial have undoubtedly enjoyed . . . we . . . desire that this our protestation may be recorded to all posterity. . . .

. . . we most truly avouch that our privileges and liberties are our rights and due inheritance no less than our very lands and goods; that they cannot be withheld from us, denied, or impaired. . . .

From these misinformed positions . . . the greatest part of our troubles, distrust and jealousy have arisen; having . . . found . . . the privileges of our house, and therein the liberties and stability of the whole kingdom, have been more universally and dangerously impugned than ever. . . . For although it may be true that in the latter times of Queen Elizabeth some one privilege was attempted against . . . yet was not the same ever by so public speech. . . . Besides that in regard to her sex and age which we had great cause to tender . . . those actions were passed over. . . .

What cause we, your poor commons, have to watch over our privileges is manifest in itself to all men. The prerogatives of princes may easily and do daily grow; the privileges of the subject are for the most part at an everlasting stand. They may be by good providence and care preserved; but, being once lost, are not recovered but with much disquiet. . . .

The right of the liberty of the commons of England in parliament consisteth chiefly in these three things; first, that they have free choice of such persons as they shall put in trust to represent them; secondly, that the persons chosen during the time of the parliament . . . be free from restraint, arrest, and imprisonment; thirdly, that in parliament they may speak freely their consciences without check or controlment. . . .

The voice of the people in things of their knowledge is said to be as the voice of God.

A Definition of the Theory of Monarchial Divine Rights
(King James I, *Speech to Parliament,* 1610)

. . . The state of monarchy is the supremest thing upon earth:

for kings are not only God's lieutenants upon earth and to sit upon God's throne, but even by God Himself they are called gods. There be three principal similitudes that illustrate the state of monarchy: one taken out of the word of God, and the two other out of the grounds of policy and philosophy. In the Scriptures kings are called gods, and so their power after a certain relation compared to the Divine Power: kings are also compared to the fathers of families for a king is truly *paren patriae,* the political father of his people. And lastly, kings are compared to the head of this microcosm of the body of man. . . .

I conclude then this point touching the power of kings with this axiom of divinity, that as to dispute what God may do is blasphemy, . . . so is it sedition in subjects to dispute what a king may do in the height of his power. But just kings will ever be willing to declare what they will do, if they will not incur the curse of God. I will not be content that my power be disputed upon; but I shall ever be willing to make the reason appear of all my doings, and rule my actions according to my laws. . . .

Now the second general ground whereof I am to speak concerns the matter of grievances. . . . First then, I am not to find fault that you inform yourselves of the particular just grievances of the people: nay I must tell you, ye can neither be just nor faithful to me or to your countries that trust and employ you, if you do it not. . . . But I would wish you to be careful to avoid three things in the matter of grievances.

First, that you do not meddle with the main points of government: that is my craft: *tractent fabrilia fabri;* to meddle with that were to lessen me. I am now an old king . . . therefore there should not be too many Phormios to teach Hannibal: I must not be taught my office. Secondly, I would not have you meddle with such ancient rights of mine as I have received from my predecessors, possessing them *more majorum*: such things I would be sorry should be accounted for grievances. All novelties are dangerous as well in a political as in a natural body: and therefore I would be loath to be quarrelled in my ancient rights and possessions: for that were to judge me unworthy of that which my predecessors had and left me.

And lastly I pray you, beware to exhibit for grievance anything that is established by a settled law, and whereunto (as you have already had a proof) you know I will never give a plausible answer: for it is an undutiful part in subjects to press their king, wherein they know beforehand he will refuse them. Now, if any law or statute be not convenient, let it be amended by Parliament, but in the meantime term it not a grievance; for to be grieved with the law is to be grieved with the king, who is sworn to be the patron and maintainer thereof. But as all men are flesh and may err in the execution of laws, so may ye justly make a grievance of any abuse of the law, distinguishing wisely between the faults of the person and the thing itself. As for example, complaints may be made unto you of the High Commissioners: if so be, try the abuse and spare not to complain upon it, but say not there shall be no Commission, for that were to abridge the power that is in me. . . .

Thomas Hobbes Defines Sovereignty
(Thomas Hobbes, *The Leviathan,* 1651)

So that in the nature of man, we find three principal causes of quarrel. First, competition; second, diffidence; third, glory.

The first, maketh men invade for gain; the second, for safety; and the third, for reputation. The first use violence, to make themselves masters of other men's persons, wives, children, and cattle; the second, to defend them; and the third, for trifles, a word, a smile, a different opinion, and any other sign of undervalue, either direct in their persons, or by reflection in their kindred, their friends, their nation, their profession, or their name.

Hereby it is manifest, that during the time men live without a common power to keep them all in awe, they are in that condition which is called war; and such a war, as it is, of every man against every man. For WAR, consisteth not in battle only, or the act of fighting; but in a tract of time, wherein the will to contend by battle is sufficiently known; and therefore the notion of *time,* is to be considered in the nature of war; as it is in the nature of weather. For as the nature of foul weather, lieth not in a shower or two of rain; but in an inclination thereto to many days together; so the nature of war, consisteth not in actual fighting; but in the known disposition thereto, during all the time there is no assurance to the contrary. All other time is PEACE.

Whatsoever therefore is consequent to a time of war, where every man is enemy to every man; the same is consequent to the time, wherein men live without other security, than what their own strength, and their own invention shall furnish them withal. In such condition there is no place for industry; because the fruit thereof is uncertain; and consequently no culture of the earth; no navigation, nor use of the commodities that may be imported by sea; no commodious building; no instruments of moving, and removing, such things require much force; no knowledge of the face of the earth; no account of time; no arts; no letters; no society; and which is worst of all, continual fear, and danger of violent death and the life of man, solitary, poor, nasty, brutish, and short.

A *commonwealth* is said to be *instituted,* when a multitude of men do agree, and *covenant, every one, with every one,* that to whatsoever *man,* or *assembly of men,* shall be given by the major part, the *right* to *present* the person of them all, that is to say, to be their *representative;* every one, as well he that *voted against it,* as he that voted for it shall *authorize* all the actions and judgments, of that man or assembly of men, in the same manner, as if they were his own, to the end, to live peaceably amongst themselves, and be protected against other men.

From this institution of a commonwealth are derived all the *rights,* and *faculties* of him, or them, on whom sovereign power is conferred by the consent of the people assembled.

First, because they covenant, it is to be understood, they are not obliged by former covenant to anything repugnant hereunto. And consequently they that have already instituted a commonwealth, being thereby bound by covenant, to own the actions, and judgments of one, cannot lawfully make a new covenant, amongst themselves, to be obedient to any other, in anything whatsoever, without his permission. And therefore, they that are subject to a monarch, cannot without his leave cast off monarchy, and return to the confusion of a disunited multitude; nor transfer their person from him that beareth it, to another man, or other assembly of men; for they are bound, every man to every man, to own, and be reputed author of all, that he that already is their sovereign, shall do, and judge fit to be done; so that any one man dissenting, all the rest shall break their covenant made to that man, which is injustice; and they have also every man given the sovereignty to him that beareth their person; and therefore if they depose him, they take from him that which is his own, and so again it is injustice. . . .

That he which is made sovereign maketh no covenant with his subjects beforehand, is manifest; because either he must make it with the whole multitude, as one party to the covenant; or he must make a several covenant with every man. With the whole, as one part, it is impossible; because as yet they are not one person; and if he make so many several covenants as there be men, those covenants after he hath the sovereignty are void; because what act soever can be pretended by any one of them for breach thereof, is the act both of himself, and of all the rest, because done in the person, and by the right of every one of them in particular. Besides, if any one, or more of them, pretend a breach of the covenant made by the sovereign at his institution; and others, or one other of his subjects, or himself alone pretend there was no such breach, there is in this case, no judge to decide the controversy; it returns therefore to the sword again; and every man recovereth the right of protecting himself by his own strength, contrary to the design they had in the institution. It is therefore in vain to grant sovereignty by way of precedent covenant. The opinion that any monarch receiveth his power by covenant, that is to say, on condition, proceedeth from want of understanding this easy truth, that covenants being but words and breath, have no force to oblige, contain, constrain, or protect any man, but what it has from the public sword. . . .

Thirdly, because the major part hath by consenting voices declared a sovereign; he that dissented must now consent with the rest.

Fourthly, because every subject is by this institution author of all the actions, and judgments of the sovereign instituted; it follows, that whatsoever he doth, it can be no injury to any of his subjects; nor ought he to be by any of them accused of injustice. . . .

Fifthly, and consequently to that which was said last, no man that hath sovereign power can justly be put to death. . . . For seeing every subject is author of the actions of his sovereign; he punisheth another for the actions committed by himself. . . .

Sixthly, it is annexed to the sovereignty, to be judge of what opinions and doctrines are averse, and what conducing to peace. . . .

Seventhly, it is annexed to the sovereignty, the whole power of prescribing the rules, whereby every man may know, what goods he may enjoy, and what actions he may do . . . and this is it men call *propriety* . . . . These rules of propriety . . . are the civil laws; that is to say, the laws of each commonwealth in particular. . . .

Eighthly, is annexed to the sovereignty, the right of judicature; that is to say, of hearing and deciding all controversies, which may arise concerning law, either civil, or natural; or concerning fact. . . .

Ninthly, is annexed to the sovereignty, the right of making war and peace with other nations, and commonwealths; that is to say, of judging when it is for the public good. . . .

Tenthly . . . the choosing of all counsellors, ministers, magistrates, and officers both in peace and war. . . .

Eleventhly, to the sovereign is committed the power of rewarding with riches, or honors, and of punishing with corporal or pecuniary punishment, or with ignominy, every subject according to the law he hath formerly made. . . .

Lastly, considering what value men are naturally apt to set upon themselves; what respect they look for from others; and how little they value other men; from whence continually arise amongst them, emulation, quarrels, factions, and at last war, to the destroying of one another, and diminuation of their strength against a common enemy; it is necessary that there be laws. . . .

A Definition of the Divine Rights of Kings by Bishop Bossuet (Bishop Bossuet, *Politics Drawn from the Very Words of Scripture,* 1660)

St. Paul said, "Let every soul be subject unto the higher powers. For there is no power but of God: the powers that be are ordained of God. Whosoever therefore resisteth power, resisteth the ordinance of God: and they that resist shall receive to themselves damnation."

We can see, then, that all political power is of God. So rulers act as the ministers of God and as his lieutenants on earth. It is through them that God exercises his empire.

Moreover, that no one may assume that the Israelites were peculiar in having Kings over them who were established by God, note what is said in Ecclesiasticus: "God has given to every people its ruler, and Israel is manifestly reserved to Him." God therefore governs all peoples and gives them their Kings.

It appears from all this that the person of the King is sacred, and that to attack him in any way is sacrilege. God has the Kings anointed by His priests with the holy unction in like manner as He has Bishops and altars anointed. But even without the external application in thus being anointed, they are by their very office the representatives of the Divine Majesty deputed by God for the execution of His purposes. And Kings should be guarded as holy things, and whosoever neglects to protect them is worthy of death.

But Kings, although their power comes from on high, as has been said, should not regard themselves as masters of that power to use it at their pleasure. They must employ it with fear and self restraint, as a thing coming from God and of which God will demand an account. Indeed, Kings should tremble as they use the power God has granted them; and let them think how horrible is the sacrilege if they use for evil a power which comes from God. What profanation for the unjust King to sit upon God's throne to render decrees contrary to His laws and to use the sword which God has put in his hand for deeds of violence and to slay His children.

The King need render account of his acts to no man; and no man may have a sanction against a King. Without this absolute authority the King could neither do good nor repress evil.

God is infinite, God is all. The King, as King, is not regarded as a private person; he is a public personage, all the state is in him, and all God's will. Thus the royal power is absolute. Many writers have tried to confound absolute government with arbitrary government. But the two things could not be more apart from each other. Look at the Prince in his cabinet. He is the image of God, who, seated on his throne high in the heavens, makes all nature to move. God is holiness itself, goodness itself, and power itself. In these things lies the majesty of God. In the image of these things lies the majesty of the King.

UNIT 7

The Conflicts of the Seventeenth and Eighteenth Centuries

While Elizabeth was working out her political compromises with Parliament, and the English Puritans were formulating the political principles upon which their later attack on the state would be based, and the French were unifying their state and consolidating power in the hands of the prince, another power was beginning to rise over eastern Europe—Russia.

Western civilization was little concerned with the mixed races and variant cultures which existed in the areas east of the Oder River until the English merchants and explorers, unable to deny the prior claims of Spain and France in the western Atlantic, and frustrated in their attempt to find a northwestern passage to the Orient, were forced to turn to the northeast. The first contact was made with the Russians by English sailors in the 15th century, but it was not for almost another century that an English explorer was able to give an accurate account of contemporary Russia. This lack of information was in great part the result of Russia's desire to live its own way, unmolested by the outside world, as much as due to any lack of curiosity or interest on the part of the West. And so not until 1700 did a foreign traveler in Russia open a window so that the West might take its first comprehensive view of the people who were Oriental and Occidental at the same time. Nor was this first look to beget in the West any response other than horror, revulsion, and ridicule. For in Russia the West saw institutions and customs with which it was totally unfamiliar; the absolutism of Peter the Great run riot, the utter tyranny of the aristocracy over a peasantry which was looked upon as almost less than human, a Church which feared and hated western ideals and concepts, and a government which held the lives and properties of all its subjects in its hand. A few years later when Czar Peter, intent on catching up with the West in cultural and economic development, attempted to force the ways of western culture on the people of Russia by the simple expedient of legislating out of existence a cultural heritage which had taken Russia several centuries to mature, the West was treated to the sight of the Russian aristocracy being beaten with whips for not speaking French, and of the beards of the priests being clipped by the czar's soldiers in the streets of Moscow.

If the West was only in a disinterested way aware of Russia in the middle years of the 18th century, the same was not true of Prussia. Indeed, the interest of all Europe was centered on the Germanies where Frederick the Great of Prussia and Maria Theresa, the Empress of Austria were beginning to gather their respective forces to determine which would dominate and direct the peoples of central Europe. This bitter struggle of the conflicting ideals of the *Grosse* and *Kleine* plans for German unification would absorb the energies and attention of the people of the Germanies for another century; while other states in Europe were winning empires and consolidating their holds on the waterway trade routes of the world, and attempting solutions to equally trying domestic problems.

France was one such state facing such a problem. Not since the first realization of national consciousness when Joan of Arc had tried to destroy the ties of universalism, had the proud and ancient Franks resident at the crossroads of Europe known peace. When in 1589 Henry IV assumed the throne, France for the first time in three centuries could turn its attention away from factional and religious strife and direct its vigorous energies at attaining unity and stability. *The Edict of Nantes* of 1598 brought religious peace, while Henry's determined resistance to baronial intrigue convinced the second estate that it must, for the time being, submerge itself in the national monarchy or be destroyed. However, by the beginning of the 17th century, France, like all the states of northern Europe which had accepted the Reformed Church, was once again to feel the stirring of religious passion. The Catholic Church, reinvigorated by the Council of Trent and the Society of Jesus, was seeking once again to re-establish its claim to the religious allegiance of western civilization; and with a degree of success. Cardinal Richelieu, chief minister to King Louis XIII in 1624, began the process of constructing an absolute monarchy in France by repudiating the whole of the program of Henry IV, including the balance of religious forces guaranteed by the *Edict of Nantes.*

In England, too, religious distemper was again becoming a political issue. The Reformed Church of Henry VIII had been rejected by his daughter Queen Mary Tudor, and her religious settlement was in turn repudiated by her younger half-sister, Elizabeth, after 1558. The first of the Stuart dynasty, James I, lacking the sense of disciplined diplomacy of Elizabeth, unable to compromise in matters of principle, and unwilling to accept the dictum laid down by John Calvin that kings were merely minor magistrates in the eyes of God, could hardly have escaped conflict with the Puritans. Nor did he try. Placed, as king, in an untenable political position by the compromises Elizabeth had been forced to make with the Puritans and common lawyers and merchants and Parliamentarians, James could retreat no further. Yet his very resistance to Puritan demands that the English Reformation be carried farther toward the radical left and away from Rome marked him as a tyrant. Thus King James, the proponent of divine right, and Calvinism, which contained within itself the seed of future doctrines of resistance to immoral authority and revolution, were, by 1647, drawn into irrevocable positions from which neither, in light of its accepted belief, could retreat.

Peter the Great Attempts to Force Western Ways on the Russian People
(Ivan Nestesuranoi, *Memoirs,* 1703)

The Tsar labored at the reform of fashions, or, more properly speaking, of dress. Until that time the Russians had always worn long beards, which they cherished and preserved with much care, allowing them to hang down on their bosoms, without even cutting the moustache. With these long beards they wore the hair very short, except the ecclesiastics, who, to distinguish themselves, wore it very long. The tsar, in order to reform that custom, ordered that gentlemen, merchants, and other subjects, except priests and peasants, would each pay a tax of one hundred rubles a year if they wished to keep their beards; the commoners had to pay one kopeck each. Officials were stationed at the gates of the towns to collect that tax, which the Russians regarded as an enormous sin on the part of the tsar and as a thing which tended to the abolition of their religion.

These insinuations, which came from the priests, occasioned the publication of many pamphlets in Moscow, where for that reason alone the tsar was regarded as a tyrant and a pagan; and there were many old Russians who, after having their beards shaved off, saved them preciously, in order to have them placed in their coffins, fearing that they would not be allowed to enter heaven without their beards. As for the young men, they followed the new custom with the more readiness as it made them appear more agreeable to the fair sex.

From the reform in beards we may pass to that of clothes. Their garments, like those of the Orientals, were very long, reaching to the heel. The tsar issued an ordinance abolishing that costume, commanding all the boyars (nobles) and all those who had positions at the court to dress after the French fashion, and likewise to adorn their clothes with gold or silver according to their means.

As for the rest of the people, the following method was employed. A suit of clothes cut according to the new fashion was hung at the gate of the city, with a decree enjoining upon all except peasants to have their clothes made on this model, under penalty of being forced to kneel and have all that part of their garments which fell below the knee cut off, or pay two grives every time they entered the town with clothes in the old style. Since the guards at the gates executed their duty in curtailing the garments in a sportive spirit, the people were amused and readily abandoned their old dress, especially in Moscow and its environs, and in the towns which the tsar oftenest visited.

The dress of the women was changed, too. English hairdressing was substituted for the caps and bonnets hitherto worn; bodices, stays, and skirts, for the former undergarment.

The same ordinance also provided that in the future women, as well as men, should be invited to entertainments, such as weddings, banquets, and the like, where both sexes should mingle in the same hall, as in Holland and England. It was likewise added that these entertainments should conclude with concerts and dances, but that only those should be admitted who were dressed in English costumes. His Majesty set the example in all these changes.

Maria Theresa, Empress of Austria, on European Diplomacy (Letter: *Maria Theresa to Marie Antoinette,* 1779)

As I desire nothing else in this world but the good of our holy religion, the happiness of my dear, and more than dear, children, the welfare of our states, and the felicity of our peoples, whom I love just as sincerely as my children, so I long to see not only our houses and our interests bound together closely and indissolubly, as indeed they already are, but a cordial personal friendship as well, which will bear every test and which no minister or other envious power shall ever be able to change or diminish. The emperor and the king are both so young, and both have such good and generous hearts, that I believe my hopes to be well founded if only they can learn to know each other and establish that mutual confidence which will be so useful and so necessary to them in their political careers, for their own happiness and that of their countries, indeed, for all Europe.

These reflections of a doting old mother and sovereign have led me to send off new instructions to Mercy, directing him to furnish you with information and arrange with you as to the policy to be adopted toward your ministers. There are matters of the highest importance which I can only touch upon in passing. The quarrels between the Turks and the Russians and between Spain and Portugal, as well as the war in America, may well bring about a general conflagration into which I shall be drawn in spite of myself; particularly as it is necessary to act with the greatest caution on account of our bad neighbor, whose persistent enmity toward us is greatly increased since we have ventured to oppose his unjust designs in Poland and elsewhere. He is performing the impossible in the effort to frustrate, or at least to weaken, our influence in all the courts of Europe; he sticks at no calumny, and especially in France, and it is this that makes me doubly regret that the interview between Joseph II and Louis XVI has not taken place. The delight of the king of Prussia is a sure sign of the importance he attached to it, and should serve to unite us all the closer, for united neither he nor any one dare molest us.

I cannot conceal from you that scandal has not spared you personally, and I have mentioned to Mercy several darts of slander that have long disquieted me in regard to your amusements, games, excursions; that you were on bad terms with the king, that you no longer share his bed, but want to sit up all night playing cards, which the king does not like; that you were alarmed at the prospect of your brother's visit, that you did not in the least desire it, and that you are now delighted to be left free to pursue your pleasures. Such are the tales that are sent out from Berlin to Saxony, Poland, everywhere; and I confess that for several months they have caused me increasing dismay. My only consolation is that, as atrocious slanders are promulgated about the emperor and myself, it must be the same with you; but my dear daughter, the newspapers but confirm these accounts of the various amusement in which my dear queen joins without her sisters-in-law or the king, and they give me many sad hours. I love you so tenderly that I cannot but look ahead into the future, and I entreat you to do the same.

On Religious and Political Toleration in France (*The Edict of Nantes,* 1598)

Henry, by the Grace of God, King of France and Navarre;

When we came to the throne this our Kingdom was divided into several factions and many parts and our subjects beset by great trouble and peril. And, since all problems relating to state and society could not be at once attended we chose the single necessary course: to seek out and set end to those demanding force—and only then those which could be solved by the application of reason and righteousness.

Among the most pressing of those problems postponed for consideration and reason were those relating to the distemper expressed by some of the Catholic towns and cities that the Catholic religion had yet to be re-established according to prior edicts; and, the demands of those followers of the Reformed groups that past promises stated in the prior edicts be fully enacted and fulfilled: that is, as to the guarantees of their liberty of belief and profession, safety and the security of their possessions, the non-performance of which led them to fear greatly that we were plotting their destruction.

In our awareness of the singular importance of these conflicting claims we have studied the records of complaints of the Catholics and have instructed our Reformed subjects to gather in session to prepare similar lists of complaints. We have examined all former laws and discussed openly the problem with both factions. In this knowledge our opinion is that a simple and sovereign law must be stated by the government by which all present and future conflicts in this sphere may be fully resolved.

Therefore in council with the Curia Regis we in this perpetual and unbreakable Edict declare and order:

That the recollection of everything done by one party or the other during all the preceding period of troubles, remain obliterated and forgotten, as if no such things had happened.

And in order to leave no occasion for trouble or difference between our subjects, we have permitted, and herewith do so, those of the said religion Reformed to live and abide in all the cities and places of this our kingdom and territories in our hold, without being annoyed, molested, or compelled to do anything in the name of religion contrary to their consciences, upon bargain that they act in other ways according to the content of this edict.

It is lawful for all lords, nobility, gentlemen, and others making profession of the Reformed religion holding feudal rights to also hold meetings of the Reformed religion in their domiciles.

We also allow those of the said religion to hold exercise of it in the villages and places of our kingdom where it was exercised by the people prior to the year 1597.

It is expressly forbidden to those of the said religion to meet for religious purposes in this our kingdom and lands otherwise than in the places permitted and granted by the present edict.

It is also stated that there shall be no difference or prejudice made regarding the said religion in admitting students to be instructed in universities, colleges, and schools, nor in receiving the sick and poor into places of public charity.

We absolutely forbid the taking of children of the Reformed religion from them by force by the Catholics for the purpose of religious instruction.

We desire here to append that all of the Reformed group as well as the Catholic shall be enabled henceforth to hold all public, Royal, and civil offices—and no oath save loyalty to the laws shall be demanded of them.

Cardinal Richelieu's Program for Strengthening the French Monarchy

(Letter: *Richelieu to King Louis XIII of France,* 1624)

At the time when your Majesty resolved to admit me both to your council and to an important place in your confidence for the direction of your affairs, I may say that the Huguenots shared the state with you; that the nobles conducted themselves as if they were not your subjects, and the most powerful governors of the provinces as if they were sovereign in their offices.

I may say that the bad example of all of these was so injurious to this realm that even the best regulated *parlements* were affected by it, and endeavored, in certain cases, to diminish your royal authority as far as they were able in order to stretch their own powers beyond the limits of reason.

I may say that every one measured his own merit by his audacity; that in place of estimating the benefits which they received from your Majesty at their proper worth, all valued them only in so far as they satisfied the extravagant demands of their imagination; that the most arrogant were held to be the wisest, and found themselves the most prosperous.

I may also say that the foreign alliances were unfortunate, individual interests being preferred to those of the public; in a word, the dignity of the royal majesty was so disparaged, and so different from what it should be, owing to the malfeasance of those who conducted your affairs, that it was almost impossible to perceive its existence.

It was impossible, without losing all, to tolerate longer the conduct of those to whom your majesty has intrusted the helm of state; and, on the other hand, everything could not be changed at once without violating the laws of prudence, which do not permit the abrupt passing from one extreme to another.

The sad state of your affairs seemed to force you to hasty decisions, without permitting a choice of time or of means; and yet it was necessary to make a choice of both, in order to profit by the change which necessity demanded from your prudence.

Thoughtful observers did not think that it would be possible to escape all the rocks in so tempestuous a period; the court was full of people who censured the temerity of those who wished to undertake a reform; all well knew that princes are quick to impute to those who are near them the bad outcome of the undertakings upon which they have been well advised; few people consequently expected good results from the change which it was announced that I wished to make, and many believed my fall assured even before your Majesty had elevated me.

Notwithstanding these difficulties which I represented to your Majesty, knowing how much kings may do when they make good use of their power, I ventured to promise you, with confidence, that you would soon get control of your state, and that in a short time your prudence, your courage, and the benediction of God would give a new aspect to the realm.

I promised your Majesty to employ all my industry and all the authority which it should please you to give me to ruin the Huguenot party, to abase the pride of the nobles, to bring back all your subjects to their duty, and to elevate your name among foreign nations to the point where it belongs.

A Statement of Puritan Doctrine
(*The Humble Advice of the Assembly of Divines of Westminster,* 1647)

God from all eternity did, by the most wise holy Council of his own will, freely, and unchangeably ordain whatsoever comes to pass. . . .

By the decree of God, from the manifestation of his glory, some men and angels are predestined unto everlasting life, and others fore-ordained to everlasting death.

Those of mankind that are predestined unto Life, God, before the foundation of the world was laid, according to his eternal and immutable purpose, and the secret Council and good pleasure of his will, hath chosen in Christ unto everlasting glory, out of his mere free grace and love, without any foresight of Faith, or good works, or perseverance in either of them, or any other thing in the creature, as conditions, or causes moving him thereunto, and all to the praise of his glorious grace.

As God has appointed the Elect unto Glory, so hath he, by the eternal and most free purpose of his Will, fore-ordained all means thereunto. Wherefore they who are elected, being fallen in Adam, are redeemed by Christ, are effectually called unto Faith in Christ. . . . Neither are any other redeemed by Christ, effectually called, justified, adopted, sanctified and saved, but the Elect only.

The rest of man-kind God was pleased, according to the unsearchable Council of his own Will . . . for the Glory of his Sovereign Power over his creatures, to pass by, and to ordain them to dishonor and wrath for their sin, to the praise of his glorious justice.

This effectual call is of God's free, and special grace alone, not from anything at all foreseen in man, who is altogether passive therein, until being quickened and renewed by the holy Spirit, he is thereby enabled to answer this call and to embrace the grace offered, and conveyed in it.

Elect infants, dying in infancy, are regenerated, and saved by Christ. . . . Others, not elected . . . cannot be saved; much less can men not professing the Christian Religion, be saved in any way whatsoever, be they never so diligent to frame their lives according to the light of Nature, and the law of the religion they do profess. And, to assert and maintain that they may, is very pernicious. . . .

God did from all eternity, decree to justify all the Elect, and Christ did, in the fullness of time, die for their sins; nevertheless men are not all justified.

The Invitation of the Combined Whig and Tory Parties to William of Orange and Mary to Come to England
(Letter: *Certain Gentlemen to William of Orange,* 1688)

We have great satisfaction to find by Lord Russell's report from you that your Highness is so ready and willing to give us such assistance as he has related to us. We have great reason to believe we shall be every day in a worse condition than we are and less able to defend ourselves. The people are so generally dissatisfied with the present conduct of the government in relation to their religion, liberties, and properties, all of which have been greatly invaded, that your Highness may be assured, there are nineteen parts out of twenty of the people who would contribute to it, if, they had such protection to countenance their rising as would secure them from being destroyed before they could get to be in a position able to defend themselves.

Much the greatest part of the gentry are as much dissatisfied and many of the officers are so discontented that they continue in their service only for a subsistence, and very many of the common soldiers do daily show such an aversion to the Popish religion that there is the greatest probability imaginable of great numbers of deserters which would come from them, should there be such an occasion; and amongst the seamen, it is almost certain, there is not one in ten who would do them any service in such a war. If upon a due consideration of all these circumstances, Your Highness shall think fit to adventure upon the attempt, there must be no time lost, in letting us know your resolution concerning it, and in what time we may depend upon all the preparations will be ready.

A Definition of "Methodism"
(John Wesley, *The Character of a Methodist,* 1738)

The distinguishing marks of a Methodist are not his opinions of any sort. His assenting to this or that scheme of religion, his embracing any particular set of notions, his enspousing the judgment of one man or of another are all quite wide of the point. Whosoever, therefore, imagines that a Methodist is a man of such or such an opinion is grossly ignorant of the whole affair. . . .

We believe, indeed, that "all Scripture is given by the inspiration of God," and herein we are distinguished from Jews, Turks, and infidels. We believe the written word of God to be the only and sufficient rule both of Christian faith and practice; and herein we are . . . distinguished from those of the Roman Church. We believe Christ to be the eternal supreme God; and herein we are distinguished from the Socinians and Arians. But as to all opinions which do not strike at the root of Christianity, we think and let think. . . .

We do not place our religion, or any part of it, in being attached to any peculiar mode of speaking, any quaint or uncommon set of expressions. . . . We never . . . deviate from the most usual way of speaking. . . .

Nor do we desire to be distinguished by actions, customs, or usages of an indifferent nature. Our religion does not lie in doing what God has not enjoined, or abstaining from what He hath not forbidden. It does not lie in the form of our apparel, or in the posture of our body, or the covering of our heads, nor yet in abstaining from marriage, or from meats and drinks. . . .

Nor, lastly, is he distinguished by laying the whole stress of religion on any single part of it. If you say, "Yes, he is; for he thinks [he is] 'saved by faith alone,'" I answer, "You do not understand the terms." By salvation he means holiness of heart and life. And this he affirms to spring from true faith alone. . . .

"What, then, is the mark? Who is a Methodist according to your own account?" I answer, "A Methodist is one who has the love of God shed abroad in his heart by the Holy Ghost given unto him"; one who "loves the Lord his God with all his heart, and with all his soul, and with all his mind, and with all his strength. . . ."

He is therefore happy in God. . . . He "rejoices . . . in the Father through Our Lord Jesus Christ by whom he hath now received the atonement. . . ."

And while he thus always exercises his love of God . . . this commandment is written in his heart, "That he who loveth God, love his brother also." And he accordingly loves his neighbor as himself. . . .

Lastly. As he has time he "does good unto all men," unto neighbors and strangers, friends and enemies; and that in every possible kind, not only to their bodies by "feeding the hungry, clothing the naked, visiting those that are sick or in prison," but much more does he labor to do good to their souls as of the ability which God giveth, to awaken those that sleep in death; to bring those who are awakened to the atoning blood that, "being justified by faith, they may have peace with God. . . ."

UNIT 8

The Enlightenment and the French Revolution

The impact of new modes of thought on economic, religious, and political institutions, which were part of the heritage of the people of Europe, in the 15th and 16th centuries had set man against man, and state against state. Uneasy peace had followed the spasmodic expressions of force, and new institutions and new social concepts had been substituted for those old and tried. Now, in the 18th and 19th centuries, man must stop and assay the returns on his tremendous investment of blood, thought, and treasure in what he had accepted as "Progress."

The results of this investigation were both satisfying and disquieting. There had been change. But was it possible that change and progress had been confused? The middle class of Europe was uncertain as to exactly what gains had been made. Power in the state had shifted from the aristocracy to the monarch, and mercantilistic control had increased commerce and wealth; yet the political liberties and the social equality so long coveted by the class of wealth had been proven to be no more than a chimera. Benevolent despotism had shown itself to be just what is was—paternalistic in its purposes but despotic in its methods—and, like the mercantilism it enforced, it was based on a philosophy of despair: it denied by its very existence what the liberal spokesmen of the Enlightenment were already beginning to affirm: that man in society was capable, of himself, without superimposed authority, of maintaining that society in an orderly and just manner.

Among the earliest of the enlightened theorists to raise his voice against existing conditions was Jean Jacques Rousseau. In his work, the *Social Compact,* Rousseau decried the institutional bonds which he felt chained and degraded man who was born a free and uncorrupted child of nature, and whose present misery could be traced to his loss of liberty. Voltaire, also in full attack on social disorganization, was unwilling to accept such radical ideals. His purpose was reform through the existing institutions of government, and his method was biting sarcasm rather than Reason. Denis Diderot, the Encyclopedist, was convinced that neither debate nor criticism was the most effective method for improving institutions, but rather the gathering together of all scientific knowledge so that all might read and study. Thus in an intellectual parliament of all men, reform could be accomplished. One thing most of the social critics held in common was the belief that all social institutions must be held up for close scrutiny in the cold and critical light of Reason and Nature and judged with the gauge of human utility rather than with the old measure of tradition and antiquity.

The Enlightenment *per se* was not solely a French movement, but just as it was stimulated most by French reformers, so did it have its first concrete effects in France. A half century of constant debate and social ferment was productive of such criticism of conditions in France that Louis XVI was forced to take the first step on the fatal road to revolution. For when the king opened the way to popular expression and popular expectation of reform by calling for the lists of grievances, or *Cahiers,* he weakened the barriers to popular action to the extent that they would give way at the first test of strength. And it followed almost naturally that a people so long in thought of liberty should follow its first revolutionary action with a document so expressive of the liberal concept as the *Declaration of the Rights of Man and the Citizen,* which stated without equivocation that man had certain "natural, inalienable, and sacred rights."

Although the *Declaration* spoke of the rights of the citizen, its authors never considered the revolution a merely national movement. To them it was dedicated to universal liberty; it was an attack on tyranny wherever it existed. The Revolution in France had meaning for the majority of the people of Europe, and it aroused both critical and sympathetic interest and expression. Edmund Burke, the English Parliamentarian, fearing the general effect of the catastrophic destruction of so great a part of France's social and political institutions on the general stability of the states of Europe, set out in his *Reflections on the Revolution in France* the classic arguments of the conservative forces of Europe. The answers to this criticism were immediate, many, and violent. Thomas Paine, the American, met Burke's attack with his *Rights of Man* which had all the emotional and rational apeal of his earlier work against the English in America, *Common Sense.*

Still, while the debate raged on the intellectual level, the revolution continued in France. And, if international boundaries did not prevent interest and debate, they similarly did not prevent the other states of Europe from becoming involved in the struggle in France. Coalitions were formed, policies drawn up, treaties signed, and always with the purpose of crushing the radical republican government of France before it could infect the rest of Europe with its highly volatile and appealing doctrines of liberty, equality, and fraternity. Yet, each treaty and each coalition only served to stimulate the French people to greater resistence. A good example of this is the *Manifesto* of the Duke of Brunswick in 1792, which threatened to wreak terrible vengeance on the Republicans unless they gave up whatever gains had been made.

The cumulative effect of these external pressures which were brought to bear on France was perhaps as much responsible for the Reign of Terror as any other single factor. Confronted simultaneously with the problems of national defense and internal security, the Jacobin party engaged France in a blood bath which Robespierre attempted to justify on the grounds that the only way to victory for the revolution was in the destruction of all elements which *might* complicate further the problems of the revolutionaries. Yet, in the end, the Terror consumed the Revolution itself. Unable to maintain itself morally after 1800, the movement turned once again toward a strong executive —Napoleon Bonaparte. This most obvious denial of the early ideals of the Revolution had many corollaries which are not at once so apparent. The French people of 1800 were, after 10 years of chaos and uncertainty, more than willing to trade policital liberty for economic and emotional security.

However, Napoleon was no more acceptable to the conservative forces of Europe than had been Robespierre, and the continued resistance by England caused Bonaparte to institute the Continental System with the *Berlin Decree* of 1806 and the *Milan Decree* of 1807. Britain's reaction to these is to be found in the several *Orders in Council,* which closed all French-dominated ports to the ships of all nations, and which in the final analysis disrupted and weakened the continental economy to the point where it could not support the continued exactions of Napoleon. Russia encouraged by England and Austria was the first to break with the dictator and Napoleon's speech to his troops at the beginning of the ensuing war with Russia was in reality his farewell as the arbiter of Europe.

Montesquieu on Political Organization
(Charles Montesquieu, *The Spirit of the Laws,* 1748)

Besides the law of nations relating to all societies, there is a polity or civil constitution for each particularly considered society. No society can subsist without a form of government. The united strength of individuals constitutes what we call the body politic.

The general strength may be in the hands of a single person, or of many. Some think that nature having established paternal authority, the most natural government was that of a single person—the father. But the example of paternal authority proves nothing. For if the power of a father relates to a single government, that of brothers after the death of a father, and that of cousins after the demise of the brothers refer to a government of many. The political power necessarily comprehends the union of several families.

Better it is to say, that the government most conformable to nature is that which best agrees with the humor and disposition of the people in whose favour it is established.

The strength of individuals cannot be united without a conjunction of their wills. The conjunction of those wills, is what is called the Civil State.

Law in general is human reason, inasmuch as it governs all the inhabitants of the earth; the political and civil laws of each nation ought to be only the particular cases in which human reason is applied.

They should be adapted in such a manner to the people for whom they are framed that it should be a great chance if those of one nation in any way suited another nation.

They should be in relation to the nature and principle of each government; whether they form it, as may be said of political laws; or whether they support it, as in the case of Civil Institutions.

They should be in relation to the climate of each country, to the quality of the soil, to its situation and extent, to the principal occupation of the natives, whether husbandmen, huntsmen, or shepherds; they should have relation to the degree of liberty which the constitution will bear; to the religion of the inhabitants, to their inclination, riches, numbers, commerce, manner, and customs. In fine, they have relations to each other, as also to their origin, to the intent of the legislator, and to the order of things on which they are established; in all of which different lights ought to be considered.

Rousseau on Political Organization
(Jean Jacques Rousseau, *Du Contrat Social,* 1750)*

Man is born free; yet he is everywhere in chains. One man holds himself the sovereign master of other men—but he is a slave in greater part than they.

What was the mode of this change?

Is it legitimate?

I cannot answer the first question but I can answer the second.

Should we seek an answer in force and the most obvious results which spring from force, we should retort; "If a people obeys through force it does well; but immediately it is able to shake off its yoke, it does better; for in this way a people regains its liberty just as it lost that liberty. Thus the people is acting in a just way for there was no justification in the act which took their liberty from them.

And yet man's right to join other men in social order is the sacred right from which all others grow. And this right is not an extension of Nature; it rests altogether on man's own contracting power.

Suppose that men (in the state of Nature) have arrived at such a point where the obstacles which endanger their existence overcome by their strength those forces which each individual can employ to maintain himself in that state. Then the human race perishes if it does not change its mode of life. As men cannot themselves create new forces, but only unify and direct those which exist, they have no other means of preserving themselves than to form together a force which can overcome resistance. . . . To find a form of assocation which defends and protects with all its combined forces the person, and goods of each member, and by means of which each person, uniting with all, yet remains as free as before,—such is the problem of which the *Social Contract* gives the solution. . . .

Each one in giving himself to all, gives himself to none. For whereas there is no associate to whom one does not concede the same rights which he concedes himself, one gains the equivalent of what one loses, and more force to retain what one possesses. If one discards from the Social Contract all that is

* Translated by George L. Mosse. Used with permission of the translator.

not essential, one will find it reduced to the following terms: each one of us in common puts his person and his powers under supreme direction of the general will. . . . At once, instead of the individual personality of each person, this act of association produces a collective and moral body, composed of as many members as have a voice in the assembly . . . I say that sovereignty, being nothing else than the exercise of the general will, can never be alienated, and that the sovereign who is only a collective being can not be represented but by himself. Powers can be delegated, but not sovereignty.

Voltaire's Concept of Deism and Political Organization (Voltaire, *Dictionnaire Philosophique*, 1770)

Man is a creature of reason and intelligence, and as such a being he could not owe his existence to the creative efforts of a directionless force less potent than himself. We may be certain that there is a great variance between the cogitative force of an Isaac Newton and the noisy voice of an animal of the barn-yard. The intellectual capacity and the Reason of Newton derives therefore in a higher intellectual force.

When there is set down before us a delicate and accurate mechanical contrivance which operates within its capacity according to the governing laws of nature, we are prone to say that the mechanism was the result of the efforts of a mechanic —and that the mechanic had excellent command of his craft. It is just as certainly apparent to us that the world is such an excellent product. It follows then that there exists in certainty a force, a creative intelligence, whose capacity is sufficient to such creation. Although ancient, this argument is sound.

All living organisms are the total of many variant parts which operate and cooperate in accord with the natural laws of mechanical leverage. For instance, liquids move and circulate as directed by the laws which govern hydraulic motion. Yet, when one recalls that all organisms of the higher orders have perceptions and feelings which are not immediately dependent on physical structure, one is even more greatly amazed.

The movement of the planets, and the gravitational force of the earth as it revolves around the sun—all follow precisely immutable and profound mathematical regulations. We know that even the eloquent Plato, ignorant of even the basic laws of spheres and trigonometry, was sufficient in genius to name

God the "eternal geometrician." Even the ancients realized the existence of some formative power operating within the laws of nature and the universe. Who then would dispute what is clearly the truth—truth which encompasses us and presses in upon us from every side.

It is not possible that even a political state existed wherein the first government tried was not republican in form. That form of polity is the result of nature working in man. Perhaps men and their families came into political agreement for protection against the wild animals—or perhaps one had grain to exchange for wood. In any case their union was that of political equals seeking the furtherance of mutual happiness. When Europe discovered America the peoples there were united into republics generally, but there did exist two monarchies. In an area of one thousand states only two were politically oppressed.

The question is—of the two types—Monarchy and Republic, which should we choose for ourselves? This question is as old as man himself. If one inquires of those who are materially wealthy they will demand an aristocratic political state. When one asks the masses they are told democracy. Kings, of course, love Monarchy best. Why then is it true that practically the entire earth is ruled by Kings? Because only in rare instances are men capable of self-government.

Equality, which is man's birthright, does exist in the Swiss state. But by the term "equality" one must not understand what is foolish and wrong—that the servant is equal to his master, or that the judge and the seeker for justice are the same—but rather that equality whenever citizens all have recourse to the same laws in identical way—laws which must defend the weak against the usurpations of the strong.

An example of the Demands for Reform Made by the People of France Prior to the Revolution

(*Cahiers of the Representatives of the Third Estate of the District of Bordeaux,* 1789)

The Third Estate of the electoral district of Bordeaux, desiring to give to a beloved Monarch the most unmistakable proof of its love and respect, and desiring to cooperate with the whole nation in repairing the successive misfortunes which have overwhelmed it, and with the hope of reviving once more its ancient glory, declares that the happiness of the nation must, in their opinion, depend upon that of its King, upon stability of the Monarchy, and upon the preservation of the orders which compose it and of the fundamental laws which govern it.

The Third Estate of the electoral district of Bordeaux very humbly petitions his Majesty to take into consideration these several matters following:

Public worship should be confined to the Roman Catholic religion.

Nevertheless the civil rights of those of the King's subjects who are not Catholics should be confirmed, and they should be admitted to positions and offices in the public administration.

The nation should consider some means of abolishing the annates and all other dues paid to the Holy See, to the prejudice and against the protests of the whole French people.

The rights of the nation should be consecrated as fundamental principles and their perpetual enjoyment should be assured by a solemn law, which should so define the rights both of the monarch and of the people that their violation should hereafter be impossible.

These following rights should be especially noted:

The nation should hereafter be subject only to such laws and taxes as it shall itself freely ratify.

The meetings of the Estates General of the Kingdom should be fixed for definite periods, and the monies judged necessary for the support of the State and the public service should be voted for no longer a period than to the close of the year in which the next meeting of the Estates General is to occur.

In order to assure to the Third Estate the influence to which it is entitled in view of the number of its members, the amount of its contributions to the public treasury, and the manifold interests which it has to defend or promote in the national assemblies, its votes in the assembly should be taken and counted by head.

No order, corporation, or individual citizen may lay claim to any tax exemption.

Feudal dues exacted from those holding fiefs should be abolished, along with all regulations which exclude members of the lower estate from positions, offices, and ranks which have hitherto been bestowed on nobles either for life or hereditarily.

Freedom should be granted also to the press, which should however be subjected, by means of strict regulations, to the principles of religion, morality, and public decency.

The Idealism of the French Revolutionaries
(*The Declaration of the Rights of Man and of the Citizen,* 1791)

The representatives of the French people, organized in National Assembly, considering that ignorance, forgetfulness, or contempt of the rights of man, are the sole causes of the public miseries and of the corruption of governments, have resolved to set forth in a solemn declaration the natural, inalienable, and sacred rights of man, in order that this declaration, being ever present to all the members of the social body, may unceasingly remind them of their rights and their duties; in order that the acts of the legislative power and those of the executive power may be each moment compared with the aim of every political institution and thereby may be more respected: and in order that the demands of the citizens, grounded henceforth upon simple and incontestable principles, may always take the direction of maintaining the constitution and the welfare of all.

In consequence, the National Assembly recognizes and declares, in the presence and under the auspices of the Supreme Being, the following rights of man and citizen.

1. Men are born and remain free and equal in rights. Social distinctions can be based only upon public utility.

2. The aim of every political association is the preservation of the natural and imprescriptible rights of man. These rights are liberty, property, security, and resistance to oppression.

3. The source of all sovereignty is essentially in the nation; no body, no individual can exercise authority that does not proceed from it in plain terms.

4. Liberty consists in the power to do anything that does not injure others; accordingly, the exercise of the natural rights of each man has no limits except those that secure to the other members of society the enjoyment of these same rights. These limits can be determined only by law.

5. The law has the right to forbid only such actions as are injurious to society. Nothing can be forbidden that is not interdicted by the law, and no one can be constrained to do that which it does not order.

6. Law is the expression of the general will. All citizens have the right to take part personally, or by their representatives, in its formation. It must be the same for all whether it protects or punishes. All citizens being equal in its eyes, are equally eligible to all public dignities, places, and employments, accord-

ing to their capacities, and without other distinction than that of their virtues and their talents.

7. No man can be accused, arrested, or detained, except in the cases determined by the law and according to the forms that it has prescribed. Those who procure, expedite, execute, or cause to be executed arbitrary orders ought to be punished; but every citizen summoned or seized in virtue of the law ought to render instant obedience; he makes himself guilty by resistance.

8. The law ought to establish only penalties that are strictly and obviously necessary, and no one can be punished except in virtue of a law established and promulgated prior to the offense and legally applied.

9. Every man being presumed innocent until he has been pronounced guilty, if it is thought indispensable to arrest him, all severity that may not be necessary to secure his person ought to be strictly suppressed by law.

10. No one should be disturbed on account of his opinions, even religious, provided their manifestation does not derange the public order established by law.

11. The free communication of ideas and opinions is one of the most precious of the rights of man; every citizen then can freely speak, write, and print, subject to responsibility for the abuse of this freedom in the cases determined by law.

12. The guarantee of the rights of man and citizens requires a public force; this force then is instituted for the advantage of all and not for the personal benefit of those to whom it is entrusted.

13. For the maintenance of the public force and for the expenses of administration a general tax is indispensable; it ought to be equally apportioned among all the citizens according to their means.

14. All citizens have the right to ascertain by themselves or by their representatives, the necessity of the public tax, to consent to it freely, to follow the employment of it, and to determine the quota, the assessment, the collection, and the duration of it.

15. Society has the right to call for an account of his administration from every public agent.

16. Any society in which the guarantee of the rights is not secured, or the separation of powers not determined, has no constitution at all.

17. Property being a sacred and inviolable right, no one can be deprived of it, unless a legally established public necessity

evidently demands it, under the condition of a just and prior indemnity.

The Classic Statement of the Conservative Viewpoint in the Late Eighteenth Century

(Edmund Burke, *Reflections on the Revolution in France,* 1791)

Abstractly speaking, government, as well as liberty, is good; yet could I, in common sense, ten years ago, have felicitated France on her enjoyment of a government (for she then had a government), without inquiry what the nature of the government was, or how it was administered? Can I now congratulate the same nation upon its freedom? Is it because liberty in the abstract may be classed amongst the blessings of mankind, that I am seriously to felicitate a madman, who has escaped from the protecting restraint and wholesome darkness of his cell, on his restoration to the enjoyment of light and liberty? Am I to congratulate a highwayman and murderer who has broken prison upon the recovery of his natural rights? . . . .

When I see the spirit of liberty in action, I see a strong principle at work; and this, for a while, is all I can possibly know of it. . . . I must be tolerably sure, before I venture publicly to congratulate men upon a blessing, that they have really received one. Flattery corrupts both the receiver and the giver; and adulation is not of more service to the people than to kings.

I should therefore suspend my congratulations on the new liberty of France until I was informed how it was combined with government, with public force, with discipline and obedience of armies, with the collection of an effective and well-distributed revenue, with morality and religion, with solidity and property, with peace and order, with civil and social manners. All these, in their way, are good things, too; and without them liberty is not a benefit while it lasts and is not likely to continue long. The effect of liberty to individuals is that they may do what they please: we ought to see what it will please them to do, before we risk congratulations, which may soon be turned into complaints. . . .

You will observe that, from Magna Carta to the Declaration of Rights, it has been the uniform policy of our constitution to claim and assert our liberties as an entailed inheritance derived to us from our forefathers, and to be transmitted to our posterity, as an estate specially belonging to the people of this kingdom, without any reference whatever to any other more general or prior right. By this means our constitution preserves an unity in so great a diversity of its parts. We have an inheritable crown, an inheritable peerage, and a House of Commons, and a people inheriting privileges, franchises, and liberties from a long line of ancestors.

Would it not, my worthy friend, have been wiser to have you thought what I for one always thought you, a generous and gallant nation, long misled to your disadvantage by your high and romantic sentiments of fidelity, honor, and loyalty; that events had been unfavorable to you, but that you were not enslaved through any illiberal or servile disposition, that, in your most devoted submission, you were actuated by a principle of public spirit: and that it was your country you worshipped, in the person of your king? Had you made it to be understood that, in the delusion of this amiable error, you had gone further than your wise ancestors—that you were resolved to resume your ancient privileges, whilst you preserved the spirit of your ancient and your recent loyalty and honor; or, if diffident of yourselves, and not clearly discerning the almost obliterated constitution of your ancestors, you had looked to your neighbors in this land, who had kept alive the ancient principles and models of the old common law of Europe, meliorated and adapted to its present state—by following the wise examples you would have given new examples of wisdom to the world.

You would have rendered the cause of liberty venerable in the eyes of every worthy mind in every nation. You would have shamed despotism from the earth by showing that freedom was not only reconcilable but, as when well disciplined it is, auxiliary to law. You would have had an unoppressive but a productive revenue. You would have had a flourishing commerce to feed it. You would have had a free constitution, a potent monarchy, a disciplined army, a reformed and venerated clergy, a mitigated but spirited nobility, to lead your virtue, not to overlay it; you would have had a liberal order of commons to emulate and recruit that nobility; you would have had a protected, satisfied, laborious, and obedient people, taught to seek and to recognize the happiness that is to be found by virtue in all conditions, in which consists the true moral equality of mankind, and not in that monstrous fiction which, by inspiring false ideas and vain expectations into men destined to travel in the obscure walk of laborious life, serves only to aggravate and embitter that real inequality which it never can remove, and which the order of civil life establishes as much for the benefit of those whom it must leave in an humble state as those whom it is able to exalt to a condition more splendid but not more happy. . . .

It is now sixteen or seventeen years since I saw the queen of France, then the dauphiness, at Versailles; and surely never lighted on this orb, which she hardly seemed to touch, a more delightful vision. . . . Little did I dream that I should have lived to see such disasters fallen upon her in a nation of gallant men, in a nation of men of honor and of cavaliers! I thought ten thousand swords must have leaped from their scabbards to avenge even a look that threatened her with insult.

But the age of chivalry is gone. That of sophisters, economists, and calculators has succeeded; and the glory of Europe is extinguished forever. Never, never more shall we behold that generous loyalty to rank and sex, that proud submission, that dignified obedience, that subordination of the heart, which kept alive, even in servitude itself, the spirit of an exalted freedom! The unbought grace of life, the cheap defense of nations, the nurse of manly sentiment and heroic enterprise, is gone! It is gone, that sensibility of principle, that chastity of honor, which felt a stain like a wound which inspired courage whilst it mitigated ferocity, which ennobled whatever it touched, and under which vice itself lost half its evil by losing all its grossness!

A Defense of Revolution. Thomas Paine's Answer to Edmund Burke

(Thomas Paine, *The Rights of Man,* 1791)

It has been thought a considerable advance towards establishing the principles of Freedom to say that Government is a compact between those who govern and those who are governed; but this cannot be true, because it is putting the effect before the cause; for as man must have existed before Governments existed, there necessarily was a time when Governments did not exist, and consequently there could originally exist no governors to form such a compact with. The fact therefore must be that the *individuals themselves,* each in his own personal and sovereign right, *entered into a compact with each other* to produce a Government: and this is the only mode in which Governments have a right to arise, and the only principle on which they have a right to exist.

To possess ourselves of a clear idea of what Government is, or ought to be, we must trace it to its origin. In doing this we shall easily discover that Governments must have arisen either *out* of the people or *over* the people. Mr. Burke has made no distinction. He investigates nothing to its source, and therefore he confounds everything; but he has signified his intention of undertaking a comparison between the Constitutions of England and France.

But it will be first necessary to define what is meant by a *Constitution.* It is not sufficient that we adopt the word; we must fix also a standard signification to it.

A Constitution is not a thing in name only, but in fact. It has not an ideal, but a real existence; and wherever it cannot be produced in visible form, there is none. A Constitution is a thing *antecedent* to a Government, and a Government is only the creature of a Constitution. The Constitution of a country is not the act of its Government, but of the people constituting a Government. It is the body of elements, to which you can refer, and quote article by article; and which contains the principles on which the Government shall be established, the manner in which it shall be organized, the powers it shall have, the mode of elections, the duration of parliaments, the powers which the Executive part of the Government shall have; and in fine, everything that relates to the complete organization of a civil Government, and the principles on which it shall act, and by which it shall be bound.

Can, then, Mr. Burke produce the English Constitution? If he cannot, we may fairly conclude that though it has been so much talked about, no such thing as a Constitution exists, or ever did exist, and consequently that the people have a Constitution yet to form.

Mr. Burke will not, I presume, deny the position I have already advanced—namely, that Governments arise either *out* of the people or *over* the people. The English Government is one of those which arose out of a conquest, and not out of society, and consequently it arose over the people; and though it has been much modified from the opportunity of circumstances since the time of William the Conqueror, the country has never yet regenerated itself, and is therefore without a Constitution. . . .

Reason and Ignorance, the opposite to each other, influence the great bulk of mankind. If either of these can be rendered sufficiently extensive in a country, the machinery of Government goes easily on. Reason obeys itself; and Ignorance submits to whatever is dictated to it.

The two modes of Government which prevail in the world, are—*First,* Government by election and representation; *Secondly,* Government by hereditary succession.

The former is generally known by the name of Republic; the latter by that of Monarchy and Aristocracy.

As the exercise of Government requires talents and abilities, and as talents and abilities cannot have hereditary descent, it is evident that hereditary succession requires a belief from man to which his reason cannot subscribe, and which can only be established upon his ignorance; and the more ignorant any country is, the better it is fitted for this species of Government.

On the contrary, Government, in a well-constituted Republic, requires no belief from man beyond what his reason can give. He sees the *rationale* of the whole system, its origin and its operation; and it is best supported when best understood. . . .

What we formerly called Revolutions were little more than a change of persons, or an alteration of local circumstances . . . and had nothing in their existence or their fate that could influence beyond the spot that produced them. But what we now see in the world, from the Revolutions of America and France, are a renovation of the natural order of things, a system of principles as universal as truth and the existence of man, and combining moral with political happiness and national prosperity.

"I. Men are born, and always continue, free and equal in respect of their rights. Civil distinctions, therefore, can be founded only on public utility.

"II. The end of all political associations is the preservation of the natural and imprescriptible rights of man; and these rights are liberty, property, security, and resistance of oppression.

"III. The Nation is essentially the source of all sovereignty; nor can ANY INDIVIDUAL, *or* ANY BODY OF MEN, *be entitled to any authority which is not expressly derived from it. . . ."*

The European Reaction to the Violence of the French Revolutionaries
(*The Manifesto of the Duke of Brunswick,* 1792)

Their Majesties the emperor and the king of Prussia having intrusted to me the command of the united armies which they have collected on the frontiers of France, I desire to announce to the inhabitants of that kingdom the motives which have determined the policy of the two sovereigns and the purposes which they have in view.

After arbitrarily violating the rights of the German princes in Alsace and Lorraine, disturbing good and legitimate government in the interior of the realm, committing against the sacred person of the king and his family brutalities which continue to be renewed daily, those who have usurped the reins of government have at last completed their work by declaring an unjust war on his Majesty the emperor and attacking his provinces situated in the Low Countries. Some of the territories of the German empire have been affected by this oppression, and others have only escaped the same fate by yielding to the threats of the dominant party and its emissaries.

His Majesty the king of Prussia, united with his Imperial Majesty by the bonds of a strict defensive alliance, and himself a preponderant member of the Germanic body, would have felt it inexcusable to refuse to march to the help of his ally and fellow-member of the empire.

To these important interests should be added another aim equally important and very close to the hearts of the two sovereigns—namely, to put an end to the anarchy in the interior of France, to check the attacks upon the throne and the altar, to reestablish the legal power, to restore to the king the security and the liberty of which he is now deprived and to place him in a position to exercise once more the legitimate authority which belongs to him.

In accordance with these views, I, the undersigned, the commander in chief of the two armies, declare:

That, drawn into this war by circumstances beyond their control, the two allied courts entertain no other aims than the welfare of France, and have no intention of enriching themselves by conquests.

That they do not propose to meddle in the internal government of France, and that they merely wish to deliver the king, the queen, and the royal family from their captivity, and to procure for the King of France the necessary security to enable him, as he shall see fit, to work for the welfare of his subjects.

That the allied armies will protect the towns and villages, and the persons and goods of those who shall submit.

That, on the contrary, the members of the National Guard who shall fight against the troops of the two allied courts, and who shall be taken with arms in their hands, shall be treated as enemies and punished as rebels.

That the inhabitants of the towns and villages who dare to defend themselves shall be punished immediately, and their houses burned and destroyed.

The city of Paris and all its inhabitants without distinction shall be required to submit at once and without delay to the king, to place that prince in full and complete liberty, and to assure to him, as well as to the other royal personages, the inviolability and respect which the law of nature and of nations demands of subjects toward sovereigns. And if their safety and their liberty be not immediately assured, they will inflict an ever memorable vengeance by delivering over the city of Paris to militay execution and complete destruction.

Robespierre Justifies the Terror*
(Robespierre, *Speeches and Writings,* 1794)

It is time to state clearly the goal of the Revolution. . . . It is time to take stock, and face the obstacles which are still in our way, and the means which we must adopt to reach our goal. . . . What is our goal? The enjoyment of Liberty and Equality, the reign of that eternal justice whose laws are not engraved in stone and marble but in the hearts of all men, even in the heart of the slave who has forgotten those laws, and of the tyrant who denies them. We want a state of things where all cruel and base passions are enchained, all beneficial and generous passions are supported by the Laws, where ambition is the wish to deserve glory and to serve the fatherland, where social distinction rests on equality itself, where the Citizen obeys the Magistrate, the Magistrate obeys the people and the people obey the dictates of justice.

[We want a state] where the fatherland assures the well being of each individual and where each individual takes part in the prosperity and the glory of the fatherland . . . where commerce is the source of public wealth and not merely benefits the monstrous opulence of a few.

Democracy is a state where the sovereign people, guided by the laws which it has made, does itself all that it can do, and delegates to its representatives all that which it can not do itself. . . . As the essence of a Democracy is equality, it follows that love of fatherland includes necessarily love of equality. It has been said

* Translated by George Mosse, used with permission of the translator.

that the terror belongs to a despotic government. Does our terror have anything in common with despotism? Yes, just as the sword which glitters in the hands of the heroes of liberty resembles that with which the servants of Tyranny are armed. . . . The Government of the Revolution is the Despotism of Liberty against Tyranny. Nature imposes on all physical and moral beings the duty to preserve themselves. . . . If the Tyranny rules a single day there will not be a Patriot alive the next morning. How much one is concerned for the oppressors and how little for the oppressed. . . . One or the other must perish. Indulgence for the Royalists cry some men, mercy for the scoundrels. No, mercy and compassion for the innocents . . . for humanity.

The protection of society is due only to Citizens, and in a Republic there are no other citizens than republicans. The Royalists, the Conspirators, are to them . . . enemies. The war of Liberty against Tyranny, is it not one and indivisible? Our internal enemies are they not the allies of our foreign foes?

The Napoleonic "Continental" System (Napoleon, *Milan Decree,* 1807)

Napoleon, Emperor of the French, King of Italy, Protector of the Confederation of the Rhine. In view of the measures adopted by the British government on the 11th of November last by which vessels belonging to powers which are neutral or are friendly and even allied with England are rendered liable to be searched by British cruisers, detained at certain stations in England, and subject to an arbitrary tax of a certain percent upon their cargo to be regulated by English legislation.

Considering that by these acts the English government has denationalized the vessels of all the nations of Europe and that no government may compromise in any degree its independance or its rights—all the rulers of Europe being jointly responsible for the sovereignty and independence of their flags—and that, if through unpardonable weakness which would be regarded by posterity as an indelible stain, such tyranny should be admitted and become consecrated by custom, the English would take steps to give it the force of law as they have already taken advantage of the toleration of the governments to establish the infamous principle that the flag does not cover the goods and to give the right of blockade an arbitrary extension which threatens the sovereignty of every state:

We have decreed and do decree as follows:

Every vessel of whatever nationality which shall submit to be searched by an English vessel or shall consent to a voyage to England, or shall pay any tax whatever to the English government is *ipso facto* declared denationalized, loses the protection afforded by its flag, and becomes English property.

Should these vessels which are thus denationalized through the arbitrary measures of the English government enter our ports or those of our allies or fall into the hands of our ships of war or of our privateers they shall be regarded as good and lawful prizes.

The British Isles are proclaimed to be in a state of blockade. Every vessel of whatever nation or whatever may be its cargo, that sails from the ports of England or from those of the English colonies or of countries occupied by English troops, or destined for England or for any of the British colonies or any country occupied by England's troops, becomes, by violating the present decree, a lawful prize, and may be captured by our ships of war and adjudged to the captor.

These measures, which are only a just retaliation against the barbarous system adopted by the English government, which models its legislation upon that of Algiers, shall cease to have any effect in the case of those nations which shall force the English to respect their flags. They shall continue in force so long as that government shall refuse to accept the principles of international law which regulates the relations of civilized states in a state of war. The provisions of the present decree shall be *ipso facto* abrogated and void so soon as the English government shall abide again by the principles of the law of nations, which are at the same time those of justice and honor.

Britain's Answer to the Continental System
(*British Order in Council,* 1807)

Whereas certain orders establishing an unprecedented system of warfare against this kingdom, and aimed especially at the destruction of its commerce and resources, were some time since issued by the Government of France, by which "the British islands were declared to be in a state of blockade," thereby subjecting to capture and condemnation all vessels, with their cargoes, which should continue to trade with His Majesty's dominions:

And, whereas, by the same order, "all trading in English merchandise is prohibited, and every article of merchandise belonging to England, or coming from her colonies, or of her manufacture, is declared lawful prize:"

And whereas, the nations in alliance with France, and under her control, were required to give, and have given, and do give effect to such orders:

And whereas, His Majesty's order of the 7th of January last has not answered the desired purpose, either of compelling the enemy to recall those orders, or of inducing neutral nations to interpose, with effect, to obtain their revocation, but on the contrary, the same have been recently reinforced with increased rigor:

And, whereas, His Majesty under these circumstances, finds himself compelled to take further measures for asserting and vindicating his just rights, and for supporting that maritime power which the exertions and valor of his people have, under the blessings of Providence, enabled him to establish and maintain; and the maintenance of which is not more essential to the safety and prosperity of His Majesty's dominions, than it is to the protection of such states as still retain their independence, and to the general intercourse and happiness of mankind:

His Majesty is therefore pleased, by and with the advice of his privy council, to order, and it is hereby ordered, that all the ports and places of France and her allies, or of any other country at war with His Majesty, and all other ports or places in Europe, from which the British flag is excluded, and all ports or places in the colonies belonging to His Majesty's enemies, shall, from henceforth, be subject to the same restrictions in point of trade and navigation, with the exceptions hereinafter mentioned, as if the same were actually blockaded by His Majesty's naval forces, in the most strict and rigorous manner: and it is hereby further ordered and declared, that all trade in articles which are of the produce or manufacture of the said countries or colonies shall be deemed and considered to be unlawful; and that every vessel trading from or to the said countries or colonies together with all goods and merchandise on board, and all articles of the produce or manufacture of the said countries or colonies, shall be captured and condemned as a prize to the captors.

Fichte Lectures to the German People on Nationalism (Fichte, *Reden an die Deutsche Nation*, 1808)*

I speak for Germany and about Germans, not acknowledging

* Translated by G. L. Mosse.

but rejecting all those divisions which unhappy events have for centuries brought forth within the one nation. You, distinguished hearers, are to my eyes the first and immediate representatives of the beloved nation, and the visual focal point which lights the flame of my speech; but my spirit collects here the cultured element of the whole nation, though it be spread over many nations, analyzes and thinks about our common position . . . only for Germans and about Germans, as I have mentioned. We will show that no other bond or descriptive term has ever had validity or truth . . . and that it is only the common basis of Germanism through which we have fought off the absorption of our nation into foreign countries, and by which we can regain our self-contained and independent nature.

I will, because I am only talking about Germans, say some things as valid for all Germans. I see in that spirit, whose outcome are these lectures, the growing unity, in which no member regards another member's fate as a foreign thing, not concerning himself. . . . I view this unity as already risen, perfected, and existing.

Selfishness (on the other hand) is developed to the highest degree, if, once it has taken hold of the governed, it spreads to the governing and becomes their only desire. In such a government you have first the loosening of all bonds by which the security of one state is linked to that of another, the abandoning of the whole nation. Such government cares only that it be not disturbed in its peace and quiet. (We have here the sad delusion that (a nation) has peace as long as its own frontiers are not attacked, and in internal affairs, the effeminate leadership of government which dignifies itself with foreign words, Humanitarianism, Liberality and Popularity, but which can be called in the true German language: Effeminacy, Weakness and Behavior without Dignity. . . .

Through a new education we want to weld Germans into one unity, which is driven and made alive by all its members through the same primary concern. But if we create by this, once again, a cultured class . . . apart from the mass of the population . . . this would work against us, not for us, and the rest of the nation would be lost to our cause. Therefore, we have no choice but to reeducate all that is German, so that this should be not the education of a special class but of the whole nation.

Reform Activity by the Prussian Government
(Frederick William, *Edict,* 1807)

We, Frederick William, by the grace of God king of Prussia . . . hereby make known and proclaim that: since peace has been established we have been occupied before everything else with the care for the depressed condition of our faithful subjects and the speediest revival and greatest possible improvement in this respect. We have considered that, in face of the prevailing want, the means at our disposal would be insufficient to aid each individual, and even if they were sufficient, we could not hope to accomplish our object; and that, moreover, in accordance with the imperative demands of justice and with the principles of a judicious economic policy, it behooves us to remove every obstacle which has hitherto prevented the individual from attaining such a state of prosperity as he was capable of reaching. We have further considered that the existing restrictions, both on the possession and enjoyment of landed property and on the personal condition of the agricultural laborer, especially interfere with our benevolent purpose and disable a great force which might be applied to the restoration of agriculture, the former, by their prejudicial influence upon the value of landed property and the credit of the proprietor; the latter, by diminishing the value of labor. We desire, therefore, to reduce both kinds of restrictions so far as the common well-being demands, and we accordingly ordain the following.

Every inhabitant of our states is competent, without any limitation on the part of the state, to own or mortgage landed property of every kind. The noble may therefore own not only noble, but also non-noble, citizen, and peasant lands of every kind, and the citizen and peasant may possess not only citizen, peasant, and other non-noble, but also noble tracts of land without in any case needing special permission for any acquisition whatever, although henceforth, as before, every change of ownership must be announced to the authorities. All privileges which are possessed by noble over citizen inheritances are entirely abolished.

Every noble is henceforth permitted, without any derogation from his station, to engage in citizen occupation, and every citizen or peasant is allowed to pass from the citizen into the peasant class or from the peasant into the citizen class.

From the date of this ordinance no new relation of serfdom, whether by birth or marriage, or by assuming the position of a serf, or by contract, can be created.

With the publication of the present ordinance the existing relations of serfdom of those serfs, with their wives, and children, who possess their peasant holdings by inheritance, or in their own right, or by perpetual leases, or of copyhold, shall cease entirely, together with all mutual rights and duties.

From Martinmas, one thousand eight hundred and ten (1810) all serfdom shall cease throughout our whole realm. From Martinmas, 1810, there shall be only free persons, as is already the case upon the royal domains in all our provinces, free persons, however, still subject, as a matter of course, to all obligations which bind them, as free persons, by reason of the possession of an estate or by virtue of a special contract.

To this declaration of our supreme will every one whom it may concern, and in particular our provincial authorities and other officials, are exactly and dutifully to conform, and the present ordinance is to be universally made known.

The Declaration of Purpose by the Allies after Napoleon's Return from the Island of Elba (*British State Papers,* 1815)

The powers who signed the treaty of Paris, reassembled in the Congress of Vienna, having been informed of the escape of Napoleon Bonaparte and of his entrance into France with an armed force, owe to their dignity and the interest of social order the solemn declaration of the sentiments which that event has inspired in them.

In thus violating the convention which established him in the island of Elba, Bonaparte has destroyed the only legal title to his existence. By reappearing in France with projects of disorder and destruction, he has cut himself off from the protection of the law, and has shown in the face of all the world that there can be neither peace nor truce with him.

Accordingly, the powers declare that Napoleon Bonaparte is excluded from civil and social relations, and as an enemy and disturber of the tranquility of the world he has incurred public vengeance.

At the same time, being firmly resolved to preserve intact the Treaty of Paris of May 30, 1814, and the arrangements sanctioned by that treaty, as well as those which have been or shall be arranged hereafter in order to complete and consolidate it, they declare that they will employ all their resources and unite all their efforts in order that the general peace, the object of the desires of Europe and the constant aim of their labors, may not be again disturbed, and in order to secure themselves from all attempts which may threaten to plunge the world once more into the disorders and misfortunes of revolutions.

And although fully persuaded that all France, rallying around its legitimate sovereign, will strive unceasingly to bring to naught this last attempt of a criminal and impotent madman, all the sovereigns of Europe, animated by the same feeling and guided by the same principles, declare that if, contrary to all expectation, there shall result from that event any real danger, they will be ready to give to the king of France and the French nation, or to any government which shall be attacked, as soon as shall be required all the assistance necessary to reestablish the public tranquillity, and to make common cause against all who may attempt to compromise it.

The present declaration, inserted in the protocol of the Congress assembled at Vienna, March 13, 1815, shall be made public.

UNIT 9

The Reaction and Its Opposites: Liberalism and Nationalism

The defeat of Napoleon by the forces of the conservative governments of Europe in 1815, was, it was felt, the final act in the destruction of radical ideology in Europe, for not only was militarism discredited, but the whole system of liberal republicanism and nationalism for which France stood in the eyes of the people of Europe was shown by the victory of the allies to have been invalid. And at once, certain in victory of the moral validity of its own political profession, the conservative group met at Vienna in a congress for concerted action in preserving future peace and stability. One of the first fruits of the meeting of the victors in the capital of Austria was the formation of the Holy Alliance. By combining the motivating force of Christian idealism with the selfish and reactionary concept of "legitimacy," the Alliance hoped to construct a solid basis not only for peace among themselves, but one which would guarantee continued domination of Europe by themselves. Yet, though unified and successful in war, the Congress began almost immediately to show signs of stress due to disagreement in peace. Tallyrand, the clever and brilliant representative of the restored King of France, Louis XVIII, at Vienna, was already, by the end of 1815, beginning to report his success at exploiting, in the interest of defeated France, the cracks apparent in the unity of the victor powers.

The programs and aspirations of the powers represented at Vienna were further weakened by certain realities which, in the first burst of victorious optimism, had been overlooked. Liberalism and nationalism in Europe had been defeated but not destroyed. The wars against France had been merely treatments of symptoms rather than cure of the disease; and by 1819 it was apparent that nationalism had grown strong in the German states. *The Carlsbad Decrees,* promulgated by the Diet of the German Confederation, were a crude attempt at controlling liberal and nationalistic tendencies by the application of various types of censorship to the works of faculties and students of the universities and by limiting the public press in its expression. And while the Congress was attempting to force its will in this way on the German reformers, a violent revolution against arbitrary authority broke out in the Greek portion of the Ottoman Empire. In 1820, the Spanish people, unwilling to accept the absolute monarchy re-established over them by the Viennese reaction also sought reform in revolution. In 1830 both France and Belgium set aside the congressional settlement in search of greater personal liberty and right of national self-expression. Thus blow after painful blow was struck against the Metternich system by the revived liberals of Europe.

France, in this period the very nerve center of continental liberal thought, not only stimulated ferment in other areas but herself maintained the pace of action. Charles X, the last of the Bourbons, was driven from the throne in 1830, and his successor, Louis Philippe, unable to match the ever-growing demands of the liberals for additional reforms, was unseated by revolution in 1848. The rejection of the "do-nothing" king, Louis Philippe, opened the way for the revival of the Napoleonic myth which would in turn, because of its emotional and dramatic appeal to the French people, produce first the Presidency, and then the Emperorship of Louis Napoleon in 1851.

In the same time period the German liberal nationalists were working toward similar objectives. Frederick William, King of Prussia, was offered the crown of a unified Germany provided he would accept it under a constitution limiting his authority. The king, despising all constitutions as mere radical devices for illegimately controlling governments, accused the German National Assembly which had tendered the crown as having offered it from the "gutter" with the intention of upsetting the "order of things established by both divine and human sanction."

From the general pattern of events in Europe in this period it can be safely deduced that the reform movements were in certain ways limited and weakened by inherent defects. The two components, liberalism and nationalism, were as yet not truly joined in purpose. They tended to emphasize their divergent goals at the expense of harmonious interaction. Also, neither was willing to clearly disassociate itself from monarchy; and in every case where revolution was successful the institution of limited monarchy was refurbished and established. The same defective thinking is visible in the program of the German liberals and nationalists in 1849, and also in Italy in 1860.

This apparent inability of the liberals to establish and maintain purposeful goals and programs resulted in its rejection by the romantic nationalists who developed the concept of cultural unity as the best means of attaining political homogeneity. Hegel, Fichte, and Gobineau were among the first of those who held that the German people, united as they were linguistically, culturally, and esthetically, were somehow unique; and in their difference from other peoples, set aside by the force of history and given a special mission to save civilization by Germanizing it. If the factors and interests in Germany could not agree on political programs and methods they *could* agree that the "volk" was a romantic reality that had greater vitality and deeper purpose than mere political unity. This new emotional basis upon which to rest unity was also appealing to the people of Italy, and it is to be noted that the new emotional stimulation to reform and unity was not without effect on Russian thought. In 1861, in the name of unity, and because he found his duty in the "sacred heritage" of his ancestors, the Czar, Alexander II, began the process of liberating the serfs from medieval bondage with the *Emancipation Ukase* of that year.

Prince Metternich's Defense of Reaction (Metternich, *Memoirs,* 1838)

The world desires to be governed by facts and according to justice, not by phrases and theories; the first need of society is to be maintained by strong authority (no authority without real strength deserves the name) and not to govern itself. In comparing the number of contests between parties in mixed governments, and that of just complaints caused by aberrations of power in a Christian State, the comparison would not be in favor of the new doctrines. The first and greatest concern for the immense majority of every nation is the stability of the laws and their uninterrupted action—never their change. Therefore let the governments govern, let them maintain the foundations of their institutions, both ancient and modern; for if it is at all times dangerous to touch them, it certainly would not now, in the general confusion, be wise to do so.

Let the governments announce this determination to their people, and demonstrate it by facts. Let them reduce the doctrinaires to silence within their States, and show their contempt for them abroad. Let them not encourage by their attitude or actions the suspicion of being, favorable or indifferent to error; let them not allow it to be believed that experience has lost all its rights to make way for experiments which at the least are dangerous. Let them be precise and clear in all their words, and not seek by concessions to gain over those parties who aim at the destruction of all power but their own, whom concessions will never gain over, but only further embolden in their pretensions to power.

Let them in these troublous times be more than usually cautious in attempting real ameliorations, not imperatively claimed by the needs of the moment, to the end that good itself may not turn against them—which is the case whenever a government measure seems to be inspired by fear.

Let them not confound concessions made to parties with the good they ought to do for their people, in modifying, according to their recognized needs, such branches of the administration as require it.

Let them give minute attention to the financial state of their kingdoms, so that their people may enjoy, by the reduction of public burdens, the real, not imaginary, benefits of a state of peace.

Let them be just, but strong; beneficent, but strict.

Let them maintain religious principles in all their purity, and not allow the faith to be attacked and morality interpreted according to the social contract or the visions of foolish sectarians.

Let them suppress secret societies, that gangrene of society.

In short, let the great monarchs strengthen their union, and prove to the world that while it exists, it is beneficent, and insures the political peace of Europe; that it is powerful only for the maintenance of tranquillity at a time when so many attacks are directed against it; that the principles which they profess are paternal and protective, menacing only the disturbers of public tranquillity.

The Idealism of the Reaction
(*The Holy Alliance,* 1815)

In the Name of the Holy and Indivisible Trinity.

Their majesties, the Emperor of Austria, the King of Prussia, and the Emperor of Russia, in view of the great events which the last three years have brought to pass in Europe and in view especially of the benefits which it has pleased Divine Providence to confer upon those states whose governments have placed their confidence and their hope in Him alone, having reached the profound conviction that the policy of the powers, in their mutual relations, ought to be guided by the sublime truths taught by the eternal religion of God our Saviour, solemnly declare that the present act has no other aim than to manifest to the world in the government of their respective countries or in their political relations with other governments, than the precepts of the holy religion, the precepts of justice, charity, and peace.

Hence their majesties have agreed upon the following articles:

Conforming to the words of Holy Scripture which command all men to look upon each other as brothers, the three contracting monarchs will continue united by the bonds of a true and indissoluble fraternity, and regarding themselves as compatriots, they will lend aid and assistance to each other on all occasions and in all places, viewing themselves, in their relations to their subjects and to their armies, as fathers of families, they will direct them in that spirit of fraternity by which they are animated, for the protection of religion, peace, and justice.

Hence the sole principle of conduct, be it between the said governments or their subjects, shall be that of rendering mutual service, and testifying by unceasing good-will, the mutual affection with which they should be animated. Considering themselves all as members of one great Christian nation, the three allied princes look upon themselves as delegates of Providence called upon to govern three branches of the same family, i.e., Austria, Russia, and Prussia. They thus confess that the Christian nation, of which they and their people form a part, has in reality no other sovereign than Him alone to whom belongs by right the power, for in Him alone are to be found all the treasures of love, of knowledge and of infinite wisdom, that is to say God, our Divine Saviour, Jesus Christ, the Word of the most High, the Word of life.

All these powers who wish solemnly to make avowal of the sacred principles which have dictated the present act, and who would recognize how important it is to the happiness of nations, too long agitated, that these truths should hereafter exercise upon human destiny all the influence belonging to them, shall be received into this Holy Alliance with as much cordiality as affection.

The Efforts of the German Bund to Check Liberal and Nationalistic Expression in Germany
(*The Carlsbad Decrees,* 1819)

It is decreed that, with a view to the fundamental improvement of the whole system of schools and universities, a series of provisional measures shall be adopted without delay. This law of the Confederation shall go into force immediately in all the States of the Confederation.

Concerning Educational Institutions

A special representative of the Prince of each state shall be appointed for each university with appropriate instructions and extended powers. The function of this agent shall be to see to the strictest enforcement of existing laws and disciplinary regulations; to observe carefully the spirit shown by the professors in public lectures and regular courses, to give salutary direction to the instruction.

The confederated governments mutually pledge themselves to remove from the universities or other public institutions all teachers who, by deviation from duty, or by exceeding the limits of their function, or by the abuse of their influence over youthful minds, or by propagating doctrines hostile to public order or subversive of existing governmental institutions, shall have proved their unfitness for such important office.

No teacher who shall have been removed in this manner shall again be appointed to a position of learning in any other State in the Union.

Those laws which have for a long period been directed against secret and unauthorized societies in the universities shall be strictly enforced. Those laws apply especially to that association established under the name of the Universal Student Union *(Burschenschaft).*

The governments mutually agree that such persons shall, after publication of the present decree, be shown to have remained in secret associations, shall not be admitted to any public office.

No student, who shall be expelled from a university by a decision of the University Senate, or shall have left the institution in order to escape expulsion, shall be admitted to any other university.

Concerning Press Regulations

So long as this decree shall remain in force no publication which appears in the form of daily issues or as a serial shall go to press in any State of the Union without previous knowledge and approval of the State officials.

Each State of the Union is responsible to the whole Confederation for every publication appearing under its supervision in which the honor or security of other States is infringed or their constitution or administration attacked.

The Diet shall have the right to suppress on its own authority all such writings in whatever German State they appear, if in the opinion of the commission appointed by it, they are inimical to the honor of the Union, the safety of the States or the maintenance of peace and quiet in Germany.

The Revolutionary Chamber of Deputies Invites Louis Philippe to Accept the Title of "King of the French People" (Chamber of Deputies, *Records,* 1830)

The Chamber of Deputies, in view of the imperative necessity resulting from the events of July 26, 27, 28, and 29, and the following days, and the general situation of France due to the violation of the Constitutional Charter:

In view also of the fact that, in consequence of this violation and of the heroic resistance of the citizens of Paris, his Majesty Charles X and his Royal Highness Louis Antoine, the dauphin, and all the members of the older branch of the royal house are at this moment leaving French territory, declares that the throne is vacant in fact and right and that it is indispensable to provide therefor.

The Chamber of Deputies declares, secondly, that, in accordance with the wish and in the interest of the French people, the preamble of the Constitutional Charter is suppressed as wounding the national dignity, since it appears to grant to Frenchmen the rights which are inherently theirs, and that the following articles of the same character must be suppressed or modified in the manner below indicated.

On condition of the acceptance of these arrangements and propositions, the Chamber of Deputies declares that the general and pressing interest of the French people summons to the throne his Royal Highness Louis Philippe of Orleans, duke of Orleans, lieutenant general of the kingdom, and his descendants forever, from male to male, in order to primogeniture, to the perpetual exclusion of women and their descendants. Accordingly his Royal Highness Louis Philippe of Orleans shall be invited to accept and swear to the clauses and engagements above enumerated, and to the observation of the Constitutional Charter including the modifications indicated, and, after having done this in the presence of the assembled chambers, to take the title of King of the French.

Louis Napoleon's Appeal to the "Napoleonic Myth" (Louis Napoleon, *Works,* 1839)

Napoleon, advancing upon the state of the world, saw that it was his part to be the testamentary executor of the Revolution. The destructive fire of parties was extinct; and when the Revolution, dying but not vanquished, bequeathed to Napoleon the accomplishment of its last wishes, it should have addressed him as follows: "Establish upon solid foundations the results of my efforts; reunite the divided people of France; repulse feudal Europe; heal my wounds; enlighten the nation; extend in breadth that which I have done in depth. Be for Europe what I have been to France; and even though you water the tree of civilization with your blood, though you see your projects misinterpreted, and your family wandering about the world without a native land to own them, never abandon the sacred cause of the French people."

The emperor Napoleon contributed more than any other man to accelerate the reign of liberty by preserving the moral influence of the Revolution. He sobered the Revolution, consolidated the dynasties of kings, and ennobled the people.

The emperor, while restoring the old forms, rested his authority upon a new and firm basis, and upon new conditions and interests. This was done by public demand, and with public confidence. In fact had these things not been demanded by the sentiments of the majority, Napoleon would not have accomplished them, for he possessed accurate powers of divination. And never were such changes effected with so little effort. Napoleon had but to say, "Let the churches be opened," and the faithful rushed to the churches in crowds. He said to the nation, "Do you desire an hereditary monarchy?" and the nation replied in the affirmative, by four millions of votes.

The improvement of the condition of the poor classes was one of the first considerations of the emperor. He had workhouses established; forty-two already existed in 1809. In order to ascertain the effectual means of relieving the misery of the people, he sought information from all the public writers. Napoleon created homes for the veterans, and a Maternal Society with many branches, and re-instituted the Sisters of Charity to receive the orphan daughters. . . .

The emperor desired that everything connected with worship should be free, and that the poor be allowed freely to enjoy the theatre and French art, and French literature.

Let us repeat in conclusion: the Napoleonic idea is not an idea of war, but a social, industrial, commercial idea—an idea of humanity. If to some men it seems still to threaten new conflicts, the reason is that it was, indeed, long enveloped in the smoke of cannon and the dust of battles. But now the clouds have dispersed and men discern a civil glory greater and more enduring. Let the ashes of the emperor repose in peace! His memory spreads wider and wider every passing day. Each wave that breaks on the rock of St. Helena brings with the breath of Europe an homage to his memory, a regret to his ashes; and the breezes repeat over his tomb, "The free nations of the earth everywhere labor to carry on thy work."

Decree of the Provisional Government Relating to the Overthrow of Louis Philippe

(Records of the Chamber of Deputies of the Provisional Government of France, 1848)

A reactionary and oligarchical government has just been overthrown by the heroism of the people of Paris. That government has fled, leaving behind it a trail of blood that forbids it ever to retrace its steps.

The blood of the people has flowed as in July; but this time this noble people shall not be deceived. It has won a national and popular government in accord with the rights, the progress, and the will of this great and generous nation.

A provisional government, the result of pressing necessity and ratified by the voice of the people and of the deputies of the departments, in the session of February 24, is for the moment invested with the task of assuring and organizing the national victory. It is composed of Messieurs Dupont (de l'Eure), Lamartine, Cremieux, Arago (of the Institute), Ledru-Rollin, Garnier-Pages, Marie, Armand Marrast, Louis Blanc, Ferdinand Flocon, and Albert (a workingman).

These citizens have not hesitated a moment to accept the patriotic commission which is imposed upon them by the pressure of necessity. With the capital of France on fire, the justification for the present provisional government must be sought in the public safety. All France will understand this and will lend it the support of its patriotism. Under the popular government which the provisional government proclaims, every citizen is a magistrate.

Frenchmen, it is for you to give to the world the example which Paris has given to France; prepare yourselves by order and by confidence in your destiny for the firm institutions which you are about to be called upon to establish.

The provisional government wishes to establish a republic, subject, however, to ratification by the people, who shall be immediately consulted.

The unity of the nation (formed henceforth of all the classes of citizens who compose it); the government of the nation by itself; liberty, equality, and fraternity, for fundamental principles, and "the people" for our emblem and watchword; these constitute the democratic government which France owes to itself, and which our efforts shall secure for it.

Louis Napoleon Seeks Popular Support in the French Presidential Elections (Louis Napoleon, *Address,* 1848)

The purpose of this journey, as you know, was to see for myself our beautiful provinces of the south and familiarize myself with their needs. It has, however, given rise to a much more important result. Indeed, and I say it with a candor as far removed from arrogance as from false modesty, never has a people testified in a manner more direct, spontaneous, and unanimous, the longing to be freed from anxiety as to the future by concentrating in a single person an authority which shall accord with their desires. They realize now both the false hopes with which they have been deluded and the dangers which threaten them.

France today encompasses me with her sympathies because I do not belong to the group of dreamers. In order to benefit the country it is not necessary to resort to new systems, but, above all, to establish confidence in the present and security for the future. This is why France seems to wish to revert to the empire.

There is, nevertheless, one apprehension, and that I shall set at rest. A spirit of distrust leads certain persons to say that the empire means war. I say, the empire means peace. France longs for peace, and if France is satisfied the world is tranquil. Glory is rightly handed down hereditarily, but not war.

I concede, nevertheless, that, like the Emperor, I have many conquests to make. I would, like him, conquer, for the sake of harmony, the warring parties and bring into the great popular current the wasteful and conflicting eddies. I would conquer, for the sake of religion, morality, and material ease, that portion of the population, still very numerous, which, in the midst of a country of faith and belief, hardly knows the precepts of Christ; which, in the midst of the most fertile country of the world, is hardly able to enjoy the primary necessities of life. We have immense uncultivated districts to bring under cultivation, roads to open, harbors to construct, rivers to render navigable, canals to finish, and our network of railroads to bring to completion.

This is what I understand by the empire, if the empire is to be re-established. These are the conquests which I contemplate, and all of you who surround me, who, like myself, wish the good of our common country, you are my soldiers.

The King of Prussia, Frederick William, Refuses the Offer of the Crown of Germany

(Communication: *Frederick William to the people of Germany,* 1849)

Taking as a pretense the interests of Germany, the enemies of the fatherland have raised the standard of revolt, first in the neighboring Saxony, then in several districts of south Germany. To my deep chagrin, even in parts of our own land some have permitted themselves to be seduced into following this standard and attempting, in open rebellion against the legal government, to overturn the order of things established by both divine and human sanction. In so serious and dangerous a crisis I am moved publicly to address a word to my people.

I was not able to return a favorable reply to the offer of a crown on the part of the German National Assembly, because the Assembly has not the right, without the consent of the German governments, to bestow the crown which they tendered me, and moreover, because they offered the crown upon condition that I would accept a constitution which could not be reconciled with the rights and safety of the German states.

I have exhausted every means to reach an understanding with the German National Assembly. Now the Assembly has broken with Prussia. The majority of its members are no longer those men upon whom Germany looked with pride and confidence.

The greater part of the deputies voluntarily left the Assembly when they saw that it was on the road to ruin, and yesterday I ordered all the Prussian deputies who had not already withdrawn to be recalled. The other governments will do the same.

A party now dominates the Assembly which is in league with the terrorists. While they urge the unity of Germany as a pretense, they are really fighting the battle of godlessness, perjury, robbery, and kindling a war against monarchy; but if monarchy were overthrown it would carry with it the blessings of law, liberty, and property. The horrors committed in Dresden, Breslau, and Elberfeld under the banner of German unity afford a melancholy proof of this. New horrors are occurring and are in prospect.

While such crimes have put an end to the hope that the Frankfort Assembly can bring about German unity, I have, with a fidelity and persistence suiting my royal station, never lost hope. My government has taken up with the more important German states the work on the German constitution begun by the Frankfort Assembly.

This is my method. Only madness or deception will dare, in view of these facts, to assert that I have given up the cause of German unity, or that I am untrue to my earlier convictions and assurances.

Gobineau's Racial Theory
(Comte de Gobineau, *Essay on the Inequalities of the Human Races*, 1853)*

Since the last half of the previous century, the eighteenth, one reasons on the basis of general principles and one pretends, also, to relate all phenomena . . . to fixed laws. . . . The prosperity or the misfortune of a nation, its greatness and decadence, were related to the obvious vices and virtues relating to the point of examination. An honest people were necessarily a famous people, and, on the contrary, a society which attracted too many easy consciences, was doomed without mercy to the ruin of . . . an Athens or a Rome. . . .

With such keys one sought to open all the mysteries; but in reality they remained unsolved. Those virtues necessary to big groups must have a peculiar collective egoism which is not parallel to individual virtue. . . . One must recognize and avow that

* Comte de Gobineau, *Essai sur l'Inegalite de Races Humaines*, 1853. Translated G. L. Mosse.

here those merits and demerits which concern Christian consciences are beside the point, but instead certain aptitudes of soul and body determine or paralyze the life of nations. This leads us to inquire why some nations can be powerful and others cannot, and thus one is forced to acknowledge that this is a matter resulting from the particular race. . . .

I reject those groups whose social system is not vigorous enough to impose itself, with the fusion of blood, upon great multitudes. I come to those whose constituting principle has such strength that it can embrace all others who are near to its center of operations, incorporate them and lift them up to the great vistas of uncontested domination of its ideas and action. . . . In one word such a people can call themselves a civilization. . . .

Is there an inequality of forces? It goes without saying that the American savages as well as the Hindus are our inferiors on that score. . . , but we must distinguish between muscular force and that power of resistance whose most remarkable feat is its staying power . . . Even feeble races have muscular power. Among peoples in the matter of force, as in the matter of beauty, there is a difference . . . though not so obvious. The Italians are more beautiful than the Germans or the Swiss, more beautiful than are the Frenchmen and the Spaniards. Thus the English have a bodily beauty which is superior to that of the Slavs. . . .

The Germans made their appearance in the midst of Roman society. At the same time they occupied the extreme northwest of Europe, which, little by little, became their base of operations. Successive marriage with Celts and Slavs . . . multiplied the expansion of the new arrivals without degrading too rapidly their force of initiative. Modern society was born; it began to perfect its members and to further the work of its creators. We have seen it discover America in practically our own day, uniting itself with the native society to lead it toward a new birth. . . .

The German people were filled with all the energy of the Aryan races; that was necessary so that it could fulfill the duty to which it was called. . . . It was indispensable that the last workers sent to the earth leave nothing difficult unaccomplished, as no one exists except themselves to accomplish such feats . . . they achieve the conquest of the globe. . . . Here we have the existence of the best human species, of the whole white race . . . result of the evolution of faculties which is like a peak, like a summit, like the final goal of history. But religion itself has not promised us eternity; only science in showing us what we have commenced to do seems to hold out hope that we might finish it. There is therefore no ground for astonishment to find once again confirmation of a fact no longer doubtful. The sad fact is not death, it is the certitude to arrive there degenerated; and perhaps that fear, reserved for our descendants, could leave us cold if we did not feel, with secret horror, that the hands of destiny are already upon us.

The Emancipation Ukase of Czar Alexander II (Alexander, *Proclamation,* 1861)

I, Alexander II, by the Grace of God Emperor of the Russias, summoned to the throne by Divine Providence and the ancient law of heredity, have felt constrained to extend greetings and affection to all faithful subjects, whatever their rank or condition.

As we consider the various classes of which the State is composed, it is apparent that the laws of the empire well and wisely provide for the upper Estates and classes; fixing with justice their rights and burdens, and yet, that those laws have not justly affected the peasants bound through ancient law or custom, to the lands and hereditarily subjected to the domination of the landlords. Relationships between the lord and peasant have been determined in great part, not by law, but by the good will of the Lord or by the affectionate docility of the peasant.

We become convinced, therefore, that the task of reforming the extant conditions of the peasant is for us a sacred heritage from our predecessors. And, we have begun this task by demonstrating our great confidence in the nobility; which of itself must accept some material loss if the proposed reforms are to be carried out. Nor has this confidence been deceived. We find the aristocracy ready to make the necessary sacrifices voluntarily; particularly so far as it involves their loss of the ancient rights of personal services from their dependents.

The peasants now bound to the land shall, in the term fixed by law, be vested with the full rights of freemen. The landed lords, while they shall continue to hold their present lands, shall transfer to the peasant *Zemstvos,* in return for the rent fixed by law, their cottages, farm buildings, and gardens. And to further insure the security of the peasants, the landlords shall turn over to the peasants a quantity of arable land.

At the same time the peasants are granted the right of purchasing their cottages and gardens, and with the consent of the landlords they shall be able to claim full ownership of the arable land given them should they be able to make the required payment.

In order to facilitate the transactions which are hereby made legal and binding, the government will grant them assistance, according to a special regulation, through the loans of money and aid in transferring mortgages and encumbrances on land and buildings.

The "Syllabus of Errors"
(Pope Pius IX, Encyclical *Quanta Cura,* 1864)

Note: *The following list, appended to the papal encyclical, contains the specific propositions condemned by the document.*

1. There exists no supreme, all wise, provident Divine Being apart from the universe; God and nature are one, and God is therefore subject to change. . . .

4. All truths of religion derive in the natural force of human reason; therefore reason is the fundamental rule by which man can . . . attain the knowledge of all truths. . . .

7. Prophecies and miracles, established in Holy Scripture, are poetical fictions; the mysteries of the Christian faith are the result of philosophic investigation . . . and Jesus Christ Himself is a . . . fiction. . . .

9. . . . All the dogmas of the Christian religion are the object of natural science and philosophy; and human reason, developed solely by history, can by its own natural power . . . arrive at true knowledge of even the more complex dogmas. . . .

15. Every man is free to accept and profess that religion which, directed by the light of reason, he shall believe true. . . .

20. The ecclesiastical institution must not exercise its authority without the permission and agreement of civil government. . . .

27. The officials of the church and the Roman Pope ought to be absolutely excluded from all care and dominion over temporal affiairs. . . .

55. The church should be separated from the state, and the state from the church.

56. Moral law does not require a divine sanction, nor is there any necessity for human laws to be in agreement with the law of nature. . . .

57. The sciences of philosophy and morals, as well as that of civil government, should be withdrawn from divine and ecclesiastical authority. . . .

67. The bond of marriage is not indissoluble . . . and in some cases divorce . . . may be commissioned by the civil authority. . . .

77. Today it is not necessary that the Catholic religion should be the only religion of the state to the exclusion of all other forms. . . .

80. The Roman Pope can and should reconcile and align himself with progress, liberalism, and modern civilization.

UNIT 10

Radicalism, Labor, and Reform

The struggle of the middle class in Europe for liberty and equality in the 18th and 19th centuries ended in victory for that class. Representative institutions came to be the accepted rather than the unusual system of political society in many of the states. Yet, awareness of its own long disenfranchisement did not lead the bourgeoisie to a deeper sympathy for the classes beneath itself. To the laboring masses the result of the shift in power from aristocrat to king to middle class represented all too often no positive gain, either in a rise in economic status or in a broadening of the basis of its political liberties. In fact in England once the Industrial Revolution was under way the middle class imposed a severer type of bondage on labor than ever kings or barons had been capable of imposing. This imposition was the more inhuman because, with the doctrine preached by the high priests of classical liberalism, the middle class was given a basis of natural scientific law upon which to rest its selfish disregard for the lower classes. A good example of the contempt with which the lower classes were held is to be found in the works of John Howard concerning prison reform in England in this period. That such treatment of man by his fellow man as is stated by Howard was a reality cannot be doubted—and that it grew in some part from liberal doctrine is equally true. Adam Smith's concept of *laissez faire* which denied the state the right to stand between the economically strong and the economically weak was based on the supposed Law of Nature under which each individual of society would seek his own level of productivity, and each man would ascertain the amount he might consume of society's total product. Thomas Malthus, a liberal much interested in population, and in the influence of population on wages, rents, and economic production, argued that labor, as a class, was forever bound to suffer the natural consequences of its depressed status. And, he pointed out, since Natural Law had established the pattern, the state dared not infringe on the immutable pattern by tampering with the law. Stripped of useless verbiage and shown in its essentials only, classical liberalism as applied in Europe was no more than the law of the jungle imposed on the social organization. That the liberal was, however, successful in convincing society to accept this rationale for social irresponsibility is easily ascertained by a mere survey of the records of Parliamentary investigating committees in the period. As late as 1840 the evil of child labor in mines and factories not only existed but was on the increase. For all time there is set down against the year 1842 in the English *Parliamentary Papers* the simple testimony of a child, "I am Sarah Gooder. I am eight years old. I'm a coal-carrier in the Gawber mine. . . . I go at half-past three in the morning, and come out at half-past five in the evening." This happened during a year of unusual economic prosperity in England.

Labor in the 19th century was beginning to challenge the patterns imposed by the dominant middle class. Between 1825 and 1832 labor in England used the political tool in seeking reform. When the Parliamentary Reform Bill of 1832 failed to guarantee the political equality sought by the lower classes they turned toward the old right of petition, with the Chartist movement. This proved a failure also, and only then, in 1845, did English labor turn to the use of economic action in gaining its ends. This was the beginning of real labor unionism in England. Meantime, while the English lower classes were applying the several methods to the problems of reform, certain groups and individuals were, independently, attempting still other solutions. In 1846 Karl Marx, finding a large and bitter element of the population crowded into the filthy slums of the English industrial towns at which to aim his appeal, published the most infectious of all radical doctrines, scientific socialism, in his *Communist Manifesto*. In France, one of the groups responsible for the revolution against Louis Philippe in 1848, was the Socialist party, which accepted the doctrine of Louis Blanc which was based on the program of the national workshops, a radical concept which held, with Marx, that private property was the cause of all social ills, and as such, must be obliterated. The middle class, brought under ever more violent attack by the increasing complex of radical-socialist idealogies, defended the *status quo* as vigorously in the 19th century as it had attacked the vested social interests in the 17th and 18th centuries, and it used quite as efficiently the same tools that had been used against itself: the law, the court decision, propaganda—and force. In 1862, when, hailed before a German court on charges of socialistic activity aimed at destruction of the state, Ferdinand Lassalle gave a classic definition of socialism which had seldom occurred to the people of the West: a definition which pointed out that while revolutionary, all socialist activity was not inevitably based on force as was Marxism. Some relied on concerted political action, some on moral persuasion; and some on the inherent goodness of man which would eventually lead him into agreement with the socialist concept of social justice. The Fabian movement in England, for example, was one of the radical professions which rested its program for reform on education and the logical use of the franchise which had been gained by labor in 1867.

All socialist movements, while they disagreed as to method, agreed as to end and purpose: the abolition of private property and the establishment of a classless society. All were economic determinists and all accepted the concept of historical inevitability, which was essentially a denial of free will. Thus, all were equally, and solely, interested in purely materialistic goals.

As the struggle between radical and liberal professions became productive of disregard for human liberty and rights, a new and moderating voice was heard appealing for rational consideration of social ills and methods of reform, that of the Papacy. In several messages to civilization various Popes pointed out the fallacies upon which both socialism and liberalism were based, and emphasized the factor of Christianity in social reform. Leo XIII in 1891 warned the West of the pitfalls of socialism, and forty years later Pius IX placed the Catholic Church in contention for leadership of world reform; which, he pointed out, must be accomplished in the way of love and respect for the individual's rights as well as property rights.

In the states of western Europe such moderation was possible; social and political reform was assured in time in that area, because the necessary legal and constitutional frameworks had been long established, and the masses had, usually, by 1900, free right to political participation. This was not true in Russia. Hedged in by antiquated law forms, bereft of any real constitution, dominated by the isolationistic philosophy of slavophilism which held passionately to distrust of any western idea, and hunted by the secret police, the reforming elements of Russia found no such legal or constitutional channels of activity open to them. It was in part because of this lack of representative institutions through which they might have acted that the radicals of Russia turned to force. The revolution of 1905 was the first breach of the peace in a revolution which would culminate in 1917 with the victory of Lenin and Trotsky, and the emergence of Bolshevism.

A "Classical English Liberal" on the "Law of Diminishing Returns"

(Thomas Malthus, *An Essay on the Principle of Population,* 1798)

In an inquiry concerning the improvement of society, the mode of conducting the subject which naturally presents itself, is;

1. To investigate the causes that have hitherto impeded the progress of mankind towards happiness; and,
2. To examine the probability of the total or partial removal of these causes in the future.

The principal object of the present essay is to examine the effects of one great cause . . . and . . . the cause to which I allude is the constant tendency in all animated life to increase beyond the nourishment prepared for it.

This is incontrovertibly true. That population has this constant tendency to increase beyond the means of subsistence will sufficiently appear from a review of the different states of society in which man has existed.

In the northern states of America, where the means of subsistence have been ample, the manners of the people are more pure . . . the population has been found to double itself, for above a century and a half successively, in less than twenty-five years.

In the back settlements, where the sole employment is agriculture, the population has been found to double itself in fifteen years.

According to a table of Euler, calculated on a mortality of 1 to 36, if the births be to the deaths in the proportion of 3 to 1, the period of doubling will be only 12 years and four-fifths.

It may safely be pronounced, therefore, that population, when unchecked, goes on doubling itself every twenty-five years, or increases in a geometrical ratio.

The rate according to which the production of food may be supposed to increase . . . must be of a totally different nature from the ratio of the increase of population. When acre has been added to acre till all the fertile land is occupied, the yearly increase of food must depend upon the melioration of the land already in possession. This is a fund, which, from the nature of all soils, instead of increasing, must be gradually diminishing. But population, could it be supplied with food, would go on with unexhausted vigour; and the increase of one period would furnish the power of a greater increase the next, and this without any limit.

Let us consider at what rate the produce of England might be supposed to increase under circumstances the most favourable to improvement.

In the next twenty-five years, it is impossible to suppose that the produce could be quadrupled. The improvement of the barren parts would be a work of time and labour; and it must be evident to those who have the slightest acquaintance with agricultural subjects, that in proportion as cultivation is extended, the additions that could yearly be made to the former average produce must be gradually and regularly diminishing.

Let us suppose that the yearly additions which might be made to the former average food produce, instead of decreasing, which they certainly would do, were to remain the same; and that the produce of this island might be increased every twenty-five years, by a quantity equal to what it at present produces. The most enthusiastic speculator cannot suppose a greater increase than this.

If this supposition be applied to the whole earth, and if it be allowed that the subsistence for man which the earth affords might be increased every twenty-five years by a quantity equal to what it at present produces this will be supposing a rate of increase much greater than we can imagine that any possible exertions of mankind could make it.

It may be fairly pronounced, therefore, that, considering the present average state of the earth, the means of subsistence, under circumstances the most favourable to human industry, could not possibly be made to increase faster than in an arithmetical ratio.

The necessary effects of these two different rates of increase, when brought together will be very striking. Let us call the population of this island eleven millions; and suppose the present produce equal to the support of such a number. In the first twenty-five years the population would be twenty-two millions, and the food being also doubled, the means of subsistence would be equal to this increase. In the next twenty-five years the population would be forty-four millions, and the means of subsistence only equal to the support of thirty-three millions. In the next period the population would be eighty-eight millions, and the means of subsistence just equal to the support of half that number. And, at the conclusion of the first century, the population would be a hundred and seventy-six millions, and the means of subsistence only equal to the support of fifty-five millions, leaving a population of a hundred and twenty-one millions totally unprovided for.

Taking the whole earth, and supposing the present population equal to a thousand millions, the human species would increase as the numbers 1, 2, 4, 8, 16, 32, 64, 128, 256, and subsistence as 1, 2, 3, 4, 5, 6, 7, 8, 9. In two centuries the population would be to the means of subsistence as 256 to 9; in three centuries as 4096 to 13, and in two thousand years the difference would be almost incalculable.

The Extension of Political Liberty to the Roman Catholics of England

(Statutes of the Realm: The Roman Catholic Emancipation Act of 1829)

An act for the relief of his majesty's Roman Catholic subjects. Whereas by various acts of Parliament certain restraints and disabilities are imposed on the Roman Catholic subjects of his majesty to which other subjects of his majesty are not liable . . . and whereas by various acts certain oaths and certain declarations . . . are or may be required to be taken, made, and subscribed by the subjects of his majesty, as qualifications for sitting and voting in Parliament, and for the enjoyment of certain offices, franchises, and civil rights; be it enacted . . . that, from and after the commencement of this act, all such parts of the said acts as require the said declarations . . . as a qualification for sitting and voting in Parliament, or for the exercise or enjoyment of any office, franchise, or civil right, be and the same are (save as hereinafter provided and excepted) hereby repealed.

And be it enacted that, from and after the commencement of this act, it shall be lawful for any person professing the Roman Catholic religion, being a peer or who shall after the commencement of this act be returned as a member of the House of

Commons, to sit and vote in either house of Parliament, respectively, being in all other respects duly qualified to sit and vote therein, upon taking and subscribing the following oath, instead of the oaths of allegiance, supremacy and abjuration: "I, A.B., do sincerely promise and swear that I will be faithful and bear true allegiance to his majesty King George IV and will defend him to the utmost of my power against all conspiracies and attempts whatever which shall be made, against his person, crown, or dignity. . . . And I do faithfully promise to maintain, support and defend to the utmost of my power the succession of the crown, which . . . stands limited to the princess Sophia, electress of Hanover, and the heirs of her body being Protestants, hereby utterly renouncing and abjuring any obedience or allegiance unto any other person claiming or pretending a right to the crown of this realm. And I further declare that it is not an article of my faith, and that I do denounce, reject, and abjure the opinion, that princes excommunicated or deprived by the Pope, or any other authority of the See of Rome, may be deposed or murdered by their subjects or by any person whatsoever. And I do declare that I do not believe that the Pope of Rome or any other foreign prince, prelate, person, state, or potentate hath or ought to have any temporal or civil jurisdiction, power, superiority, or pre-eminence, directly or indirectly, within this realm. I do swear that I will defend to the utmost of my power the settlement of property, within this realm as established by the laws. And I do hereby disclaim, disavow, and solemnly abjure any intention to subvert the present church establishment as settled by law within this realm. And I do solemnly swear that I will never exercise any privilege to which I am or may become entitled, to disturb or weaken the Protestant religion or Protestant government in the united kingdom . . . So help me God."

And be it further enacted that it shall be lawful for persons professing the Roman Catholic religion to vote at elections of members to serve in Parliament for England and for Ireland, and also to vote at the elections of representative peers of Scotland and of Ireland, and to be elected such representative peers, being in all other respects, duly qualified, upon taking and subscribing the oath herein before appointed.

Child Labor in an English Textile Factory
(*Testimony of William Henden to a Parliamentary Committee,* 1832)

Where do you live? At Leeds. Are your father and mother living? No; they are dead. What time did you begin to work at a mill? When I was six years old. What sort of a mill? A woolen mill. Whose? Mr. John Good's, at Hunslett. What were the hours of work? We used to start at five and work till nine at night. What time had you for your dinner? Half an hour. What time for breakfast and drinking? A quarter of an hour at each end of the day. What wages had you? Two shillings and sixpence.

Where did you remove to afterwards? My father and mother removed to Leeds, and I had a brother working at Tetley, Tatham, and Walker's, and they got me work there. How long did you stop there? Three years and a half. What were the hours of working there? We used to start at half past five and work till half past nine at night. What time had you for dinner? Forty minutes. What time for breakfast and drinking? Nothing for either. What is Tetley, Tatham, and Walker's mill? A flax mill. What were the wages there? I had three shillings and sixpence there. What was your business? A doffer.

Where did you go then? To Mr. Hammond's flax mill, at Leeds. At about what age? About ten years of age. At what time did you begin work at that mill in the morning? We used to start at half past five and work till eight at night. What time was allowed for breakfast and dinner and drinking? Forty minutes a day was all that was allowed. How were you kept up to your work during the latter part of the day? The overlooker used to come with a strap and give us a rap or two, or if they caught us asleep they would give us a pinch of snuff till we sneezed; they would give us a slap with a strap if we did not mind our work. Was the strap an instrument capable of hurting you badly? It was a heavy strap with a small handle to it.

Where did they strike you with it? Generally in the small of the back and over the head. Did they strike the young children as well as the older ones? Yes. And the females as well as the males? Yes. State the effect upon your health at those long hours of labor. I was pretty fair in health but happened with two or three misfortunes. State, in the first place, the effect upon your health and limbs of those long hours of labour? It produced a weakness in my knees; I was made crooked with standing the long hours. Just show the gentlemen your limbs. (The witness exhibited to the committee his limbs, which appeared exceedingly crooked).

Are you quite sure you were, as a child, perfectly straight and well formed? Yes. How old were you before your limbs began to fail you? About eight years and a half old. Had you any brother or sister working at the mill? Yes, I had two sisters and a brother. Have those long hours of labor had any effect upon the rest of your family? Yes, upon one of my sisters. Is she crippled? She is nearly as bad as I am. Was she originally perfectly straight and well formed? Yes. To what age did she continue to be perfectly well formed? Till she was about nine years old. How tall are you? About four feet nine inches. Were the children unhappy at the state in which they were? Yes, they were. Have you seen them crying at their work? Yes. Had you time to go to a day school or a night school during this labor? No. Can you write? No, not at all. Had you to work by gaslight? Yes. What effect do you think that has upon the eyes? It nearly made me blind; I was forced to go into the infirmary . . . and the doctors said . . . they did not expect they could cure me. What do you do now? I sell potatoes.

Social Aspects of the English Industrial Revolution (Statements of witnesses before the Ashley Mines Investigation Commission. *Parliamentary Papers,* 1842)

I am Sarah Gooder, I am 8 years old. I'm a coal carrier in the Gawber Mine. It does not tire me, but I have to trap without a light and I'm scared. I go at four and sometimes half past three in the morning, and come out at five and half past in the evening. I never go to sleep. Sometimes I sing when I've light, but not in the dark; I dare not sing then. I don't like being in the pit. I am very sleepy when I go in the morning. I go to Sunday-school and learn to read. They teach me to pray. I have heard tell of Jesus many a time. I don't know why he came on earth, I don't know why he died, but he had stones for his head to rest on.

I am Isabella Read, 12 years old, coal-bearer. I am brought with sister and brother; it is very sore work; cannot say how many rakes or journeys I make from the pit's bottom to wall face and back. I carry out about one hundred and thirty pounds of coal on my back, but have to stoop so much and creep through water, which is up to the calves of my legs. I do not like the work, nor do the other girls, but they are made to like it.

I am Mary Barrett, I am 14 years old. I have worked down in the pit five years. Father is working next pit. I have 12 brothers and sisters—all of them but one live at home. They weave, and wind, and hurry, and one is a counter. One of them can read; none of the rest can or write. They never went to day-school, but three of them go to Sunday-school. I carry for my brother John, and come down at seven o'clock. I go up at six, sometimes seven. I do not like working in the pit, but I am obliged to get a living. I work always without stockings, or shoes, or trousers. I wear nothing but my underwear. I have to go up to the headings with the men. They are all naked there; I am got well used to that, and don't care now much about it. I was afraid at first, and did not like it.

I am Patience Kershaw, I am 17 years old. My father has been dead about a year. My mother is living and has ten children, five lads and five lassies; the oldest is thirty, the youngest is four. All my sisters have been coal carriers but three went to the mill. Alice went because her legs swelled from carrying in cold water. I never went to school. I go to Sunday-school, but cannot read or write. I go to the pit at five o'clock in the morning and come out at five in the evening. I get my breakfast of porridge and milk first. I take my dinner with me, a loaf, and eat it as I go. I do not stop or rest any time for that purpose. I get nothing else until I get home, and then have potatoes and meat, not meat every day, though.

The bald place upon my head is made by pushing the coal cart. I push the cart a mile and more under ground and back; they weigh over three hundred pounds; I push 11 a day. I wear a belt and chain at the workings to get the cart out. The men that I carry for are naked except their caps. They pull off all their clothes. I see them at work when I go up. Sometimes they beat me, if I am not quick enough, with their hands. They strike me upon my back. The boys take liberties with me; sometimes they pull me about. I am the only girl in the pit. There are about 20 boys and 15 men. All the men are naked.

On Conditions in the English Industrial Centers in 1845 (*State Papers: The Second Report of the Commissioners for Inquiring into the State of Large Towns and Populous Districts,* 1845)

Birmingham, containing 189,000 inhabitants, is perhaps one of the most healthy of our large towns. The houses of the richer and middle classes appear generally dry and airy. The supply of water for these classes is good, and the drainage and cleansing is little complained of, though susceptible of considerable improvement.

The state of the habitations of the working and poorer classes is often widely different. I am obliged, however reluctantly, to say that many, if not most of the narrow streets, alleys, and courts in which their habitations are situated, are much neglected as regards drainage, paving, and cleansing, and though wells are found in most of them, they are frequently found out of order, or the water indifferent.

The courts in the parish of Birmingham alone are above 2,000 in number, and their inhabitants exceed 50,000. The ingress to most of the courts is by a narrow entry, from the houses fronting the street. The ventilation of the court is by this narrow and covered state of the entry very much impeded. The number of houses in each court varies from four or five to twenty or thirty. At the end, or on one side, there is often a wash-house, sometimes an ash-pit, and always one or two privies, or sets of privies, close to which there is often one or more pig-sties, tubs full of hog-slop, and heaps of offensive manure. In the midst of the court stands the pump of supply for the inhabitants. These courts are frequently unpaved, and the open channel for dirty water ill-defined, so that stagnant puddles in wet weather are the consequence.

In many, the overflowings from the privy vaults, pig sties, and dirt-heaps, trickling down the court, pass close to the well, and no doubt often enter it. Many of these courts are unpaved. There appears to be no system of sweeping or cleansing of any kind, except what is from time to time done by the inhabitants themselves. The smaller streets are also much neglected in this respect; and this remark applies to every town visited.

The neglect of all public regulations for draining, cleansing, or paving the courts in which the poorer classes reside, prevails in all the towns and districts visited. In a few towns, there are by-laws or regulations to prevent nuisances and ensure cleanliness, but none of these regulations are enforced.

The "Middle" Class Abandons Labor in the Struggle for Parliamentary Reform
(The Parliamentary Reform Bill of 1832)

An act to amend the representation of the people in England and Wales. Whereas it is expedient to take effectual measures for correcting divers abuses that have long prevailed in the choice of members to serve in the commons house of Parliament; to deprive many of the inconsiderable places of the right of returning members; to grant such privilege to large, populous and wealthy towns; to increase the number of knights of the shire; to extend the elective franchise to many of his majesty's subjects who have not heretofore enjoyed the same; and to diminish the expense of elections; be it therefore enacted that each of the boroughs enumerated in the schedule marked A to this act annexed shall, from and after the end of this present Parliament, cease to return any member or members to serve in Parliament.

And be it enacted that each of the boroughs enumerated in the schedule marked B shall return one member and no more to serve in Parliament.

And be it enacted that each of the places named in the schedule marked C shall for the purpose of this act be a borough, and shall return two members to serve in Parliament.

And be it enacted that each of the places named in the schedule marked D shall for the purposes of this act be a borough, and shall return one member to serve in Parliament.

And be it enacted that in all future Parliaments there shall be four knights of the shire, instead of two, to serve for each of the counties (enumerated in the schedule marked F) and that in all future parliaments there shall be three knights of the shire, instead of two, to serve for each of the counties enumerated in the schedule marked F2 and two knights of the shire, instead of one to serve for each of the counties of Carmarthen, Denbigh, and Glamorgan.

And be it enacted that every male person of full age and not subject to any legal incapacity who shall be seized at law or in equity of any lands or tenements or copyhold, or any other tenure whatever except freehold, for his own life or for the life of another or for any lives whatsoever, of the clear yearly value of not less than £10 shall be entitled to vote in the election of a knight or knights of the shire for the county in which such lands or tenements shall be respectively situate.

And be it enacted that every male person of full age and not subject to any legal incapacity who shall be entitled, either as lessee or assignee, to any lands or tenements for the unexpired residue of any term originally created for a period of not less than sixty years . . . of the clear yearly values of not less than £10, or for the unexpired residue of any term originally created for a period of not less than twenty years of the clear yearly value of not less than £50, or who shall occupy as tenant any lands or tenements for which he shall be *bona fide* liable to a yearly rent of not less than £50, shall be entitled to vote in the election of a knight or knights of the shire to serve in any future Parliament for the county in which such lands shall be respectively situate. And be it enacted that, notwithstanding anything hereinbefore contained, no person shall be entitled to vote in the election of a knight or knights of the shire to serve in any future Parliament unless he shall have been duly registered according to the provisions hereinafter contained.

And be it enacted that, in every city or borough which shall return a member or members to serve in any future Parliament, every male person of full age and not subject to any legal incapacity who shall occupy within such city or borough, as owner or tenant, any house, warehouse, counting-house, shop, or other building of the clear yearly value of not less than £10 shall, if duly registered according to the provisions hereinafter contained, be entitled to vote in the election of a member or members to serve in any future Parliament for such city or borough. Provided always that no such person shall be so registered unless he shall have occupied such premises for twelve calendar months; nor unless such person shall have been rated in respect of such premises to all rates for the relief of the poor made during the time of such his occupation; nor unless such person shall have paid all the poor rates and assessed taxes which shall have become payable from him in respect of such premises.

And be it enacted that every person who would have been entitled to vote in the election of a member or members to serve in any future Parliament for any city or borough, not included in the schedule A, either as a burgess or freeman, if this Act had not been passed, shall be entitled to vote in such election, provided such person shall be duly registered.

And be it enacted that all booths erected for the convenience of taking polls shall be erected at the joint and equal expense of the several candidates, that the expense to be incurred for the booth or booths to be erected at the principal place of election for any county or division of a county shall not exceed the sum of £40; and that the expense to be incurred for any booth or booths to be erected for any parish, district, or part of any city or borough shall not exceed the sum of £25.

Provided always that nothing in this act contained shall in any wise affect the election of members to serve in Parliament for the Universities of Oxford or Cambridge.

The English Parliament's First Step in Abolishing Slavery
(*The Act Abolishing Slavery,* 1833)

An Act for the abolition of slavery throughout the British colonies. . . .

Be it enacted that, subject to the obligations imposed by this act, all persons who on the first day of August, 1834, shall be holden in slavery within any British colony shall upon and from and after the said first day of August, 1834, become and be to all intents and purposes free and discharged of and from all manner of slavery, and shall be absolutely and forever manumitted; and that the children thereafter to be born to any such persons, and the offspring of such children, shall in like manner be free from their birth; and that from and after the said first day of August, 1834, slavery shall be and is hereby utterly and forever abolished and declared unlawful throughout the British colonies, plantations, and possessions abroad.

An Attempt by English Labor to Win the Franchise
(*A Chartist Petition to Parliament,* 1839)

Your petitioners dwell in a land whose merchants are noted for their enterprise, whose manufacturers are very skillful, and whose workmen are proverbial for their industry. The land itself is goodly, the soil rich, and the temperature wholesome. It is abundantly furnished with the materials of commerce and trade. It has numerous and convenient harbors. In facility of internal communication it exceeds all others. For three and twenty years we have enjoyed a profound peace.

Yet with all the elements of national prosperity, and with every disposition and capacity to take advantage of them, we find ourselves overwhelmed with public and private suffering. We are bowed down under a load of taxes, which, notwithstanding, fall greatly short of the wants of our rulers. Our traders are trembling on the verge of bankruptcy; our workmen are starving. Capital brings no profit, and labor no remuneration. The home of the artificer is desolate, and the warehouse of the pawnbroker is full. The workhouse is crowded, and the manufactory is deserted. We have looked on every side; we have searched diligently in order to find out the causes of distress so sore and so long continued. We can discover none in Nature or in Providence.

It was the fond espectations of the friends of the people that a remedy for the greater part, if not for the whole, of their grievances would be found in the Reform Act of 1832. They regarded that act as a wise means to a worthy end, as the machinery of an improved legislation, where the will of the masses would be at length potential. They have been bitterly and basely deceived. The Reform Act has effected a transfer of power from one domineering faction to another, and left the people as helpless as before. We come before your honorable house to tell you, with all humility, that this state of things must not be permitted to continue.

Required as we are universally, to support and obey the laws, nature and reason entitle us to demand that in making the laws the universal voice shall be implicitly listened to. We perform the duties of freemen; we must have the privileges of freemen. Therefore we demand universal suffrage. The suffrage, to be exempt from the corruption of the wealthy and the violence of the powerful, must be secret. We ask for the reality of a good, not for its semblance; therefore we demand the ballot. The connection between the representatives and the people, to be beneficial, must be intimate. The legislative and constituent powers, for correction and for instruction, ought to be brought into frequent contact. Errors which are comparatively light when susceptible of a speedy popular remedy may produce the most disastrous effects when permitted to grow inveterate through years of compulsory endurance. To public safety, as well as public confidence, frequent elections are essential. Therefore we demand annual parliaments.

With power to choose, and freedom in choosing, the range of our choice must be unrestricted. We are compelled by the existing laws to take for our representatives men who are incapable of appreciating our difficulties, or have little sympathy with them; merchants who have retired from trade and no longer feel its harassings; proprietors of land who are alike ignorant of its evils and its cure; lawyers by whom the notoriety of the senate is courted only as a means of obtaining notice in the courts. The labors of a representative who is sedulous in the discharge of his duty are numerous and burdensome. It is neither just, nor reasonable, nor safe, that they should continue to be gratuitously rendered. We demand that in the future election of members of your honorable house, the approbation of the constituency shall be the sole qualification, and that to every representative so chosen shall be assigned out of the public taxes a fair and adequate remuneration for the time which he is called upon to devote to the public service . . . granting to every male of lawful age, sane mind, and unconvicted of crime, the right of voting for members of parliament, and directing all future elections of members of parliament to be in the way of secret ballot, and ordaining that the duration of parliament, so chosen, shall in no case exceed one year, and abolishing all property qualifications in the members, and providing for their due remuneration while attendant on their parliamentary duties.

The Social-Political Theory of Communism
(Karl Marx, *The Communist Manifesto,* 1846)

Communists of various nationalities have assembled in London, and sketched the following manifesto, to be published in the English, French, German, Italian, Flemish, and Danish languages.

The history of all hitherto existing society is the history of class struggles. The modern bourgeois society that has sprouted from the ruins of feudal society, has not done away with class antagonisms. It has but established new classes, new conditions of oppression, new forms of struggle in place of the old ones.

Our epoch, the epoch of the bourgeoisie, possesses this distinctive feature; it has simplified the class antagonism. Society as a whole is more and more splitting up into two great classes directly facing each other; bourgeoisie and proletariat.

The bourgeoisie, wherever it has got the upper hand, has put an end to all feudal, patriarchal, idyllic relations. It has pitilessly torn asunder the motley feudal ties that bound man to his "natural superiors," and has left remaining no other nexus between man and man than naked self-interest, than callous "cash payment."

In proportion as the bourgeoisie, i.e., capital, is developed, in the same proportion is the proletariat, the modern working class, developed; a class of laborers, who live only so long as they find work, and who find work only so long as their labor increases capital. These laborers, who must sell themselves piecemeal, are a commodity, like every article of commerce and are consequently exposed to all the vicissitudes of competition, to all the fluctuations of the market.

Modern industry has converted the little work shop of the patriarchal master into the great factory of the industrial capitalist. Masses of laborers crowded into the factory are organized like soldiers. As privates of the industrial army they are placed under the command of a perfect hierarchy of officers and sergeants. Not only are they the slaves of the bourgeois class and of the bourgeois State, they are daily and hourly enslaved by the machine, by the over-looker, and, above all, by the individual bourgeois manufacturer himself.

The unceasing improvement of machinery, ever more rapidly developing, makes their livelihood more and more precarious; the collisions between individual workmen and individual bourgeois take more and more the character of collisions between two classes. Thereupon the workers begin to form combinations or Trades' Unions against the bourgeois.

The organization of the proletarians into a class and consequently into a political party, is continually being upset again by the competition between workers themselves. But it ever rises again stronger, firmer, mightier.

It has become evident that the bourgeoisie is unfit any longer to be the ruling class in society and to impose its conditions of existence upon society as an over-riding law. It is unfit to rule because it is incompetent to secure an existence to its slave within his slavery, because it cannot help letting him sink into such a state that it has to feed him, instead of being fed by him. Society can no longer live under this bourgeoisie; in other words, its existence is no longer compatible with society.

The essential condition for the existence and for the sway of the bourgeois class, is the formation and augmentation of capital; the condition for capital is wage-labor. Wage-labor rests exclusively on competition between the laborers. The advance of industry, whose involuntary promoter is the bourgeoisie, replaces the isolation of the laborers, due to competition by their involuntary combination, due to association. The development of Modern Industry, therefore, cuts from under its feet the very foundation on which the bourgeoisie produces, and appropriates products.

What the bourgeoisie therefore produces, above all, are its own grave-diggers. Its fall and the victory of the proletariat are equally inevitable.

The immediate aim of the Communists is the same as that of all other proletarian parties; formation of the proletariat into a class, overthrow of the bourgeois supremacy, conquest of political power by the proletariat.

The distinguishing feature of Communism is not the abolition of property generally, but the abolition of bourgeois property. But modern bourgeois private property is the final and most complete expression of the system of producing and appropriating products, that is based on class antagonism, on the exploitation of the many by the few.

In this sense, the theory of the Communists may be summed up in the single sentence: Abolition of private property.

The working men have no country. We cannot take from them what they have not got. Since the proletariat must first of all acquire political supremacy, must rise to be the leading class of the nation, must constitute itself the nation, it is, so far, itself national, though not in the bourgeois sense of the word.

National differences and antagonisms between peoples are daily more and more vanishing, owing to the development of the bourgeoisie, to freedom of commerce, to the world-market, to uniformity in the mode of production and in the conditions of life corresponding thereto.

The supremacy of the proletariat will cause them to vanish still faster. United actions of the leading civilized countries at least, is one of the first conditions for the emancipation of the proletariat.

The proletariat will use its political supremacy to wrest by degrees, all capital from the bourgeoisie, to centralize all instruments of production in the hands of the State, i.e., of the proletariat organized as the ruling class; and to increase the total productive forces as rapidly as possible.

Of course, in the beginning this cannot be effected except by means of despotic inroads on the rights of property and on the conditions of bourgeois production; by means of measures, therefore, which appear economically insufficient and untenable, but which, in the course of the movement, outstrip themselves, necessitate further inroads upon the old social order and are unavoidable as a means of entirely revolutionizing the mode of production.

When, in the course of development, class distinctions have disappeared and all production has been concentrated in the hands of a vast association of the whole nation, the public power will lose its political character. Political power, properly so called, is merely the organized power of one class for oppressing another. If the proletariat during its contest with the bourgeoisie is compelled by the force of circumstances to organize itself as a class, if, by means of a revolution it makes itself the ruling class and, as such, sweeps away by force the old conditions of production, then it will, along with these conditions, have swept away the conditions for the existence of class antagonism and of classes generally and will thereby have abolished its own supremacy as a class.

In place of the old bourgeois society with its classes and class antagonism, we shall have an association in which the free development of each is the condition for the free development of all.

The Communists disdain to conceal their views and aims. They openly declare that their ends can be attained only by the forcible overthrow of all existing social conditions. Let the ruling classes tremble at a Communistic revolution. The proletarians have nothing to lose but their chains. They have a world to win. Workingmen of all countries, unite!

The Social-Political Theory of Anarchism
(Pierre Proudhon, *Property and Anarchism,* 1848)

I ought not to conceal the fact that property and communism have been considered always the only possible form of society. This deplorable error has been the life of property. The disadvantages of communism are so obvious that its critics never have needed to employ much eloquence to thoroughly disgust men with it. The pious and stupid uniformity which it enforces upon the free, active, reasoning, unsubmissive personality of man, have shocked common sense, and condemned communism by an irrevocable decree.

Communism is inequality, but not as property is. Property is the exploitation of the weak by the strong. Communism is the exploitation of the strong by the weak.

Anarchism is the only solution. By means of self-instruction and the acquisition of ideas, man finally acquires the idea of *science*—that is, of a system of knowledge in harmony with the reality of things, and inferred from observation. He searches for the science, or the system, of inanimate bodies—the system of organic bodies, the system of the human mind, and the system of the universe: why should he not also search for the *system* of society? But, having reached this height he comprehends that political truth, or the science of politics, exists quite independently of the will of sovereigns, the opinion of the majorities, the popular beliefs that kings, ministers, magistrates, and nations, have no connection with science, and are worthy of no consideration. He comprehends, at the same time, that if man is born a social being, the authority of his father over him ceases on the day when, his mind being formed and his education finished, he becomes the associate of his father; that his true chief and his king is demonstrable truth; that politics is a science, not a strategem; and that the function of the legislator is reduced, in the last analysis, to the methodical search for truth.

Just as the right of force and the right of artifice retreat before the steady advance of justice, and must finally be extinguished in equality, so the sovereignty of the will yields to the sovereignty of the reason, and must at last be lost in scientific socialism. Property and royalty have been crumbling to pieces ever since the world began. As man seeks justice in equality, so society seeks true order in anarchy.

Anarchy—the absence of a master, of a sovereign—such is the form of government to which we are every day approximating, and which our accustomed habit of taking man for our rule, and his will for law, leads us to regard as the height of disorder and the expression of chaos. As long as we live, we want a chief or chiefs; and at this very moment I hold in my hand a brochure, whose author, a zealous communist, dreams of dictatorship. The most advanced among us are those who wish the greatest possible number of sovereigns, their most ardent wish is for the royalty of the National Guard. Soon, undoubtedly, some one, jealous of the citizen militia, will say, "Everybody is king." But, when he has spoken, I will say, in my turn, "Nobody is king; we are, whether we will or not, associated." Every question of domestic politics must be decided by scientifically ascertained statistics; every question of foreign politics is an affair of international statistics. The science of government rightly belongs to one of the sections of the Academy of Sciences, whose permanent secretary is necessarily Prime Minister; and, since every citizen may address a note to the Academy, every citizen is a legislator. But, as the opinion of no one is of any value until its truth has been proven by science, nobody is king.

All matters of legislation and politics are matters of science, not of opinion. The legislative power belongs only to Reason, methodically recognized and demonstrated. To attribute to any power whatever, the right of veto or of sanction, is the last degree of tyranny. Justice and legality are two things independent of our approval as is mathematical truth. To compel, they need only to be known, they need only to be considered and studied. What, then, is the nation, if it is not the sovereign, if it is not the source of that legislative power? The nation is the guardian of the law; the nation is the *executive power*. Every citizen may assert: "This is true; that is just"; but his opinion controls no one but himself. That the truth which he proclaims may become a law it must be recognized. Now, what is it to recognize a law? It is to verify a mathematical or metaphysical calculation; it is to repeat an experiment, to observe a phenomenon, to establish a fact. Only the nation has the right to say, "Be it known and decreed."

I confess that this is an overturning of old ideas, and that I seem to be attempting to revolutionize our political system. I do not see how the liberty of citizens would be endangered by entrusting to their hands, instead of the pen of the legislator, the sword of the law. The executive power, belonging properly to the people, cannot be confided to too many proxies. That is the true sovereignty of the nation.

Louis Blanc on the National Workshop Program of the French Socialist Party During the Revolutionary Period of 1848 (Louis Blanc, *Historical Revelations,* 1852)

The socialist workshops according to my suggestion were to have consisted of tradesmen of the same trade working within the framework of their own profession. The National Workshops as finally put into practice by the Provisional Government were collections of laborers thrown together without regard for occupations or skills, and every one was put at the same task. The program as suggested by myself had been consistent with the division of labor. Each group of producers was to have followed its own trade. This was to have been made possible by the loans allowed the groups by the State; loans which would have been paid back at logical interest rates in a stipulated time period. Yet, each group, confined to production within its own sphere for the purpose of common profit, would be motivated by a unity of spirit and personal interest.

In the Workshop Plan as managed and directed by the Provisional Government the State entered only as a contractor; and the workers operated as simple wage-earners. And the type of labor expended in the shops was foolish, unproductive, and humiliating. Most of the men were set to projects they were unfamiliar with; which resulted in the State squandering public funds entrusted to it. Its direct subsidy program put a high return on idleness, its wages were no more than charity.

This program impoverished the national treasury and embarrassed the laborers by reducing them to the point where they were forced to accept charity instead of wages; and worse, this program discredited the whole Socialist program of State control of industry. This was done consciously. Those who hold to the doctrine of *laissez faire* desired to tie to the Socialist Party all the mischief that had been done, and thus educate the public to hatred for us. Thus the whole program so nobly begun ended in a travesty.

An English Liberal on the Meaning of Liberty (John Stuart Mill, *On Liberty,* 1859)

The object of this Essay is to assert one very simple principle, as entitled to govern absolutely the dealings of society with the individual in the way of compulsion and control, whether the means used by physical force in the form of legal penalties, or the moral coercion of public opinion. That principle is that the sole end for which mankind are warranted, individually or collectively, in interfering with the liberty of action of any of their number, is self-protection. That the only purpose for which power can be rightfully exercised over any member of a civilized community, against his will, is to prevent harm to others. His own good, either physical or moral, is not a sufficient warrant. He cannot rightfully be compelled to do or forbear because it will be better for him to do so, because it will make him happier, because, in the opinion of others, to do so would be wise, or even right. These are good reasons for remonstrating with him, or reasoning with him, or persuading him, or entreating him, but not for compelling him, or visiting him with any evil in case he do otherwise. To justify that, the conduct from which it is desired to deter him must be calculated to produce evil to some one else. The only part of the conduct of any one, for which he is amenable to society, is that which concerns others. In the part which merely concerns himself, his independence is, of right, absolute. Over himself, over his own mind and body, the individual is sovereign.

It is, perhaps, hardly necessary to say that this doctrine is meant to apply only to human beings in the maturity of their faculties. We are not speaking of children, or of young persons below the age which the law may fix as that of manhood or womanhood.

There is a sphere of action in which society, as distinguished from the individual, has, if any, only an indirect interest; comprehending all that portion of a person's life and conduct which affects only himself, or if it also affects others, only with their free, voluntary, and undeceived consent and participation. This, then, is the appropriate region of human liberty. It comprises, first, the inward domain of consciousness, demanding liberty of conscience in the most comprehensive sense; liberty of thought and feeling; absolute freedom of opinion and sentiment on all subjects, practical or speculative, scientific, moral, or theological. Secondly, the principle requires liberty of tastes and pursuits; of framing the plan of our life to suit our own character; of doing as we like, subject to such consequences as may follow without impediment from our fellow-creatures, so long as what we do does not harm them, even though they should think our conduct foolish, perverse, or wrong. Thirdly, from this liberty of each individual, follows the liberty, within the same limits, of combination among individuals; freedom to unite, for any purpose not involving harm to others, the persons combining being supposed to be of full age, and not forced or deceived.

No society in which these liberties are not, on the whole, respected, is free, whatever may be its form of government; and none is completely free in which they do not exist absolute and unqualified. The only freedom which deserves the name, is that of pursuing our own good in our own way, so long as we do not attempt to deprive others of theirs, or impede their efforts to obtain it. Each is the proper guardian of his own health, whether bodily, *or* mental and spiritual. Mankind are greater gainers by suffering each other to live as seems good to themselves, than by compelling each to live as seems good to the rest.

A German Socialist Defines "Revolution" Before a Prussian Court of Justice when Charged with Radical Activity (Ferdinand Lassalle, *Gesammelte Reden und Schriften,* 1862)*

What is the scientific meaning of the word "revolution" and how can revolution be distinguished from reform?

Revolution means fundamental change, and when a revolution occurs a new governing principle is substituted for the old, whether through force or without it; the means are not relevant here. Reform, on the other hand, occurs when the principles underlying existing conditions (of Society) are kept and are only modified or developed in more reasonable and just directions. Again, this is not a question of the means. A reform can come about through insurrection and the spilling of blood, and a revolution can occur peacefully. The development of industry was a revolution which took place in the most peaceful manner possible, for a new (social) principle was substituted for the hitherto existing conditions. If I myself, then, had spoken of a "coming social revolution" would this have to mean that I was thinking of a bloody overthrow (of the existing order) with pitchforks and bayonets?

But anyway, how could any mention of a coming social revolution, even with pitchforks, stimulate hate and lead to the despising of the bourgeoisie? One can only hate and despise own's own actions.

Every class in society is entitled to desire domination over the state, as long as it does not use illegal means to gain its ends. No (longing towards a social) goal can be punished by the state, only the means used to get there (are within the reach of punishment.) The appeal to work for the domination over other classes would stimulate the working classes to greater ambition, but never to hate and despise the bourgeoisie.

The Attitude of the Catholic Church on the Condition of Labor in the Late Nineteenth Century (Pope Leo XIII, *Encyclical, Rerum Novarum,* 1891)*

The ancient workmen's Guilds were destroyed in the last century, and no other organization took their place. Public in-

* From: "Die Wissenschaft und die Arbeiter," *Gesammelte Reden und Schriften,* ed. Eduard Bernstein. Translated by and used with the permission of G. L. Mosse.

* Pope Leo XIII, *Encyclical Rerum Novarum,* Translated in *Two Basic Social Encyclicals,* Benzinger Brothers, New York. Used with the permission of the publisher.

stitutions and the laws have repudiated the ancient religion. Hence by degrees it has come to pass that working men have been given over, isolated and defenseless, to the callousness of employers and the greed of unrestrained competition. And to this must be added the custom of working by contract, and the concentration of so many branches of trade in the hands of a few individuals, so that a small number of very rich men have been able to lay upon the masses of the poor a yoke little better than slavery itself.

To remedy these evils the *Socialists,* working on the poor man's envy of the rich, endeavor to destroy private property, and maintain that individual possessions should become the common property of all, to be administered by the State or by municipal bodies. They hold that, by thus transferring property from private persons to the community, the present evil state of things will be set to rights, because each citizen will then have his equal share of whatever there is to enjoy. But their proposals are so clearly futile for all practical purposes, that if they were carried out the working man himseslf would be among the first to suffer. Moreover they are emphatically unjust, because they would rob the lawful possessor, bring the State into a sphere that is not its own, and cause complete confusion in the community.

The *Socialists* in endeavoring to transfer the possessions of individuals to the community, strike at the interests of every wage earner, for they deprive him of the liberty of disposing of his wages, and thus of all hope and possibility of increasing his stock or of bettering his condition in life.

What is of still greater importance, however, is that the remedy they propose is manifestly against justice. For every man has by nature the right to possess property as his own. The authority of the Divine Law adds its sanction, forbidding us in the gravest terms even to covet that which is another's.

Thus, it is clear *that the main tenet of Socialism, the community of goods, must be utterly rejected;* for it would injure those whom it is intended to benefit, it would be contrary to the natural rights of mankind, and it would introduce confusion and disorder into the commonwealth. Our first and most fundamental principle, therefore, when we undertake to alleviate the condition of the masses, must be the inviolability of private property. This laid down, we go on to show where we must find the remedy that we seek.

The great mistake that is made in the matter now under

consideration, is to possess oneself of the idea that class is naturally hostile to class; that rich and poor are intended by nature to live at war with one another. So irrational and so false is this view, that the exact contrary is the truth. Just as the symmetry of the human body is the result of the disposition of the members of the body, so in a State it is ordained by nature that these two classes should exist in harmony and agreement, and should, as it were, fit into one another, so as to maintain the equilibrium of the body politic. Each requires the other; capital cannot do without labor, nor labor without capital. Mutual agreement results in pleasantness and good order; perpetual conflict necessarily produces confusion and outrage. Now, in preventing such strife as this, and in making it impossible, the efficacy of Christianity is marvelous and manifold. Religion teaches the laboring man and the workman to carry out honestly and well all equitable agreements freely made, never to injure capital, nor to outrage the person of an employer; never to employ violence in representing his own cause, nor to engage in riot and disorder; and to have nothing to do with men of evil principles, who work upon the people with artful promises, and raise foolish hopes which usually end in disaster and in repentance when too late. Religion teaches the rich man and the employer that their work people are not their slaves; that they must respect in every man his dignity as a man and as a Christian; that labor is nothing to be ashamed of, if we listen to right reason and to Christian philosophy, but is an honorable employment, enabling a man to sustain his life in an upright and creditable way; and that it is shameful and inhuman to treat men like chattels to make money by, or to look upon them merely as so much muscle or physical power. His great and principal obligation is to give to every one that which is just. Doubtless before we can decide whether wages are adequate many things have to be considered; but rich men and masters should remember this —that to exercise pressure for the sake of gain upon the indigent and destitute, and to make one's profit out of the need of another, is condemned by all laws, human and divine. To defraud anyone of wages that are his due is a crime that cries to the avenging anger of Heaven. Finally, the rich must religiously refrain from cutting down the workman's earnings, either by force, fraud, or by usurious dealing; and with the more reason because the poor man is weak and unprotected, and because his slender means should be sacred in proportion to their scantiness.

A Nineteenth Century Discussion of Fabian Socialism (G. B. Shaw, *Fabian Essays in Socialism,* 1889)

What then does a gradual transition to Social Democracy mean specifically? It means the gradual extension of the franchise; and the transfer of rent and interest to the State, not in one lump sum, but by installments. Looked at in this way, it will at once be seen that we are already far on the road, and are being urged further by many politicians who do not dream that they are touched with Socialism—nay, who would earnestly repudiate the touch as a taint. Let us see how far we have gone. In 1832 the political power passed into the hands of the middle class; and in 1838 Lord John Russell announced finality. Meanwhile, in 1834, the middle class had swept away the last economic refuge of the workers, the old Poor Law, and delivered them naked to the furies of competition. Ten years turmoil and active emigration followed; and then the thin end of the wedge went in. The Income Tax was established; and the Factory Acts were made effective. The Income Tax (1842), which is on individualist principles an intolerable spoliative anomaly, is simply a forcible transfer of rent, interest, and even rent of ability, from private holders to the State without compensation. It excused itself to the Whigs on the ground that those who had most property for the State to protect should pay *ad valorem* for its protection. The Factory Acts swept the anarchic theory of the irresponsibility of private enterprise out of practical politics; made employers accountable to the State for the well-being of their employees; and transferred a further installment of profits directly to the worker by raising wages. An extension of the Franchise, which was really an installment of Democracy, and not, like the 1832 Reform Bill, only an advance towards it, was gained in 1867; and immediately afterwards came another installment of Socialism in the shape of a further transfer of rent and interest from private holders to the State for the purpose of educating the people. In the meantime, the extraordinary success of the postoffice, which, according to the teaching of the Manchester school, should have been a nest of incompetence and jobbery, had not only shown the perfect efficiency of State enterprise when the officials are made responsible to the class interested in its success, but had also proved the enormous convenience and cheapness of socialistic or collectivist charges over those of private enterprise.

After 1875, leaping and bounding prosperity, after a final spurt during which the Income Tax fell to twopence, got out of breath, and has not yet recovered it. Russia and America, among other competitors, began to raise the margin of cultivation at a surprising rate. Education began to intensify the sense of suffering, and to throw light upon its causes in dark places. The capital needed to keep English industry abreast of the growing population began to be attracted by the leaping and bounding of foreign loans and investments, and to bring to England, in payment of interest, imports that were not paid for by exports—a phenomenon inexpressibly disconcerting to the Cobden Club. The old pressure of the eighteen-thirties came back again. Numbers of young men, pupils of Mill, Spencer, Comte, and Darwin, roused by Mr. Henry George's "Progress and Poverty," left aside evolution and free-thought; took to insurrectionary economics; studied Karl Marx; and were so convinced that Socialism had only to be put clearly before the working classes to concentrate the power of their immense numbers in one irresistible organization, that the Revolution was fixed for 1889—the anniversary of the French Revolution—at the latest. However, the ensuing years sifted and sobered us. "The Socialists," as they were called, have fallen into line as a Social Democratic Party, no more insurrectionary in its policy than any other party.

The Biological Interpretation of Social Organization as Expressed by a Late Nineteenth Century "Darwinian" Social Philosopher
(Herbert Spencer, *Man vs. the State,* 1902)

Be it or be it not true that Man is shapen in iniquity and conceived in sin, it is unquestionably true that Government is begotten of aggression and by aggression. We find proofs that, at first recognized but temporarily during leadership in war, the authority of a chief is permanently established by continuity of war; and grows strong where successful war ends in subjection of neighboring tribes. And thence onwards, examples furnished by all races, put beyond doubt the truth, that the coercive power of the chief developing into king, the king of kings (a frequent title in the ancient East), becomes great in proportion as conquest becomes habitual and the union of subdued nations extensive. Comparisons disclose a further truth which should be ever present to us—the truth that the aggressiveness of the ruling power inside a society increases with its aggressiveness outside society.

An obvious implication is that political ethics originally identical with the ethics of war, must long remain akin to them; and can diverge from them only as warlike activities and preparations become less. Current evidence shows this. At present on the Continent, the citizen is free only when his services as a soldier are not demanded; and during the rest of his life he is largely enslaved in supporting the military organization. Even among ourselves a serious war would, by the necessitated conscription, suspend the liberties of large numbers and trench on the liberties of the rest by taking from them through taxes whatever supplies were needed—that is, forcing them to labor so many days more for the State. Inevitably the established code of conduct in the dealing of Governments with citizens must be allied to their code of conduct in their dealings with one another.

Among men's desires seeking gratifications, those which have prompted their private activities and their spontaneous cooperation, have done much more toward social development than those which have worked through governmental agencies. That abundant crops now grow where once only wild berries could be gathered is due to the pursuit of individual satisfaction through many centuries. Perpetually, governments have thwarted and deranged the growth but have in no way furthered it; save by partially discharging their proper function and maintaining social order. So, too, with those advances of knowledge and those improvements of appliances by which these structural changes and these increasing activities have been made possible. It is not to the State that we owe the multitudinous useful inventions from the spade to the telephone; it was not the State which made possible extended navigation by a developed astromony; it was not the State which made the discoveries in physics, chemistry, and the rest which guide modern manufacturers. The world-wide transactions conducted in merchants' offices, the rush of traffic filling our streets, the retail distributing system which brings everything within easy reach and delivers the necessaries of life daily at our doors, are not of governmental origin. All these are results of the spontaneous activities of citizens, separate or grouped.

And then a truth to which the foregoing one introduces us, is that the spontaneously formed social organization is so bound together that you cannot act on one part without acting more or less on all parts. We see this unmistakably when a cotton-famine first paralyzing certain manufacturing districts and then affecting the doings of wholesale and retail distributors throughout the kingdom, as well as the people they supply, goes on to affect the makers and distributors, as well as the wearers of other fabrics—woolen, linen, etc. Or we see it when a rise in the price of coal, besides influencing domestic life everywhere, hinders many of our industries, raises the prices of the commodities produced, alters the consumption of them, and changes the habits of the consumers. What we see clearly in these marked cases happens in every case, in sensible or in insensible ways. And manifestly Acts of Parliament are among those factors which, beyond the effects directly produced, have countless other effects of multitudinous kinds. As I heard remarked by a distinguished professor, whose studies give ample means of judging—"when once you begin to interfere with the order of Nature there is no knowing where the results will end." And if this is true of that subhuman order of Nature to which he referred, still more is it true of that order of Nature existing in the social arrangements of human beings.

One of the most familiar facts is that animals of superior types, comparatively slow in reaching maturity, are enabled when they have reached it, to give more aid to their off-spring than animals of inferior types. The adults foster their young during periods more or less prolonged, while yet the young are unable to provide for themselves; and it is obvious that maintenance of the species can be secured only by this parental care. It requires no proving that the blind, unfledged hedge-bird, or the young puppy even after it has acquired sight, would forthwith die if it had to keep itself warm and obtain its own food. The gratuitous aid must be great in proportion as the young one is of little worth either to itself or to others; and it may diminish as fast as, by increasing development, the young one acquires worth, at first for self-sustentation and by and by for sustentation of others. That is to say, during immaturity benefits received must vary inversely as the power or ability of the receiver. Clearly if during the first part of life benefits were proportioned to merits, or rewards to deserts, the species would disappear in a generation.

From this regime of the family group, let us turn to the regime of that larger group formed by adult members of the species. Ask what happens when the new individual acquiring complete use of its powers and ceasing to have parental aid is left to itself. Now there comes into play a principle just the reverse of that above described. Throughout the rest of its life each adult gets benefits in proportion to merit—reward in proportion to desert; merit and desert in each case being understood as ability to fulfill all the requirements of life—to get food, to find shelter, to escape enemies. Placed in competition with members of its own species and in antagonism with members of other species, it dwindles and gets killed off or thrives and propagates, according as it is ill-endowed or well-endowed. Manifestly an opposite regime, could it be maintained, would, in the course of time, be fatal. If the benefits received by each individual were proportionate to its inferiority—if, as a consequence, multiplication of the inferior was furthered and multiplication of the superior hindered, progressive degradation would result; and eventually the degenerate species would fail to hold its ground in the presence of antagonistic species and competing species.

The broad fact then, here to be noted, is that Nature's modes of treatment inside the family group and outside the family group are diametrically opposed to one another; and that the intrusion of either mode into the sphere of the other, would be destructive either immediately or remotely.

Does any one think that the like does not hold of the human species? He cannot deny that within the human family, as within any inferior family, it would be fatal not to proportion benefits to merits. Surely none can fail to see that were the principle of family to be adopted and fully carried out in social life—were reward always great in proportion as desert was small, fatal results to the society would quickly follow; and if so, then even a partial intrusion of the family regime into the regime of the State will be slowly followed by fatal results. Society in its corporate capacity cannot without immediate or remoter disaster interfere with the play of these opposed principles under which every species has reached such fitness for its mode of life as it possesses and under which it maintains that fitness.

And yet, notwithstanding the conspicuousness of these truths, which should strike everyone who leaves his lexicons and his law-deeds, and his ledgers, and looks abroad into that natural order of things under which we exist, and to which we must conform there is continual advocacy of paternal government. The intrusion of family ethics into the ethics of the State, instead of being regarded as socially injurious, is more and more demanded as the only efficient means to social benefits. So far as this delusion now gone, that it vitiates the beliefs of those who might, more than all others, be thought safe from it. In the essay to which the Cobden Club awarded its prize in 1880, there occurs the assertion that "the truth of Free Trade is clouded over by the *laissez faire* fallacy"; and we are told that "we need a great deal more parental government—that bugbear of the old economists."

The process of "natural selection," as Mr. Darwin called it, cooperating with a tendency to variation and to inheritance of variations, he has shown to be a chief cause (though not, I believe, the sole cause) of that evolution through which all living things, beginning with the lowest and diverging and re-diverging as they evolved, have reached their present degree of organization and adaptation to their modes of life. So familiar has this truth become that some apology seems needed for naming it. Any yet, strange to say, now that this truth is recognized by most cultured people—now that the beneficent working of the survival of the fittest has so impressed itself on them that much more than people in past times, they might be expected to hestitate before neutralizing its action—now more than ever before in the history of the world, are they doing all they can to further the survival of the unfittest.

The Attitude of the Catholic Church on the Condition of Labor and the Meaning of Socialism in the Twentieth Century (Pope Pius XI, *Encyclical, Quadragesimo Anno,* 1931)*

Study and investigation caused Pope Leo's teaching to become widely known throughout the world, and steps were taken to apply it to practical use . . . in a spirit of active beneficence, every effort was made to lift up a class of men, who owing to the expansion of modern industry, had enormously increased in numbers, but whose rightful position in society had not yet been determined, and who in consequence were the objects of much neglect and contempt. In answer to the appeal of the Pontiff, works of beneficence and charity began to multiply. Under the direction of the Church, and frequently under the guidance of her priests, there sprang up further an ever increasing number of new institutions, by which working men, craftsmen, husbandmen, wage-earners of every class could give and receive mutual assistance and support.

With regard to the Civil power, Leo XIII boldly passed be-

* From: Pope Pius XI, *Encyclical, Quadragesimo Anno,* 1931. Translated in *Two Basic Social Encyclicals,* Benzinger Brothers, Inc., New York, 1943. Used with the permission of the publishers.

yond the restrictions imposed by Liberalism, and fearlessly proclaimed the doctrine that the Civil power is more than the mere guardian of law and order, and that it must strive with all zeal "to make sure that the laws and institutions, the general character and administration of the commonwealth, should be such as of themselves to realize public well-being and private prosperity." It is true, indeed, that a just freedom of action should be left to individual citizens and families; but this principle is only valid as long as the common good is secure and no injustice is entailed. The duty of rulers is to protect the community and its various elements; and in protecting the rights of individuals they must have special regard for the infirm and needy. "For the richer class have many ways of shielding themselves and stand less in need of help from the State, whereas the mass of the poor have no resources of their own to fall back upon and must chiefly depend upon the assistance of the State. And for this reason wage-earners, since they mostly belong to that class, should be especially cared for and protected by the government."

At that period (of which Pope Leo XIII wrote) rulers of not a few nations were deeply infected with Liberalism and regarded Unions of workingmen with disfavor, if not with open hostility. While readily recognizing and patronizing similar corporations among other classes, with criminal injustice they denied the innate right of forming associations to those who needed them most for self-protection against oppression by the more powerful.

Eager to carry out to the full the program of Leo XIII, the clergy and many of the laity devoted themselves everywhere with admirable zeal to the creation of worker's unions, which in turn became instrumental in building up a body of truly Christian workingmen. These happily combined the successful plying of their trade with deep religious convictions; they learned to defend their temporal rights and interests energetically and efficiently, retaining at the same time a due respect for justice and a sincere desire to collaborate with other classes. Thus they prepared the way for a Christian renewal of the whole social way of life.

These unions of workingmen have everywhere so flourished, that in our days, though unfortunately still inferior in number to the organizations of Socialists and Communists, they already muster an imposing body of wage-earners able to maintain successfully both in national and international assemblies, the rights and legitimate demands of Catholic laborers, and to assert the saving priniciples on which Christian society is based.

Let it be made clear beyond all doubt that neither Leo XIII, nor those theologians who have taught under the guidance and direction of the Church, have ever denied or called in question the two-fold aspect of ownership, which is individual or social accordingly as it regards individuals or concerns the common good. Their unanimous contention has always been that the right to own property has been given to man by nature or rather by the Creator Himself, not only in order that individuals may be able to provide for their own needs and those of their families, but also that by means of it, the goods which the Creator has destined for the human race may truly serve this purpose. Now these ends cannot be secured unless some definite and stable order is maintained.

There is, therefore, a double danger to be avoided. On the one hand, if the social and public aspect of ownership be denied or minimized, the logical consequence is "Individualism" as it is called; on the other hand, the rejection or diminuation of its private and individual character necessarily leads to some form of "Collectivism."

However, when civil authority adjusts ownership to meet the needs of the public good it acts not as an enemy, but as the friend of private property, intended by Nature's Author, in His Wisdom for the sustaining of human life, from creating intolerable burdens and so rushing to its own destruction. It does not therefore abolish, but protects private ownership, and, far from weakening the right of private property, it gives it new strength.

Not every kind of distribution of wealth and property amongst men is such that it can at all, and still less adequately, attain the end intended by God. Wealth, therefore, which is constantly being augmented by social and economic progress, must be so distributed amongst the various individuals and classes of society that the common good of all, of which Leo XIII spoke, be thereby promoted. In other words, the good of the whole community must be safeguarded. By these principles of social justice one class is forbidden to exclude the other from a share in the profits. This sacred law is violated by an irresponsible wealthy class, who, in the excess of their good fortune, deem it a just state of things that they should receive everything and the laborer nothing; it is violated also by a property-less wage-earning class who demand for themselves all the fruits of production, as being the work of their hands. Such men, vehemently incensed against the violation of justice by capitalists, go too far in vindicating the one right of which they are conscious; they attack and seek to abolish all forms of ownership and all profits not obtained by labor, whatever be their nature or significance in human society, for the sole reason that they are not acquired by toil.

Each class, then, must receive its due share and the distribution of created goods must be brought into conformity with the demands of the common good and social justice, for every sincere observer is conscious that the vast differences between the few who hold excessive wealth and the many who live in destitution constitute a grave evil in modern society.

An Eye-Witness Account of the Events of "Bloody Sunday" in St. Petersburg, on January 22, 1905
(*An Anonymous Account,* 1905)

The first trouble began at eleven o'clock, when the military tried to turn back some thousands of strikers at one of the bridges. The same thing happened almost simultaneously at other bridges, where the constant flow of workmen pressing forward refused to be denied access to the common rendezvous in the Palace Square. The Cossacks at first used their whips, then the flat of their sabers, and finally they fired. The strikers in the front ranks fell on their knees and implored the Cossacks to let them pass, protesting that they had no hostile intentions. They refused, however, to be intimidated by blank cartridges, and orders were given to load with bullets.

The passion of the mob broke loose like a bursting dam. The people, seeing the dead and dying carried away in all directions, the snow on the streets and pavements soaked with blood, began to cry for vengeance. Meanwhile the situation at the Palace was becoming momentarily worse. The troops were reported to be unable to control the masses which were constantly surging forward. Reinforcements were sent, and at two o'clock the order was given to fire. Men, women, and children fell at each volley, and were carried away in sledges and carts. The indignation and fury of every class was aroused. Students, merchants, all classes of the population alike were inflamed.

Father Gapon, marching at the head of a large body of workmen, carrying a cross and other religious emblems, was wounded in the arm and shoulder. The two forces of workmen were separated. Those on the other side of the river were arming with swords, knives, and other instruments, and were erecting barricades. The troops were apparently firing in every direction without reason or purpose. The rioters continued to appeal to them saying, "You are Russians! Why play the part of bloodthirsty butchers?"

A night of terror is in prospect.

The Russian Revolution (The Representative Assembly of the Workers' and Peasants' Soviets, *The Declaration of the Workers and Exploited Peoples,* 1918)

The Representative Assembly of the Russian People declares:

I. That Russia is a Republic of Soviets of Laborers', Soldiers', and Peasants' Deputies;

That all political power in the Republic resides in the Soviets and in the provinces of the Soviets;

That the Republic of Soviets is based on free union and consists of free states federated together.

II. The Representative Assembly of the Russian People, aware of its further duty, in order to destroy class divisional lines, and to eliminate the continued exploitation of the Workers, and to insure the establishment of world Socialism—and to guarantee the victory of that Socialism in all the countries and areas of the earth, resolves in addition;

To bring about the immediate socialization of all land,

To abolish private ownership of property,

To declare all land the property of all the people in common, and to force its transfer to the Workers without payment.

Therefore, it is declared that all mineral deposits and forests, all water-ways, all animate and inorganic property, all private lands and estates, and all agrarian projects to be the property of the nation.

The Soviet Laws relative to control of Labor and the Committee of the National Economy are confirmed to facilitate the authority of the Workers over the exploiting classes, as the initial act in carrying out the transfer of mines, mills, factories, transport and communication facilities, and other tools of production, to the ownership of the Workers Soviet Republic.

In accord with such plan all banking and credit institutions are given into the possession of the Workers' and Peasants' Soviet States, that being one of the necessary acts in freeing the exploited workers from the yoke of capital.

The necessity for eradicating the exploiting classes and the necessity for reorganizing the national economy according to Socialistic theory makes it imperative that universal labor service be established.

Since it is essential to secure complete political control in the possession of the Workers, and to establish functionable barriers against a resurgence of the defeated exploiters, the Workers must be given arms. Thus the immediate disarmament of all those other than Workers is decreed, and an army consisting only of Workers and Peasants is called into being.

III. Expressing its indestructible determination to rescue all mankind from the claws of capitalism and imperialism, which have soaked the earth with human blood in criminal war, this Assembly, representative of all the peoples of Russia, declares itself to be unanimous in agreement on the policy of repudiating all secret treaties which have been heretofore binding on the State of Russia.

The Assembly further unanimously accepts the policy adopted by the Soviet Government of furthering and broadening friendly contact with the Workers of the armies of the world now mutually struggling against each other, and this humane contact bringing into being a democratic peace without territorial annexations or monetary indemnities, based on the freely expressed self-determination of the peoples of the states.

For these reasons the Representative Assembly demands a total disruption with the barbarian policies of the bourgeois civilization which has consciously constructed the massive wealth of the exploiters of the few favored states directly upon the slave labor of many millions of proletarians in Asia, in Colonies, and in weaker nations.

The Representative Assembly accords sincere welcome to the expression of the policy of the Assembly of People's Commissaries relative to the immediate proclamation of the independence of Finland, to the withdrawal of armies from Persia, and which accords liberty to Armenia.

The Representative Assembly holds that the law of the Soviets relative to repudiation of all indebtedness contracted by the Czarist state, and by the land-owning class, and the Bourgeoisie, as the initial and necessary blow against banking, finance, and capital, and desires to express the hope that the efforts of the Soviets will continue such policy until the inevitable struggle between international labor and exploitive capitalism is resolved in favor of the Worker.

UNIT 11

The New Imperialism

In the history of modern Europe three types of imperialism are visible in operation in succeeding periods. The first commercial revolution of the 16th and 17th centuries begot a commercial imperialism that was seldom more than a beachhead process wherein the states of Europe attempted to control the natural trade outlets of extraterritorial areas. The 18th century, bringing the Industrial Revolution, also produced imperialistic devices suited to the needs of Europe. Penetration of land masses and control of peoples replaced the "factory" system of contact between the Europeans and the producers of the backward areas. Indeed, the aboriginal peoples now played a dual role; producer and consumer. The 19th and 20th centuries were to be forced by the peculiar circumstances of the times to forge and apply yet a third method of interaction between peoples of dominating and dominated areas; and to find and apply, also, new rationales of justification. This historic period, from 1800 to 1918, might well be termed the period of "psychological" imperialism, for its main stimulus was rooted in the emotional and psychological needs rather than in the economic desires of Europe's peoples, and it satisfied esthetic rather than materialistic drives. The German-French competition in North Africa, the French-English race to absorb the provinces of the decadent Ottoman Empire, the Pan-Slavic drive of Russia into the Balkans area, even the competition between the several states to complete the conquest of the polar regions, might be included in this expression of conquest, wherein the states of Europe tended to adjudge each its relative importance by the number of square miles of the earth's surface it controlled.

This type of expansive activity had its continental expression also. In 1832 the Russian Czar incorporated the helpless Poles into his own domain on the plea that the "union of the two nations committed by Divine Providence to our care" might prosper and be secure. Between 1862 and 1890 Otto von Bismarck, the outstanding proponent of continental imperialism, was instrumental in facilitating many boundary changes in Europe. Yet, apart from the formation of the German state and the exclusion of Austria from that state, which were altogether political objectives, it is difficult to explain certain of Bismarck's foreign policies outside the psychological area. If it is agreed, for instance, that the Franco-Prussian war of 1870 was a conscious expression of Prussia's will to reconstruct the continental balance of power, what does that signify in regard to Bismarck's wresting of Alsace and Lorraine from France? Although these provinces were producers of an amount of economic wealth, it is demonstrably true that neither the positive material gain to Germany, nor the loss of that wealth by France, or even both in combination, could be equivalent to the importance this conquest would assume as a formative influence on future French policy. The same holds true of the French-German struggle for dominion in northwest Africa. However, it is equally obvious that German pride and nationalism, as psychological factors, could not take into account their own antithesis: the same reaction by another people. That the French response was a long-term hope for revenge—and that vengeance colored all of France's foreign policy thereafter—is indisputable, for France, too, was psychologically, though negatively so in this case, involved in the process of German imperialism in Europe. Thus World War I, unlike the second great war, was not a conflict of ideologies so much as the immediate result of fatal disregard for the psychological factors involved in the processes of territorial acquisition.

It is usually conceded that British imperialism in this period was solidly based on economic motives. This, too, will bear closer scrutiny. The overriding arrogance of the British foreign office in its dealings with the princes of India and the peoples of South Africa in the 19th century suggests rather that here was a people which, in its own eyes, had a Messianic duty imposed on it by higher authority to save less fortunate peoples from themselves. Thus the "white man's burden" became a pious rationale for coloring large areas of the world map with the royal purple of the British Empire. However, the late 19th century brought with it a clear change in tone. The inexpressible contempt for the conqueror and the continued resistance to foreign rulers on the part of certain of the dominated peoples began to have their effects. An important indication of this change in policy is Gladstone's speech in the House of Commons in 1886 advocating home rule for Ireland. And this speech is symbolic, too, of new policies of pro-liberation beginning to evolve in many of the chancellories of Europe. Yet modification of over-all and traditional policy is a matter of much thought and long periods of time. It was not until 1931, with the Statute of Westminster, that the British government would lead the way in expressing the new philosophy of Empire: that whatever bonds exist among the different peoples of the earth they must be consistent with common sense. Respect and mutual trust and need can weld an empire into a unity of tremendous resiliance, while force binds with a rope of sand.

Otto von Bismarck's Political Concepts
(Letter: *Bismarck to the Prussian Ambassador in Paris,* 1863)*

The question is this: are we a great power or merely a member of the German federation, are we to be ruled monarchically like a great power, or, as conceivable, for a mere small state, ruled by professors, judges, and small town politicians? Our strength cannot spring from cabinet or newspaper politics, but only from the actions of a great, armed power. I am not afraid of a war. I am also indifferent towards being called "Revolutionary" or "Conservative" as I am toward all mere slogans. If one were to apply the standards of morality and justice to European politics, such standards would have to be abolished.

Letter: *Bismarck to the North German Diet,* 1867*

I have never in my life asserted that I am an enemy of the freedom of the people, but have only qualified it according to the state of my affairs: my interest in foreign policy is not only stronger, but at the moment the only decisive one—so that, as much as lies in my power, I will overcome any obstacle which stands in the way of the arrival at the goal, which, as I believe, must be reached for the good of the fatherland. This does not exclude . . . that it is the duty of every honest government to work for that highest degree of freedom for the people, and the individual, which is compatible with the safety of the State.

(Address: *To the Secondary School Teachers,* 1895)*

Man cannot himself create or guide the flow of destiny, he can only ride upon it and steer himself with more or less experience and ability. One can suffer shipwreck and be cast upon the shores, or land in good harbors. Political development is as slow as geological formations, layers form on top of each other and produce new hills and mountains. Do not succumb too much to the German love for criticism, accept what God has given you, and what we have with much labor brought into safe harbor under the threat of war from all other Europeans. As for myself I try to be satisfied with God's will, and the passage "Thy will be done" in the Lord's Prayer is always decisive for me. I try to understand Him, but I do not always understand Him.

Bismarck's Account of How he Held the Prussian Government in Check After the Victory in the Austro-Prussian War of 1866

(Otto von Bismarck, *Works*)

On July 23, under the presidency of the King a council of war was to be held in which the question to be studied was whether we should demand high indemnities from the Austrian Government.

I thereupon set to work to commit to paper the reasons which, in my opinion, spoke for the conclusion of a peace easy for the Austrian government to accept.

We had to avoid wounding Austria too severely; we had to avoid leaving behind in her any unnecessary bitterness of feeling or desire for revenge; we ought rather to reserve the possibility of becoming friends again with our adversary of the moment, and in any case to regard the Austrian state as a piece on the European chessboard and the renewal of friendly relations as a move open to us. If Austria were severely injured, she would become the ally of France and of every other opponent of ours; she would even sacrifice her anti-Russian interests in the Balkans for the sake of revenge on Prussia.

On the other hand I could not see any guarantee for us in the future should we insist upon splitting up the Austrian Empire. Fresh formations here would only be of a revolutionary nature, while the acquisition of provinces like Austrian Silesia and portions of Bohemia could not strengthen the Prussian

---

* Translated by and used with the permission of G. L. Mosse.

state, since it would not lead to an amalgamation of German Austria with Prussia.

To all this the King raised no objection, but declared the terms to be inadequate; but he put forth no plan of his own. Only this was clear; he said that the chief culprit could not be allowed to escape unpunished, and that justice once satisfied, we could let the misled backsliders off more easily, and he insisted on the cession of much territory from Austria.

I replied that we were not there to sit in judgment, but to pursue the German policy.

Passing on to the German states, the King spoke of various acquisitions by cutting down the territories of all our opponents. I repeated that we were not there to administer retributive justice, but to pursue a policy; that I wished to avoid in the German federation of the future the sight of mutilated territories, whose princes and peoples might very easily retain a lively wish to recover their former possessions by means of foreign aid.

Further, I begged the King, in the event of his not accepting the advice for which I was responsible, to relieve me of my functions.

Bismarck's Explanation of the Incident of the "Ems Dispatch" of 1870
(Otto von Bismarck, *Works*)

All things led me to believe that Prussia could avoid war with France only be sacrificing her honor and the inspiration the whole German people found in her. With this conviction uppermost in my mind I made use of the authority given me by the King to publish the contents of the telegram from Ems; and in the presence of my two guests, Generals Moltke and Roon, I reduced the context by simply deleting certain words, but without adding or rearranging any that were left.

The form of the message was finally this:

"After the news of the renunciation of the hereditary prince of Hohenzollern had been officially communicated to the imperial government of France by the royal government of Spain, the ambassador of France at Ems made the further demand of his Majesty the King that he should authorize him to telegraph to Paris that his Majesty the King of Prussia bound himself for all the future never again to give his consent if the

Hohenzollerns should put forth their candidate for the Spanish throne. His Majesty the King thereupon decided not to receive the French ambassador again, and sent to tell him, through the aide-de-camp on duty, that his Majesty had nothing further to communicate to the ambassador."

The difference in the effect of the abbreviated text of the dispatch as compared with that produced by the original was not the result of stronger words, but of the form, which made it appear that the refusal had been decisive.

When I read out the edited edition to my two guests, Moltke said: "Now it has a different sound; in the first form it sounded like a discussion of possibilities; but now it is more like an answer to a challenge."

I explained to him further; "If I now send this text, which contains no alteration or addition, but only the deletions, not only to the news organs, but also by wire to all our embassies, it will be known in Paris before midnight, and because of its method of distribution it will have the effect of a red flag on a French bull. And this is as it should be, for we must fight if we do not desire to act the part of a people defeated without even a battle. However, our success depends on the impression which the beginning of the war makes on popular opinion. It is important that we appear the ones attacked; and French touchiness and insolence will make this possible; and further will allow the fruition of our policy without our going through the Reichstag."

The Process of English Imperialism in India (Great Britain, *Treaties,* 1849)

Terms granted to the Maharajah Dulleep Sing Bahadoor, on the part of the Honorable East India Company, by Henry Meirs Elliot, Esq., Foreign Secretary to the Government of India, and Lieutenant Colonel Sir Henry Montogomery Lawrence, K.C.B., Resident, in virtue of full powers vested in them by the Right Honorable James, Earl of Dalhousie, Knight of the Most Ancient and Most Noble Order of the Thistle, one of Her Majesty's Most Honorable Privy Council.

His Highness the Maharajah Dulleep Sing shall resign for himself, his heirs, and his successors, all right, title, and claim to the sovereignty of the Punjab, or to any sovereign power whatever.

All the property of the State, of whatever description and wheresoever found, shall be confiscated to the Honorable East India Company, in part payment of the debt due by the State of Lahore to the British government, and of the expenses of the war.

The gem called the Koh-i-noor, which was taken from Shah Shoojaool-Moolk by Maharajah Runjeet Sing, shall be surrendered by the Maharajah of Lahore to the Queen of England.

His Highness Dulleep Sing shall receive from the Honorable East India Company, for the support of himself, his relatives, and servants, a pension of certain monies from the Honorable East India Company.

His Highness shall be treated with respect and honor. He shall retain the title of Maharajah Dulleep Sing Bahadoor, and he shall continue to receive, during his life the pension above named, provided he shall remain obedient to the British government and shall reside at such place as the Governor General of India may select.

The Process of English Imperialism in Africa
(*British Foreign and State Papers,* 1887)

Proclamation by his Excellency Sir Theophilus Shepstone, Her Majesty's Special Commissioner for certain purposes in South Africa:

Whereas at a meeting held on the 16th day of January, in the year 1852, at the Sand River, between her Majesty's commissioners, Major Hogge and C. M. Owne, on the one part, and a deputation from the emigrant farmers then residing north of the Vaal River, under the headship of General A. W. J. Pretorious, on the other part, the said Commissioners of her Majesty did "guarantee in the fullest manner on the part of the British government to the emigrant farmers north of the Vaal River, the right to manage their own affairs and to govern themselves according to their own laws, without any interference on the part of the British government."

And whereas the evident objects and inciting motives of the commissioners in granting such guarantee were "to promote peace, free trade, and friendly intercourse" with the inhabitants of the Transvaal.

And whereas the hopes and expectations upon which this mutual compact was reasonably and honorably founded have been disappointed, and the circumstances show that increasing weakness in this area itself on the one side, and more than corresponding growth of real strength and confidence among the native tribes on the other, have produced their natural and inevitable consequences.

And whereas the ravaging of an adjoining friendly State by warlike savage tribes cannot for a moment be contemplated by Her Majesty's government without the most earnest and painful solicitude.

And whereas I have been satisfied by numerous addresses and letters I have received from the inhabitants of the Transvaal who desire the establishment within and over it of Her Majesty's authority and rule.

Now therefore I do, in virtue of the power and authority conferred upon me by Her Majesty's Royal Commission, proclaim and make known, that the territory heretofore known as the South African Republic, shall be taken to be British territory.

And I further proclaim and make known that the Transvaal will remain a separate government, with its own laws and legislature, and that it is the wish of Her Most Gracious Majesty that it shall enjoy the fullest legislative privileges compatible with the circumstances of the country and the intelligence of its people.

Equal justice is guaranteed to the persons and property of both white and colored; but the adoption of this principle does not and should not involve the granting of equal civil rights, such as the exercise of voting by savages, or their becoming members of a legislative body.

The native tribes living within the jurisdiction and under the protection of the government must be taught due obedience to the paramount authority, and be made to contribute their fair share towards the support of the State that protects them.

Gladstone's Address to Commons Advocating "Home Rule" for Ireland

(*Parliamentary Debates,* 1886)

Gentlemen:

The principle that I am laying down I am not laying down only for Ireland. It is the very principle on which, within my recollection, to the immense advantage of the country, we have not only altered, but revolutionized our method of governing the colonies. Fifty years ago the colonies were governed from Downing Street. It is true that some of them had legislative assemblies; but with these we were always in conflict. England tried to pass good laws for the colonies at that period; but the colonies said, "We do no want your good laws; we want our own."

We admitted the reasonableness of that principle, and it is now coming home to us from across the seas. We have to consider whether it is applicable to the case of Ireland. Do not let us disguise this from ourselves. We stand face to face with what is termed Irish nationality. Irish nationality vents itself in the demand for local autonomy, or separate and complete self-government in Irish, not in imperial, affairs. Is this a thing that we should view with horror or fear? I hold that there is such a thing as local patriotism, which, in itself, is not bad, but good. Englishmen are eminently English; Scotchmen are profoundly Scotch; and, if I read Irish history aright, the Irishman is profoundly Irish; but it does not follow that, because his local patriotism is keen, he is incapable of imperial patriotism.

I say that the Irishman is as capable of loyalty as another man. I say that if his loyalty has been checked in its development, why is it? Because the laws by which he is governed do not present themselves to him, as they do to us in England and Scotland, with a native and congenial aspect. Have you a braver or a more loyal man in your armies than the Irishman, who has shared every danger with his Scotch and English comrades, and who has never been behind them, when confronted by peril, for the sake of the honor and safety of his empire?

Looking forward, I ask the House to assist us in the work which we have undertaken. I ask you to show to Europe and to America that we, too, can face political problems which other countries have not feared to deal with. I ask that in our own case we should practice, with firm and fearless hand, what we have so often preached, namely, that the concession of local self-government is not the way to sap or impair, but the way to strengthen and consolidate, unity.

Typical American Expressions Concerning Imperialism in the Nineteenth Century

(President McKinley's reasons for annexing the Philippine Islands; President McKinley, *Address to Congress,* 1898)*

When I realized that the Philippines had dropped into our

* From: Charles S. Olcott, *The Life of William McKinley,* II, pp. 110–111, Houghton Mifflin and Company, 1916. Used with the permission of the publisher.

laps I confess I did not know what to do with them. I sought counsel from all sides—Democrats as well as Republicans—but got little help. I thought first we would take only Manila; then Luzon; then other islands, perhaps, also. I walked the floor of the White House night after night until midnight; and I am not ashamed to tell you, gentlemen, that I went down on my knees and prayed Almighty God for light and guidance more than one night. And one night late it came to me this way—I don't know how it was, but it came: (1) That we could not give them back to Spain— that would be cowardly and dishonorable; (2) that we could not turn them over to France or Germany—our commercial rivals in the Orient—that would be bad business and discreditable; (3) that we could not leave them to themselves—they were unfit for self-government—and they would soon have anarchy and misrule over there worse than Spain's was; and (4) that there was nothing left for us to do but to take them all and to educate the Filipinos and uplift and civilize and Christianize them. . . .

A Typical American Expression Opposed to Imperialism (*The Platform of the American Anti-Imperialist League,* 1899)

We hold that the policy known as imperialism is hostile to liberty and tends toward militarism, an evil from which it has been our glory to be free. We regret that it has become necessary in the land of Washington and Lincoln to reaffirm that all men of whatever race or color are entitled to life, liberty, and the pursuit of happiness. We maintain that governments derive their just powers from the consent of the governed. We insist that the subjugation of any people is "criminal aggression" and open disloyalty to the distinctive principles of our government.

We hold with Abraham Lincoln that "no man is good enough to govern another man without that man's consent. When the white man governs himself, that is self-government, but when he governs himself and also governs another man, that is more than self-government—that is despotism. Our defense is in the spirit which prizes liberty as the heritage of all men in all lands. Those who deny freedom to others deserve it not for themselves and under a just God cannot long retain it."

A Typical Expression of "Manifest Destiny" (*New York News,* 1845)

Away, away with all these cobweb tissues of rights of discovery, exploration, settlement, continuity etc. To state the truth at once in its neglected simplicity, we are free to say that were the respective cases and arguments of the two parties, as to all these points of history and law, reversed—had England all ours, and we nothing but hers—our claim to Oregon would still be best and strongest. And that claim is by the right of our manifest destiny to overspread and to possess the whole of the continent which Providence has given us for the development of the great experiment of liberty and federated self-government entrusted to us.

The *Statute of Westminster* as a New Departure in Imperialism (*Statutes of the Realm,* 1931)

Whereas it is meet and proper to set out by way of preamble to this Act that, inasmuch as the Crown is the symbol of the free association of the members of the British Commonwealth of Nations, and as they are united by a common allegiance to the Crown, it would be in accord with the established constitutional position of all the members of the Commonwealth in relation to one another that any alteration in the law touching the Succession to the Throne or the Royal Style and Titles shall hereafter require the assent as well of the Parliaments of all the Dominions as of the Parliament of the United Kingdom:

And whereas it is in accord with the established constitutional position that no law hereafter made by the Parliament of the United Kingdom shall extend to any of the said Dominions as part of the law of that Dominion otherwise than at the request and with the consent of that Dominion:

And whereas it is necessary for the ratifying, confirming, and establishing of certain of the said declarations and resolutions of the said Conferences that a law be made and enacted in due form by authority of the Parliament of the United Kingdom:

And whereas the Dominion of Canada, the Commonwealth of Austrialia, the Dominion of New Zealand, the Union of South Africa, the Irish Free State, and Newfoundland have severally requested and consented to the submission of a measure to the Parliament of the United Kingdom for making such provision with regard to the matters aforesaid as is hereafter in this Act contained:

Now, threfore, be it enacted by the King's most Excellent Majesty by and with the advice and consent of the Lords Spiritual and Temporal, and Commons, in this present Parliament assembled, and by the authority of the same, as follows:

1. In this Act the expression "Dominion" means any of the following Dominions, that is to say, the Dominion of Canada, the Commonwealth of Australia, the Dominion of New Zealand, the Union of South Africa, the Irish Free State, and Newfoundland.

2. (1) The Colonial Laws Validity Act, 1865, shall not apply to any law made after the commencement of this Act by the Parliament of a Dominion.

(2) No law and no provision of any law made after the commencement of this Act by the Parliament of a Dominion shall be void or inoperative on the ground that it is repugnant to the law of England, or to the provisions of any existing or future Act of Parliament of the United Kingdom, or to any order, rule, or regulation made under any such Act, and the powers of the Parliament of a Dominion shall include the power to repeal or amend any such Act, order, rule, or regulation in so far as the same is part of the law of the Dominion.

3. It is hereby declared and enacted that the Parliament of a Dominion has full power to make laws having extraterritorial operation.

4. No Act of Parliament of the United Kingdom passed after the commencement of this Act shall extend, or be deemed to extend, to a Dominion as part of the law of that Dominion, unless it is expressly declared in that Act that that Dominion has requested, and consented to, the enactment thereof. . . .

UNIT 12

The Failure of the Balance of Power: World War I and its Consequences

After the Congress of Vienna the major states of Europe enjoyed a period of comparative peace. True, there were spasmodic outbreaks of violence, such as the Crimean War, the Franco-Prussian War, and various "incidents" in the struggle for empire, but none of these, bloody as they were, approached the dimensions of a world war in space or in time. This uneasy peace was maintained in large part after the rise of Prussia by shifting but fairly well-balanced systems of alliances.

Thus in the opening years of the 20th century the great powers found themselves divided into two groups: the Triple Alliance—Germany, Austria-Hungary, and Italy; and the Triple Entente—France, Russia, and Great Britain. Both groups loudly proclaimed their devotion to peace, and indeed, did actually lay the foundations of modern world organization in a series of meetings beginning with the Hague Conference of 1897, but at the same time they displayed their inherent lack of confidence in each other (a result of the amoral basis of politics since the Renaissance) by seeking to outdo one another in size of military establishments.

The stability of Europe was further compromised by the abnormal growth of highly emotional factors such as rampant nationalism, decadent liberalism, revolutionism, racism, revenge sentiment, and imperialism, which tended to counteract the largely intellectual peace movement, and to tie the hands of governments that could foresee the horrible consequences of a major conflict. In short, by 1914 Europe found itself in a situation where almost any inflammatory occurrence might cause an uncontrollable explosion.

The incident which finally ballooned into a major war was the assassination of the heir to the throne of Austria-Hungary. Although it was an insignificant event in itself, the death of the Austrian archduke unleashed the destructive forces that society had been barely holding in check. During the hot summer months that followed the royal murder, the leading nations sent note after note to each other, some feverishly striving to avert an outbreak of bloodshed, others blustering and threatening. In the end the declarations of war came so unexpectedly that the public in the United States was completely stunned.

Once begun, however, the war quickly developed into as savage and costly a conflict as the world had ever known. The shock of the neutral nations turned into horror. And in the United States official neutrality became enmeshed in emotional and economic involvements too powerful for a pacifistic president to handle. President Wilson gradually turned the whole rationale of his idealism into an argument for active participation by the United States in a war "to make the world safe for democracy" and "to end all war." Future wars, he decided, could be prevented by a permanent association of nations.

In many noteworthy documents and speeches the scholarly president argued his cause. But brilliant as was his language, he failed to secure in the Treaty of Versailles an agreement fully acceptable to any one of the great powers. And most bitter of all his defeats was the failure of his own people to accept his idea of a League of Nations, although the Covenant of the League did become a part of the postwar treaty settlement.

The League of Nations began its life under favorable augury despite the nonparticipation of the United States. The devastating effect of the war on victor and vanquished alike had infused renewed vigor into the age-old hope that man could find a way to maintain permanent peace among nations. To many who had listened to the inspired phrases of Woodrow Wilson, this ideal seemed to have become a bright reality in the postwar years when the great powers in conference after conference tried painstakingly to build up a legal structure for the pacific settlement of international disputes and the outlawry of violence as an instrument of policy. Only a few of the able leaders who worked for peace could or would realize that the virile seeds of war were not being sterilized by legal documents and idealistic speeches.

Yet, in many places the seeds—nationalism, colonialism, militarism, and others—rested in fertile soil working toward a certain germination. In Germany, Italy, and Japan the friction of frustration rubbing against ambition warmed them; and in all the western world a ferment of ideological revolution spreading from Bolshevik Russia imbued them with synthetic energy. Bolshevism, Fascism, and National Socialism were but new forms of old historical forces which had not been devitalized by the peace settlement of 1919 and after.

The warning voices of the few statesmen who saw the rising menace during the 1920's were lost among the loud chorus of peacemakers, or were diverted by the threat of economic catastrophe to the warped postwar business organization. Only when the menace had grown into a young giant did the elder statesmen of western Europe seek to frustrate it by legal action of the League of Nations, and failing in that, to placate it by appeasement.

General Treaty of Peace Between Great Britain, Austria, France, Prussia, Russia, Sardinia, and Turkey, at Paris (1856) (Great Britain, *Treaties*)

Article I. From the day of the exchange of the ratifications of the present Treaty there shall be peace and friendship between Her Majesty the Queen of the United Kingdom of Great Britain and Ireland, His Majesty the Emperor of the French, His Majesty the King of Sardinia, His Imperial Majesty, the Sultan of Turkey, on the one part and His Majesty the Emperor of all the Russias, on the other part; as well as between their heirs and successors, their respective dominions and subjects, in perpetuity.

Article II. Peace being happily re-established between their said Majesties, the territories conquered or occupied by their armies during the late war shall be evacuated.

Article III. His Majesty the Emperor of all the Russias engages to restore to his Majesty the Sultan the town and citadel of Kars, as well as the other parts of the Ottoman territory of which the Russian troops are in possession.

Article VII. In combined approval their Majesties declare the Sublime Porte admitted to participate in the Concert of Europe. Their Majesties further mutually engage to respect the Independence and the territorial integrity of the Turkish Empire, and they will consider any act in violation of this a question of general interest.

Article VIII. If there should arise between the Sultan and anyone of the signatory Powers any misunderstanding which might serve to endanger their peaceful relations, both parties shall, before having recourse to force, permit the other Power the opportunity of preventing such extremity by means of mediation.

Article IX. His Imperial Majesty, the Sultan, having in his constant solicitude for the welfare of his subjects issued a Decreetal, which records his generous intentions towards the Christian population of his Empire, has resolved to communicate to the Contracting Powers the said Decreetal.

The contracting Powers recognize the high value of this communication. Yet it is clearly apparent that it cannot in any case give the said powers the right of interference in the relations of His Majesty the Sultan with his Subjects, nor in the internal administration of his Empire.

Article X. The Convention of the 13th of July, 1841, which maintains the ancient rule of the Ottoman Empire relative to the closing of the Straits of the Bosphorus and Dardanelles, has been revised by common interest.

Article XI. The Black Sea is neutralized; its Waters and its Ports are thrown open to the usage of every nation, and are formally and forever interdicted to the flag of war.

Article XV. The Act of the Congress of Vienna, having established the principles intended to regulate the navigation of Rivers which separate or traverse different States, the Contracting Powers stipulate that these principles shall in the future be equally applied to the Danube and its mouths. Consequently there shall not be levied any toll founded solely upon the fact of the navigation of the river, nor any duty upon the goods which may be on board vessels.

Article XIX. In order to insure the execution of the above regulations which are established by common agreement, each of the contracting Powers shall have the right to station, at all times, two light vessels at the mouths of the Danube.

Article XX. In order to more fully secure the freedom of the navigation of the Danube, His Majesty the Emperor of all the Russias consents to the ratification of the modification of his frontier in Bessarabia.

Article XXI. The territory ceded by Russia shall be annexed to the Principality of Moldavía, under the Suzerainty of the Sultan.

Article XXII. The Principalities of Wallachia and Moldavia shall continue to enjoy under the Suzerainty of the Sultan, the powers, privileges, and immunities of which they are in possession.

Article XXIV. His Majesty the Sultan promises to convoke immediately in each of the two provinces a Council composed in such a manner as to express the wishes of the people in regard to the definitive organization of the Principalities.

Article XXV. His Majesty the Emperor of all the Russias and

His Majesty the Sultan maintain in its integrity the state of their possessions in Asia such as it legally existed before the war.

In order to prevent all local disputes a mixed Commission, composed of two Russian Commissioners, two Ottoman Commissioners, one English, and one French Commissioner, shall be sent to any troubled area to re-establish diplomatic relations in good order.

Treaty of Peace Between Austria and Prussia, Prague, August, 1866
(Royal Austrian Chancellory, State Records)

Article I. There shall be Peace and Friendship between his Majesty the Emperor of Austria and His Majesty, the King of Prussia, and between their heirs and successors, as well as between their respective States and Subjects, henceforth and forever.

Article II. For the purpose of carrying out Article VI of the *Preliminaries of Peace* concluded at Nikolsburg on the 26th of July, 1866, and as His Majesty the Emperor of the French officially declared through his accredited Ambassador to His Majesty, King of Prussia, on the 29th of July, 1866, "qu'en ce qui concerne le Gouvernement de l'Empereur, la Venetie est acquise a l'Italie pour lui etre remise a la Paix," His Majesty the Emperor of Austria also accedes on his part to that Declaration and gives his consent to the union of the Lombard-Venetian Kingdom with the Kingdom of Italy, without any other burdensome condition than that the liquidation of those debts which being charged on the territories ceded, are to be recognized in accordance with the precedent of the Treaty of Zurich.

Article IV. His Majesty the Emperor of Austria acknowledges the dissolution of the Germanic Confederation as hitherto constituted, and gives his consent to a new organization of Germany without the participation of the Imperial Austrian State. His Majesty likewise promises to recognize the more restricted Federal relations which His Majesty the King of Prussia will establish to the north of the line of the Main River; and he declares his concurrence in the formation of an Association of the German States situated to the south of that line, whose national connection with the North German Confederation is reserved for further arrangement between the parties, and which will have independent international existence.

Article V. His Majesty the Emperor of Austria transfers to his Majesty, the King of Prussia, all the rights which he acquired by the Vienna Treaty of October, 1864, over the Duchies of Holstein and Schleswig, with the condition that the population of the northern Districts of Schleswig, shall be ceded to Denmark if, by plebicite, they express the desire to be so united to Denmark.

Article VI. At the desire of his Majesty the Emperor of Austria, His Majesty the King of Prussia declares his willingness to let the present territorial condition of the Kingdom of Saxony remain to the same extent as before in the alterations which are about to be made in Germany; but he reserves to himself the right of arranging the contribution of Saxony to the expenses of the war, and the future position of the Kingdom of Saxony in the North German Confederation, by a special treaty with His Majesty, the King of Saxony.

His Majesty the Emperor of Austria promises to recognize the new arrangements that will be made by His Majesty the King of Prussia in North Germany.

Article VII. For the purpose of making arrangements respecting the late Federal Property, a commission will meet at Frankfort-on-the-Main within six weeks from ratification of this treaty . . . which will liquidate all claims and demands on the German Confederation within six months.

Article VIII. Austria has the right of removing or otherwise disposing of the Imperial Property in the Federal Fortresses belonging to her according to specifications.

Article X. No one belonging to the Duchies of Schleswig and Holstein and no subject of either of Their Majesties will be prosecuted or molested in his person or property on account of his political belief or conduct during the late events and the war.

Article XI. His Majesty the Emperor of Austria undertakes to pay to His Majesty the King of Prussia the sum of 40,000,000 Prussian thalers, to cover part of the expenses which Prussia has been put to by the war. From that sum is to be deducted the amount of the War expenses which His Majesty the Emperor of Austria has still to demand from the Duchies of Schleswig and Holstein, to the extent of 15,000,000 Prussian thalers, as well as the additional sum of 5,000,000 thalers as the sum equal to the free maintenance which the Prussian Army is to have in those parts of the Austrian territories which it will occupy until the conclusion of the peace; so that there remain 20,000,000 thalers to be paid in ready money.

Article XII. The evacuation of the Austrian territories held by Prussian troops shall be completed within three weeks after the ratification of this Treaty.

Article XIII. All the treaties and conventions concluded between the contracting parties prior to 1866 are again brought into force, insofar as they must not, by their nature, lose their effect by the dissolution of the relations of the Germanic Confederation.

The Frankfort Treaty of Peace Between France and Germany (1871)

Article I. The distance between the town of Belfort and the line of the frontier . . . is considered as describing the radius which, by virtue of the clause relating thereto in Article I of the Preliminaries, is to remain to France with the town and the fortifications of Belfort.

The German Government is disposed to extend that radius so as to exclude the Cantons of Belfort, Delle, and Giromogny, as well as the western part of the Canton of Fontaine, to the west of a line to be traced from the spot where the canal from the Rhone to the Rhine leaves the Canton of Delle to the south of Montreux-Chateau, to the northern limits of the Canton between Bourg and Fenlon where that line would join the eastern limit of the Canton of Giromogny.

The German Government will, nevertheless, not cede the above territories unless the French Republic agrees, on its part, to a ratification of the frontier along the western limits of the Cantons of Cattenom and Thionville which will give to Germany the territory to the east of a line starting from the frontier of Luxomberg between Hussigny and Redingen, leaving to France the villages of Thil and Villerupt, extending between Erronville and Aumetz between Beuvillers and Boulange, between Trieux and Lomeringen, and joining the line of frontier between Arril and Moyeuvre.

The International Commission, mentioned in Article I of the Preliminaries, shall proceed to the spot immediately after the ratification of this Treaty to execute the works entrusted to them in tracing and establishing the new frontier.

Article II. French subjects, natives of the ceded territories, actually domiciled on that territory, who shall preserve their nationality, shall, up to the first of October, 1872, and on their making a previous statement to that effect, be allowed to change their domicile into France and to remain there, that right in no way infringing on the laws of military service.

They shall also be allowed to preserve their real properties in the ceded zone.

Article III. The French government shall deliver to the German government the archives, documents, and civil and military records relating to the ceded areas.

Article IV. The French government shall give over to the German government within six months:

1. The amount of the sum deposited by the departments, communes, and public establishments of the ceded territories.
2. The amount of payment for enlistment and discharge bonuses belonging to soldiers and sailors native to the ceded territories who shall choose German citizenship.

Article V. The two nations shall enjoy equal rights as regards navigation on the Moselle, the Marne-Rhine canal, the Rhone-Rhine canal, and the canal of the Sorre and the Navigable Waters connecting these channels of maritime movement.

Article VI. The communities belonging either to the Reformed Church or to the Augsburg Confession, established on the ceded territories, shall cease to be under French Ecclesiastical authority.

Article VII. The payment of 500,000,000 francs shall be made within 30 days after the re-establishment of the authority of the French Government in the city of Paris. 1,000,000,000 francs shall be paid in the course of the year, and 500,000,000 francs on the first of May, 1872. The last 3,000,000,000 are payable on the second of March, 1874. From the second of March of the present year the interest on those 3,000,000,000 francs shall be paid each year on the third of March, at the rate of 5 per cent annually.

Payment can only be made in the principal German towns of commerce, and shall be altogether in metal, gold or silver, in notes of the Bank of England, Prussian Bank notes, in first class negotiable bills to order or letters of exchange.

The German government, having fixed in France the value of a Prussian thaler at 3 francs 75 centimes, the French government accepts the conversion at the rate stated.

After payment of the first 500,000,000 francs and the ratification of this treaty, the Departments of the Somme, Seine Inferieure, and Eure shall be evacuated by the German Armies. The evacuation of the Departments of the Oise, Seine-et-Oise, Seine-et-Marne, and Seine, as well as the forts of Paris, shall take place as soon as the German government shall consider the re-establishment of order in France and Paris sufficient to guarantee the execution of the commitments contracted by the French government.

Article VIII. German soldiers shall abstain from taking contributions either in produce or money in the occupied territories; that obligation on their part being correlative to the obligations contracted for their support by the French government, in case the French government, notwithstanding the repeated demands of the German government, is remiss in the execution of the obligation, the German soldiers will have the right to procure what is necessary to their needs by taking taxes and levies in the occupied areas, and even outside those territories if necessary.

The Constitution of the German Empire (1871)
(Constitution)

1. Territory of the Confederation

Article I. The Territory of the Confederation is comprised of the States of Prussia with Lauenburg, Bavaria, Saxony, Wurtemberg, Baden, Hesse, Mecklenburg-Schwerin, Saxe-Weimar, Mecklenburg-Strelitz, Oldenburg, Brunswick, Saxe-Meiningen, Saxe-Altenburg, Saxe-Coburg-Gotha, Anhalt, Schwarzburg-Rudolstat, Schwarzburg-Sondershausen, Waldeck, Reuss Elder, Reuss Younger, Schaumburg-Lippe, Lippe, Lubeck, Bremen, and Hamburg.

2. Legislature of the Empire

Article II. Within this Confederate Territory the Empire exercises the right of legislation according to this Constitution, and with the effect that the Imperial laws take precedence of the laws of the States. The Imperial laws receive their binding power by their publication in the name of the Empire.

Article III. For entire Germany one common nationality exists with the effect, that every person belonging to any one of the Confederated States is to be treated in every other State as a born native, to have the right to hold public office, property, and to enjoy all other civil rights.

No German may be restricted from the exercise of these rights by the authorities of his own State or by any of the Confederated States.

What is needful for the fulfillment of military duty in regard to the entire country will be ordered by the way of Imperial Legislation.

Article IV. The following affairs are subject to the superintendence and legislation of the Empire:

1. The regulation as to freedom of translocation, domicile, citizenship, passport and police regulation for foreigners, and as to transacting business, including insurance affairs.

2. The customs and commercial legislation, and Imperial taxation.

3. The regulation of the system of coinage, weights, and measures.

4. The general regulations as to banking.

5. The granting of patents.

6. The protection of intellectual property.

7. The organization of the common protection of German commerce in foreign countries, of German ships and their flags at sea, and the arrangement of a common consular representation.

8. Railway affairs and the construction of land and water communications for general intercourse and defence.

10. Postal and telegraph affairs.

11. The general legislation as to obligatory rights, penal law, commercial and bill-of-exchange laws, and judicial procedure.

14. The military and naval affairs of the Empire.

16. The regulation of the press and of labor unions and societies.

Article V. The legislation of the Empire is carried on by the Council of the Confederation and the Imperial Diet. The accordance of the majority of votes in both assemblies is necessary and sufficient for a law of the Empire.

3. The Council of the Confederation

Article VI. The Council of the Confederation consists of the Representatives of the Members of the Confederation, among which the votes are divided in such a manner that Prussia has, with the former votes of Hanover, Electoral Hesse, Holstein, Nassau, and Frankfort, seventeen votes. The other States have:

Bavaria	6
Saxony	4
Wurtemberg	4
Baden	3
Hesse	3
Mecklenburg-Schwerin	2
All others	1 each
Total votes in the Council	58

Article VII. The Council of the Confederation determines what bills are to be brought before the Imperial Diet. Every member of the Confederation has the right to propose bills and to recommend them, and the Presidency is bound to bring them under debate.

Article VIII. The Council of the Confederation forms permanent Committees from its own members:

1. For land army and defense,
2. For naval affairs,
3. For customs and taxes,
4. For railways, post, telegraph, commerce, and intercourse,
5. For affairs of Justice,
6. For finances.

In each of these Committees at least four of the States will be represented and each state has one vote. In the Committee of land army and defense Bavaria has a permanent seat, the other members of that Committee as well as the Committee for naval affairs are nominated by the Emperor. The members of the other Committees are elected by the Council of the Confederation.

4. The Presidency

Article XI. The Presidency of the Confederation belongs to the King of Prussia, who bears the name of German Emperor. The Emperor has to represent the Empire internationally, to declare war, and to conclude peace in the name of the Empire, and to enter into alliances and other treaties with foreign powers.

The consent of the Council of the Confederation is necessary for the declaration of war in the name of the Empire.

Article XII. The Emperor has the right to summon, to open, to prorogue, and to close both the Council of the Confederation and the Imperial Diet.

Article XIII. The summoning of the Council of the Confederation, and of the Imperial Diet, takes place once each year.

Article XV. The Presidency in the Council of the Confederation and the directorship of its business belong to the Chancellor of the Empire, who is to be appointed by the Emperor.

Article XVII. The expedition and proclamation of the laws of the Empire and the care of their execution belong to the Emperor.

Article XVIII. The Emperor nominates the Imperial Officials, and when necessary decrees their dismissal.

5. Imperial Diet

Article XX. The Imperial Diet is elected by universal and direct election with secret votes.

Article XXIII. The Imperial Diet has the right to propose laws within the competency of the Empire, and to forward petitions which have been addressed to it to the Council of the Confederation, or to the Chancellor.

Article XXIV. The Imperial Diet meets for three years. In case of a dissolution by the Emperor the meeting of the Electors must be called within a period of 60 days, and within a period of 90 days the Imperial Diet must be summoned.

Article XXVII. The members of the Imperial Diet must not receive any salary or remuneration in that capacity.

6. Customs and Commercial Affairs

XXXIII. Germany forms one customs and commercial territory. All articles of free trade in any one of the States may be introduced freely into any other State.

Article XXXVI. The collection and administration of the duties and consumptive taxes remain in the hands of each State.

The Emperor oversees the observance of the legal procedures through Imperial officials whom he attaches to the customs or excise offices.

11. Military Affairs

Article LVII. Every German is liable to military service.

Article LVIII. The expenses and burdens of the whole of the military of the Empire are to be born equally by all of the States of the Confederation.

Article LIX. Every German capable of service belongs for seven years to the standing army, between his twentieth and twenty-eighth year: that is, three years active and four years reserve status, then the following five years with the Landwehr.

Article LXI. After the publication of this Constitution the whole Prussian Military Code of Laws is to be introduced throughout the Empire without delay.

12. Finances of the Empire

Article LXIX. All the receipts and disbursements of the Empire must be estimated for each year, and be brought into the Imperial Estimate. These are to be fixed by law.

13. Settlement of Differences and Penal Stipulations

Article LXXIV. Every undertaking against the existence, the integrity, the safety, or the Constitution of the German Empire; finally, insulting the Council of the Confederation or the Imperial Diet, or a member of the Council of the Confederation or of the Imperial Diet, or any authority, or any public functionary of the Empire, while in the exercise of their vocation, or in reference to their vocation, by word, in writing, printing, drawing, figurative or other representation, will be sentenced and punished according to the fixed law.

14. General Stipulations

Article LXXVIII. Alterations in the Constitution take place by way of legislation. Proposals of alteration are rejected if they have fourteen votes against them in the Council of the Confederation.

The Schonbrunn Treaty Between Russia and Austria (1873)

His Majesty the Emperor of Austria, and His Majesty the Emperor of the Russias, wishing to give substance to their mutual hopes for the consolidation and protection of the peace of the peoples of Europe, and having in their hearts the full desire to reduce the prospects of war—and convinced that this object could in no surer way be assured than by a direct understanding between them, have agreed on the following points:

1. Their Majesties mutually promise, even though the interests of their States should present some divergences respecting special problems, to discuss together such things in order that problems of minor consideration may not prevail over other considerations of higher virtue. Their respective Majesties are determined to prevent any one from succeeding in dividing them on the matter of the principles which they feel are alone able to impose the continuation of the European peace against all subverting forces opposed to peace.

2. In case an aggression coming from a third Power should threaten to shatter the peace of Europe, Their Majesties engage to come to a preliminary agreement between themselves without coming into any agreement with any third Power.

3. If, as a result of this present Agreement, a military action should become necessary, it should be directed by a special convention to be established by Their Majesties.

4. If one of the parties to this contract should wish to regain its liberty of action by denouncing this contract, it must notify the other power two years prior to such act.

Treaty of Alliance (Dual Alliance) Between Germany and Austria (1879)

Considering that their Majesties the German Emperor, King of Prussia, and the Emperor of Austria, King of Hungary, must esteem it as their incontestable duty as Sovereigns to take care in all circumstances, for the security of their Empires and for the tranquility of their peoples;

Considering that the two monarchs as in the previously existing Confederation will be in a position, by a firm alliance of the two Empires, to fulfill their duty more easily and more efficaciously;

Considering, finally, that an intimate accord between Germany and Austria-Hungary can menace nobody, but is, on the contrary, qualified to consolidate the peace of Europe created by the stipulations of the Treaty of Berlin in 1878:

Their Majesties the German Emperor and the Emperor of Austria, King of Hungary, promising one another never to give any aggressive tendency in any direction to their purely defensive agreement, have resolved to conclude an alliance of peace and reciprocal protection.

With this object their Majesties have agreed . . . to the following principles.

Article I. If, contrary to expectations and against the sincere desire of both the high contracting parties, one of the two Emperors shall be attacked on the part of Russia, the contracting parties are bound to assist each other with the whole of the military power of their Empire, and to conclude peace thereafter conjointly, only, and by agreement.

Article II. Should one of the contracting parties be attacked by another power, the other contracting party hereby engages not only not to assist the aggressor against his ally, but at the least to observe a benevolent neutral attitude with regard to the other contracting party.

If, however, in such a case the attacking Power should be supported by Russia, by way of active cooperation or by military measures which menace the contracting party under attack, then the obligation of reciprocal assistance with full military power, which is stipulated in the first Article of this treaty, will in this case enter immediately into effect, and the conduct of the war by both the contracting parties shall then be in common until the joint conclusion of peace.

Article III. This treaty, in conformity with its pacific character and to prevent any misconstruction, shall be kept secret by both contracting parties, and it will be communicated to a third Power only with the consent of both parties, and strictly according to a special agreement.

Both contracting parties, in view of the sentiments expressed by the Emperor Alexander hope that the preparations of Russia will not prove in reality to be a menace to them, and for this reason they have for the present no occasion for a communication. But if, contrary to expectation, this hope shall prove a vain one, the two contracting parties will recognize it as a loyal obligation, to inform the Emperor Alexander of Russia at least confidentially that they must consider an attack against one of them as directed against both.

The Three Emperors' League (1881)

The Courts of Austria-Hungary, of Germany, and of Russia, animated by a common desire to safeguard the peace of Europe by an understanding intended to assure the defensive position of their respective States, have come into agreement on certain questions which more especially concern their mutual interests. To facilitate this understanding they have agreed on the following Articles:

Article I. In case one ot the high contracting parties should find itself at war with a fourth power, the other two shall maintain toward it a benevolent neutrality and shall devote their efforts to the localization of the conflict.

This stipulation shall also apply to any war between one of the three powers and Turkey, but only in the case where a previous agreement shall have been reached between the three Courts as to the results of this war.

In the special circumstance where one of them should obtain a more positive support from one of its two allies, the obligatory character of this treaty shall remain in force for the third friendly power.

Article II. Russia, in agreement with Germany, declares her firm resolution to respect the interests arising from the new position assured to Austria-Hungary by the Treaty of Berlin.

The three Courts, wishing to avoid all dissonance between them, engage to take account of their respective interests in the Balkan area. They further contract that any innovations in the territorial *status quo* of Turkey in Europe can be accomplished only by a common agreement among them.

In order to facilitate the agreement contemplated by the present Article, an agreement of which it is difficult to foresee all possible conditions, the three Courts from the present moment record in the Protocol annexed to this Treaty the points on which an understanding has already been established in principle.

Article III. The three Courts recognize the European and mutually obligatory character of the principle of the closing of the Straits of the Bosphorus and of the Dardanelles, founded on international law and confirmed by treaties, and as stated by the Congress of Berlin.

They will take care in common that Turkey shall make no exception to this rule in favour of the interests of any Government whatsoever, by lending to warlike operations of a belligerent Power the portion of its empire constituted by the Straits.

In case of infringement, or to prevent a threatened infringement, the three Courts will inform Turkey that they regard her, in that event, as putting herself in a state of war toward the injured party.

Article IV. This treaty shall remain in valid force for three years.

Article V. The contracting parties mutually promise secrecy as to the contents and the existence of the present Treaty.

Article VI. The secret conventions concluded between Austria-Hungary and Russia, and between Germany and Russia in 1873 are replaced by the present treaty.

Secret Protocol Appended to the Treaty as Stated in Article II Above

The undersigned plenipotentiaries of His Majesty the

Emperor of Austria, His Majesty the Emperor of Germany, and His Majesty the Emperor of Russia, having recorded in accordance with Article II of the Secret Treaty the points affecting the interests of the three Courts in the Balkans area, have agreed to the following Protocol:

1. Bosnia and Herzegovinia

Austria-Hungary shall have the right to occupy and take these provinces at her best convenience.

2. Eastern Rumelia

The three Powers agree in regarding the eventuality of an occupation of either Eastern Rumelia or of the Balkans as full of danger for European peace. Should this occur, they will employ their efforts to keep the Sultan from such an enterprise. Yet, the three Powers agree that Bulgaria and Eastern Rumelia should not unduly antagonize the Sultan by attacks originating in their territories against any other province of the Turkish Empire.

3. Bulgaria

The three Powers will not oppose the reunion of Bulgaria and Eastern Rumelia within the limits set forth by the Treaty of Berlin. They will, however, dissuade the Bulgarians from attacking any neighboring province, especially Macedonia—and to inform the Bulgarians that in such case they act at their own risk and peril.

The Triple Alliance (1882)

Their Majesties the Emperor of Austria, King of Bohemia, and Apostolic King of Hungary, the Emperor of Germany, King of Prussia, and the King of Italy, in the desire to further the guarantees of the general peace of Europe, and to insure the Monarchial principle and social and political order in their respective realms, have agreed to enter a Treaty, which, by its defensive nature pursues only the hope of forestalling the danger which might threaten their States and the peace of Europe.

To this end Their Majesties . . . have agreed upon the following articles:

Article I. The high contracting parties promise each the other mutual peace and friendship, and that they will not enter into alliance or agreement with any other power against any one of the contracting parties.

They engage to exchange ideas and knowledge on political and economic questions which in the future may arise, and further to support one another within the limits of their own best interests.

Article II. In case Italy is attacked by any non-signatory power without direct provocation on her part, or by France for any cause, the other two parties to this agreement shall be bound to lend full and complete assistance to the party attacked.

Article III. In case one or two of the contracting parties, without direct provocation on their part, should be attacked by one or more great powers not signatory of the present treaty and should become involved in a war with them, the *casus foederis* would rise simultaneously for all the high contracting parties.

Article IV. In case a great power not signatory of the present treaty should threaten the state security of one of the contracting parties, and in case the threatened party should thereby be compelled to declare war against that great power, the other two contracting parties engage themselves to maintain benevolent neutrality toward their ally. Each of them reserves the right, in this case, to take part in the war if it thinks fit in order to make common cause with its Ally.

Article V. If the security or peace of any of the high contracting parties should be threatened under circumstances as set forth in the preceding Articles, the contracting parties shall counsel together in sufficient time concerning military measures to be taken regarding cooperative action.

Also, they engage hereby, in all cases of common war activity never to conclude armistice, peace, or treaty except by mutual agreement.

Article VI. The high contracting parties herewith mutually promise to hold the contents and existence of the present treaty in secret.

Article VII. Austria-Hungary and Italy, who are in accord as to the maintenance, as far as possible, of the territorial *status quo* in the East, engage themselves to use their influence to prevent all territorial changes which might be disadvantageous to the one or the other of the Powers signatory to the present treaty. To this end they will give reciprocally all information calculated to enlighten each other concerning their own intentions and those of other powers.

Should, however, the case arise that, in the course of events, the maintenance of the *status quo* in the Balkans or of the Ottoman coasts and islands in the Adriatic or Aegean Seas become impossible and that, either in consequence of the action of a third power or for any other reason, Austria-Hungary or Italy should be obliged to change the *status quo* on their part by a temporary or permanent occupation, such occupation would only take place after previous agreement between the two Powers, which would have to be based upon the principle of a reciprocal compensation for all territorial or other advantages that either of them might acquire over and above the existing *status quo,* and would have to satisfy the interests and rightful claims of both parties.

The "Reinsurance" Treaty Between Germany and Russia (1887)

The Imperial Courts of Germany and Russia, animated by an equal desire to strengthen the general peace by an understanding destined to assure the defensive position of their respective States, have resolved to confirm the agreement established between them by a special arrangement, in view of the expiration on June 15/24, 1887, of the validity of the secret treaty and protocol, signed in 1881 and renewed in 1884 by the three Courts of Germany, Russia, and Austria-Hungary. They have therefore agreed on the following Articles:

Article I. In case one of the high contracting parties should find itself at war with a third power, the other would maintain a benevolent neutrality toward it, and would devote its effort to the localization of the conflict. This provision would not apply to a war against Austria or France in case such a war should result from the attack directed by one of the contracting powers against either one of the other two powers mentioned.

Article II. Germany fully recognizes the historically valid rights acquired by Russia in the Balkans area, and particularly the legitimacy of her preponderant influence in Bulgaria and in Eastern Rumelia. The two Courts engage to admit no modification of the territorial *status quo* of the said area without a previous agreement between them, and to oppose every attempt to disturb this *status quo* or to modify it without their mutual agreement.

Article III. The two Courts recognize the European and mutually obligatory character of the principle of the closing of the Straits of the Bosphorus and of the Dardanelles, as founded on international law and confirmed by treaties.

They agree that Turkey shall make no exception to this rule in favor of any other Government, by lending to warlike operations of a belligerent power the portion of its Empire constituted by these Straits. In case of infringement or to prevent any threatened infringement, the two courts will inform Turkey that they would regard her, in that event, as placing herself in a state of hostilities with the injured Party, and as depriving herself thenceforth of the benefits of the security assured to her territorial *status quo* as set forth in the Treaty of Berlin.

Article V. The contracting parties mutually promise secrecy as to the contents and the existence of the present treaty and of the protocol annexed thereto.

Additional and Very Secret Protocol Annexed as Stated in Article V Above

In order to complete the stipulations of Articles II and III of the secret treaty now concluded, the two Courts have come to agreement on the points following:

1. Germany, as in the past, will lend her assistance to Russia in order to re-establish a regular and legal government in Bulgaria. She promises in no case to give her consent to the restoration of the Prince of Battenberg.
2. In case His Majesty the Emperor of Russia should find himself under the necessity of defending the entrance of the Black Sea in order to safeguard the interests of Russia, Germany engages to accord her benevolent neutrality and moral and diplomatic support to the measures which His Majesty may deem it necessary to take to guard his Empire.
3. The present protocol forms an integral part of the secret treaty signed on this day at Berlin.

The Berlin Treaty Between Germany and Italy (1887)

Their Majesties, the King of Italy and the Emperor of Germany, desiring to further good understanding and tighten the bonds already existing between their peoples and realms, have desired, and hereby do enact, a separate treaty which is more in keeping with present political conditions in Europe.

Their Majesties have agreed on the following Articles:

Article I. The contracting parties, having in mind the maintenance of the territorial *status quo* in the East, engage to forestall, in as far as they are able, on the Ottoman coasts and islands in the Adriatic and Aegean Seas, any territorial modifications which might be injurious to either of them.

Article II. Should France attempt to extend her occupation, or her protectorate or sovereignty, in any manner in the North African Territories, and in consequence of this Italy, in order to protect her position in the Mediterranean, should feel that she must herself undertake action in North Africa, or even to move against French territory in Europe, the resultant state of hostilities between Italy and France would constitute *ipso facto,* on the demand of Italy the *casus foederis* . . . for joint action by both parties.

Article IV. If the fortunes of any war undertaken in common against France should cause Italy to seek for territorial guarantees with respect to France for the security of the frontiers of the Kingdom and of her maritime position, as well as with a view to the stabilization of peace, Germany will present no obstacle thereto; and, if need arise, compatible with circumstances, will apply herself to aiding in finding the means for attaining this purpose.

Article V. The contracting parties promise, mutually, secrecy as to the contents of the present treaty.

Documents Relating to the Formation and Functioning of the "Dual Entente" (1891)

M. de Mohrenheim, Ambassador of Russia at Paris to M. Ribot, Minister of Foreign Affairs of France.

Paris
August 23, 1891.

Sir:

During my recent visit to my homeland as ordered by duty, it much pleased the Emperor of the Russias to instruct me especially, as per the copy of his letter enclosed, regarding certain communications I am to make to the Government of the Republic of France.

In carrying out this command I hold it my first duty to bring this letter to the knowledge of your Excellency, in the hope that its contents, agreed upon fully by my government, will meet with your full approval and that of your most August government; and that you will be kind enough, Mr. Minister, to honor me with a reply testifying to the perfect understanding existing from now on between our two governments.

M. de Giers, Minister of Foreign Affairs of Russia, to de Mohrenheim, Ambassador of Russia to France.

Petersburg.
August 20, 1891.
Sir:

The situation brought to Europe by the public renewal of the Triple Alliance and the more or less probable adhesion of Great Britain to the aims which that Alliance pursues, have . . . prompted an exchange of ideas between the Ambassador of France and myself, tending to define the attitude which, as things now stand and in the presence of certain eventualities, might best favour our respective governments. While we have entered no league or alliance, we are none the less greatly interested in bulwarking the European peace with every functionable guarantee.

In this we have formulated two points:

1. In order to more clearly define the friendly understanding which unites them, and hoping to contribute in mutual accord to the protection of peace which forms the object of their sincerest aspirations, the two governments declare that they will discuss together every question of a nature to threaten the general peace.

2. In the event the peace should be actually endangered, and more especially should one of the two parties be threatened with any aggression, the two parties undertake to reach an understanding on the measures whose immediate and simultaneous adoption would be imposed upon the two governments by the realization of this eventuality.

Having submitted to the Emperor the facts of this exchange of ideas and this text, I have the great pleasure to inform you now that His Majesty has deigned to approve fully these principles of agreement, and would view with approval their adoption by the two Governments.

I beg that you . . . bring these things to the attention of the French Government and immediately communicate to me the decisions which it may make concerning them.

M. Ribot, French Minister of Foreign Affairs, to de Mohrenheim, the Russian Ambassador at Paris.

Paris.
August 28, 1891.

Sir:

You were kind enough, by order of your government, to communicate to me the text of the letter of the Minister of Foreign

Affairs of the Russian Empire, wherein are set forth the special instructions with which the Emperor Alexander, through M. de Giers, the Foreign Minister, provided you in relation to the general situation in Europe.

Your Excellency was instructed to express at the same time the hope that the contents of this document would meet with the approval of the government of the French Republic.

The Government of the Republic can only take the same view as does the Imperial Government of the situation brought about in Europe by the renewal of the Triple Alliance, and too, the French Government holds that the time has arrived to define the attitude which, in light of possible eventualities, might seem best to the two governments, who are equally hopeful of assuring the guarantees for the maintenance of the peace which results from the balance of power.

I am happy to inform you that the government of France gives its entire support to the two points which form the substance of the communication from your government relative to these developments.

I furthermore am at your complete disposal for the examination of all questions which, under present political conditions, should be examined by the two governments.

I further presume that the Imperial Government will appreciate as we do the importance of confiding to special envoys which should be delegated at once, the practical measures for meeting the possible eventualities as set forth in the second point of your communication.

In begging you to bring the reply of my Government to the attention of the Imperial Government, I wish to emphasize how desirous I am of eventual participation in the consecration of an understanding which has been the constant object of our common efforts.

The Military Convention Between France and Russia (1892)

France and Russia, being animated by an equal desire to preserve peace, and having no other object than to meet the necessities of a defensive war, provoked by an attack of the forces of the Triple Alliance against one or the other of them, herewith agree upon the following provisions:

1. If France is attacked by Germany, or by Italy supported by Germany, Russia shall employ all her available forces to attack Germany. If Russia is attacked by Germany, or by Austria

supported by Germany, France shall employ all her forces to fight Germany.

2. Should the forces of the Triple Alliance, or any one of the powers composing it, mobilize, France and Russia shall immediately and without the need of any discussion, also mobilize their whole force and simultaneously each shall move its full force to its frontier common with the opposing force.

3. The available forces to be employed against Germany shall be, for France, 1,300,000 soldiers; for Russia 700,000 to 800,000 soldiers.

These forces shall engage immediately, to the fullest extent, the forces of Germany so that Germany shall be required to fight at once in both the West and the East.

4. The General Staffs of the Armies of the two countries shall cooperate at all times in preparation, facilitation, and execution of all measures of security and action.

They shall, in peace as well as war, communicate all available information relative to the armies of the Triple Alliance.

5. France and Russia shall not conclude peace separately.

6. The present Convention shall have the same duration as the Triple Alliance.

7. All the clauses above stated shall be kept totally secret.

The Fourteen Points
(Woodrow Wilson, *Address to Congress,* January 8, 1918)

We entered this war because violations of right had occurred which touched us to the quick and made the life of our own people impossible unless they were corrected and the world secured once and for all against their recurrence. What we demand in this war, therefore, is nothing peculiar to ourselves. . . . All the peoples of the world are in effect partners in this interest, and for our own part we see very clearly, that unless justice be done to others, it will not be done to us. The program of the world's peace, therefore, is our program; and that program, the only possible program, as we see it is this:

I. Open covenants of peace, openly arrived at, after which there shall be no private international understandings of any kind but diplomacy shall proceed always frankly and in the public view.

II. Absolute freedom of navigation upon the seas, outside territorial waters, alike in peace and in war, except as the seas may be closed in whole or in part by international action for the enforcement of international covenants.

III. The removal, so far as possible, of all economic barriers and the establishment of an equality of trade conditions among all the nations consenting to the peace and associating themselves for its maintenance.

IV. Adequate guarantees given and taken that national armaments will be reduced to the lowest point consistent with domestic safety.

V. A free, open-minded, and absolutely impartial adjustment of all colonial claims, based upon a strict observance of the principle that in determining all such questions of sovereignty the interests of the populations concerned must have equal weight with the equitable claims of the government whose title is to be determined.

VI. The evacuation of all Russian territory and such a settlement of all questions affecting Russia as will secure the best and freest cooperation of the other nations of the world in obtaining for her an unhampered and unembarrassed opportunity for the independent determination of her own political development and national policy and assure her of a sincere welcome into the society of free nations under institutions of her own choosing. . . .

VII. Belgium . . . must be evacuated and restored, without any attempt to limit the sovereignty which she enjoys in common with all other free nations. . . .

VIII. All French territory should be freed and the invaded portions restored, and the wrong done to France by Prussia in 1871 in the matter of Alsace-Lorraine, which has unsettled the peace of the world for nearly fifty years, should be righted, in order that peace may once more be made secure in the interest of all.

IX. A readjustment of the frontiers of Italy should be effected along clearly recognizable lines of nationality.

X. The peoples of Austria-Hungary, whose place among the nations we wish to see safeguarded and assured, should be accorded the freest opportunity of autonomous development.

XI. Rumania, Serbia, and Montenegro should be evacuated; occupied territories restored; Serbia accorded free and secure access to the sea . . . and international guarantees of the political and economic independence and territorial integrity of the several Balkan states should be entered into.

XII. The Turkish portions of the present Ottoman Empire should be assured a secure sovereignty, but the other nationalities which are now under Turkish rule should be assured an undoubted security of life and an absolutely unmolested opportunity of autonomous development, and the Dardanelles should be permanently opened as a free passage to the ships and commerce of all nations under international guarantees.

XIII. An independent Polish state should be erected which should include the territories inhabited by indisputably Polish populations, which should be assured a free and secure access to the sea, and whose political and economic independence and territorial integrity would be guaranteed by international covenant.

XIV. A general association of nations must be formed under specific covenants for the purpose of affording mutual guarantees of political independence and territorial integrity to great and small states alike.

An Official Statement by the German Government Relative to the Charge that the German People "Stabbed in the Back" the Victorious German Armies in 1917 and 1918 (General von Kuhl, *Report to the Reichstag,* 1918)

To say, as is often the case, that the people were guilty of the "stab-in-the-back" of the German Armies, just as though the people had attacked those armies, is untrue. There was a complex of reasons for Germany's loss of the war.

Nevertheless, it is true that a certain amount of pacifism, antimilitarism, defeatism, and revolutionism, behind the front lines among the civilian population helped to undermine the morale and unity of the German armies. Yet even this does not attach to the majority of the people—which suffered heroically the miseries of almost five years of the conflict. It rather pertains to a minority of professional agitators and trouble-makers who for political considerations desired to infect the courageous soldiers of our armies.

This is most clearly apparent, when, after our great series of attacks along the western front had failed to provide complete victory, the war appeared lost. And yet, the treasonous activities of this minority had begun long before the summer of 1918. It is far better that one should thus speak of a "poisoning" of the armies rather than a "stab-in-the-back."

However, that pernicious phrase could well be applied to the terrible impact of the revolution when it came with such unexpected fierceness; for it did, actually, attack our soldiers from the rear, disrupting military communications and transport, and bringing to an end all order and discipline. Indeed, it was this act which forced Germany to lay down her arms and seek whatever terms the enemy would extend. The leftist revolution was not caused by the defeat of our armies in the offensive of 1918—on the contrary, it was causal to that defeat and had been prepared and planned long before.

The Treaty of Versailles, June 28, 1919

Section III
Left Bank of the Rhine
Article 42

Germany is forbidden to maintain or construct any fortifications either on the left bank of the Rhine or on the right bank to the west of a line drawn 50 kilometers to the east of the Rhine.

Article 43

In case Germany violates in any manner whatever the provisions of Article 42 she shall be regarded as committing a hostile act against the powers signatory of the present Treaty.

Section IV
Saar Basin
Article 45

As compensation for the destruction of the coal mines in the north of France and as part payment towards the total reparation due from Germany for the damage resulting from the war, Germany cedes to France in full and absolute possession, with exclusive rights of exploitation, unencumbered and free from all debts and charges of any kind the coal mines situated in the Saar Basin.

Article 49

Germany renounces in favour of the League of Nations, in the capacity of trustee, the government of the territory defined above.

At the end of fifteen years from coming into force of the present Treaty the inhabitants of the said territory shall be called upon to indicate the sovereignty under which they desire to be placed.

Annex
Chapter III
34

At the termination of a period of fifteen years from the coming into force of the present Treaty, the population of the territory of the Saar Basin will be called upon to indicate their desires in the following manner:

A vote will take place by communes or districts, on the three following alternatives: (a) maintenance of the regime established by the present Treaty and by this annex; (b) union with France; (c) union with Germany.

36

If the League of Nations decides in favour of the Union of the whole or part of the territory of the Saar Basin with Germany, France's rights of ownership in the mines situated in such part of the territory will be repurchased by Germany in their entirety at a price payable in gold. The price to be paid will be fixed by three experts, one nominated by Germany, one by France, and one nominated by the Council of the League of Nations; the decision of the experts will be given by a majority.

Section VI
Austria
Article 80

Germany acknowledges and will respect strictly the independence of Austria, within the frontiers which may be fixed in a Treaty between that State and the Principal Allied and Associated Powers; she agrees that this independence shall be inalienable, except with the consent of the Council of the League of Nations.

Article 84

German nationals habitually resident in any of the territories recognized as forming part of the Czecho-Slovak State will obtain Czecho-Slovak nationality *ipso facto* and lose their German nationality.

Section XI
Free City of Danzig
Article 102

The principal Allied and Associated Powers undertake to establish the town of Danzig. It will be placed under the protection of the League of Nations.

PART IV

German Interests and Rights Outside Germany

Section I

German Colonies

Article 119

Germany renounces in favour of the Principal Allied and Associated Powers all her rights and titles over her oversea possessions.

PART V

Military, Naval, and Air Clauses

Section I

Chapter I

Article 160

By a date which must not be later than March 31, 1920, the German Army must not comprise more than seven divisions of infantry and three divisions of cavalry.

After that date the total number of effectives in the Army of the States constituting Germany must not exceed one hundred thousand men, including officers. The Army shall be devoted exclusively to the maintenance of order within the territory.

The total effective strength of officers, including the personnel of staffs, whatever their composition, must not exceed four thousand.

The Great German General Staff and all similar organizations shall be dissolved and may not be reconstituted in any form.

Section II

Naval Clauses

Article 181

After the expiration of a period of two months from the coming into force of the present treaty the German naval forces in commission must not exceed:

6 battleships of the Deutschland or Lothringen type
6 light cruisers
12 destroyers
12 torpedo boats

No submarines are to be included.

Section IV

Article 203

All the military, naval, and air clauses contained in the present treaty, for the execution of which a time limit is prescribed, shall be executed by Germany under the control of Inter-Allied Commissions specially appointed for this purpose by the Principal Allied and Associated Powers.

Article 207

The upkeep and cost of the Commissions of Control and the expenses involved by their work shall be borne by Germany.

PART VII

Penalties

Article 227

The Allied and Associated Powers publicly arraign William II of Hohenzollern, formerly German Emperor, for a supreme offence against international morality and the sanctity of treaties.

A special tribunal will be constituted to try the accused, thereby assuring him the guarantees essential to the right of defence. It will be composed of five judges, one appointed by each of the following powers: namely, the United States of America, Great Britain, France, Italy, and Japan.

The Allied and Associated Powers will address a request to the Government of the Netherlands for the surrender to them of the ex-Emperor in order that he may be put on trial.

PART VIII

Reparation

Section I

Article 231

The Allied and Associated Governments affirm and Germany accepts the responsibility of Germany and her Allies for causing all the loss and damage to which the Allied and Associated Governments and their nationals have been subjected as a consequence of the war imposed upon them by the aggression of Germany and her allies.

Article 232

The Allied and Associated Governments recognize that the resources of Germany are not adequate, after taking into account permanent diminutions of such resources which will result from other provisions of the present treaty, to make complete reparation for all such loss and damage.

The Allied and Associated Governments, however, require, and Germany undertakes that she will make compensation for all damage done to the civilian population of the Allied and Associated Powers and to their property during the period of the belligerency of each as an Allied or Associated Power against Germany by such aggression by land, by sea, and from the air.

In accordance with Germany's pledges, already given, as to complete restoration for Belgium, Germany undertakes, in addition to the compensation for damage elsewhere in this part provided for, as a consequence of the violation of the Treaty of 1839, to make reimbursement of all sums which Belgium has borrowed from the Allied and Associated Governments up to November 11, 1918, together with interest at the rate of five per cent per annum on such sums.

Annex I

Compensation may be claimed from Germany under the following categories:

(1) Damage to injured persons and to surviving dependents by personal injury to or death of civilians caused by acts of war.

(2) Damage caused by Germany or her allies to civilian victims of acts of cruely, violence or maltreatment.

(3) As damages caused to the peoples of the Allied and Associated Powers, all pensions and compensation in the nature of pensions to naval and military victims of war, whether mutilated, wounded, sick, or invalided, and to the dependents of such victims.

(6) Allowance by the Governments of the Allied and Associated Powers to the families and dependents of mobilized persons or persons serving with the forces.

Annex IV

6

As an immediate advance on account of the animals referred to in a prior article of this Treaty, Germany undertakes to deliver in equal monthly instalments in the three months following the coming into force of the present Treaty the following quantities of live stock:

(1) To the French Government.

500 stallions (3 to 7 years)

30,000 fillies and mares of the type Ardennais, Boulonnais, or Belgian

2,000 bulls

90,000 milch cows

1,000 rams

100,000 sheep

10,000 goats

PART XII

Ports, Waterways and Railways

Chapter III

Article 331

The following rivers are declared international:

The Elbe, the Oder, the Niemen, the Danube, along with all navigable parts of these river systems which naturally provide more than one state with access to the sea.

PART XIV

Guarantees

Section 1

Article 428

As a guarantee for the execution of the present treaty by Germany, the German territory situated to the west of the Rhine, together with the bridgeheads, will be occupied by Allied and Associated troops for a period of fifteen years from the coming into force of the present treaty.

Covenant of the League of Nations, 1919

The High Contracting Parties

In order to promote international cooperation and to achieve international peace and security

by the acceptance of obligations not to resort to war,

by the prescription of open, just and honorable relations between nations,

by the firm establishment of the understandings of international law as the actual rule of conduct among Governments, and by the maintenance of justice and a scrupulous respect for all treaty obligations in the dealings of organized peoples with one another,

agree to this Covenant of the League of Nations.

Article 2

The action of the League under this Covenant shall be effected through the instrumentality of an Assembly and of a Council, with a permanent Secretariat.

Article 8

1. The members of the League recognize that the maintenance of peace requires the reduction of national armaments to the lowest point consistent with national safety and the enforcement

by common action of international obligations.

2. The Council . . . shall formulate plans for such reduction for the consideration and action of the several Governments. . . .

5. The Members of the League agree that the manufacture by private enterprise of munitions and implements of war is open to grave objections. . . .

6. The Members of the League undertake to interchange full and frank information as to the scale of their armaments . . . and the condition of such of their industries as are adaptable to warlike purposes.

Article 10

The Members of the League undertake to respect and preserve as against external aggression the territorial integrity and existing political independence of all Members of the League. In case of any such aggression or in case of any threat or danger of such aggression the Council shall advise upon the means by which this obligation shall be fulfilled.

The Unsuccessful German Attempt at Republican Government (*The Weimar Constitution,* 1919)

Article 1. The German Reich is a Republic.

Article 25. The Reich President may dissolve the Reichstag, but only once for any one cause. A new election will take place not later than the sixtieth day following the dissolution.

Article 43. The term of office of the Reich President is seven years. He may be legally elected thereafter.

Before the expiration of the term, the Reich President, upon motion of the Reichstag, may be recalled by a popular vote.

Article 48. The Reich President may, in the event that the public order and security are seriously disturbed or endangered, take the measures necessary for their restoration, intervening, if necessary, with the aid of the armed forces. For this purpose he may temporarily abrogate, wholly or in part, the fundamental principles laid down in the *Bill of Rights* of the *Constitution.*

Article 50. All orders and decrees of the Reich President, including those relating to the armed forces, must, in order to be valid, be countersigned by the Reich Chancellor or the competent Reich Minister. Through the countersignature the responsibility is assumed.

Article 54. The Reich Chancellor and the Reich Ministers require the confidence of the Reichstag for the administration of their offices. Each one of them must resign when the Reichstag, by means of an espress resolution, withdraws its confidence.

Article 73. A law of the Reichstag must be submitted to popular referendum before its proclamation, if the Reich President, within one month of its passage, so decides.

Article 109. All Germans are equal before the law. Men and women have the same fundamental civil rights and duties.

Article 165. Statutory bodies representative of workmen and employees are to be created for the protection of their social and economic interests, namely, local workers' councils, district workers' councils, organized so as to correspond with industrial areas, and a National Workers' Council.

The district workers' councils and the National Workers' Council are to join with representatives of employers and other interested sections of the community to form district economic councils and a National Economic Council for the accomplishment of the economic tasks in general and to collaborate in the execution of the socialization laws in particular.

The Statement of Indemnity Presented by the Allies to Germany after the Treaty of Versailles Had Been Accepted (*The German Reparation Bill,* 1921)

The Reparation Commission: To the *Kriegslastenkommission.*

The Reparation Commission has the honour to notify to the German Government, in the enclosed document, the Schedule of Payments prescribing the time and manner for securing and discharging the entire obligation of Germany for Reparation under the Treaty of Versailles.

Article 1

Germany will perform in the manner laid down in this Schedule her obligation to pay the total fixed in accordance with Articles 231, 232, and 233 of the Treaty of Versailles by the Commission, *viz.,* 132 milliards of gold marks less:

(a). The amount already paid on account of Reparation,

(b). Sums which may from time to time be credited to Germany in respect of State properties in ceded territories, and

(c). Any sums received from other enemy or ex-enemy Powers in respect of which the Commission may decide that credit should be given to Germany.

Article 2

Germany shall create and deliver to the Commission the bonds hereafter described.

(a). Bonds for the amount of 12 milliards gold marks.
(b). Bonds for a further amount of 38 milliards gold marks.
(c). Bonds for 82 milliards of gold marks.

Article 4

Germany shall pay in each year until the redemption of the bonds provided for in Article 2;

(1). The sum of 2 milliard gold marks.
(2). A sum equivalent to 25 percent of the value of her exports in each period of twelve months.

Article 5

Germany shall pay within 25 days from this notification one milliard gold marks in gold or approved foreign currencies or approved foreign bills or in drafts at three months on the German Treasury.

Article 8

Germany shall on demand, subject to the prior approval of the Commission, provide such materials and labour as any of the Allied Powers may require towards the restoration of the devastated areas of that Power, or to enable any Allied Power to proceed with the restoration or the development of its industrial or economic life.

The Nine-Power Treaty of Washington (1922)
(United States Statutes at Large)

Article I

The Contracting Powers, other than China, agree:

1. To respect the sovereignty, the independence, and the territorial and administrative integrity of China,

2. To provide the fullest and most unembarrassed opportunity to China to develop and maintain for herself an effective and stable government,

3. To use their influence for the purpose of effectually estab-

lishing and maintaining the principle of equal opportunity for the commerce and industry of all nations throughout the territory of China,

4. To refrain from taking advantage of conditions in China in order to seek special rights or privileges which would abridge the rights of subjects or citizens of friendly States, and from countenancing action inimical to the security of such States.

Article II

The Contracting Powers, the Governments of Great Britain, France, the United States, Japan, Italy, Portugal, Belgium, the Netherlands, and China, agree not to enter into any treaty, agreement, arrangement, or understanding, either with one another, or, individually or collectively, with any Power or Powers, which would infringe or impair the principles stated in Article I.

Article III

With a view to applying more effectually the principles of the Open Door or equality of opportunity in China for the trade and industry of all nations, the Contracting Powers, other than China, agree that they will not seek nor support their respective nationals in seeking:

1. Any arrangement which might purport to establish in favour of their interests any general superiority of rights with respect to commercial or economic development in any designated region of China;

2. Any such monopoly or preference as would deprive the nationals of any other Power of the right of undertaking any legitimate trade or industry in China, or of participating with the Chinese Government, or with any local authority, in any category of public enterprise, or which by reason of its scope, duration, or geographical extent is calculated to frustrate the practical application of the principle of equal opportunity.

It is understood that the foregoing stipulations of this Article are not to be so construed as to prohibit the acquisition of such properties or rights as may be necessary to the conduct of a particular commercial, industrial, or financial undertaking or to the encouragement of invention and research.

China undertakes to be guided by the principles stated in the foregoing stipulations of this Article in dealing with applications for economic rights and privileges from Governments and nationals of all foreign countries whether parties to the present Treaty or not.

Article IV

The Contracting Powers agree not to support any agreements by their respective nationals with each other designed to create spheres of influence or to provide for the enjoyment of mutually exclusive opportunities in designated parts of Chinese territory.

Article V

China agrees that, throughout the whole of the railways in China, she will not exercise or permit unfair discrimination of any kind.

The Contracting Powers, other than China, assume a corresponding obligation in respect of any of the aforesaid railways over which they or their nationals are in a position to exercise any control in virtue of any concession, special agreement or otherwise.

Article VI

The Contracting Powers, other than China, agree fully to respect China's rights as a neutral in time of war to which China is not a party; and China declares that when she is a neutral she will observe the obligations of neutrality.

Article VII

The Contracting Powers agree that, whenever a situation arises which in the opinion of any one of them involves the application of the stipulations of the present Treaty, and renders desirable discussion of such application, there shall be full and frank communication between the Contracting Powers concerned.

Article VIII

Powers not signatory to the present Treaty shall be invited to adhere to the present Treaty.

The Final Protocol of the Locarno Conference (League of Nations, *Treaty Series,* 1926)

The representatives of the German, Belgian, British, French, Italian, Polish, and Czechoslovak Governments, who have met at Locarno from the 5th to 16th October, 1925, in order to seek by common agreement means for preserving their respective nations from the scourge of war and for providing for the peaceful settlement of disputes of every nature which might eventually arise between them, have given their approval to the drafts, treaties, and conventions which respectively effect them and which, framed in the course of the present conference, are mutually interdependent:

Treaty between Germany, Belgium, France, Great Britain and Italy.

Arbitration Convention between Germany and Belgium.

Arbitration Convention between Germany and France.

Arbitration Treaty between Germany and Poland.

Arbitration Treaty between Germany and Czechoslovakia.

Annex A: Treaty of Mutual Guarantee between Germany, Belgium, France, Great Britain, and Italy:

Article 1

The high contracting parties collectively and severally guarantee, in the manner provided in the following articles, the maintenance of the territorial *status quo* resulting from the frontiers between Germany and Belgium and between Germany and France and the inviolability of the said frontiers as fixed by or in pursuance of the Treaty of Peace signed at Versailles on the 28th June, 1919, and also the observance of the stipulations of articles 42 and 43 of the said treaty concerning the demilitarized zone.

Article 2

Germany and Belgium, and also Germany and France, mutually undertake that they will in no case attack or invade each other or resort to war against each other.

This stipulation shall not, however, apply in the case of:

1. The exercise of the right of legitimate defense.
2. Action pursuant to Article 16 of the Covenant of the League of Nations.

3. Action as the result of a decision taken by the Assembly or by the Council of the League of Nations or in pursuance of Article 15, paragraph 7, of the Covenant of the League of Nations, provided that in this last event the action is directed against a State which was the first to attack.

Article 3

In view of the undertakings entered into in Article 2 of the present Treaty, Germany and Belgium and Germany and France undertake to settle by peaceful means and in the manner laid down herein all questions of every kind by the normal methods of diplomacy.

Article 4

1. If one of the high contracting parties alleges that a violation of Article 2 of the present Treaty or a breach of Articles 42 or 43 of the Treaty of Versailles has been or is being committed, it shall bring the question at once before the Council of the League of Nations.

2. As soon as the Council of the League of Nations is satisfied that such violation or breach has been committed, it will notify its finding without delay to the Powers signatory of the present Treaty, who severally agree that in such case they will each of them come immediately to the assistance of the Power against whom the act complained of is directed.

3. In case of a flagrant violation of Article 2 of the present Treaty or of a flagrant breach of Articles 42 or 43 of the Treaty of Versailles by one of the high contracting parties, each of the other contracting parties hereby undertakes immediately to come to the help of the party against whom such a violation or breach has been directed as soon as the said Power has been able to satisfy itself that this violation constitutes an unprovoked act of aggression and that by reason either of the crossing of the frontier or of the outbreak of hostilities or of the assembly of armed forces in the demilitarized zone immediate action is necessary. Nevertheless, the Council of the League of Nations, which will be seized of the question in accordance with the first paragraph of this article, will issue its findings, and the high contracting parties undertake to act in accordance with the recommendations of the Council provided that they are concurred in by all the members other than the representatives

of the parties which have engaged in hostilities.

The Pact of Paris
(*United States Treaty Series,* 1928)

The President of the German Reich, the President of the United States of America, His Majesty the King of the Belgians, the President of the French Republic, His Majesty the King of Great Britain, Ireland, and the British Dominions beyond the Seas, Emperor of India, His Majesty the King of Italy, His Majesty the Emperor of Japan, the President of the Republic of Poland, the President of the Czechoslovak Republic,

Persuaded that the time has come when a frank renunciation of war as an instrument of national policy should be made to the end that the peaceful and friendly relations now existing between the peoples may be perpetuated;

Convinced that all changes in their relations with one another should be sought only by pacific means and be the result of a peaceful and orderly process, and that any signatory Power which shall hereafter seek to promote its national interests by resort to war should be denied the benefits furnished by this Treaty;

Hopeful that, encouraged by their example, all the other nations of the world will join in this humane endeavor and by adhering to the present Treaty as soon as it comes into force bring their people within the scope of its beneficent provisions, thus uniting the civilized nations of the world in a common renunciation of war as an instrument of their national policy;

Have decided to conclude a Treaty for that purpose.

Article 1

The High Contracting Parties solemnly declare in the names of their respective peoples that they condemn recourse to war for the solution of international controversies, and renounce it as an instrument of national policy in their relations with one another.

Article 2

The High Contracting Parties agree that the settlement or solution of all disputes or conflicts of whatever nature or of whatever origin they may be, which may arise among them, shall never be sought except by pacific means.

Benito Mussolini on Fascism
(Benito Mussolini, *Fascism,* 1922)*

Fascism was not the nursling of a doctrine worked out beforehand with detailed elaboration. It was born of the need for action and from the beginning it was practical rather than theoretical. It was not just another political party, but even in the first two years it was a living movement in opposition to all political parties as such.

Fascism repudiates the doctrine of Pacifism—born of a renunciation of struggle and an act of cowardice in the face of sacrifice. War alone brings up to its highest tension all human energy and puts the stamp of nobility upon the peoples who have the courage to meet it.

This anti-pacifist spirit is carried by Fascism into the life of the individual. The proud motto of the *Squadrista,* "Me ne frego" (never mind), written on the bandage of a wound, is an act of philosophy not only stoic, the summary of a doctrine not only political—it is the education to combat, the acceptance of the risks which combat implies, and a new way of life for Italy. Thus the fascist conceives of life as duty and struggle and conquest, life which should be high and full, lived for oneself, but above all for others—those who are near and those who are far distant, those of the present and those who will come after.

Such a conception of life makes Fascism the complete opposite of that basic doctrine of so-called scientific and Marxian Socialism, the materialistic conception of history. Fascism now and always believes in actions inspired by religious and patriotic motives, that is to say, above all, Fascism denies that class-war can be the preponderant force in the transformation of society.

Fascism also combats the whole complex system of democratic ideology and repudiates its practical application. Fascism denies that the majority, by the simple fact that it is a majority, can direct human society. Fascism denies, in democracy, the absurd conventional untruth of political equality dressed out in the garb of collective irresponsibility and the myth of "happiness" and indefinite progress. But, if democracy may be conceived in

* From: Article by Benito Mussolini in the *Enciclopedia Italiana,* 1932. Authorized English translation printed in *International Conciliation,* No. 306, January, 1935. Used with the permission of the Carnegie Endowment for International Peace.

diverse forms—that is to say, taking democracy to mean a state of society in which the populace are not reduced to impotence in the State—Fascism may write itself down as "an organized, centralized, and authoritative democracy."

But the Fascist negation of Socialism and Liberal Democracy must not be taken to mean that Fascism desires to lead the world back to the state of affairs before 1789. A party which governs a nation is a fact entirely new to history.

The foundation of Fascism is the conception of the State. The Fascist State is self-conscious, it has a will and a personality —and it may therefore be called the "ethical" state. The individual in the Fascist State is not annulled but rather multiplied, just as a soldier in a regiment is not diminished but rather increased by the number of his fellow soldiers. The Fascist State organized the nation, but leaves a goodly margin of freedom to the individual citizen. The latter is deprived of all surplus and perhaps harmful liberties but retains that which is essential. The deciding power in this distribution of rights cannot be the individual, but the State alone.

The Fascist State is not indifferent to the fact of religion in general, or to that particular and positive faith, Italian Catholicism. The State professes no theology, but only a morality.

The Fascist State is an embodied will to power and government. Here the Roman tradition is an ideal of force in action. For Fascism, the growth of empire, that is to say the expansion of the nation, is an essential manifestation of vitality and its opposite a sign of decadence. Fascism is the doctrine best adapted to represent the tendencies and aspirations of a people, like the people of Italy, who are rising again after many centuries of abasement and foreign servitude.

The Twenty-Two Syndicates and Their Councils as Established in Fascist Italy by Benito Mussolini in 1934
(Italian Ministry of Justice, *Decree Concerning Producers Corporations; Relative to Structure,* 1934)

The *Duce* brought into order and being, on May 29, 1934, with the Eight Decrees, eight Corporations, i.e., the Corporations of Cereals, of Fruit and Vegetables, of Wine and Beverages, of Edible Oils, of Sugar Beets and Sugar, of Livestock and Fishes, of Lumber, and of Textiles.

The *Duce* brought into order and being, on June 9, 1934,

with the Eight Decrees, eight Corporations embracing industry and commerce, i.e., the Corporations of Metals and Engineering, of Building Construction, of Clothing Trades, of Glassware and Pottery, of Chemical Trades, of Paper and Printing, of Mining, and of Water, Gas, and Electric power.

The *Duce* brought into order and being, on June 23, 1934, with Six Decrees, six Corporations covering services, i.e., the Corporations of Arts and Professions, representing the four parts; legal, medical, and technical professions and the arts, of Internal Communications, representing rail and tramways and inland navigation, motor transport, telephone, radio, and cable, of Sea and Air Transport, of Hospitality, representing restaurants, hotels, and travel, of Credit and Insurance, and of Amusements.

Each is decreed to have its own Council according to the following example;

Corporation of Cereals. This Council shall consist of a President and 36 representatives;

3 representatives of the National Fascist Party,

7 employers and 7 workers representing cereal growers,

1 employer and 1 worker representing the threshing industry,

3 employers and 3 workers representing milling of grain edibles,

1 employer and 1 worker representing the baking industries,

3 employers and 3 workers representing trade and cereal commerce,

1 representative of cooperative societies of consumers of cereals,

1 representative of agricultural experts,

1 representative of small industries,

The total number of employers includes 3 representatives of persons managing agricultural, industrial and commercial concerns.

The League of Nations Declaration of Italy to be an Aggressor against Ethiopia
(League of Nations, *Report of the Council Committee,* Oct. 7, 1935)

1. At its meeting on October 5, the Council, after hearing the statements of the representatives of Italy and Ethiopia and taking cognizance of the grave facts laid before it, set up a Committee of the Council "to study the situation and report to the

Council so as to enable it to take decisions with full knowledge of the matters involved."

2. In order to study this situation, brought about by events subsequent to October 2, it was the Committee's duty to specify these events and to determine their character in relation to the obligations of the Covenant.

The Committee accordingly considered whether there had been a resort to war in disregard to Articles 12, 13, or 15 of the Covenant.

After an examination of the facts stated above, the Committee have come to the conclusion that the Italian Government has resorted to war in disregard of its covenants under Article 12 of the Covenant of the League of Nations.

The President—"In the name of the members of the Council, I am obliged to repeat the declaration which I made from the chair at the private meeting. It is as Follows: The report of the Committee which is before the Council describes the facts from official sources and draws attention to the provisions of the Covenant.

Today, October 7, five days after the opening of hostilities, the establishment of the existence of a state of war, in relation to the obligations of the Covenant, compels the members of the Council to face their responsibilities. This obligation does not in any way prejudice the rights of the parties to make known their observations subsequently at another meeting of the Council. However anxious the members of the Council may be courteously to take account of the convenience of one of their colleagues, they cannot allow that anxiety to take precedence over a primary duty.

I take note of the protest made by the representative of Italy, and, in the name of the Council, I declare, as its president and as its moderator, and with, therefore, the unanimous consent of my colleagues other than the parties—that the members of the Council will be called upon at today's meeting to state their views as to the conclusions of the Council Committee, and that the Council will hear the Representative of Italy, should he so desire, at another meeting.

We will proceed by roll call to the consultation of the members of the Council and of the two parties.

I will begin by consulting the members of the Council other than the parties."

(The members of the Council other than the parties involved, consulted by roll call, declared themselves in agreement with the conclusions of the report.)

The President—"I will now consult the parties."

Baron Aloisi of Italy—"While making every reservation as to the procedure which is now being followed, I state, for all useful purposes, that I do not approve of the conclusions of the report. I also reserve my right to submit, at a later meeting, any observations I may have to offer on the document before us."

M. Tecle-Hawariate of Ethiopia—"I accept the report."

The President—"I take note that fourteen members of the League of Nations represented on the Council consider that we are in the presence of a war begun in disregard of the obligations of Article 12 of the Covenant.

Accordingly, the report of the Council Committee and the minutes of the present meeting will be sent to all the members of the League of Nations.

The Council has now to assume its duty of co-ordination in regard to the measures to be taken."

Prime Minister Neville Chamberlain Argues for Appeasement of the Axis Powers
(Neville Chamberlain, *Address to Commons,* 1938)

On a former occasion I described British foreign policy as being based upon three principles—first upon the protection of British interests, secondly on the maintenance of peace, and, as far as we can influence it, the settlement of differences by peaceful means and not by force, and thirdly the promotion of friendly relations with other nations who are willing to reciprocate our friendly feelings and who will keep those rules of international conduct without which there can be neither security nor stability.

If we truly desire peace it is necessary to make a sustained effort to ascertain, and if possible to remove the causes which threaten peace. We are now engaged upon a gigantic scheme of rearmament. Indeed, we are the last of the nations to rearm; but this process of general rearmament has been forced upon us all, because every country is afraid to disarm lest it should fall a victim of some armed neighbor. I recognize the force of that hard fact, but have never publicly ceased to deplore what seems to me a senseless waste of money. I cannot believe that, with a little good will and determination, it is not possible to remove genuine grievances and to clear away suspicions which may be entirely unfounded.

For these reasons, then, my colleagues and I have been anxious to find some opportunity of entering upon conversations with the two European countries with which we have been at variance, namely Germany and Italy, in order that we might find out whether there was any common ground on which we might build up a general scheme of appeasement in Europe. The peace of Europe must depend upon the attitude of the four major powers, Germany, Italy, France, and ourselves. For ourselves, we are linked to France by common ideals of democracy, of liberty, and Parliamentary government. On the other side we find Italy and Germany linked by affinity of outlook and in the forms of their government. The question that we have to think of is this: Are we to allow these two pairs of nations to go on glowering at one another across the frontier, allowing the feeling between the two sides to become more and more embittered, until at last the barriers are broken down and the conflict begins which many think would mark the end of civilization? Or can we bring them to an understanding of one another's aims and objects, and to such discussion as may lead to a final settlement? If we can do that, if we can bring these four nations into friendly discussion, into settling their differences, we shall have saved the peace of Europe for a generation.

Adolph Hitler on National Socialism (Adolph Hitler, *Works,* 1923-42)*

In that we deny the principle of parliamentary democracy we strike the strongest blow for the right of the nation to the self-determination of its own life. For in the parliamentary system we see no genuine expression of the nation's will—a will which cannot logically be anything else than a will to the maintenance of the nation—but we do see a distortion, if not a perversion, of that will. The will of a nation to the self-determination of its being manifests itself most clearly and is of most use when its most capable minds are brought forth. They form the representative leaders of a nation, they alone can be the pride of a nation—certainly never the parliamentary politician who is the product of the ballot box and thinks only in terms of votes. The constructive development of the future leadership of the

* Selections from *Hitler's Works,* edited by Gordon W. Prange (American Council of Public Affairs, Washington), 1944, pp. 34, *passim*. (Used with the permission of the Public Affairs Press.)

nation through its most able men will take years; the intelligent education of the German people will take decades (Nuremberg, Sept. 1, 1933; *Voelkischer Beobachter,* Sept. 2, 1933).

Internationalism is weakness in the life of nations. What is there that is born of internationalism? Nothing. The real values of human culture were not born of internationalism, but they were created by the whole heritage and tradition of the people (das Volkstum). When peoples no longer possess creative power they become international. Wherever there is weakness in regard :o spiritual matters in the life of nations, internationalism makes ts appearance. It is no coincidence that a people, namely, the Jews, which does not have any real creative power and talent is :he carrier of this internationalism. It is the people with the east creative power and talent. It dominates only in the field of :rooked and speculative economy.

The Jew, as a race, has a remarkable instinct for self-preservation, but as an individual he has no cultural abilities at all. He is the demon of the disintegration of nations—the symbol of :ontinual destruction of peoples. If the first of May, therefore, s to have any meaning in the life of peoples, it can be only a glorification of the national, creative idea as against the international idea of decay (Munich, May 1, 1933; *Voelkischer Beobachter,* May 3, 1933).

I do not even want to speak of the Jews. They are simply our old enemies, their plans have suffered shipwreck through us, and hey rightly hate us, just as we hate them. We realize that this var can only end either in the wiping out of the Germanic naions, or by the disappearance of Jewry from Europe. On Sepember 3rd, I spoke in the Reichstag—and I dislike premature prophecies—and I said that this war would not end the way the ews imagine, that is, in the extinction of the European Aryan ıations, but that the result of this war would be the destruction of Jewry. For the first time, it will not be the others who will bleed to death, but for the first time the genuine ancient Jewish aw, "an eye for an eye, a tooth for a tooth," is being applied. The more this struggle spreads, the more anti-Semitism will pread—and world Jewry may rely on this. It will find nourishnent in every family which is being enlightened as to why it is being called upon to make such sacrifices, and the hour will come vhen the worst enemy of the world, of all time, will have finished is part for at least one thousand years to come. (Berlin, Jan. 0, 1942).

For fourteen or fifteen years I have continuously proclaimed to the German nation that I regard it as my task before posterity to destroy Marxism, and that it is no empty phrase but a solemn oath which I shall follow as long as I live. I have made this confession of faith the confession of faith of a single man, that of a mighty organization. I know now that even if fate were to remove me, the fight would be fought to the end; this movement is the guarantee for that. This for us is not a fight which can be finished by compromise. We see in Marxism the enemy of our people which we will root out and destroy without mercy.

We must then fight to the very end those tendencies which have eaten into the soul of the German nation in the last seventeen years, which have done us such incalculable damage and which, if they had not been vanquished, would have destroyed Germany. Bismarck told us that liberalism was the pace-maker of Social Democracy. I need not say here that Social Democracy is the pace-maker of Communism. And communism is the forerunner of death, of national destruction, and extinction. We have joined battle with it and will fight it to the death (Berlin, May 10, 1933).

We are enemies of cowardly pacifism because we recognize that according to the laws of nature, struggle is the father of all things. We are enemies of democracy because we recognize that an individual genius represents at all times the best in his people and that he should be the leader. Numbers can never direct the destiny of a people. Only genius can do this. We are the deadly enemies of internationalism because nature teaches us that the purity of race and the authority of the leader alone are able to lead a nation to victory (Kulmbach, Feb. 5, 1928; *Voelkischer Beobachter,* Feb. 9, 1928).

(Today) I stand for exactly the same principles that I stood for already a year ago. We are convinced that a final showdown will come in this fight against Marxism. We are convinced that it must come, for two *Weltanschauungen* are fighting each other and there can be only one outcome! One will be destroyed and the other will win. It is the great mission of the National Socialist Movement, to give this epoch a new faith and to see to it that millions will swear by this faith, so that, when some day the hour for the showdown comes, the German people will not meet the Jewish international murderers completely unarmed (Munich May 23, 1926; *Voelkischer Boebachter,* May 26, 1926).

Geopolitics and Lebensraum
(U. S. Department of State, *Bulletin,* 1945)

The Men of Munich—those who specialized in geopolitics—have defined the subject as follows: "Geopolitics is the science of the earth's relationship to political developments. It is based on the broad foundations of geography, especially political geography, which is the science of political organisms in space and their structure. It guides practical politics to that point where it must take the step into the unknown. Geopolitics will and must become the geographical conscience of the state." Dr. Karl Haushofer has asserted that the word Politik is not preceded by the prefix geo by accident. The prefix relates to the soil.

Geopolitical concepts in Germany centered around a number of subjects. The ideas of the organic state, living space or *Lebensraum,* and the organic frontier have received considerable attention in German literature. One definition asserted that geopolitics was the scientific basis of the art of political action in the conflict of state organisms for *Lebensraum.* The political power of the state has been analyzed by the Men of Munich. One definition claimed that geopolitics was really the doctrine of the power of the state on earth. A very important idea back of the political power of the state was its location with reference to a specific concept of the distribution of land masses and ocean spaces. In accordance with relative power, a state was classified as renovating or decadent. The expression of the state in wartime involved the study of *Wehr-Geopolitik* or war geopolitics. The German geopoliticians have used the studies of an American admiral, Alfred T. Mahan, as basic source material on sea power. A Prussian general, Karl von Clausewitz, an authority on land power, inspired subsequent students of military affairs. Dr. Haushofer has quoted the definition of war given by Clausewitz, namely, that war is a continuation of policy with other means. No writer on air power assumed the stature of either Mahan or Clausewitz with the Men of Munich.

The Policy and the Application of Genocide in Nazi Germany (Testimony of A. Hoess, Commandant of the Prison Camp at Auschwitz, Germany from 1940 to 1943, before the War Crimes Trial Court at Nuremburg, 1945)*

"We had two SS doctors on duty at Auschwitz to examine the

* Office of United States Chief of Counsel for Prosecution of Axis Criminality, *Nazi Conspiracy and Aggression* (Washington, 1947).

incoming transports of prisoners. The prisoners would be marched by one of the doctors who would make spot decisions as they walked by. Those who were fit for work were sent into the camp. Others were sent immediately to the extermination plants. Children of tender years were invariably exterminated since by reason of their youth they were unable to work. Still another improvement we made over Treblinka was that at that camp the victims almost always knew they were to be exterminated and at Auschwitz we endeavored to fool the victims into thinking that they were to go through a delousing process. Of course, frequently they realized our true intentions and we sometimes had riots and difficulties due to this fact. Very frequently women would hide their children under their clothes, but of course when we found them we would send the children in to be exterminated.

It took from 3 to 15 minutes to kill the people in the death chamber, depending upon climatic conditions. We knew when the people were dead because their screaming stopped. We usually waited about one-half hour before we opened the doors and removed the bodies. After the bodies were removed our special commandos took off the rings and knocked the gold from the teeth of the corpses.

(The testimony of Herman Graebe before the court, 1945)

Then we heard shots in quick succession from behind one of the earth mounds. The people who had got off the trucks, men, women, and children of all ages, had to undress upon the orders of an SS man, who carried a riding or dog whip. Without screaming or crying, these people undressed, stood around by families, kissing each other, said farewells, and waited for the command of another SS man, who stood near the excavation, also with a whip in his hand. At that moment the SS man at the excavation called something to his comrade. The latter counted off about 20 persons, and instructed them to walk behind the earth mound. I walked around the mound and stood in front of a tremendous grave; closely pressed together, the people were lying on top of each other so that only their heads were visible. The excavation was already two-thirds full; from the far side of the grave an SS man with a machine gun took aim and shot bullets into the backs of the exposed heads. Occasionally one, not dead, would signal by moving his head or hands so as not to be left to be covered alive. I estimated the grave contained about a thousand people.

Now already the next group approached, descended into the excavation, lined themselves up against the previous victims and were shot.

UNIT 13

The Second World War and After

In a sense the second World War was a continuation of World War I. It developed essentially from the same underlying causes, some of which had been intensified by the shortcomings of the peace settlement of 1919. True, the opposing alliances of states in the two wars were not identical, but the changes are quite explainable in view of shifting national ambitions and alterations in world power structures between 1914 and 1939. Unlike the first world war, World War II, however, did not begin through a relatively insignificant event. Its immediate forerunner was a crescendo of international crises beginning in 1938 with Germany's absorption of the Czechoslovakian Sudetenland, and rising to a climax in 1939 with her invasion of Poland, the acton which set off the war. Each of the incidents in this series added to the growing conviction of Great Britain and France that there could be no appeasement of German ambtions. Russia declined to join the British and French in a formal alliance to check the growing German threat and instead entered into a five-year non-agression pact with the German government which enabled Germany to accept the challenge of the Franco-British alliance.

Following the rapid defeat of Poland by Germany in 1939, the war for a year produced so little action that some observers called it a "phony war." Then, early in 1940, Germany launched an offensive of such force and speed that in a few weeks Denmark, Norway, Belgium, and the Netherlands were occupied by her troops, and France, her army crushed, agreed on June 17 to a truce by which about half of her country would be in German hands. During the next year Great Britain was subjected to mass aerial raids on an unprecedented scale, and the war spread to other parts of Europe. Italy and the Balkan nations, through political attachment or by conquest, were allied with the German side. Russia, invaded by Germany in June, 1941, became a partner of Great Britain. The French people, along with those of other nations occupied by the German military maintained at least a nominal resistance through "governments in exile" maintained in England. The war reached global proportions with the involvement of Japan, which had been waging war on China since 1937, and the United States on December 7, 1941.

The United States had emerged from the first World War unquestionably the richest and most powerful nation on the earth. During the 1920's the giant democracy of the New World, her idealism dimmed by disillusionment, had attempted to divest herself of active interest in world politics, preferring to play a spectator's and preceptor's role. But her very wealth and power made it impossible to remain wholly aloof. The rapid rise of aggressive National Socialism in Germany and imperialism in Japan caused a revulsion of feeling among the American people; and when hostilities broke out in Europe there was no talk by the president of neutrality in thought, as there had been in 1914.. Already alarmed by the course of events in eastern Asia, the government of the United States was ready to extend the meaning of neutrality to the utmost limit when the war in Europe took a disastrous turn for the western nations. Its economy was placed at their disposal. At the same time it tightened its attitude toward Japan. Finally in December, 1941, Japan, already allied with Germany and Italy, in the Berlin-Rome-Tokyo axis, launched an aerial attack on the American naval base at Pearl Harbor. When the United States declared war on Japan, Japan's allies declared war on the United States.

The vast geographical scope of the conflict and the use of air power to annihilate cities remote from the line of battle involved civilian populations in the war on an unprecedented scale. These conditions, together with the inhuman practice of genocide and the brutal treatment of populations in many German and Japanese occupied areas, caused thoughtful men to wonder if the Western Civilization that had been so laboriously nurtured and built up since the days of ancient Greece was about to be destroyed. Their fears seemed to be on the verge of realization when the terribly destructive power of atomic fission was applied as a weapon of war.

As the war progressed and as the preponderant strength of the anti-axis nations became fully mobilized, the defeat of the axis powers seemed to be inevitable. The nature of the peace settlement, and the character of the post-war world, began to occupy much of the attention of the allied governments. In a series of unprecedented "summit" conferences, their heads of state worked out the strategy of the war and conditions of the peace. Many problems, however, remained to be solved when hostilities came to an end. While the greatest of these undoubtedly was to create some kind of international control of atomic power, most of them involved territorial settlement and the ambition of Russia to displace the United States as the leading power of the world. So intense were these problems and the hostilities they engendered that the new age of peace might aptly be called the era of the cold war.

The rivalry of the United States and Russia was complicated by rapid and revolutionary political and economic changes during the post-war years. The countries of eastern and central Europe, occupied by the Russian armies at the end of the war, perforce adopted communism and became "satellites" of the Soviet Union. Communism gained strength in other parts of the world also through internal revolution. The most important country to assume a communist government was China, which began to forge ahead under the new regime as a world power and as a source of strength for the world communist movement. In many of the countries that did not have revolutions, economic problems, intensified by the war, caused political instability and constitutional change. Finally, the remaining European colonial empires in Asia and Africa began to disintegrate, and new nations appeared on the map in considerable number.

The strategy of the cold war seemed to be aimed on the one side at making the whole world communist and on the other at destroying communism as a world movement. but actually the national ambitions of the leading powers, both communist and non-communist, have been more influential motives. The tactics of the war involve the maintaining of almost constant international tension through "incidents," hidden intrigue and subversion, economic aid by the wealthier to the poorer nations, propaganda, and scientific rivalry. On occasion the conflict broadened into local military action, but the leading powers showed considerable reluctance to risk a situation that might lead to the use of atomic weapons. The potential for the complete physical destruction of civilization became a horrifying reality after the 1950's when man became able to launch earth-girdling rockets capable of carrying atomic warheads of city-destroying force.

The principal hope of the nations of the world to avert a catastrophic war rested in the United Nations organization which had displaced the League of Nations. Profiting by the experience of the League, the United Nations took a more active role in world affairs. Its existence, however, did not prevent the formation of military alliances among the rival groups of states. The western non-communist nations, for example, formed the North Atlantic Treaty Organization, while the Russian "satellites" banded together in the Warsaw Pact. Although the most striking effect of the cold war has been the formation of rival groups of powers, not all of the states of the world have chosen to take sides officially. Some like India, elected to follow the path of "neutralism."

Treaty of Nonaggression Between the German Reich and the Union of Soviet Socialist Republics, August 23, 1939 (U.S. Department of State, *Bulletin*)

The Governments of the German Reich and the Union of Soviet Socialist Republics, directed by the wish to strengthen the cause of peace between Germany and the Union of Soviet Socialist Republics and proceeding upon the basic provisions of the treaty of neutrality concluded between Germany and the Union of Soviet Socialist Republics in April, 1926, have reached the following agreement:

The two contracting parties undertake to refrain from any sort of violence, any aggressive action, or any attack against one another whether individually or jointly with other powers.

In case one of the contracting parties should become the object of warlike acts on the part of a third power the other contracting party will not support that third power in any form.

The governments of the two contracting parties will in the future remain in contact with each other through continuous consultations in order to inform each other concerning questions affecting their mutual interests.

Neither of the two contracting parties will participate in any grouping of powers which is indirectly or directly aimed against the other party.

Should disputes or conflicts arise between the contracting parties regarding questions of any kind whatsoever, the two parties would clear away these disputes or conflicts solely by means of friendly exchanges of views or if necessary, by arbitration commissions.

The present treaty is concluded for a period of ten years with the provision that unless one of the contracting parties denounces it one year before the end of this period the duration of the validity of this treaty is to be regarded as automatically prolonged for another five years.

The present treaty is to be ratified within the shortest possible time. The documents of ratification are to be exchanged in Berlin. The treaty becomes effective immediately upon signature.

Ribbentrop
Molotov

Address by the President of the United States on September 3, 1939 Relative to the Situation in Europe (Franklin Roosevelt, *Public Address*)

Tonight my single duty is to speak to the whole of America.

Until 4:30 this morning I had hoped against hope that some miracle would prevent a devastating war in Europe and bring an end to the invasion of Poland by Germany.

For four years a succession of actual wars and constant crises have shaken the entire world and have threatened in each case to bring on the gigantic conflict which is today unhappily a fact.

I myself cannot and do not prophesy the course of events abroad—and the reason is that because I have of necessity such a complete picture of what is going on in every part of the world, I do not dare to do so.

Nor can I prophesy the immediate economic effect of this war on our Nation, but I do say that no American has the moral right to profiteer at the expense either of his fellow citizens or of the men, women, and children who are living and dying in the midst of war in Europe.

We have certain ideas and ideals of national safety, and we must act to preserve that safety today and to preserve the safety of our children in future years.

That safety is and will be bound up with the safety of the Western Hemisphere and of the seas adjacent thereto. We seek to keep war from our firesides by keeping war from coming to the Americas. For that we have historic precedent that goes back to the days of the administration of President George Washington. It is serious enough and tragic enough to every American family in every state in the Union to live in a world that is torn by wars on other continents. Today they affect every American home.

It is our national duty to use every effort to keep them out of the Americas.

And at this time let me make the simple plea that partisanship and selfishness be adjourned, and that national unity be the thought that underlies all others.

This Nation will remain neutral, but I cannot ask that every American remain neutral in thought as well. Even a neutral has a right to take account of facts. Even a neutral cannot be asked to close his mind or his conscience.

I have said not once but many times that I have seen war and that I hate war. I say that again and again.

I hope the United States will keep out of this war. I believe that it will. And I give you my assurances that every effort of your government will be directed toward that end.

As long as it remains within my power to prevent, there will be no blackout of peace in the United States.

The Appeal for Material Aid against Germany by the French Premier, Paul Reynaud, to the President of the United States, June 10, 1940 (United States Department of State, *Bulletin*)

MR. PRESIDENT: I wish first to express to you my gratitude for the generous aid that you have decided to give us in aviation and armament.

For six days and six nights our divisions have been fighting without one hour of rest against an army which has a crushing superiority in numbers and material. Today the enemy is almost at the gates of Paris.

We shall fight in front of Paris; we shall fight behind Paris; we shall close ourselves in one of our provinces to fight and if we should be driven out of it we shall establish ourselves in North Africa to continue the fight and if necessary in our American possessions.

A portion of the government has already left Paris. I am making ready to leave for the front. That will be to intensify the struggle with all the forces which we still have and not to abandon the struggle.

May I ask you, Mr. President, to explain all this yourself to your people to all the citizens of the United States saying to them that we are determined to sacrifice ourselves in the struggle that we are carrying on for all free men.

This very hour another dictatorship has stabbed France in the back. Another frontier is threatened. A naval war will begin.

You have replied generously to the appeal which I made to you a few days ago across the Atlantic. Today this 10th of June, 1940 it is my duty to ask you for new and even larger assistance.

At the same time that you explain this situation to the men and women of America, I beseech you to declare publicly that the United States will give the Allies aid and material support by all means "short of an expeditionary force." I beseech you to do this before it is too late. I know the gravity of such a gesture. Its very gravity demands that it should not be made too late.

You said to us yourself on the 5th of October, 1937: "I am compelled and you are compelled to look ahead. The peace, the freedom and the security of 90% of the population of the world is being jeopardized by the remaining 10% who are threatening a breakdown of all international order and law.

"Surely the 90% who want to live in peace and under law and in accordance with moral standards that have received almost trusty acceptance through the centuries, can and must find some way to make their will prevail."

Mr. President, *the hour has now come for these.*

"Their Finest Hour," Prime Minister Winston Churchill's Address to the House of Commons, June 18, 1940 (Great Britain, *Parliamentary Debates, House of Commons*)

What General Weygand called the "Battle of France" is over. I expect that the battle of Britain is about to begin. Upon this battle depends the survival of Christian civilization. Upon it depends our own British life and the long continuity of our institutions and our Empire. The whole fury and might of the enemy must very soon be turned on us. Hitler knows that he will have to break us in this island or lose the war. If we can stand up to him, all Europe may be free and the life of the world may move forward into broad, sunlit uplands; but if we fail, then the whole world, including the United States, and all that we have known and cared for, will sink into the abyss of a new dark age made more sinister, and perhaps more prolonged, by the lights of a perverted science. Let us therefore brace ourselves to our duty and so bear ourselves that if the British Commonwealth and Empire lasts for a thousand years, men will still say, "This was their finest hour."

Prime Minister Winston Churchill's Address to the House of Commons Relative to the Defeat of France, June 25, 1941
(Great Britain, *Parliamentary Debates, House of Commons*)

Because it was clear that the defeat and subjection of France was imminent and her fine army, on which so many hopes were set, was reeling under the German flail, M. Reynaud, the courageous Prime Minister of France, asked me to meet him at Tours, which I did on June 13, accompanied by the Foreign Secretary.

M. Reynaud, after dwelling on conditions at the Front and the state of the French Army, asked me whether Great Britain would release France from her obligation not to negotiate for an armistice or peace without the consent of her British ally.

Although I knew how great the French sufferings were and that we had not, so far, endured equal trials or made an equal contribution, I felt bound to say that I could not give assent. But there would be no use in adding mutual reproaches to other things we might have to bear.

We agreed that a further appeal should be made by M. Reynaud to the United States and that if the reply was not sufficient to enable Reynaud to go on with the fight, then we should meet again and take a decision in the light of the new facts.

On the 16th I received a message from M. Renaud, who had then moved to Bordeaux, to say that the American response had not been satisfactory and requesting a formal release for France from her obligations under the Anglo-French agreement.

The Cabinet was immediately convened and we sent a message, of which I shall not give the exact terms but the general substance. Negotiations for a separate armistice or peace were dependent upon an agreement made with the French Republic and not with any particular French administration or statesman. They, therefore, involved the honor of France.

However, in view of what France had suffered, it was nevertheless intimated that, provided the French fleet be dispatched to British ports to remain there while negotiations were being conducted, His Majesty's Government would give consent to the French Government asking what terms of armistice would be opened to them.

It was also made clear that His Majesty's Government were resolved to continue the war and altogether cut themselves out of any association with any inquiry about an armistice.

On the same evening I was preparing to go see M. Reynaud

and was, in fact, aboard the train, when I received the information that he had been overthrown and that a new government under Marshal Petain had been formed, which government was established for the prime purpose of seeking an armistice with Germany. Under these circumstances, we naturally did everything in our power to secure the proper arrangements for disposition of the French fleet.

Address by President Franklin Roosevelt to Congress Articulating the "Four Freedoms," January 6, 1941
(Congressional Record)

In the future days, which we seek to make secure, we look forward to a world founded upon four essential human freedoms.

The first is freedom of speech and expression—everywhere in the world.

The second is freedom of every person to worship God in his own way—everywhere in the world.

The third is freedom from want—which, translated into world terms, means economic understandings which will secure to every nation a healthy peacetime life for its inhabitants—everywhere in the world.

The fourth is freedom from fear—which, translated into world terms, means a world-wide reduction of armaments to such a point and in such a thorough fashion that no nation will be in a position to commit an act of physical aggression against any neighbor—anywhere in the world.

The "Atlantic Charter" Agreement Betweeen the United States and Great Britain, August 14, 1941
(White House News Release)

The President of the United States of America and the Prime Minister, Mr. Churchill, representing His Majesty's Government in the United Kingdom, being met together, deem it right to make known certain common principles in the national policies of their respective countries on which they base their hopes for a better future for the world.

First, their countries seek no aggrandizement, territorial or other;

Second, they desire to see no territorial changes that do not accord with the freely expressed wishes of the peoples concerned;

Third, they respect the right of all peoples to choose the form of government under which they will live; and they wish to see sovereign rights and self-government restored to those who have been forcibly deprived of them;

Fourth, they will endeavor, with due respect for their existing obligations, to further the enjoyment by all States, great or small, victor or vanquished, of access, on equal terms, to the trade and to the raw materials of the world which are needed for their economic prosperity;

Fifth, they desire to bring about the fullest collaboration between all nations in the economic field with the object of securing, for all, improved labor standards, economic advancement and social security;

Sixth, after the final destruction of the Nazi tyranny, they hope to see established a peace which will afford to all nations the means of dwelling in safety within their own boundaries, and which will afford assurance that all the men in all the lands may live out their lives in freedom from fear and want.

Seventh, such a peace should enable all men to traverse the high seas and oceans without hindrance;

Eighth, they believe that all of the nations of the world, for realistic as well as spiritual reasons must come to the abandonment of the use of force. Since no future peace can be maintained if land, sea, or air armaments continue to be employed by nations which threaten, or may threaten, aggression outside of their frontiers, they believe, pending the establishment of a wider and permanent system of general security, that the disarmament of such nations is essential. They will likewise aid and encourage all other practicable measures which will lighten for peace-loving peoples the crushing burden of armaments.

Franklin D. Roosevelt
Winston S. Churchill

President Franklin Roosevelt Asks Congress to Declare War against the Japanese Empire, December 8, 1941
(Congressional Record)

Yesterday, December 7, 1941—a date which will live in infamy—the United States of America was suddenly and deliberately attacked by naval and air forces of the Empire of Japan.

The United States was at peace with that nation, and, at

the solicitation of Japan, was still in conversation with its Government and its Emperor looking toward the maintenance of peace in the Pacific. It will be recorded that the distance of Hawaii from Japan make it obvious that the attack was deliberately planned many days or even weeks ago. During the intervening time the Japanese Government has deliberately sought to deceive the United States by false statements and expressions of hope for continued peace.

The attack yesterday on the Hawaiian Islands has caused severe damage to American naval and military forces. Very many American lives have been lost. Yesterday the Japanese Government also launched an attack against Malaya. Last night Japanese forces attacked Hong Kong . . . Guam . . . the Philippine Islands . . . (and) Wake Island. . . .

Japan has, therefore, undertaken a surprise offensive throughout the Pacific area. The facts of yesterday speak for themselves. Always will we remember the character of the onslaught against us. I believe I interpret the will of the congress and of the people when I assert that we will not only defend ourselves to the uttermost but will make very certain that this form of treachery shall never endanger us again. I ask that the congress declare that since the unprovoked and dastardly attack by Japan on Sunday, December seventh, a state of war has existed between the United States and the Japanese Empire.

The German Declaration of War against the United States, December 11, 1941 (U.S. Department of State, *Bulletin*)

The Government of the United States, having violated in the most flagrant manner and in ever-increasing measure all rules of neutrality in favor of the adversaries of Germany and having continually been guilty of the most severe provocations toward Germany ever since the outbreak of the European war, provoked by the British declaration of war against Germany on September 3, 1939, has finally resorted to open military acts of aggression.

On September 11, 1941, the President of the United States publicly declared that he had ordered the American Navy and Air Force to shoot on sight at any German war vessel. In his speech of October 27, 1941, he once more expressly affirmed that this order was in force. Acting under this order, vessels of the

American Navy, since early September, 1941, have systematically attacked German naval forces. Thus, American destroyers, as for instance the *Greer,* the *Kearny* and the *Reuben James,* have opened fire on German submarines according to plan. The Secretary of the American Navy, Mr. Knox, himself confirmed that American destroyers attacked German submarines.

Furthermore, the naval forces of the United States, under order of their Government and contrary to international law have treated and seized German merchant vessels on the high seas as enemy ships.

The German Government therefore establishes the following facts:

Although Germany on her part has strictly adhered to the rules of international law in her relations with the United States during every period of the present war, the Government of the United States from initial violations of neutrality has finally proceeded to open acts of war against Germany. The Government of the United States has thereby virtually created a state of war.

The German Government, consequently, discontinues diplomatic relations with the United States of America and declares that under these circumstances brought about by President Roosevelt, Germany too, as from today, considers herself as being in a state of war with the Unted States of America.

The Establishment of U.N.R.R.A., March 9, 1943
(U.S. Department of State, *Bulletin*)

The Governments or Authorities whose duly authorized representatives have subscribed hereto,

Being United Nations or being associated with the United Nations in this war,

Being determined that immediately upon the liberation of any area by the armed forces of the United Nations or as a consequence of retreat of the enemy the population thereof shall receive aid and relief from their sufferings, food, clothing, and shelter, aid in the prevention of pestilence and in the recovery of the health of the people, and that preparation and arrangements shall be made for the return of prisoners and exiles to their homes and for assistance in the resumption of urgently needed agricultural and industrial production and the restoration of essential services,

Have agreed as follows:

Article I. There is hereby established the United Nations Relief and Rehabilitation Administration.

1. The Administration shall have power to acquire, hold, and convey property, to enter into contracts and undertake obligations, to designate or create agencies and to review the activities of agencies so created, to manage undertakings, and in general to perform any legal act appropriate to its objects and purposes.

2. Subject to the provisions of Article VIII, the purposes and functions of the Administration shall be as follows:

(a) To plan, coordinate, administer or arrange for the administration of measures for the relief of victims of war in any area under the control of any of the United Nations through the provision of food, fuel, clothing, shelter and other basic necessities, medical and other essential services; and to facilitate in such areas, so far as necessary to the adequate provision of relief, the production and transportation of these articles and the furnishing of these services. The form of activities of the Administration within the territory of a member government wherein that government exercises administrative authority and the responsibility to be assumed by the member government for carrying out measures planned by the Administration therein shall be determined after consultation with and with the consent of the member government.

(b) To formulate and recommend measures for individual or joint action by any or all of the member governments for the coordination of purchasing, the use of ships and other procurement activities in the period following the cessation of hostilities, with a view to integrating the plans and activities of the Administration with the total movement of supplies, and for the purpose of achieving an equitable distribution of available supplies.

(c) To study, formulate, and recommend for individual or joint action by any or all of the member governments measures with respect to such related matters, arising out of its experience in planning and performing the work of relief and rehabilitation, as may be proposed by any of the member governments.

The Moscow Conference of Foreign Ministers, October 30, 1943 (U.S. Department of State, *Bulletin*)

Communique released November 1, 1943.

The Conference of Foreign Secretaries of the United States of America, Mr. Cordell Hull, of the United Kingdom, Mr. Anthony Eden, and of the Soviet Union, Mr. V. M. Molotov, took place at Moscow from the 19th to 30th October 1943. There were twelve meetings.

The agenda included all the questions submitted for discussion by the three Governments. Some of the questions called for final decisions and these were taken. On other questions, after discussion, decisions of principle were taken: these questions were referred for detailed consideration to commissions specially set up for the purpose, or reserved for treatment through diplomatic channels.

The three Governments have been in close cooperation in all matters concerning the common war effort. But this is the first time that the Foreign Secretaries of the three Governments have been able to meet together in conference.

In the first place there were frank and exhaustive discussions of measures to be taken to shorten the war against Germany and her satellites in Europe.

The Conference agreed to set up machinery for ensuring the close cooperation between the three governments in the examination of European questions arising as the war develops. For this purpose the Conference decided to establish in London a European Advisory Commission to study these questions to make joint recommendations to the three governments.

Provision was made to establish an Advisory Council for matters relating to Italy.

The three Foreign Secretaries declared it to be the purpose of their Governments to restore the independence of Austria. At the same time they reminded Austria that in the final settlement account will be taken of efforts that Austria may make towards its own liberation.

In the atmosphere of mutual confidence and understanding which characterized all the work of the Conference, consideration was also given to other important questions.

Declaration of Four Nations on General Security (China here included)

The Governments of the United States of America, the United Kingdom, the Soviet Union and China:

United in their determination, in accordance with the Declaration by the United Nations of January 1, 1942, to continue hostilities against those Axis powers with which they are at war until such powers have laid down their arms on the basis of unconditional surrender, jointly declare:

1. That their united action, pledged for the prosecution of the war against their respective enemies, will be continued for the organization and maintenance of peace and security.

2. That those of them at war with a common enemy will act together in all matters relating to the surrender of that enemy.

3. That they will take all measures deemed by them to be necessary to provide against any violation of the terms imposed upon the enemy.

4. That they recognize the necessity of establishing at the earliest practicable date a general international organization, based on the principle of the sovereign equality of all peace-loving states, and open to membership by all such states, for the maintenance of international peace and security.

The Declaration Regarding Italy

The Foreign Secretaries of the United States, the United Kingdom, and the Soviet Union have established that their three Governments are in complete agreement that Allied policy toward Italy must be based upon the fundamental principle that Fascism and all its evil influences and emanations shall be utterly destroyed and that the Italian people shall be given every opportunity to establish governmental and other institutions based upon democratic principles.

In the furtherance of this policy the three Governments are agreed that the following measures are to be put into effect:

1. It is essential that the Italian Government should be made more democratic by the introduction of representatives of those sections of the Italian people who have always opposed Fascism.

2. All institutions and organizations created by the Fascist regime shall be suppressed.

3. All Fascist elements shall be removed from the administration and from the institutions and organizations of a public character.

It is further understood that nothing in this resolution is to operate against the right of the Italian people ultimately to choose their own form of government.

The Declaration Regarding Austria

The three Governments are agreed that Austria, the first free country to fall a victim to Hitlerite aggression, shall be liberated from German domination.

They regard the annexation imposed upon Austria by Germany on March 15, 1938, as null and void. They consider themselves as in no way bound by any changes effected in Austria since that date. They declare that they wish to see re-established a free and independent Austria, and thereby to open the way for the Austrian people themselves, as well as those of neighboring states which will be faced with similar problems, to find that political and economic security which is the only basis for lasting peace.

The Declaration on German Atrocities

The three Governments have received from many quarters evidence of atrocities, massacres, and cold-blooded mass executions which are being perpetrated by the Hitlerite forces in the many countries they have overrun and from which they are now being steadily expelled. The brutalities of Hitlerite domination are no new thing and all the peoples or territories in their grip have suffered from the worst form of government by terror. What is new is that many of these territories are now being redeemed by the advancing armies of the liberating Powers and that in their desperation, the recoiling Hitlerite Huns are redoubling their ruthless cruelties. This is now evidenced with particular clearness by monstrous crimes of the Hitlerites on the territory of the Soviet Union which is being liberated from the Hitlerites, and on French and Italian territory.

Accordingly, the three Governments, speaking in the interests of the thirty-three United Nations, hereby solemnly declare and give full warning of their declaration as follows:

At the time of the granting of any armistice to any government which may be set up in Germany, those German officers and men and members of the Nazi Party who have been responsible for, or have taken a consenting part in the above atrocities, massacres, and executions will be sent back to the countries in which their abominable deeds were done in order that they may be judged and punished. Lists will be compiled in all possible detail from all these countries, having regard especially to invaded parts of the Soviet Union, to Poland and Czechoslovakia, to Yugoslavia and Greece, including Crete and other islands, to

Norway, Denmark, the Netherlands, Belgium, Luxemburg, France, and Italy.

Thus, the Germans who take part in wholesale shootings of Italian officers, in the execution of French, Dutch, Belgian, or Norwegian hostages or of Cretan peasants, or who have shared in the slaughters inflicted on the people of Poland or in territories of the Soviet Union which are now being swept clear of the enemy, will know that they will be brought back to the scene of their crimes and judged on the spot by the peoples whom they have outraged. Let those who have hitherto not imbrued their hands with innocent blood beware lest they join the ranks of the guilty, for most assuredly the three allied Powers will pursue them to the uttermost ends of the earth and will deliver them to their accusers in order that justice may be done.

The above declaration is without prejudice to the case of the major criminals, whose offenses have no particular geographical localization and who will be punished by the joint decision of the Governments of the Allies.

The First Cairo Conference, November 22, 1943
(U.S. Department of State, *Bulletin*)

The several military missions have agreed upon future military operations against Japan. The Three Great Allies expressed their resolve to bring unrelenting pressure against their brutal enemies by sea, land, and air. This pressure is already rising.

The Three Great Allies are fighting this war to restrain and punish the aggression of Japan. They covet no gain for themselves and have no thought of territorial expansion. It is their purpose that Japan shall be stripped of all the islands in the Pacific which she has seized or occupied since the beginning of the first world war in 1914, and that all the territories Japan has stolen from the Chinese, such as Manchuria, Formosa, and the Pescadores, shall be restored to the Republic of China. Japan will also be expelled from all other territories which she has taken by violence and greed. The aforesaid three great powers, mindful of the enslavement of the people of Korea, are determined that in the due course Korea shall become free and independent.

With these objects in view the three Allies, in harmony with those of the United Nations at war with Japan, will continue to persevere in the serious and prolonged operations necessary to procure the unconditional surrender of Japan.

The Tehran Conference, November 28, 1943
(U.S. Department of State, *Bulletin*)

We—The President of the United States, the Prime Minister of Great Britain, and the Premier of the Soviet Union, have met these four days past, in this, the Capital of our Ally, Iran, and have shaped and confirmed our common policy.

We express our determination that our nations shall work together in war and in the peace that will follow.

As to war—our military staffs have joined in our round table discussions, and we have concerted our plans for the destruction of the German forces. We have reached complete agreement as to the scope and timing of the operations to be undertaken from the east, west, and south.

The common understanding which we have here reached guarantees that victory will be ours.

And as to peace —we are sure that our concord will win an enduring peace. We recognize fully the supreme responsibility resting upon us and all the United Nations to make a peace which will command the good will of the overwhelming mass of the peoples of the world and banish the scourge and terror of war for many generations.

With our diplomatic advisors we have surveyed the problems of the future. We shall seek the cooperation and active participation of all nations, large and small, whose peoples in heart and mind are dedicated, as are our own peoples, to the elimination of tyranny and slavery, oppression, and intolerance. We will welcome them, as they may choose to come, into a world family of democratic nations.

No power on earth can prevent our destroying the German armies by land, their U boats by sea, and their war plants from the air.

Our attack will be relentless and increasing.

Emerging from these cordial conferences we look with confidence to the day when all peoples of the world may live free lives, untouched by tyranny, and according to their varying desires and their own consciences.

We come here with hope and determination. We leave here, friends in fact, in spirit and in purpose.

Roosevelt, Churchill, Stalin

The Yalta Conference, February 4, 1945
(U. S. Department of State, *Bulletin*)

Protocol of the Proceedings of the Crimea Conference.

The Crimea Conference of the Heads of the Governments of the United States of America, the United Kingdom, and the Union of Soviet Socialist Republics which took place from February 4 to 11 came to the following conclusions:

I. World Organization

It was decided:

(1) that a United Nations Conference on the proposed world organization should be summoned for Wednesdaly, 25th April, 1945, and should be held in the United States of America.

(2) the Nations to be invited to this Conference should be:

(a) the United Nations as they existed on the 8th February, 1945; and

(b) such of the Associated Nations as have declared war on the common enemy by 1st March, 1945. When the Conference on World Organization is held, the delegates of the United Kingdom and United States of America will support a proposal to admit to original membership two Soviet Socialist Republics, i.e., the Ukraine and White Russia.

(3) that the United States Government on behalf of the Three Powers should consult the Government of China and the French Provisional Government in regard to decisions taken at the present Conference concerning the proposed World Organization.

II. Declaration on Liberated Europe

The following declaration has been approved:

"The Premier of the Union of Soviet Socialist Republics, the Prime Minister of the United Kingdom and the President of the United States of America have consulted with each other in the common interests of the peoples of their countries and those of liberated Europe. They jointly declare their mutual agreement to concert during the temporary period of instability in liberated Europe the policies of their three governments in assisting the peoples of the former Axis satellite states of Europe to solve by democratic means their pressing political and economic problems.

The establishment of order in Europe and the rebuilding of

national economic life must be achieved by processes which will enable the liberated peoples to destroy the last vestiges of Nazism and Fascism."

III. Dismemberment of Germany

It was agreed that Article 12(a) of the Surrender Terms for Germany should be amended to read as follows:

"The United Kingdom, the United States of America, and the Union of Soviet Socialist Republics shall possess supreme authority with respect to Germany. In the exercise of such authority they will take such steps, including the complete disarmament, demilitarization, and dismemberment of Germany as they deem requisite for future peace and security."

V. Reparation

The following protocol has been approved:

(1) Germany must pay in kind for the losses caused by her to the Allied nations in the course of the war. Reparations are to be received in the first instance by those countries which have borne the main burden of the war, have suffered the heaviest losses, and have organized victory over the enemy.

(2) Reparation in kind is to be exacted from Germany in the three following forms:

(a) removals within two years from the surrender of Germany or the cessation of organized resistance from the national wealth of Germany located on the territory of Germany herself as well as outside herself, as well as outside her territory (equipment, machine tools, ships, rolling stock, German investments abroad, shares of industrial, transport, and other enterprises in Germany, etc.), these removals to be carried out chiefly for purpose of destroying the war potential of Germany

(b) annual deliveries of goods from current production for a period to be fixed.

(c) use of German labour.

(3) For the working out on the above principles of a detailed plan for exaction of reparation from Germany an Allied Reparation Commission will be set up in Moscow. It will consist of three representatives—one from the Union of Soviet Socialist Republics, one from the United Kingdom, and one from the United States of America.

(4) With regard to the fixing of the total sum of the repara-

tion as well as the distribution of it among the countries which suffered from the German aggression the Soviet and American delegations agreed as follows:

"The Moscow Reparation Commission should take in its initial studies as a basis for discussion the suggestion of the Soviet Government that the total sum of the reparation in accordance with the points (a) and (b) of the paragraph 2 should be 20 billion dollars and that 50 per cent of it should go to the Union of Soviet Socialist Republics."

The British delegation was of the opinion that pending consideration of the reparation question by the Moscow Reparation Commission no figures of reparation should be mentioned.

VI. Major War Criminals

The Conference agreed that the question of the major war criminals should be the subject of inquiry by the three Foreign Secretaries for report in due course after the close of the Conference.

VII. Poland

The following Declaration on Poland was agreed by the Conference:

"A new situation has been created in Poland as a result of her complete liberation by the Red Army. This calls for the establishment of a Polish Provisional Government which can be more broadly based than was possible before the recent liberation of the Western part of Poland. The Provisional Government which is now functioning in Poland should therefore be reorganized on a broader democratic basis with the inclusion of democratic leaders from Poland itself and from Poles abroad. This new Government should then be called the Polish Provisional Government of National Unity."

VIII. Yugoslavia

It was agreed to recommend to Marshal Tito and to Dr. Subasic:

(a) that the Tito-Subasic Agreement should immediately be put into effect and a new Government formed on the basis of the Agreement.

(b) that as soon as the new Government has been formed it should declare:

(i) that the anti-Fascist Assembly of National Liberation

(AUNOJ) will be extended to include members of the last Yugoslaw Skupstina who have not compromised themselves by collaboration with the enemy, thus forming a body to be known as a temporary Parliament and

(ii) that legislative acts passed by the Anti-Fascist Assembly of National Liberation (AUNOJ) will be subject to subsequent ratification by a Constituent Assembly; and that this statement should be published in the Communique of the Conference.

Agreement Regarding Japan

The leaders of the three Great Powers—the Soviet Union, the United States of America, and Great Britain—have agreed that in two or three months after Germany has surrendered and the war in Europe has terminated the Soviet Union shall enter into the war against Japan on the side of the Allies on condition that:

(1) The *status quo* in Outer Mongolia (The Mongolian People's Republic) shall be preserved;

(2) The former rights of Russia violated by the treacherous attack of Japan in 1904 shall be restored, viz:

(a) the southern part of Sakahlin as well as all the islands adjacent to it shall be returned to the Soviet Union,

(b) the commercial port of Dairen shall be internationalized, the pre-eminent interests of the Soviet Union in this port being safeguarded and the lease of Port Arthur as a naval base of the U.S.S.R. restored,

(c) the Chinese-Eastern Railroad and the South-Manchurian Railroad which provides an outlet to Dairen shall be jointly operated by the establishment of a joint Soviet-Chinese Company, it being understood that the pre-eminent interests of the Soviet Union shall be safeguarded and that China shall retain full sovereignty in Manchuria;

(3) The Kuril islands shall be handed over to the Soviet Union.

It is understood, that the agreement concerning Outer Mongolia and the ports and railroads referred to above will require concurrence of Generalissimo Chiang Kai-Shek. The President will take measures in order to obtain this concurrence on advice from Marshal Stalin. The Heads of the three Great Powers have agreed that these claims of the Soviet Union shall be unquestionably fulfilled after Japan has been defeated.

For its part the Soviet Union expresses its readiness to conclude with the National Government of China a pact of friendship and alliance between the U.S.S.R. and China in order to render assistance to China with its armed forces for the purpose of liberating China from the Japanese yoke.

Joseph V. Stalin; Franklin D. Roosevelt; Winston S. Churchill, February 11, 1945.

The Charter of the United Nations
(United Nations Publications, 1945)

Preamble

We the peoples of the United Nations determined to save succeeding generations from the scourge of war, which twice in our lifetime has brought untold sorrow to mankind, and to reaffirm faith in fundamental human rights, in the dignity and worth of the human person, in the equal rights of men and women and of nations large and small, and to establish conditions under which justice and respect for the obligations arising from treaties and other sources of international law can be maintained, and to promote social progress and better standards of life in larger freedom, *and for these ends* to practice tolerance and life together in peace and security, and to ensure, by the acceptance of principles and the institution of methods, that armed force shall not be used, save in the common interest, and to employ international machinery for the promotion of the economic and social advancement of all peoples, *have resolved to combine our efforts to accomplish these aims.* Accordingly, our respective Governments have agreed to the present Charter of the United Nations and do hereby establish an international organization to be known as the United Nations.

Article 1 – Purposes and Principles

The purposes of the United Nations are:

1. To maintain international peace and security, and to that end: to take effective collective measures for the prevention and removal of threats to the peace, and for the suppression of acts of aggression or other breaches of the peace, and to bring about by peaceful means, and in conformity with the principles of justice and international law, adjustment or settlement of international disputes or situations which might lead to a breach of the peace;

2. To develop friendly relations among nations based on respect for the principle of equal rights and self-determination of peoples, and to take other appropriate measures to strengthen universal peace;

3. To achieve international cooperation in solving international problems of an economic, social, cultural, or humanitarian character, and in promoting and encouraging respect for human rights and for fundamental freedoms for all without distinction as to race, sex, language, or religion; and

4. To be a center for harmonizing the actions of nations in the attainment of these common ends.

Article 25 – Security Council

The members of the United Nations agree to accept and carry out the decisions of the Security Council in accordance with the present Charter.

Article 27 – Security Council

1. Each member of the Security Council shall have one vote.

2. Decisions of the Security Council on procedural matters shall be made by an affirmative vote of seven members.

3. Decisions on the Security Council on all other matters shall be made by an affirmative vote of seven members including the *concurring votes of the permanent members;* provided that, in decisions under Chapter VI, and under paragraph 3 of Article 52, a party to a dispute shall abstain from voting.

Article 41 – Breaches of the Peace

The Security Council may decide what measures not involving the use of armed forces are to be employed to give effect to its decisions, and it may call upon the members of the United Nations to apply such measures. These may include complete or partial interruption of economic relations and of rail, sea, air, postal, telegraphic, radio and other means of communication, and the severance of diplomatic relations.

Article 42 – Breaches of the Peace

Should the Security Council consider that measures provided for in Article 41 would be inadequate or have proved to be inadequate, it may take such action by air, sea, or land forces as may be necessary to maintain or restore international peace and security. Such action may include demonstrations, blockade, and other operations by air, sea, or land forces of members of the United Nations.

Article 43 – Breaches of the Peace

1. All members of the United Nations, in order to contribute to the maintenance of international peace and security, undertake to make available to the Security Council, on its call and in accordance with a special agreement or agreements, armed forces, assistance, and facilities, including rights of passage, necessary for the purpose of maintaining international peace and security.

Article 62 – Economic and Social Council

1. The Economic and Social Council may make or initiate studies and reports with respect to international economic, social, cultural, educational, health, and related matters to the General Assembly, to the members of the United Nations, and to the specialized agencies concerned.
2. It may make recommendations for the purpose of promoting respect for, and observances of, human rights and fundamental freedoms for all.
3. It may prepare draft conventions for submission to the General Assembly, with respect to matters falling within its competence.

Article 76 – International Trusteeship System

The basic objectives of the trusteeship system, in accordance with the purposes of the United Nations laid down in Article 1 of the present Charter, shall be:

a. to further international peace and security

b. to promote the political, economic, social, and educational advancement of the inhabitants of the trust territories, and their progressive development towards self-government or independence as may be appropriate to the particular circumstances of each territory and its peoples and the freely expressed wishes of the peoples concerned, and as may be provided by the terms of each trusteeship agreement;

c. to encourage respect for human rights and for fundamental freedoms for all without distinction as to race, sex, language, or religion, and to encourage recognition of the interdependence of the peoples of the world; and

d. to ensure equal treatment in social, economic, and commercial matters for all members of the United Nations and their nationals, and also equal treatment for the latter in administration of justice, without prejudice to the attainment of the foregoing objectives and subject to the provisions of Article 80.

Statement by the President of the United States Regarding the Dropping of the First Atomic Bomb, August 6, 1945. (U. S. Department of State, *International Control of Atomic Energy*)

Sixteen hours ago an American airplane dropped one bomb on Hiroshima, an important Japanese Army base. That bomb had more power than 20,000 tons of T.N.T. It had more than two thousand times the blast power of the British "Grand Slam" which is the largest bomb ever yet used in the history of warfare.

The Japanese began the war from the air at Pearl Harbor. They have been repaid manyfold. And the end is not yet. With this bomb we have now added a new and revolutionary increase in destruction to supplement the growing power of our armed forces. In their present forms these bombs are now in production and ever more powerful forms are in development.

It is an atomic bomb. It is a harnessing of the basic power of the universe. The force from which the sun draws its power has been loosed against those who brought war to the Far East.

Before 1939, it was the accepted belief of scientists that it was theoreticaly possible to release atomic energy. But no one knew any practical method of doing it. By 1942, however, we knew that the Germans were working feverishly to find a way to add atomic energy to the other engines of war with which they hoped to enslave the world. But they failed. We may be grateful to Providence that the V-1's and V-2's were discovered late and produced only in limited quantities and even more grateful that they did not get the atomic bomb at all.

The battle of the laboratories held fateful risks for us as well as the battle of the air, land, and sea, and we have now won the battle of the laboratories as we have won the other battles.

Beginning in 1940, before Pearl Harbor, scientific knowledge useful in war was pooled between the United States and Great Britain, and many priceless helps to our victories have come from that arrangement. Under the general policy the research on the atomic bomb was begun. With American and British scientists working together we entered the race of discovery against the Germans.

The United States had available the large number of scientists of distinction in the many needed areas of knowledge. It had the tremendous industrial and financial resources necessary for the project and they could be devoted to it without undue impairment of other vital war work. In the United States the laboratory work and the production plants, on which a substantial start had already been made, would be out of reach of enemy bombing, while at that time Britain was exposed to constant air attack and was still threatened with the possibility of invasion. For these reasons Prime Minister Churchhill and President Roosevelt agreed that it was wise to carry on the project here. We now have two great plants and many lesser works devoted to the production of atomic power. Employment during peak construction numbered 125,000, and over 65,000 individuals are even now engaged in operating the plants. Many have worked there for two and a half years. Few know what they have been producing. They see great quantities of material going in and they see nothing coming out of these plants, for the physical size of the explosive charge is exceedingly small. We have spent two billion dollars on the greatest scientific gamble in history—and won.

But the greatest marvel is not the size of the enterprise, its secrecy nor its cost, but the achievement of scientific brains in putting together infinitely complex pieces of knowledge held by many men in different fields of science into a workable plan. And hardly less marvelous has been the capacity of industry to design, and of labor to operate, the machines and methods to do things never done before so that the brain child of many minds came forth in physical shape and performed as it was supposed to do. Both science and industry worked under the direction of the United States Army, which achieved a unique success in managing so diverse a problem in the advancement of knowledge in an amazingly short time. It is doubtful if such another combination could be got together in the world. What has been done is the greatest achievement of organized science in history. It was done under high pressure and without failure.

We are now prepared to obliterate more rapidly and completely every productive enterprise the Japanese have above ground in any city. We shall destroy their docks, their factories, and their communications. Let there be no mistakes; we shall completely destroy Japan's power to make war.

It was to spare the Japanese people from utter destruction that the ultimatum of July 26 was issued at Potsdam. Their leaders promptly rejected the ultimatum. If they do not now accept our terms they may expect a rain of ruin from the air, the like of which has never been seen on this earth. Behind this air attack will follow sea and land forces in such numbers and power as they have not yet seen and with the fighting skill of which they are already well aware.

The Secretary of War, who has kept in personal touch with all phases of the project, will immediately make public a statement giving further details.

His statement will give facts concerning the sites at Oak Ridge near Knoxville, Tennessee, and at Richland near Pasco, Washington, and an installation near Santa Fe, New Mexico. Although the workers at the sites have been making materials to be used in producing the greatest destructive force in history they have not themselves been in danger beyond that of many other occupations, for the utmost care has been taken for their safety.

The fact that we can release atomic energy ushers in a new era in man's understanding of nature's forces. Atomic energy may in the future supplement the power that now comes from coal, oil, and falling water, but at present it cannot be produced on a basis to compete with them commercially. Before that comes there must be a long period of intensive research.

It has never been the habit of scientists of this country or policy of this Government to withhold from the world scientific knowledge. Normally, therefore, everything about the work with atomic energy would be made public.

But under present circumstances it is not intended to divulge the technical processes of production or all the military applications, pending further examination of possible methods of protecting us and the rest of the world from the danger of sudden destruction.

I shall recommend that the Congress of the United States consider promptly the establishment of an appropriate commission to control the production and use of atomic power within the United States. I shall give further consideration and make further recommendations to the Congress as to how atomic power can become a powerful and forceful influence towards the maintenance of world peace.

The End of Lend-Lease Aid to Europe, August 21,1945
(U.S. Department of State, *Bulletin*)

The President has directed the Foreign Economic Administrator to take steps immediately to discontinue all lend-lease operations and to notify foreign governments receiving lend-lease of this action.

The President also directs that all outstanding contracts for lend-lease be canceled, except where Allied governments are willing to agree to take them over or where it is in the interest of the United States to complete them.

The Foreign Economic Administrator furthermore is instructed to negotiate with Allied governments for possible procurement by them of lend-lease inventories now in stockpile and in process of delivery.

If the military needs lend-lease supplies for the movement of troops or for occupation purposes the military will be responsible for procurement.

It is estimated that uncompleted contracts for non-munitions and finished goods in this country not yet transferred to lend-lease countries amount to about 2 billion dollars and that lend-lease supplies in stockpile abroad amount to between 1 and 1½ billion dollars.

The Surrender of Japan, September 2, 1945
(Government Section, Supreme Commander of the Allied Powers, *Report of Political Re-orientation of Japan*)

Imperial rescript by Hirohito, Emperor of Japan, prior to the signing of the surrender instrument. Tokyo, September 2, 1945.

Accepting the terms set forth in Declaration issued by the heads of the Governments of the United States, Great Britain, and China on July 26th, 1945, at Potsdam and subsequently adhered to by the Union of Soviet Socialist Republics, We have commanded the Japanese Imperial Government and the Japanese Imperial General Headquarters to sign on Our behalf the Instrument of Surrender presented by the Supreme Commander for the Allied Powers. We command all Our people forthwith to cease hostilities, to lay down their arms and faithfully to carry out all the provisions of Instrument of Surrender and the General

Orders issued by the Japanese Imperial Government and the Japanese Imperial General Headquarters hereunder.

Instrument of Surrender

We, acting by command of and in behalf of the Emperor of Japan, the Japanese Government and the Japanese Imperial General Headquarters, hereby accept the provisions set forth in the declaration issued by the heads of the Governments of the United States, China, and Great Britain on 26 July, 1945, at Potsdam, and subsequently adhered to by the Union of Soviet Socialist Republics, which four powers are hereafter referred to as the Allied Powers.

We hereby proclaim the unconditional surrender to the Allied Powers of the Japanese Imperial General Headquarters and of all Japanese armed forces and all armed forces under Japanese control wherever situated.

We hereby command all Japanese forces wherever situated and the Japanese people to cease hostilities forthwith, to preserve and save from damage all ships, aircraft, and military and civil property and to comply with all requirements which may be imposed by the Supreme Commander for the Allied Powers or by agencies of the Japanese Government at his direction.

We hereby command the Japanese Imperial General Headquarters to issue at once orders to the Commanders of all Japanese forces and all forces under Japanese control wherever situated to surrender unconditionally themselves and all forces under their control. . . .

We hereby command all civil, military, and naval officials to obey and enforce all proclamations, orders, and directives deemed by the Supreme Commander for the Allied Powers to be proper to effectuate this surrender and issued by him or under his authority and we direct all such officials to remain at their posts and to continue to perform their noncombatant duties unless specifically relieved by him or under his authority.

We hereby undertake for the Emperor, the Japanese Government, and their successors to carry out the provisions of the Potsdam Declaration in good faith, and to issue whatever orders and take whatever action may be required by the Supreme Commander for the Allied Powers or by any other designated representatives of the Allied Powers for the purpose of giving effect to that Declaration.

We hereby command the Japanese Imperial Government

and the Japanese Imperial General Headquarters at once to liberate all allied prisoners of war and civilian internees now under Japanese control and to provide for their protection, care, maintenance, and immediate transportation to places as directed.

The authority of the Emperor and the Japanese Government to rule the state shall be subject to the Supreme Commander for the Allied powers who will take such steps as he deems proper to effectuate these terms of surrender.

Signed at Tokyo Bay, Japan, at 0904 on the second day of September, 1945.

Presidential Statement of the Principles of American Foreign Policy (Harry S. Truman. Statement. 27 October, 1945. U.S. Department of State, *Bulletin*)

1. We seek no territorial expansion or selfish advantage. We have no plans for aggression against any other state. . . . We have no objective which need clash with the peaceful aims of any other nation.
2. We believe in the eventual return of sovereign rights and self-government to all peoples who have been deprived of them by force.
3. We shall approve no territorial changes in any friendly part of the world unless they accord with the freely expressed wishes of the people concerned.
4. We believe that all peoples who are prepared for self-government should be permitted to choose their own form of government by their own freely expressed choice, without interference from any foreign source. . . .
5. By the combined and cooperative action of our war allies we shall help the defeated enemy states establish peaceful, democratic governments of their own free choice. And we shall try to attain a world in which Nazism, Facism, and military aggression cannot exist.
6. We shall refuse to recognize any government imposed upon any nation by the force of any foreign power. In some cases it may be impossible to prevent forceful imposition of such a government. But the United States will not recognize any such government.
7. We believe that all nations should have the freedom of

the seas, and equal rights to the navigation of boundary rivers and waterways, and of rivers and waterways which pass through more than one country.

8. We believe that all states which are accepted in the society of nations should have access on equal terms to the trade and the raw materials of the world.

9. We believe that the sovereign states of the western hemisphere, without interference from outside the western hemisphere, must work together as good neighbors in the solution of their common problems.

10. We believe that full economic collaboration between all nations . . . is essential to the improvement of living conditions all over the world, and to the establishment of freedom from fear and freedom from want.

11. We shall continue to strive to promote freedom of expression and freedom of religion through the . . . world.

12. We are convinced that the preservation of peace between nations requires a United Nations Organization composed of all peace-loving nations of the world who are willing jointly to use force if necessary to insure peace.

That is the foreign policy which guides the United States now.

That is the foreign policy with which it confidently faces the future.

The Constitution of UNESCO, 1964
(U.S. Department of State, *Bulletin*)

The governments of the states parties to this *Constitution* on behalf of their peoples declare:

that since wars begin in the minds of men, it is in the minds of men that the defenses of peace must be constructed;

that ignorance of each other's ways and lives has been a common cause . . . of that suspicion and mistrust between the peoples of the world through which their differences have all to often broken into war;

that the great and terrible war which has now ended was a war made possible by the denial of the democratic principles of the dignity, equality, and mutual respect of men, and by the propagation, in their place, through ignorance and prejudice, of the doctrine of the inequality of men and races;

that the wide diffusion of culture and the education of humanity for justice and liberty and peace are indispensable to the dignity of man, and constitute a sacred duty which all the nations must fulfill in a spirit of mutual assistance and concern;

that a peace based exclusively upon the political and economic arrangements of governments would not be a peace which could secure the unanimous, lasting, and sincere support of the peoples of the world, and that the peace must therefore be founded . . . upon the intellectual and moral solidarity of mankind.

For These Reasons the states parties to this *Constitution*, believing in full and equal opportunities for education for all, in the unrestricted pursuit of objective truth, and in the free exchange of ideas and knowledge, are agreed and determined to develop and to increase the means of communication between their peoples . . . ;

In Consequence Whereof they do hereby create the United Nations Educational, Scientific and Cultural Organization for the purpose of advancing, through the educational and scientific and cultural relations of the peoples of the world, the objectives of international peace and of the common welfare of mankind for which the United Nations Organization was established and which its *Charter* proclaims.

Article I. Purposes and Functions:

1. The purpose of the organization is to contribute to peace and security by promoting collaboration among the nations through education, science, and culture in order to further universal respect for justice, for the rule of law and for the human rights and fundamental freedoms which are affirmed for the peoples of the world, without distinction of race, sex, language, or religion, by the *Charter* of the United Nations.

2. To realize this purpose the organization will:

(a) collaborate in the work of advancing the mutual knowledge and understanding of peoples through all means of mass communication . . . ;

(b) give fresh impulse to popular education and to the spread of culture . . . ;

(c) maintain, increase, and diffuse knowledge;

by assuring the conservation . . . of the world's inheritance of books, works of art, and monuments of history and science. . . .

by encouraging coöperation among the nations in all branches of intellectual activity, including the international exchange of persons active in the fields of education, science, and culture, and the exchange of publications, objects of artistic and scientific interest, and other materials of information;

by initiating methods of international cooperation calculated to give the people of all countries access to the printed and published materials produced by any of them.

The First General Report of the Secretary-General of the United Nations (United Nations, *Publications,* 1946)

Has the United Nations succeeded in capturing the imagination and in harnessing the enthusiasm of the peoples of the world? I, for one, do not feel that it has done so in the degree that might be hoped for. What is the explanation, and what measures can, or should, be taken?

Part of the explanation lies no doubt in the inevitable slowness of United Nations proceedings at this stage which, in turn, is due to preoccupation with matters of procedure and organization. Much could be done to "educate" public opinion to appreciate more fully the significance of the often undramatic but fundamental work that is being performed, and the fact that many of our difficulties are of a temporary character. The world is in the midst of a giant post-war upheaval, its economic life is dislocated, many regions still present a picture of distress and destruction, and many political frontiers and forms of government, as well as the terms of the peace settlement, are still undecided. It is too often overlooked that while such conditions remain, the working of the Charter system will inevitably be affected.

Misunderstanding of our problems and discouragement with the results so far achieved may also be attributed, in no small degree, to a lack of historical perspective in surveying the world as we find it today. Without excusing our failure to settle our problems more rapidly, it must be understood that any war on a world scale is bound to bring vast problems in its wake and that many of these problems demand careful and methodical treatment. It is unquestionably better that time be employed in the proper settlement of controversies when hasty agreement could only lead to future trouble. There is no cause for discouragement, still less for pessimism. But are there not nevertheless very real dangers facing us? Has not the lively desire of all peoples and governments to establish the authority of the United Nations, and to combine their efforts in achieving the victories of peace, sometimes been impeded by a lack of mutual trust among the members of the organization?

The United Nations is no stronger than the collective will of the nations that support it. Of itself it can do nothing. It is a machinery through which the nations can cooperate. It can be used and developed in the light of its activities and experience, to the untold benefit of humanity, or it can be discarded and broken. As in the control of atomic power, the choice is between life and death. The failure of the United Nations would mean the failure of peace, the triumph of destruction.

International Control of Atomic Power
(Joint Declaration by the President of the U.S., the Prime Minister of the United Kingdom, and the Prime Minister of Canada. **U.S. Senate Committee** ***Report.*** **November 15, 1946)**

1. We recognize that the application of recent scientifie discoveries to the methods and practice of war has placed at the disposal of mankind means of destruction hitherto unknown, against which there can be no adequate military defense, and in the employment of which no single nation can in fact have a monopoly.

2. We desire to emphasize that the responsibility for devising means to insure that the new discoveries shall be used for the benefit of mankind, instead of as a means of destruction, rests not on our nations alone, but upon the whole civilized world . . . and we have accordingly met together to consider the possibility of international action—

(a) to prevent the use of atomic energy for destructive purposes;

(b) to promote the use of recent and future advances in scientific knowledge . . . for peaceful and humanitarian ends.

3. We are aware that the only complete protection for the civilized world from the destructive use of scientific knowledge lies in the prevention of war. . . .

4. . . . We declare at the outset our willingness . . . to proceed with the exchange of fundamental scientific information

. . . for peaceful ends with any nation that will fully reciprocate.

5. . . . . In pursuance of this policy the basic scientific information essential to the development of atomic energy for peaceful purposes has already been made available to the world. . . .

6. We have considered the question of the disclosure of detailed information concerning the practical application of atomic energy. The military exploitation of atomic energy depends . . . upon the same methods and processes as would be required for industrial uses. We are not convinced that the spreading of the specialized information regarding the practical application of atomic energy, before it is possible to devise effective, reciprocal, and enforceable safeguards acceptable to all nations, would contribute to a constructive solution of the problem of the atomic bomb. . . . We are, however, prepared to share . . . detailed information concerning the practical industrial application of atomic energy just as soon as effective enforceable safeguards against its use for destructive purposes can be devised.

7. In order to [eliminate] the use of atomic energy for destructive purposes . . . a commission should be set up under the United Nations Organization to prepare recommendations for submission to the Organization.

The commission should be instructed . . . to submit recommendations . . . dealing with separate phases of its work.

In particular the commission should make specific proposals - - -

(a) for extending between all nations the exchange of basic scientific information for peaceful ends;
(b) for control of atomic energy to the extent necessary to insure its use only for peaceful purposes;
(c) for the elimination from national armaments of atomic weapons and of all other major weapons adaptable to mass destruction;
(d) for effective safeguards by way of inspection and other means to protect complying states against the hazards of violations and evasions. . . .

Harry S. Truman
Clement R. Attlee
W. L. Mackenzie King

The Truman Doctrine
(President Harry Truman, *Address to the Congress*, March 12, 1947)

The gravity of the situation which confronts the world today necessitates my appearance before a joint session of the Congress. The foreign policy and the national security of this country are involved.

One aspect of the present situation, which I wish to present to you at this time for your consideration and decision, concerns Greece and Turkey.

The United States has received from the Greek Government an urgent appeal for financial and economic assistance. Preliminary reports from the American Economic Mission now in Greece and reports from the American Ambassador in Greece corroborate the statement of the Greek Government that assistance is imperative.

The very existence of the Greek state is today threatened by the terrorist activities of several thousand armed men, led by Communists, who defy the Government's authority at a number of points, particularly along the northern boundaries. A commission appointed by the United Nations Security Council is at present investigating disturbed conditions in Northern Greece and alleged border violations along the frontiers between Greece on the one hand and Albania, Bulgaria, and Yugoslavia on the other.

Greece must have assistance if it is to become a self-supporting and self-respecting democracy.

Greece's neighbor, Turkey, also deserves our attention. The future of Turkey as an independent and economically sound state is clearly no less important to the freedom-loving peoples of the world than the future of Greece. The circumstances in which Turkey finds itself today are considerably different from those of Greece. Turkey has been spared the disasters that have beset Greece. And during the war, the United States and Great Britain furnished Turkey with material aid. Nevertheless, Turkey now needs our support.

Since the war Turkey has sought additional financial assistance from Great Britain and the United States for the purpose of effecting that modernization necessary for the maintenance of its national integrity. That integrity is essential to the preservation of order in the Middle East. As in the case of Greece, if

Turkey is to have the assistance it needs, the United States must supply it.

I am fully aware of the broad implications involved if the United States extends assistance to Greece and Turkey, and I shall discuss these implications with you at this time.

One of the primary objectives of the foreign policy of the United States is the creation of conditions in which we and other nations will be able to work out a way of life free from coercion. This was a fundamental issue in the war with Germany and Japan. Our victory was won over countries which sought to impose their will, and their way of life on other nations.

The peoples of a number of countries of the world have recently had totalitarian regimes forced upon them against their will. The Government of the United States has made frequent protests against coercion and intimidation, in violation of the Yalta Agreement, in Poland, Roumania, and Bulgaria. I must also state that in a number of other countries there have been similar developments.

At the present moment in world history nearly every nation must choose between alternative ways of life. The choice is too often not a free one.

One way of life is based upon the will of the majority, and is distinguished by free institutions, representative government, free elections, guarantees of individual liberty, freedom of speech and religion, and freedom from political oppression.

The second way of life is based upon the will of the minority forcibly imposed upon the majority. It relies upon terror and oppression, a controlled press and radio, fixed elections, and the suppression of personal freedoms.

I believe that it must be the policy of the United States to support free peoples who are resisting attempted subjugation by armed minorities or by outside pressures.

The world is not static, and the *status quo* is not sacred. But we cannot allow changes in the *status quo* in violation of the charter of the United Nations by such methods. In helping free and independent nations to maintain their freedom, the United States will be giving effect to the principles of the charter of the United Nations.

It would be an unspeakable tragedy if these countries, which have struggled so long against overwhelming odds, should lose that victory for which they sacrificed so much. Collapse of free institutions and loss of independence would be disastrous not only for them but for the world.

We must take immediate and resolute action.

In addition to funds, I ask the Congress to authorize the detail of American civilian and military personnel to Greece and Turkey, at the request of those countries, to assist in the tasks of reconstruction, and for the purpose of supervising the use of such financial and material assistance as may be furnished. I recommend that authority also be provided for the instruction and training of selected Greek and Turkish personnel.

This is a serious course upon which we embark. I would not recommend it except that the alternative is much more serious.

If we falter in our leadership, we may endanger the peace of the world—and we shall surely endanger the welfare of our own Nation.

Great responsibilities have been placed upon us by the swift movements of events.

I am confident that the Congress will face these responsibilities squarely.

The Economic Needs of Post-War Europe (Address by U.S. Secretary of State George C. Marshall, June 5, 1947)

I need not tell you gentlemen that the world situation is very serious. That must be apparent to all intelligent people. I think one difficulty is that the problem is one of such enormous complexity that the very mass of facts presented . . . by press and radio make it exceedingly difficult . . . to reach a clear appraisement of the situation. Furthermore, the people of this country are distant from the troubled areas of the earth and it is hard for them to comprehend the plight and consequent reactions of the long-suffering peoples, and the effect of those reactions on their governments in connection with our efforts to promote peace in the world.

In considering the requirements for the rehabilitation of Europe, the physical loss of life, the visible destruction of cities, factories, mines, and railroads was correctly estimated; but it has become obvious during recent months that this visible destruction was probably less serious than the dislocation of the entire fabric of European economy. For the past ten years conditions have been highly abnormal. The feverish preparation for war, and the more feverish maintenance of the war effort, engulfed all aspects of national economics. Machinery has fallen into disrepair or is entirely obsolete. Under the arbitrary and destructive Nazi rule virtually every possible enterprise was geared into the German war machine. Long-standing commercial ties, private institutions, banks, insurance companies, and shipping companies disappeared through loss of capital, absorption through nationalization, or by simple destruction. In many countries confidence in the local currency has been severely shaken. The breakdown of the business structure of Europe during the war was complete. . . .

There is a phase of this matter which is both interesting and serious. The farmer has always produced the foodstuffs to exchange with the city dweller for the other necessities of life. This division of labor is the basis of modern civilization. At the present time it is threatened with breakdown. The town and city industries are not producing adequate goods to exchange with the food-producing farmer. Raw materials and fuel are in short supply. . . . The farmer or the peasant cannot find the goods for sale which he desires to purchase. So the sale of his farm produce for money which he cannot use seems to him an unprofitable transaction. He therefore has withdrawn many fields from crop cultivation and is using them for grazing. He feeds more grain to stock and finds for himself and his family an ample supply of food, however short he may be on clothing and the other ordinary gadgets of civilization. Meanwhile people in the cities are short of food and fuel. So the governments are forced to use their foreign money and credits to procure these necessities abroad. This process exhausts funds which are urgently needed for reconstruction. Thus a very serious situation is rapidly developing which bodes no good for the world. The modern system of the division of labor upon which the exchange of products is based is in danger of breaking down.

The truth of the matter is that Europe's requirements for the next three or four years of foreign food and other essential products, principally from America, are so much greater than her present ability to pay that she must have substantial additional help; or face economic, social, and political deterioration of a very grave character. . . .

It is logical that the United States should do whatever it is able to do to assist in the return of normal economic health in the world, without which there can be no political stability and no assured peace. Our policy is directed not against any country or doctrine but against hunger, poverty, desperation, and chaos. Its purpose should be the revival of a working economy in the world so as to permit the emergence of political and social conditions in which free institutions can exist. Such assistance, I am convinced, must not be on a piecemeal basis as various crises develop. Any assistance that this Government may render in the future should provide a cure rather than a mere palliative. Any government that is willing to assist in the task of recovery will find full cooperation, I am sure, on the part of the United States Government. Any government which maneuvers to block the recovery of other countries cannot expect help from us. Furthermore, governments, political parties, or groups which seek to perpetuate human misery in order to profit therefrom politically or otherwise will encounter the opposition of the United States. . . .

The North Atlantic Treaty
(U.S. Department of State, *Bulletin,* 1949)

The Parties of this Treaty reaffirm their faith in the purposes and principles of the Charter of the United Nations and their desire to live in peace with all peoples and all governments.

They are determined to safeguard the freedom, common heritage, and civilization of their peoples, founded on the principles of democracy, individual liberty, and the rule of law.

They seek to promote stability and well-being in the North Atlantic area.

They are resolved to unite their efforts for collective defense and for the preservation of peace and security.

They therefore agree to this North Atlantic Treaty:

The Parties undertake, as set forth in the Charter of the United Nations, to settle any international disputes in which they may be involved by peaceful means in such a manner that international peace and security, and justice, are not endangered, and to refrain in their international relations from the threat or use of force in any manner inconsistent with the purposes of the United Nations.

The Parties will contribute toward the further development of peaceful and friendly international relations by strengthening their free institutions, by bringing about a better understanding of the principles upon which these institutions are founded, and by promoting conditions of stability and well-being. They will seek to eliminate conflict in their international economic policies and will encourage economic collaboration between any or all of them.

In order more effectively to achieve the objectives of this Treaty, the Parties, separately and jointly, by means of continuous and effective self-help and mutual aid, will maintain and develop their individual and collective capacity to resist armed attack.

The Parties will consult together whenever, in the opinion of any of them, the territorial integrity, political independence, or security of any of the Parties is threatened.

The Parties agree that an armed attack against one or more of them in Europe or North America shall be considered an attack against them all; and consequently they agree that, if such an armed attack occurs, each of them, in exercise of the right of individual or collective self-defense recognized by the Charter of the United Nations, will assist the Party or Parties so attacked by taking such action as it deems necessary.

The Parties hereby establish a council, on which each of them shall be represented, to consider matters concerning the implementation of this Treaty.

The Parties may, by unanimous agreement, invite any other European state in a position to further the principles of this Treaty and to contribute to the security of the North Atlantic area to accede to this Treaty. Any state so invited may become a party to the Treaty by depositing its instrument of accession with the Government of the United States of America.

After the Treaty has been in force for ten years the Parties shall consult together for the purpose of reviewing the Treaty.

After the Treaty has been in force for twenty years, any Party may cease to be a party one year after its notice of denunciation has been given to the Government of the United States of America.

Theory and Practice of Communism in China
(Address by Mao Tse-Tung, June, 1949. U.S. Department of State, *Publication*)

The Chinese found Marxism through the introduction of the Russians. Before the October Revolution the Chinese not only did not know Lenin and Stalin, but also did not know Marx and Engels. The gunfire of the October Revolution sent us Marxism and Leninism. . . .

In 1919 the May 4 Movement occurred in China, and the Communist Party of China was formed in 1921. During this period Sun Yat-sen . . . welcomed the October Revolution, welcomed Russian help to the Chinese, and welcomed the Communist Party of China to cooperate with him.

Sun Yat-sen died and Chiang Kai-shek came into power. During the long period of 22 years Chiang Kai-shek dragged China into hopeless straits. At this period the anti-fascist Second World War, with the Soviet Union as its main force, defeated three big imperialist powers, weakened two other big imperialist powers, and only one imperialist country in the world, the United States of America, suffered no loss. . . . She wanted to enslave the entire world, and she aided Chiang Kai-shek with arms to slaughter several millions of Chinese. Under the leadership of the Communist Party of China, the Chinese people, after having driven away Japanese imperialism, fought the People's War of Liberation for three years and gained a basic victory.

Twenty-four years have elapsed since Sun Yat-sen's death, and under the leadership of the Communist Party of China, Chinese revolutionary theory and practice have made big strides forward. . . . Up to the present, the Chinese people have gained the following two basic experiences:

1. To awaken the masses in the country. This is to unite the working class, the peasant class, the petty bourgeoisie, and the national bourgeoisie, into a united front under the leadership of the working class and develop into a state of the people's democratic dictatorship. . . .

2. To unite in a common struggle with those nations of the world who treat us on the basis of equality. . . . This is to ally with the Soviet Union . . . with the new democratic countries of Europe . . . with the proletariat and masses of the people in other countries to form an international united front.

"You lean to one side." Precisely so. The 40 years' experience of Sun Yat-sen and the 28 years' experience of the Communist Party have made us firmly believe that in order to win victory . . . we must lean to one side. . . . We oppose the Chiang Kai-shek reactionary clique who lean to the side of imperialism. We also oppose the illusion of a third road. Not only in China but also in the world, without exception, one either leans to the side of imperialism or to the side of socialism. Neutrality is a camouflage. . . .

"You are too provoking." We are talking of how to deal with domestic and foreign reactionaries, that is, imperialists and their running dogs, and not of any other people. . . .

Only by drawing a clear line between reactionaries and revolutionaries, only by exposing the designs and plots of the reactionaries, arousing vigilence and attention within the revolutionary ranks, and only by raising our morale and taking down the arrogance of the enemy can the reactionaries be isolated, conquered. . . .

"You are dictatorial." Yes . . . we are really that way. . . . The experiences of several decades amassed by the Chinese people tell us to carry out the people's democratic dictatorship; that is, the right of reactionaries to voice their opinion must be deprived, and only the people are allowed . . . the right of voicing their opinions.

Who are the "people" at the present stage [of Communist revolution] in China? They are the working class, the peasants, the petty bourgeoisie, and the national bourgeoisie. Under the leadership of the working class and the Communist Party these classes unite together to form their own state and elect their own government to enact dictatorships over the lackeys of imperialism—the landlords, the bureaucratic class, and the Kuomintang reactionaries and their henchmen . . . to oppress them and only allow them to behave properly and not allow them to talk and act wildly. If they talk and act wildly they will be prohibited and punished immediately.

The democratic system is to be carried out within the ranks of the people, giving them freedom of speech, assembly, and association. The right to vote is given only to the people and not to the reactionaries. These two aspects, namely, democracy among the people, and dictatorships over the reactionaries, combine to form the people's dictatorship.

Why should it be done this way? It is very obvious that if this is not done the revolution will fail. . . . "Do you not want to eliminate State authority?" Yes, but not at present. . . . Why? Because imperialism still exists, and domestic reactionaries still exist and classes . . . still exist. Our present task is to strengthen the people's State apparatus, which refers mainly to the People's Army, People's Police, and People's Court, for national defense and protection of the people's interests; and with this . . . to enable China to advance steadily under the leadership of the working class and the Communist Party from an agricultural to an industrial country, and from a new democratic to a socialist and Communist society, to eliminate classes and to realize world Communism.

Outbreak of Hostilities in Korea
(President Harry S. Truman, Statement to the press, June 27, 1950)

In Korea the Government forces, which were armed to prevent border raids and to preserve internal security, were attacked by invading forces from North Korea. The Security Council of the United Nations called upon the invading troops to cease hostilities and to withdraw to the 38th parallel. This they have not done, but on the contrary have pressed the attack. The Security Council called upon all members of the United Nations to render every assistance to the United Nations in the execution of this resolution. In these circumstances I have ordered United States air and sea forces to give the Korean Government troops cover and support.

The attack upon Korea makes it plain beyond all doubt that Communism has passed beyond the use of subversion to conquer independent nations and will now use armed invasion and war. It has defied the orders of the Security Council of the United Nations issued to preserve international peace and security. In these circumstances the occupation of Formosa by Communist forces would be a direct threat to the security of the Pacific area and to the United States forces performing their lawful and necessary functions in that area. Accordingly I have ordered the Seventh Fleet to prevent any attack on Formosa. As a corollary of this action I am calling upon the Chinese Government on Formosa to cease all air and sea operations against the mainland. The Seventh Fleet will see that this is done. The determination of the future status of Formosa must await the restoration of security in the Pacific, a peace settlement with Japan, or consideration by the United Nations.

I have also directed that United States Forces in the Philippines be strengthened and that military assistance to the Philippine Government be accelerated.

I have similarly directed acceleration in the furnishing of military assistance to the forces of France and the Associated States in Indo-China and the dispatch of a military mission to provide close working relations with those forces. . . .

Gamal Abdel Nasser Expresses Egyptian Nationalism Nationalization of the Suez Canal, July 26, 1952. Radio Speech. (U.S. Department of State, *Publication,* 1956)

Today the Suez Canal, where 120,000 of our sons had lost their lives in digging it by *corvee,*[1] and for the foundation of which we paid 8 million pounds, has become a state within a state. It has humiliated ministers and cabinets. . . .

The income of the Suez Canal Company in 1955 reached 35 million Egyptian pounds, or 100 million dollars. This is the Suez Canal which, according to the Firman[2] was dug for the sake of Egypt. . . .

Do you know how much assistance America and Britain were going to offer us over 5 years? 70 million dollars. Do you know who takes the 100 million dollars, the company's income, every year? They take them, of course. . . .

We shall not repeat the past. We shall eradicate it by restoring our rights in the Suez Canal. This money is ours. This Canal is the property of Egypt because it is an Egyptian joint stock company.

The Canal was dug by Egypt's sons and 120,000 of them died while working. The Suez Canal Company in Paris is an imposter company. . . .

But history will never repeat itself. On the contrary, we shall build the High Dam. We shall restore our usurped rights. We shall build the High Dam as we want it. We are determined to do it. . . . Thus, today, citizens, when we build the High Dam we are actually building the dam to defend our dignity, freedom, and pride, and to eradicate humiliation and submission.

Egypt . . . announces that it will fight to the last drop of its blood . . . for the sake of Egypt. We shall not let war-mongers imperialists, or those who trade in human beings dominate us. We shall depend on our hands and on our blood. . . . We shall build a strong and dignified Egypt, the Arab Egypt. . . .

Today, citizens, the Suez Canal Company has been nationalized. This order has been published in the *Official Journal.* . . . Today . . . our wealth has been restored to us. . . .

We shall work, produce, and step-up production despite all these intrigues and these talks. Whenever I hear talk from Washington I shall say, "Die of your fury."

We shall build up industry in Egypt and compete with them.

[1] As used here, forced labor.

[2] Decree of the Khedive of Egypt, Ismail, authorizing construction of the Canal.

They do not want us to become an industrial country so that they can promote the sale of their products and market them in Egypt. I never saw any American aid directed towards industrialization. . . . American aid is everywhere directed towards exploitation. . . .

On embarking upon the fifth year of the Revolution, as Farouk was expelled on July 26, 1952, the Suez Canal Company will depart on the very same day. We are conscious of accomplishing glories and achieving true dignity. Sovereignty in Egypt will belong only to her sons.

The Cult of Stalin Comes to an End
(Report by Nikita Khrushchev to the Twentieth Congress of the Communist Party of the Soviet Union. February, 1956. (U.S. Department of State, *Press Release*)

Lenin used severe methods only in the most necessary cases, when the exploiting classes were still in existence and were vigorously opposing the revolution. . . .

Stalin, on the other hand, used extreme methods and mass repressions at a time when the revolution was already victorious, when the Soviet state was strengthened, when the exploiting classes were already liquidated . . . when our party was politically consolidated . . . both numerically and ideologically. It is clear that here Stalin showed in a whole series of cases his intolerance, his brutality, and his abuse of power. . . .

Stalin was a very distrustful man, sickly suspicious: we knew this from our work with him. . . . Everywhere and in everything he saw "enemies, two-facers, and spies. . . ."

The power accumulated in the hands of one person, Stalin, led to serious consequences during the Great Patriotic War. When we look at many of our novels, films, and historical "scientific studies," the role of Stalin in the . . . War appears to be entirely improbable. Stalin had foreseen everything. The Soviet army, on the basis of a strategic plan prepared by Stalin long before, used the tactics of so-called "active defense," i.e., tactics which, as we all know, allowed the Germans to come up to Moscow and Stalingrad. Using such tactics the Soviet army, supposedly, thanks only to Stalin's genius, turned to the offensive and subdued the enemy. . . .

. . . .Stalin put forward the thesis that the tragedy which our nation experienced in the first part of the war was the result of the "unexpected" attack of the Germans against the Soviet

Union. . . .This is completely untrue. As soon as Hitler came to power in Germany he assigned himself the task of liquidating Communism. The Fascists were saying this openly; they did not hide their plans. In order to attain this aggressive end all sorts of pacts and blocs were created. . . . Many facts from the pre-war period clearly showed that Hitler was going all out to begin a war against the Soviet State and that he had concentrated large armed units . . . near the Soviet borders.

Documents which have now been published show that by April 3, 1941, Churchill . . . personally warned Stalin that the Germans had begun regrouping their armed units with the intent of attacking the Soviet Union. However, Stalin took no heed of these warnings. What is more, Stalin ordered that no credence be given to information of this sort. . . .

Had our industry been mobilized . . . to supply the army with the necessary material, our wartime losses would have been decidedly smaller. Such mobilization had not been, however, started in time. And already in the first days of the war it became evident that our army was badly armed, that we did not have enough artillery, tanks, and planes. . . .

We must state that after the war the situation became even more complicated. Stalin became even more capricious, irritable, and brutal; in particular his suspicions grew. His persecution mania reached unbelievable dimensions. . . .

Let us recall the affair of the "Doctor-Plotters." Actually there was no "affair" outside of the declaration of the woman doctor, Timashuk, who was probably influenced or ordered by someone . . . to write to Stalin a letter in which she declared that doctors were applying . . . improper methods of medical treatment.

Such a letter was sufficient for Stalin to reach an immediate conclusion that there are doctor-plotters in the Soviet Union. He issued orders to arrest a group of eminent Soviet medical specialists. He personally issued advice on the conduct of the investigation and the method of interrogation of the arrested persons. . . . [He] called the investigative judge, gave him instruction, advised him on which investigative methods should be used: those methods were simple—beat, beat, and once again, beat.

Shortly after the doctors were arrested we members of the Political Bureau received protocols on the doctors: confessions of guilt. After distributing these protocols Stalin told us, "You are blind like young kittens; what will happen without me? The country will perish because you do not know how to recognize enemies."

We felt, however, that the case of the arrested doctors was questionable. . . . When we examined this "case" after Stalin's death, we found it to be fabricated from beginning to end.

The Hungarian Revolt Against Communist Control, 1956 (U.N. General Assembly, *Report of the Special Committee on the Problem of Hungary*)

What took place in Hungary in October and November 1956 was a spontaneous national uprising due to long-standing grievances which had caused resentment among the people. One of these grievances was the inferior status of Hungary with regard to the U.S.S.R.: the system of government was in part maintained by the weapon of terror, wielded by the AVH or political police, whose influence was exercised . . . through a complex network of agents and informers permeating the whole of Hungarian society. . . . From the stifling of free speech to the adoption of a Soviet-style uniform for the Hungarian army an alien influence existed in all walks of life. . . .

The thesis that the uprising was fomented by reactionary circles in Hungary and that it drew its strength from . . . "Western Imperialists" failed to survive the Committee's examination. From start to finish the uprising was led by students, workers, soldiers, and intellectuals, many of whom were Communists or former Communists. The majority of political demands put forward during the revolution included a stipulation that democratic socialism should be the basis of the Hungarian political structure and that such social achievements as the land reform should be safeguarded. At no time was any proposal made for the return to power, or to the Government, of any figure associated with pre-war days. "Fascists" and "saboteurs," heavily armed, could not have succeeded in landing on Hungarian airfields which were under Soviet supervision, or in crossing the Austrian frontier, where a closed zone was shown by the Austrian authorities to the military attaches of France, the United Kingdom, the United States of America, and the U.S.S.R.

The uprising was not planned in advance. . . . No single explanation can determine exactly why the outbreak occurred just when it did. Communist spokesmen . . . and the members of the present government, have recognized the bitter grievances of the Hungarian people before 23 October. They have spoken of a "broad, popular movement" caused by the "bitterness and indignation" of the masses. Two factors would seem to have brought this resentment to a head. The first of these was the news received on 19 October of a successful move by Poland for greater independence from the U.S.S.R. This news was largely instrumental in bringing the Hungarian students together in the meetings of 22 October. The second factor was the acute disappointment felt by the people when Erno Gero, First Secretary of the Central Committee of the Hungarian Workers' Party, in his speech on the evening of 23 October failed to meet any of the popular demands, and adopted what was considered a truculent tone towards his hearers.

. . . . It would appear that the Soviet authorities had taken steps as early as 20 October to make armed intervention in Hungary possible. Evidence exists of troop movements . . . from that date on. It would appear that plans for action had therefore been laid some time before the students met to discuss their demands. The Committee is not in a position to say whether the Soviet authorities anticipated that the grievances of the Hungarian people . . . could no longer be contained. Signs of opposition were evident before the 23rd; the Hungarian government had reason to foresee that trouble was brewing. While the evidence shows that Soviet troops from outside Hungary were used even in the first intervention, no clause of the Warsaw Treaty provides for intervention by armed forces of the Soviet Union to dictate political developments within any signatory's frontiers.

The demonstrations on 23 October were at first entirely peaceable . . . and no evidence has been discovered that any of those who voiced the political demands or joined the demonstrators had any intention to resort to force. While disappointment at Mr. Gero's speech may have angered the crowds, it would hardly of itself have sufficed to turn the demonstration into an armed uprising. That this happened was due to the action of the AVH in opening fire on the people outside the radio building. Within a few hours Soviet tanks were in action against the Hungarians. . . .

The few days of freedom enjoyed by the Hungarian people provided abundant evidence of the popular nature of the uprising. A free press and radio came to life all over Hungary, and the disbanding of the AVH was the signal for general rejoicing, which revealed the degree of unity achieved by the people once the burden of fear had been lifted from them. . . .

Steps were taken by the Workers' Councils during this period to give the workers real control of nationalized industrial undertakings and to abolish unpopular institutions, such as the production norms. . . . During the days of freedom . . . attempts were made to clear up the streets of Budapest and life was beginning to return to normal. . . .

Following the second Soviet intervention of 4 November, there has been no evidence of popular support for Mr. Kadar's government. Mr. Kadar has successively abandoned most of the points from the revolutionary program which he had at first promised to the Hungarian people. On the central question of the withdrawal of Soviet troops he has moved from complete acceptance of the nation's wishes to a refusal to discuss the subject in present circumstances. Against the workers, he has proceeded step by step to destroy their power and that of the Workers' Councils. Capital punishment is applicable to strike activities. The processes of justice have been distorted by the institution of special police and special courts and by the ignoring of the rights of the accused. The Social Democratic Party has again been forcibly liquidated. General elections have been postponed for two years. Writers and intellectuals are subjected to repressive measures. . . . Only a small fraction of the 190,000 Hungarians . . . who fled the country have accepted his invitation to return.

The Theory of Neutralism
(Speech by Jawaharlal Nehru to the Tenth General Conference of UNESCO, November 5, 1956)

The meeting of the General Conference of UNESCO in Delhi has a certain special significance. It is a tribute, if I may say so, to the importance that is now attached by this great organization to the countries of Asia. But this conference is significant in yet another way which was not realized when this date and venue were chosen. We meet at a moment when we can hear again the dread tramp of armed men and the thunder of bombs hurled from the skies to destroy men and cities. . . .

Soon after the last great war ended, and as a result of the war and the hunger for peace of the peoples of the world, the

United Nations Organization came into being. The General Assembly of the United Nations came to represent the mind of the world community and its desire for peace. If the General Assembly mainly faced the political problems of the world, its specialized agencies were charged with work of equal, if not greater, importance in the economic, educational, scientific, and cultural spheres.

Man does not live by politics alone, nor indeed, wholly by economics. And so UNESCO came into being to represent something that was vital to human existence and progress. Even as the United Nations General Assembly represented the political will of the world community, UNESCO tried to represent the finer and the deeper sides of human life and, indeed, might be said to represent the conscience of the world community.

I should like to remind you of the preamble to the constitution of this great organization. This embodies a declaration on behalf of the governments of the States and their peoples . . . that "since wars begin in the minds of men, it is in the minds of men that the defenses of peace must be constructed. . . : Here is laid down in clear and noble language the basic approach of this organization and the way it has to travel if it is to realize its objectives of international peace and the common welfare of mankind.

UNESCO has considerable achievements to its credit during its ten years of existence. And yet after these ten years what do we find? Violence and hatred still dominate the world. The doctrine of inequality of men and races is preached and practiced. The democratic principles of dignity, equality, and mutual respect are denied or ignored. Some countries dominate over others and hold their people in subjection, denying them freedom and the right to grow; and armed might is used to suppress the freedom of countries. . . .

* * *

We see today in Egypt, as well as in Hungary, both human dignity and freedom outraged, and the force of modern arms used to suppress peoples and to gain political objectives; old colonial methods which we had thought . . . belonged to a more unenlightened age are revived and practiced: in other parts of the world also movements for freedom are crushed by superior might. . . .

* * *

You will forgive me, I hope, if I speak with some feeling.

I would be untrue to . . . this distinguished gathering if I did not refer to something which has moved us deeply and which must be in the minds of all of us here. We use brave phrases to impress ourselves and others, but our actions belie those noble sentiments, and so we live in a world of unreality where profession has little to do with practice. . . .

At present it would appear that great countries think that the only reality is force and violence and that fine phrases are merely the apparatus of diplomacy. This is a matter which concerns all of us, whichever quarter of the world we may live in. But, in a sense, it concerns us in Asia and Africa more than in other countries because some of our countries have recently emerged into freedom and independence and we cherish them with all our strength and passion. We are devoting ourselves to serving our people and to bettering their lives and making them grow in freedom and progress. We have bitter memories of the past when we were prevented from so growing and we can never permit a return to that past age. And yet we find an attempt made to reverse the current of history and of human development. We find that all our efforts at progress might well be set at nought by the ambitions and conflicts of other peoples.

Many of the countries in Asia laid down a set of Five Principles, which we call Panchsheel, for the governance of international relations and for the peaceful coexistence of nations . . . so that each nation and people might grow according to its own genius and in cooperation with others. . . . We see now that these Five Principles are also words without meaning to some countries who claim the right of deciding problems by superior might.

I have called this great assembly the conscience of the world community. . . . May I also . . . point out to you that a world organization like this cannot be properly constituted or function adequately if a large section of the world remains unrepresented here? I hope that three countries which have recently attained their independence—the Sudan, Tunisia, and Morocco—will find a place soon in this organization to share the burdens and responsibilities of its labors. But I would especially refer to the People's Government of China and the six hundred million people who live in that great country who have so far not been represented here.

The countries of Europe and America are fortunate in some ways for they have attained a measure of well-being. We in

Asia and Africa still lack the primary necessities of life. To obtain these becomes, therefore, our first task; and we cannot do so with war and violence. I earnestly trust that the meeting of this organization in this ancient city of Delhi will turn your minds more to the needs of those under-developed countries of the world, which hunger for bread and education and health; but which, above all, cherish freedom and will not part with it at any price.

Our country is a large one and our population is considerable. But we have no desire to interfere with any other country. We have no hatreds and we have been nurtured under the inspiring guidance of our great leader, Mahatma Gandhi, in the ways of peace. We want to be friends with all the world. . . .

The Problem of German Reunification (Declaration of the Western Powers, July 29, 1957)

Twelve years have elapsed since the end of the war in Europe. The hopes of the peoples of the world for the establishment of a basis for a just and lasting peace have nevertheless not been fulfilled. One of the basic reasons for the failure to reach a settlement is the continued division of Germany. . . .

The governments of France, the United Kingdom, and the United States, which share with the Soviet Union responsibility for the reunification of Germany and the conclusion of a peace treaty, and the government of the Federal Republic of Germany, as the only government qualified to speak for the German people as a whole, wish to declare their views on these questions, including the question of European security, and the principles which motivate their policies in this regard.

1. A European settlement must be based on freedom and justice. Every nation has the right to determine its own way of life in freedom; to determine for itself its political, economic, and social system; and to provide for its security with due regard to the legitimate interests of other nations. Justice requires that the German people be allowed to re-establish their national unity on the basis of this fundamental right.

2. The reunification of Germany remains the joint responsibility of the four powers who in 1945 assumed supreme authority in Germany; a responsibility which was reaffirmed in the *Directive* issued by the four heads of government in Geneva in July, 1955. . . .

3. The unnatural division of Germany and of its capital, Berlin, is a continuing source of international tension. So long as Germany remains divided there can be no German peace treaty and no assurance of stability in Europe. . . .

4. Only a freely elected all-German government can undertake . . . obligations which will inspire confidence on the part of other countries and which will be considered just and binding in the future by the people of Germany themselves.

6. There should be no discrimination against a reunified Germany. Its freedom and security should not be prejudiced by an imposed status of neutralization or demilitarization. Its government should be free to determine its foreign policy and to decide on its international associations. It should not be deprived of the right . . . to participate in collective measures of self-defense.

7. Re-establishment of the national unity of Germany . . . would not in itself constitute a threat to Germany's neighbors nor would it prejudice their security. . . .

8. The western powers have never required as a condition of German reunification that a reunified Germany should join the North Atlantic Treaty Organization. . . .

9. If the all-German government . . . should elect to join NATO, the western powers after consultation with other members of NATO, are prepared to offer . . . to the government of the Soviet Union . . . assurances of a significant and far-reaching character. . . .

11. The reunification of Germany . . . would facilitate the achievement of a comprehensive disarmament agreement. . . . The western powers do not intend to enter into any agreement on disarmament which would prejudice the reunification of Germany.

12. Any measures of disarmament applicable to Europe must have the consent of the European nations concerned and take into account the link between European security and German reunification. . . .

Through this declaration the western powers, in full accord with the Federal Republic, wish again to manifest their sincere desire to enter into negotiations with the Soviet Union in order to reach a European settlement and to give evidence that the paramount objective of their policy is the attainment of a just and lasting peace.

President Charles DeGaulle Outlines the Problems of the Fifth Republic (Radio and Television Broadcast to the French Nation, June 13, 1958)

French unity was breaking up. Civil war was about to begin. In the eyes of the world France seemed on the verge of dissolution. It was then that I assumed responsibility for governing our country.

The tragedy of Algeria . . . was inevitable, because for twelve years the party system, insecurely based on a deeply divided people, in the midst of a . . . dangerous world, showed itself totally unfit to insure the conduct of affairs. This was by no means due to . . . incompetence. . . . Those who held positions of power under the Fourth Republic were able. . . , honest and patriotic. But, as they never represented anything but small fractions of the population these men who governed did not identify themselves with the general interest. Moreover, divided amongst themselves. . . , struggling against the encroachments of the Parliamentary Assembly . . . subjected to the demands of the parties they represented—they were doomed to live . . . faced with huge problems which they could not possibly solve.

I said huge problems. They were indeed huge, those problems which confronted them. So are those which we shall have to brace together: to pacify Algeria . . . in such a way that it will forever be body and soul with France; to organize in the federal manner the ties between our metropolitan country and the associated countries in Africa and Madagascar; to establish on the basis of cooperation our relations with Morocco, Tunisia, and the States of Indo-China.

In the western world to which we belong . . . to take a place that is our own; to perform an action that is our action, with a view to serving . . . both peace and security.

At home, to succeed in making the very difficult . . . effort to restore the equilibrium of our finances and our economy, lacking which our country would be heading for . . . disaster. . . .

Women and men of France, this is what we must do first of all. To start out with . . . I request you earnestly to insure a triumphal success for the loan which we are about to float: first phase of our recovery, first test of national confidence that you will give to yourselves and . . . that you will grant me who needs it so very badly.

"Isn't all this too much for us?" complain those who . . . have, as their secret motto, that of Mephistopheles, the eloquent demon of despair, "I am the spirit which denies everything." No, it is not too much for France . . . which, in spite of past trials and the confusion in her affairs of state, can manage to hold in her hand all the cards for an extraordinary regeneration: a population that is growing; an economy that has . . . overcome the obstacle of routine; a technology that is forging ahead; new sources of ability that are ready to spring from the deepest layers of the populations; the Sahara, which holds a fortune for us and the territories bordering it . . . ; an army that is very fine and very good; lastly the world which wishes . . . to see us play the part that is rightfully ours. . . .

Ah, I do not pity our youth which sees all these resources of life, all these incentives to activity offered to it; but there is not a single Frenchman who does not know that any future is barred to us if France does not have to guide her a state which is capable of doing so.

. . . . It is my task . . . to propose to our people new institutions of such a kind that they will provide for the Republic powers that are strong enough, stable enough, effective enough to be responsible for its destiny. I shall do so at the beginning of the autumn. . . .

Act of Bogota. September 13, 1960
(U.S. Department of State, *Bulletin*)

The Special Committee to Study the Formulation of New Measures for Economic Cooperation

Recognizing that the preservation and strengthening of free and democratic institutions in the American republics requires the acceleration of social and economic progress in Latin America adequate to meet the legitimate aspirations of the peoples of the Americas . . .;

Recognizing that the success of a cooperative program of economic and social progress will require maximum self-help efforts on the part of the American republics . . .;

Believing it opportune to give further practical expression to the spirit of Operation Pan-America by immediately enlarging the opportunities of the people of Latin America for social progress . . .;

Recommends to the Council of the Organization of American States:

I. MEASURES FOR SOCIAL IMPROVEMENT. An inter-American program for social development should be established which should be directed to the carrying out of the following measures of social improvement in Latin America. . . .

A. *Measures for the improvement of conditions of rural living and land use—*

1. The examination of existing legal and institutional systems with respect to:
   a. land tenure legislation and facilities with a view to insuring a wider and more equitable distribution and ownership of land . . .;
   b. agricultural credit institutions with a view to providing adequate financing to individual farmers or groups of farmers;
   c. tax systems and procedures and fiscal policies with a view to assuring equity of taxation and encouraging improved use of land, . . .
2. The initiation or acceleration of appropriate programs to modernize and improve the existing legal and industrial framework to insure better conditions of land tenure, extend more adequate credit facilities. . . .
3. The acceleration of the preparation of projects and programs for:
   a. land reclamation and land settlement . . .;
   b. the increase of the productivity of land already in use . . .;
   c. the construction of farm-to-market and access roads.
4. The adoption or acceleration of other government service programs designed . . . to assist the small farmer. . . .

C. *Measures for the improvement of educational systems and training facilities—*

1. The re-examination of educational systems, giving particular attention to:
   a. the development of modern methods of mass education . . .;
   b. the adequacy of training in the industrial arts and sciences . . .;

c. the need to provide instruction in rural schools not only in basic subjects but also in agriculture, health, sanitation, nutrition, and in methods of home and community improvement;
d. the broadening of courses of study in secondary schools to provide the training . . . for clerical and executive personnel in industry, commerce, public administration, and community service;
f. vocational agricultural instruction;
g. advanced education of administrators, engineers, economists, and other professional personnel of key importance to economic development.

D. *Measures for the improvement of public health—*

1. The re-examination of programs and policies of public health, giving particular attention to:
a. strengthening the expansion of national and local health services . . .;
b. the progressive development of health insurance systems . . .;
c. the provision of hospital and health service in areas located away from main centers of population;
e. the strengthening of campaigns for the control or elimination of communicable diseases [and] malaria;
f. the provision of water supply facilities for purposes of health and economic development;
g. the training of public health officials and technicians;
h. the strengthening of programs of nutrition for low-income groups. . . .

III. MEASURES FOR ECONOMIC DEVELOPMENT

The Special Committee Recommends:

1. That special attention be given to an expansion of long-term lending, particularly in view of the instability of exchange earnings of countries exporting primary products. . . .
2. That urgent attention be given to the search for effective and practical ways . . . to deal with the problem of the instability of exchange earnings of countries heavily dependent upon the exportation of primary products. . . .

The Problem of Neutrality in Laos (Statement by U.S. Secretary of State Dean Rusk, May 17, 1961. U.S. Department of State, *Bulletin*)

There is only one problem of peace in southeast Asia and, indeed, in many other parts of the world. It is whether those who have wrapped around themselves the doctrine of the historical inevitability of world domination by their own particular political system merely believe it or will attempt to impose it upon others by all the means at their disposal. The real issue is whether peaceful coexistence is what normal language would indicate it means, or whether it means an all-out and continuous struggle against all those not under Communist control. . . .

We note the statement made by the representative from Peiping that he "is ready to work jointly with the delegations of all the other countries participating in this conference to make contributions to the peaceful settlement of the Laotian question." We ourselves are prepared to work diligently to discover whether there is agreement in the conference on the questions before us.

Promptly after assuming office President Kennedy said: "We strongly and unreservedly support the goal of a neutral and independent Laos, tied to no outside power or group of powers. . . ." In early exchanges with Chairman Khrushchev, the latter affirmed his commitment to a neutral and independent Laos. . . . Other spokesmen of other governments . . . have declared their desire for a neutral Laos.

The King of that country, on February 19 of this year, declared: "We desire to proclaim once more the policy of true neutrality that Laos has always sought to follow. . . . We appeal to all countries to respect the independence, sovereignty, territorial integrity, and neutrality of Laos."

We believe the most immediate problem is to insure an effective cease-fire, to give the International Control Commission the necessary and relevant instructions, and to give it the resources required to carry out its vital task.

Next we must turn to the problem of insuring a genuinely neutral Laos. . . .

But what does this mean? Neutrality is not simply a negative concept. A neutral Laos should be a dynamic, viable Laos, making progress toward more stable political institutions, economic well-being, and social justice. A truly neutral Laos must have the right to choose its own way of life. . . .

It is, of course, too early in the conference to present detailed proposals for achieving this end. But it is not too early to begin considering the broad outlines of a program directed to the goal.

As my Government sees it, such an outline would involve three separate points:

1. A definition of the concept of neutrality, as it applies to Laos, which all of us gathered here could pledge ourselves to respect. . . .

2. The development of effective international machinery for maintaining and safeguarding that neutrality against threats to it from within as well as without.

3. Laos will need, if it wishes to take its place in the modern world, a substantial economic and technical aid program. We believe that such aid could be most appropriately administered by neutral nations from the area, and that it should be supported by contributions from many states and agencies. . . .

Alliance for Progress
(The Charter of Punta Del Este. August 17, 1961. U.S. Department of State, *Bulletin*)

We, the American republics, hereby proclaim our decision to unite in a common effort to bring our people accelerated economic progress and broader social justice within the framework of personal dignity and political liberty.

Almost two hundred years ago we began in this hemisphere the long struggle for freedom which now inspires people in all parts of the world. Today, in ancient lands, men moved to hope by the revolutions of our young nations search for liberty. . . . The men and women of our hemisphere are reaching for the better life which today's skills have placed within their grasp. They are determined for themselves and their children to . . . end those conditions which benefit the few at the expense of the needs and dignity of the many. . . .

Inspired by these principles . . . the American republics hereby resolve to adopt the following program of action to establish and carry forward an Alliance for Progress.

Title I. Objectives of the Alliance for Progress

1. To achieve in the participating Latin American countries

a substantial and sustained growth of per capita incomes at a rate designed to attain . . . levels of income capable of assuring self-sustaining development. . . .

It is recognized that, in order to reach these objectives within a reasonable time, the rate of economic growth in any country of Latin America should be not less than 2.5 per cent per capita per year. . . .

2. To make the benefits of economic progress available to all citizens of all economic and social groups through a more equitable distribution of national income . . . at the same time that a higher proportion of the national product is devoted to investment.

4. To accelerate the process of . . . industrialization so as to increase the productivity of the economy as a whole . . . providing productive and remunerative employment for unemployed or part-time workers. . . .

5. To raise greatly the level of agricultural productivity. . . .

6. To encourage . . . programs of comprehensive agrarian reform leading to the effective transformation . . . of unjust structures and systems of land tenure and use, with a view to replacing latifundia and dwarf-holdings by an equitable system of land tenure. . . .

7. To eliminate adult illiteracy, and by 1970 to assure, as a minimum, access to six years of primary education for each . . . child in Latin America; to modernize and expand vocational, secondary, and higher educational and training facilities; to strengthen the capacity for basic and applied research. . . .

8. To increase life expectancy at birth by a minimum of five years. . . .

9. To increase the construction of low-cost houses for low-income families. . . .

10. To maintain stable price levels, avoiding inflation or deflation and the consequent social hardships and maldistribution of resources. . . .

11. To strengthen existing agreements on economic integration, with a view to the ultimate fulfillment of aspirations for a Latin American common market. . . .

Chapter II. National Development Programs

1. Latin American countries agree to introduce or strengthen systems for the preparation, execution, and periodic revision of national programs for economic and social development consistent with the principles, objectives, and requirements con-

tained in this document.

2. National development programs should incorporate self-help efforts directed to:

(a) The improvement of human resources and widening of opportunities through raising general standards of education and health; improving and extending technical education and the training of professionals . . . ; encouraging managerial, entrepreneurial, and salaried talent; providing more productive employment for underemployed manpower; establishing effective systems of labor relations. . . .

(b) The wider development and more efficient use of natural resources. . . .

(c) . . . . Insuring in countries with Indian populations the integration of these populations into the economic, social, and cultural processes of modern life. . . .

(d) The more effective . . . and equitable mobilization and use of financial resources through the reform of tax structures, including fair and adequate taxation of large incomes and real estate. . . .

(e) The promotion . . . of conditions that will encourage the flow of foreign investments. . . .

Chapter III. Immediate and Short-Term Action Measures

1. Recognizing that a number of Latin American countries . . . may require emergency financial assistance, the United States will provide assistance . . . for such purposes. . . .

2. Participating Latin American countries should immediately increase their efforts to accelerate their development, giving special emphasis. . . . to the following objectives:

(a) The completion of projects already under way and the initiation of projects for which the basic studies have been made in order to accelerate their financing and execution.

(c) The facilitation of the preparation . . . of long-term programs . . . designed:

i. to train teachers, technicians, and specialists
ii. to provide accelerated training to workers and farmers
iii. to improve basic statistics
iv. to establish needed credit and marketing facilities
v. to improve services and administration

3. . . . . The United States will provide assistance under the Alliance . . . totalling more than one billion dollars in the year ending March 1962.

Title III. Economic Integration of Latin America

The American republics consider that the broadening of present national markets in Latin America is essential to accelerate the process of economic development in the hemisphere. . . . The broadening of markets will also make possible the better use of resources under the Alliance for Progress. Consequently, the American republics recognize that . . . :

11. The promotion and coordination of transportation and communications systems is an effective way to accelerate the integration process . . . ;

12. In working toward economic integration and complimentary economies, efforts should be made to achieve an appropriate coordination of national plans, or to engage in joint planning for various economies through the existing regional integration organizations . . . ;

14. The active participation of the private sector is essential to economic integration and development, and except in those countries in which free enterprise does not exist, development planning by the pertinent national public agencies, far from hindering such participation, can facilitate and guide it. . . .

15. As the countries of the hemisphere still under colonial domination achieve their independence, they should be invited to participate in Latin American economic integration programs.

President John F. Kennedy: Cuban Missile Speech (John F. Kennedy: *Address to the Nation,* 1963)

This government . . . has maintained the closest surveillance of the Soviet military build-up on the island of Cuba. Within the past week unmistakable evidence has established the fact that a series of offensive missile sites is now in preparation on that imprisoned island. . . .

The characteristics of these new missile sites indicate two distinct types of installations. Several of them include medium range ballistic missiles capable of carrying a nuclear warhead for a distance of more than one thousand nautical miles. . . . Additional sites not yet completed appear to be designed for intermediate-range ballistic missiles—capable of traveling more than twice as far. . . .

This urgent transformation of Cuba into an important strategic base . . . constitutes an explicit threat to the peace and security of all the Americas, in flagrant and deliberate defiance of the Rio Pact of 1947, the traditions of this nation and hemisphere, the joint resolution of the 97th Congress, the Charter of the United Nations, and my own public warnings to the Soviets on September 4 and 13. . . .

The size of this undertaking makes clear that it has been planned for some months. Yet only last month . . . the Soviet government publicly stated . . . that, and I quote, "the armaments and military equipment sent to Cuba are designed exclusively for defensive purposes. . . ." That statement was false.

Only last Thursday, as evidence of this rapid offensive build-up was already in my hand, Soviet Foreign Minister Gromyko told me in my office that he was instructed to make it clear once again . . . that Soviet assistance to Cuba "pursued solely the purpose of contributing to the defense capabilities of Cuba . . ." and that "if it were not otherwise the Soviet government would never become involved in rendering such assistance." That statement also was false.

This secret, swift, and extraordinary build-up of Communist missiles—in an area well known to have a special and historical relationship to the United States and the nations of the Western Hemisphere, in violation of Soviet assurances, and in defiance of American and hemispheric policy—this sudden, clandestine decision to station strategic weapons . . . outside of Soviet soil—is a deliberately provocative and unjustified change in the *status quo* which cannot be accepted by this country, if our courage and our commitments are ever to be trusted again by either friend or foe.

The 1930's taught us a clear lesson: Aggressive conduct, if allowed to grow unchecked and unchallenged, ultimately leads to war. This nation is opposed to war. We are also true to our word. Our unswerving objective, therefore, must be to . . . secure their withdrawal or elimination from the Western Hemisphere.

Acting, therefore, in the defense of our own security and of the entire Western Hemisphere, and under the authority entrusted to me by the Constitution . . . I have directed that the following initial steps be taken immediately:

First: To halt this offensive build-up a strict quarantine on all offensive military equipment under shipment to Cuba is being initiated. All ships of any kind bound for Cuba from whatever nation or port will, if found to contain cargoes of offensive weapons, be turned back. . . .

Second: I have directed the continued and increased close surveillance of Cuba and its military build-up. . . . The foreign ministers of the OAS in their communique of October 6, rejected secrecy on such matters in this hemisphere. . . . I have directed the armed forces to prepare for any eventualities. . . .

Third: It shall be the policy of this nation to regard any nuclear missile launched from Cuba against any nation in the Western Hemisphere as an attack by the Soviet Union on the United States, requiring a full retaliatory response upon the Soviet Union.

Fourth: As a necessary military precaution I have reinforced our base at Guantanamo. . . .

Fifth: We are calling tonight for an immediate meeting of the organ of consultation under the Organization of American States to consider this threat to hemispheric security and to invoke Articles 6 and 8 of the Rio Treaty. . . . Our other allies around the world have also been alerted.

Sixth: Under the Charter of the United Nations we are asking tonight that an emergency meeting of the Security Council be convoked. . . . Our resolution will call for the prompt dismantling and withdrawal of all offensive weapons in Cuba under the supervision of UN observers, before the quarantine can be lifted.

Seventh and finally: I call upon Chairman Khrushchev to halt and eliminate this clandestine, reckless, and provocative threat to world peace. . . . I call upon him further to abandon this course of world domination. . . .

Finally, I want to say a few words to the captive people of Cuba. . . . I speak to you as a friend, as one who knows of your deep attachment to your fatherland, as one who shares your aspirations for liberty and justice for all. And I have watched, and the American people have watched, with deep sorrow how your nationalist revolution was betrayed—and how your fatherland fell under . . . puppets and agents of an international conspiracy. . . .

These new weapons are not in your interest. They contribute nothing to your peace and well-being. They can only undermine it. But this country has no wish to cause you to suffer or to impose any system upon you. . . .

Many times in the past the Cuban people have risen to throw

out tyrants who destroyed their liberty. And I have no doubt that most Cubans today look forward to the time when they will be truly free—free from foreign domination, free to choose their own leaders, free to select their own system, free to own their own land, free to speak, and write, and worship without fear or degradation. . . .

My fellow citizens, let no one doubt that this is a difficult and dangerous effort on which we have set out. No one can foresee precisely what course it will take or what costs or casualties will be incurred. Many months of sacrifice and self-discipline lie ahead—months in which both our patience and our will will be tested. . . . But the greatest danger of all would be to do nothing.

The path we have chosen for the present is full of hazards . . . but it is the one most consistent with our character and courage as a nation and our commitments around the world. The cost of freedom is always high—but Americans have always paid it. And one path we shall never choose, and that is the path of surrender or submission.

APPENDIX I

Simplified Genealogical Chart
The Carolingian Dynasty

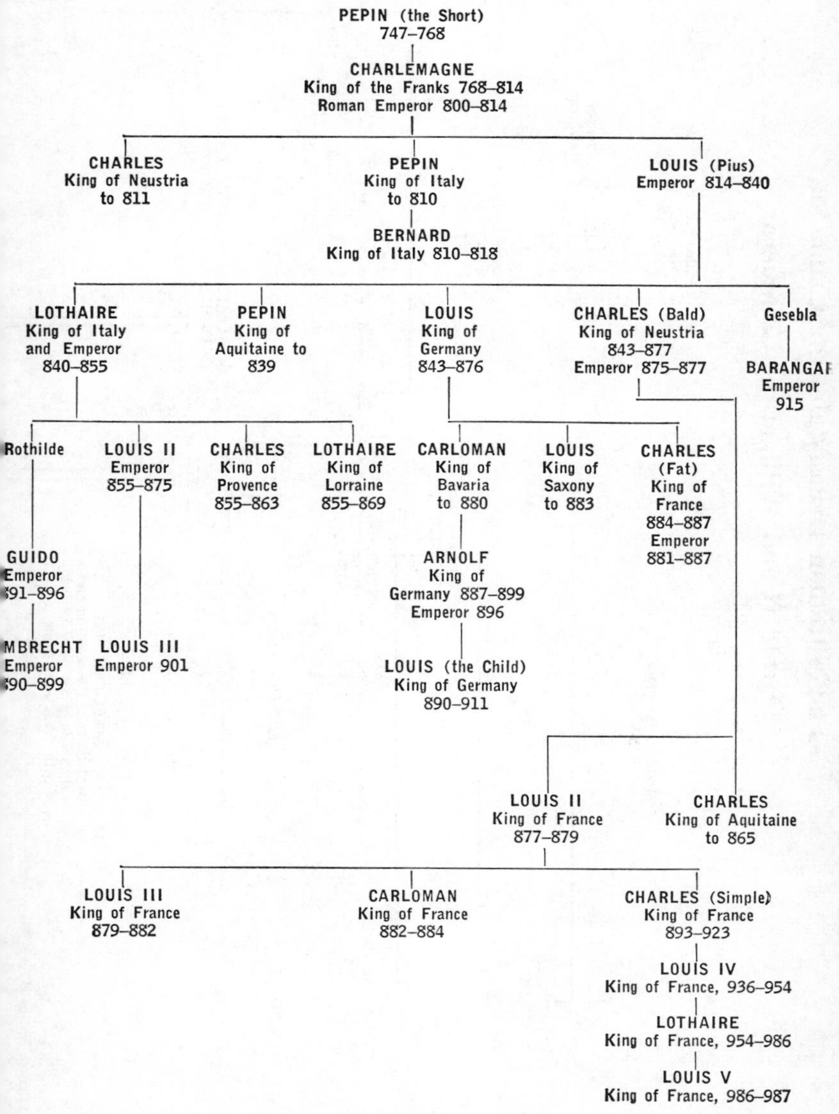

The Alfredian Dynasty and the Claims of Harold II and William the Conqueror

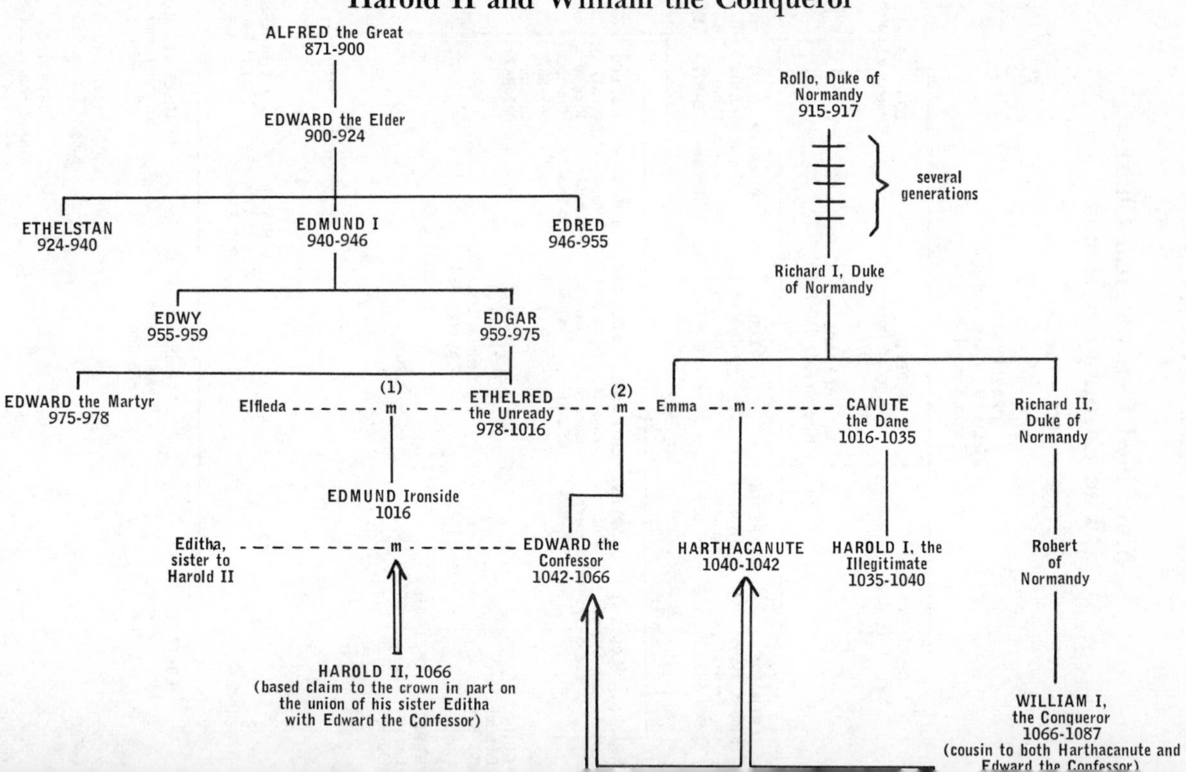

Simplified Genealogical Chart
The Capetian Kings of France

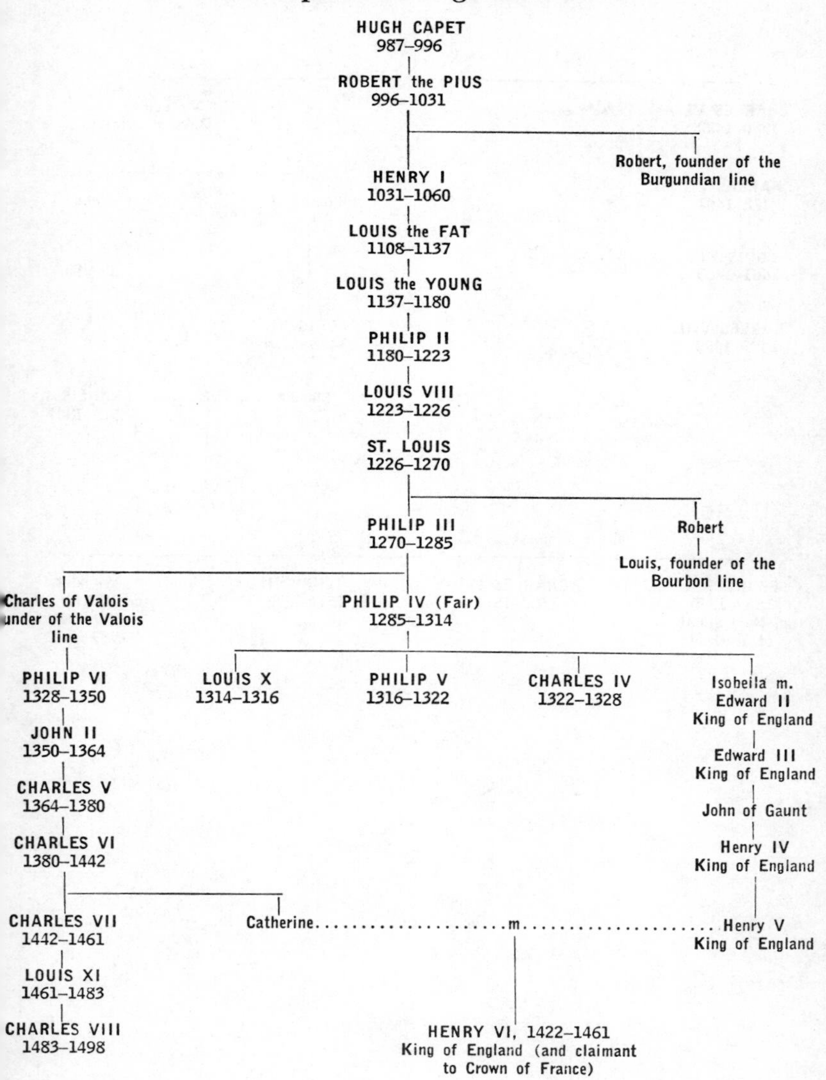

Simplified Genealogical Chart
The House of Valois (1364-1609)

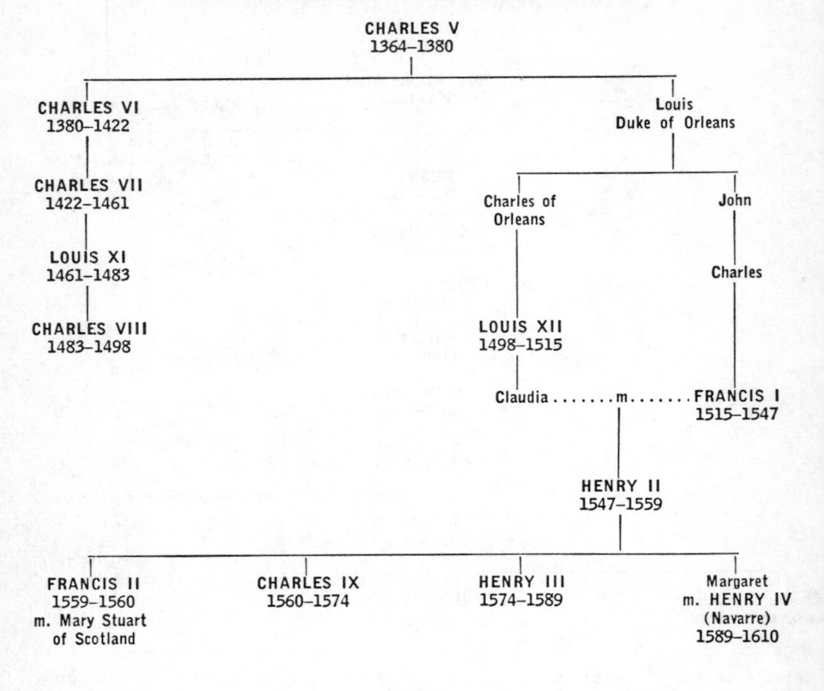

Simplified Genealogical Chart
The House of Hohenzollern (1415-1918)

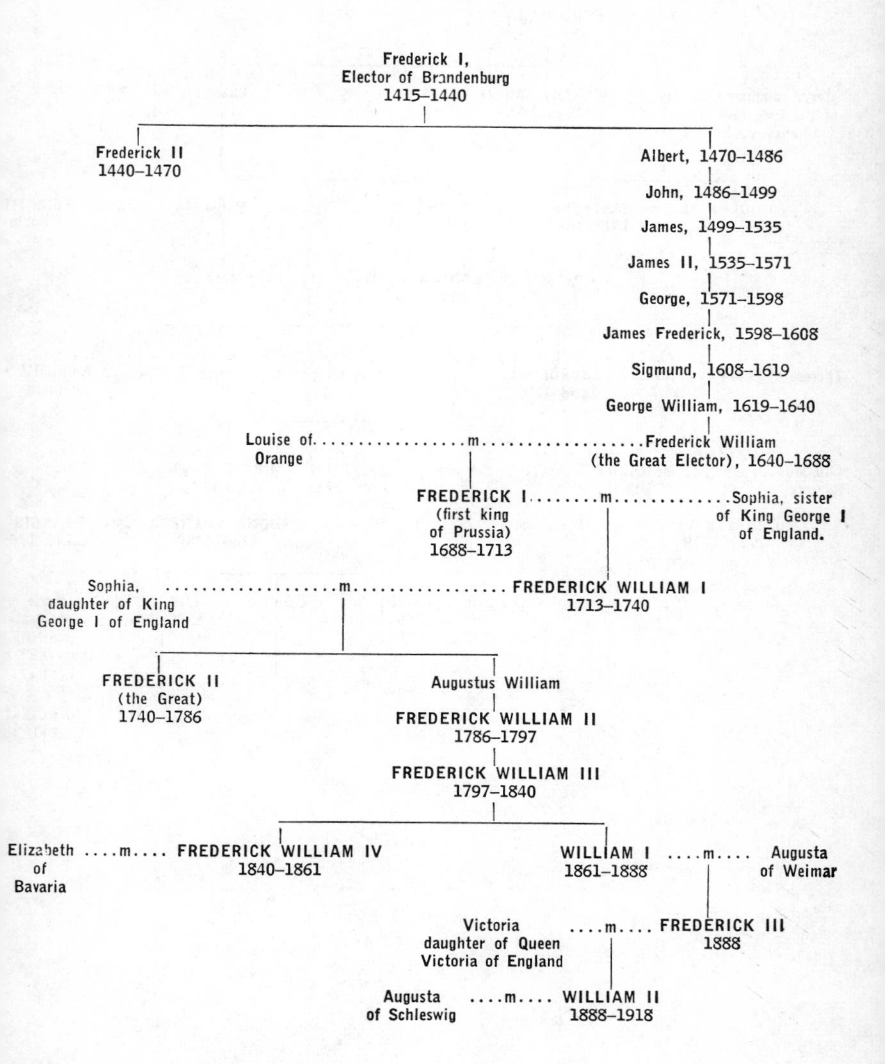

Simplified Genealogical Chart
The Austrian Hapsburgs (1556-1835)

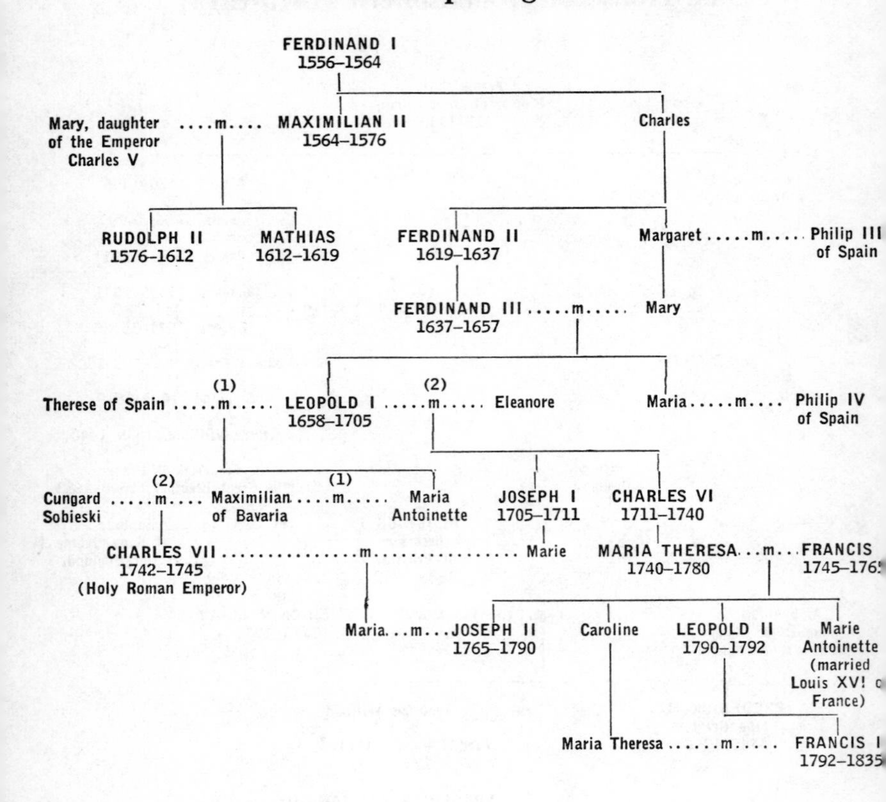

Simplified Genealogical Chart
The French Bourbon Kings and the House of Orleans (1589-1848)

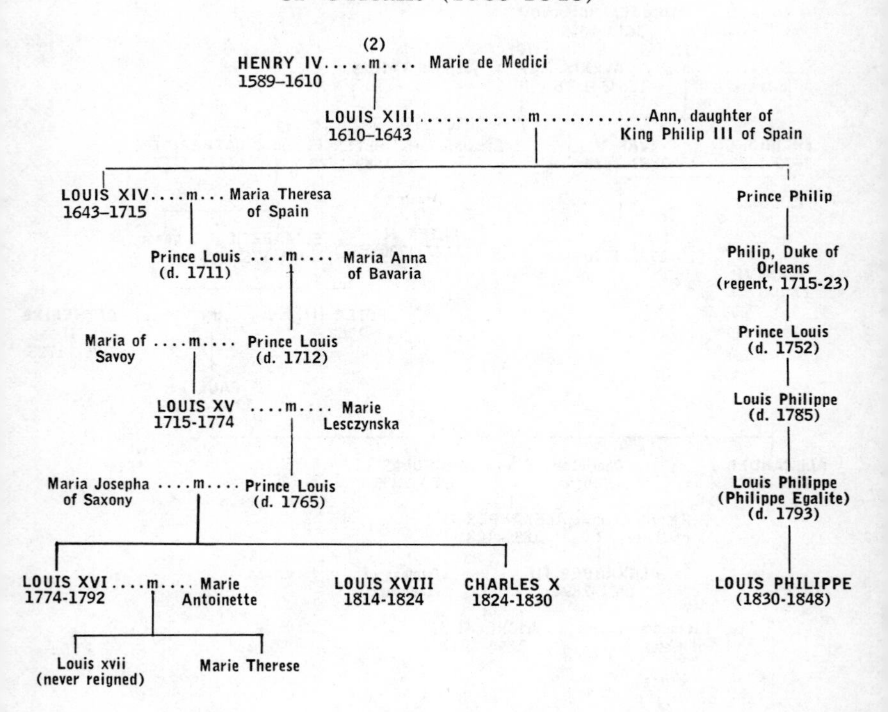

Simplified Genealogical Chart
The House of Romanov (1613-1917)

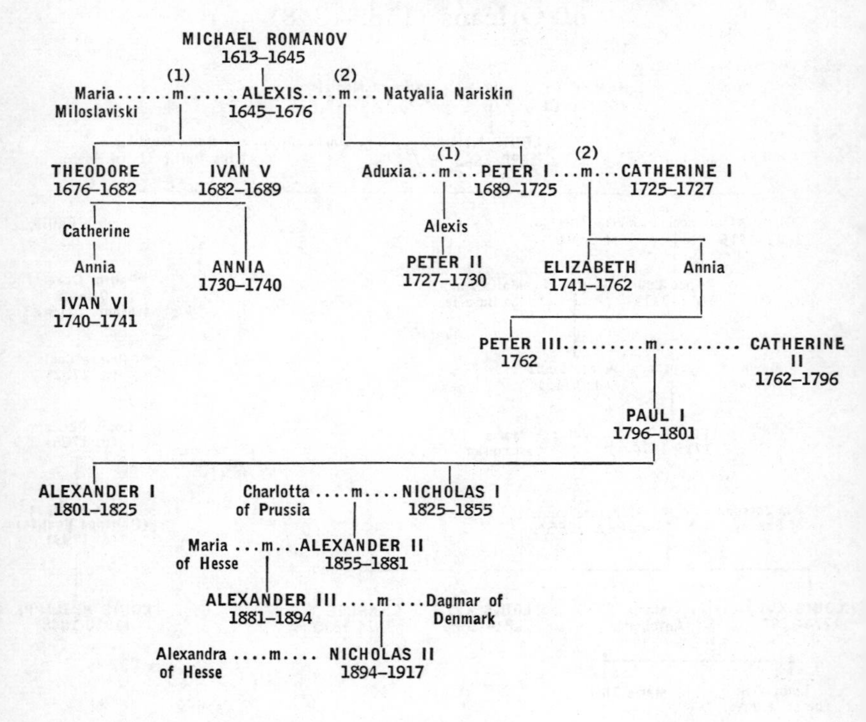

Simplified Genealogical Chart
Norman and Plantagenet Kings of England

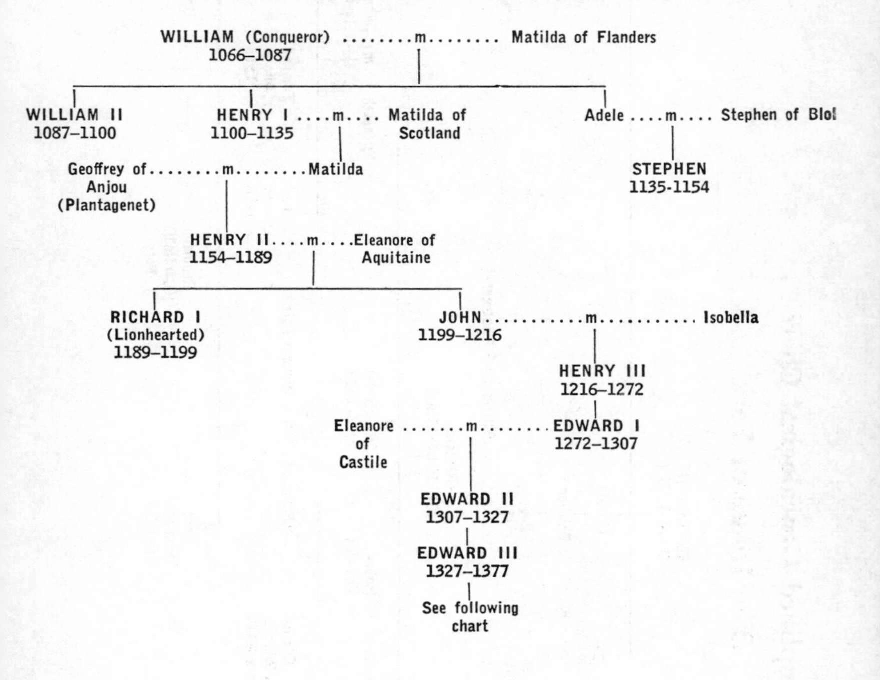

Simplified Genealogical Chart

The House of York

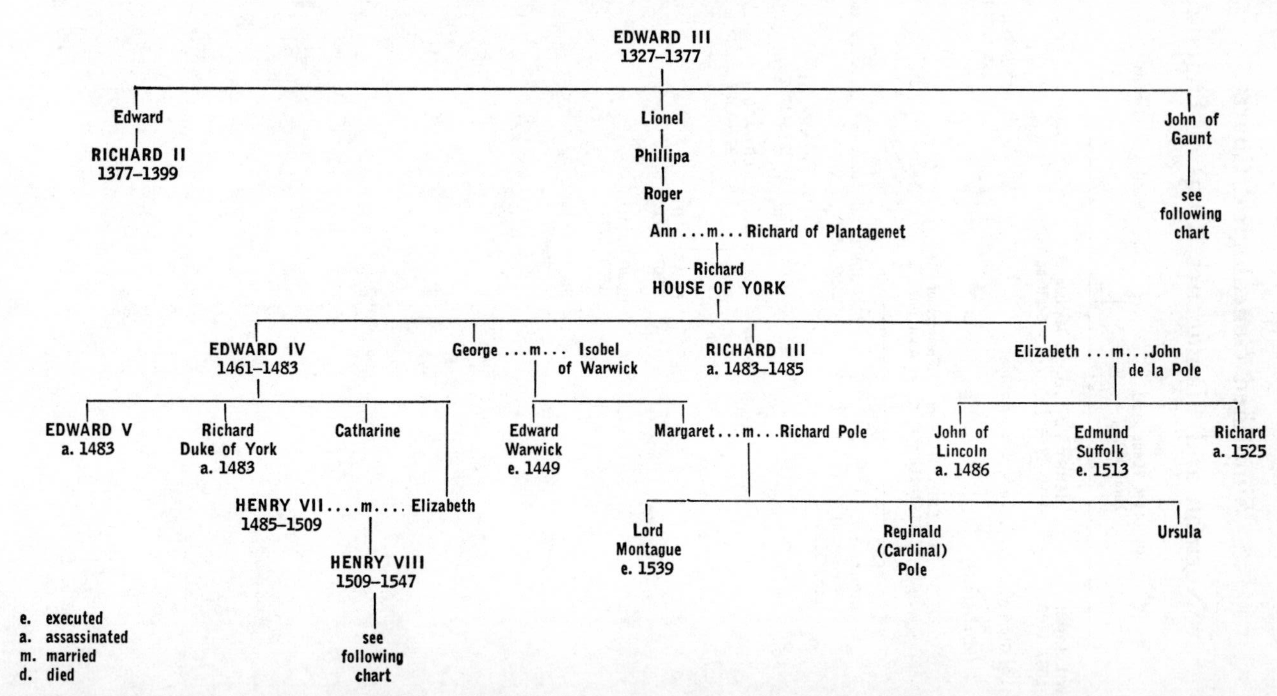

Houses of Lancaster and York

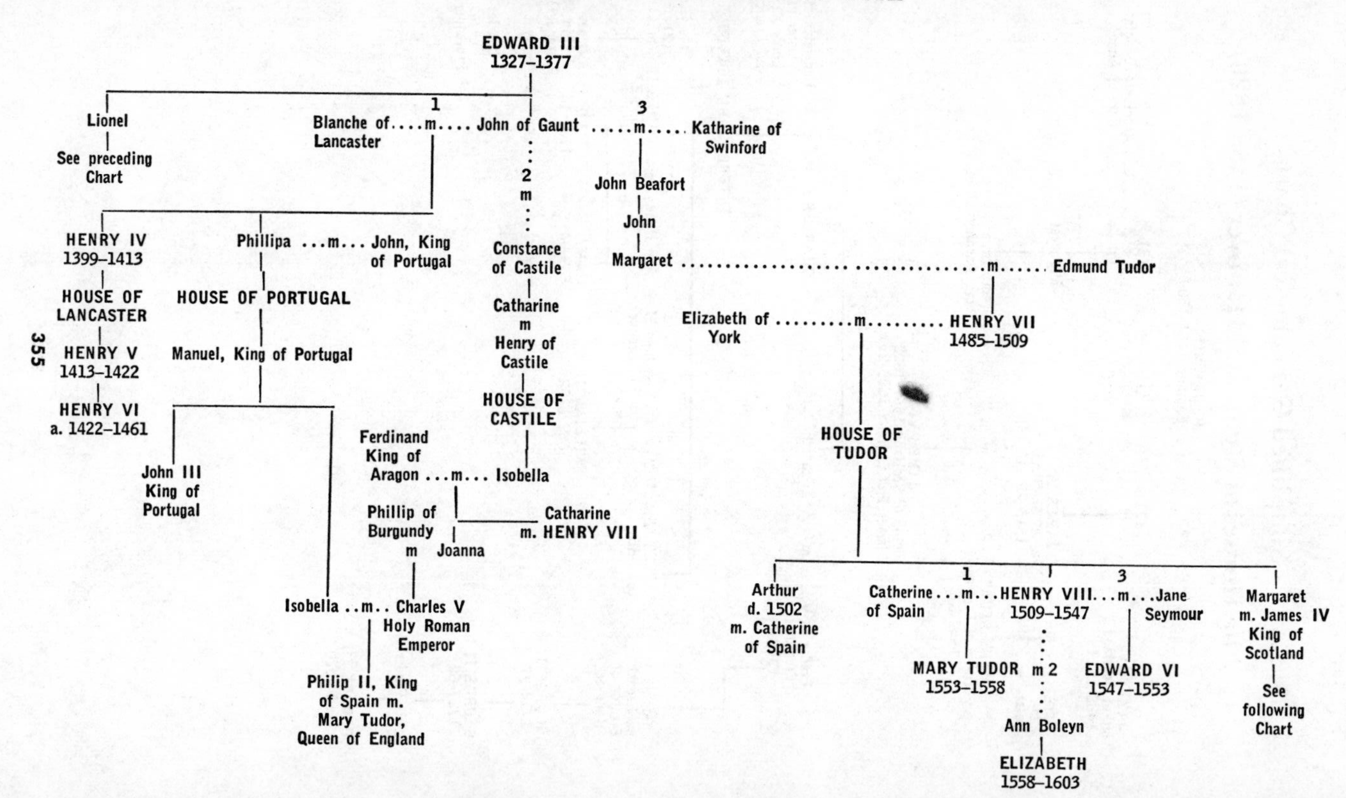

Simplified Genealogical Chart

The Houses of Stuart and Hanover (1488-1820)

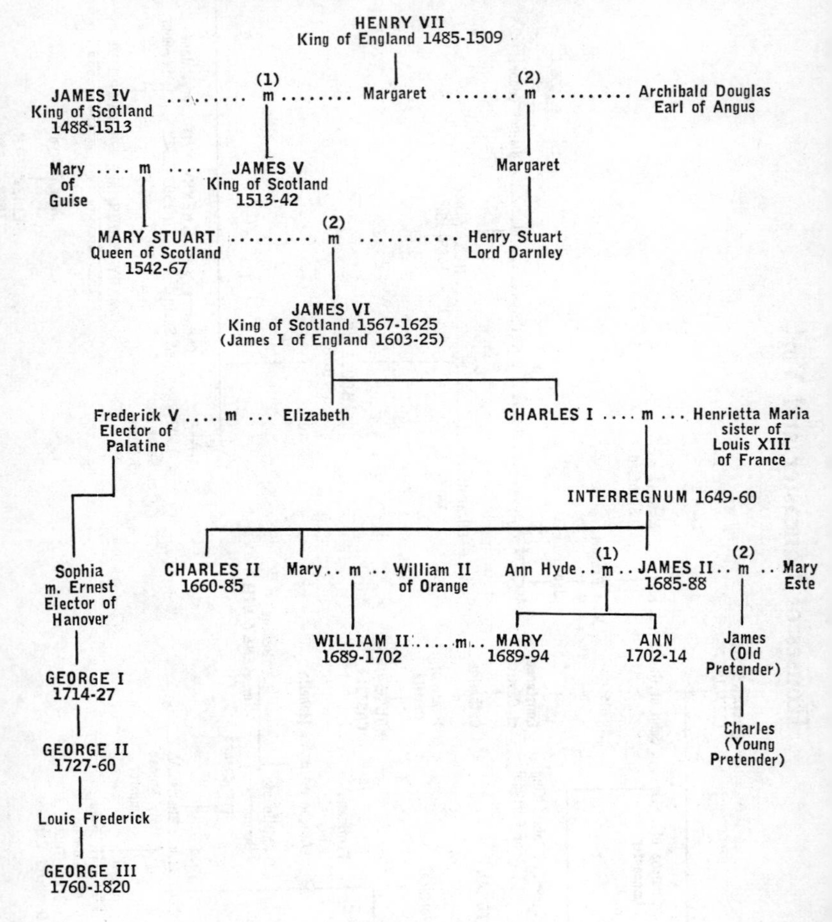

Simplified Genealogical Table

House of Hanover-Windsor

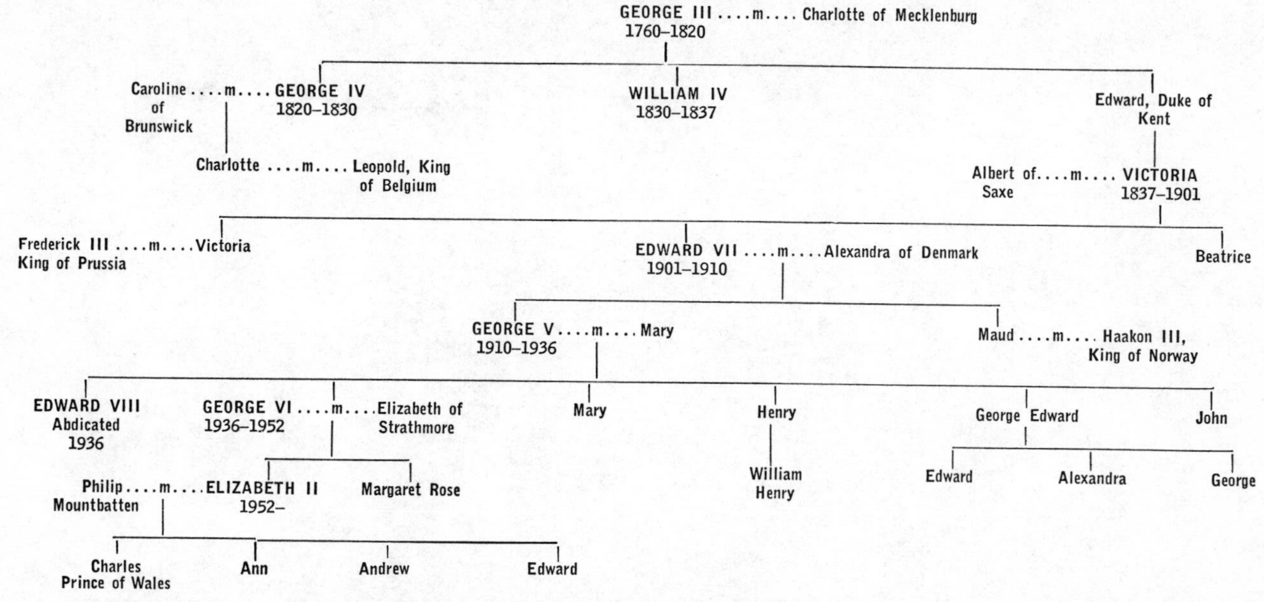

APPENDIX II

Roman Emperors

27 B.C.–14 A.D.	Augustus
14–37	Tiberius
37–41	Caligula
41–54	Claudius
54–68	Nero
68–69	Galba
69	Otho
69	Vitellius
69–79	Vespasian
79–81	Titus
81–96	Domitian
96–98	Nerva
98–117	Trajan
117–138	Hadrian
138–161	Antoninus Pius
161–180	Marcus Aurelius
161–169	Lucius Verus
180–192	Commodus
193	Pertinax
193	Didius Julian
193–211	Septimius
211–217	Caracalla
209–211	Geta
217–218	Marcus Opellius
218–222*	Marcus Varius
222–235	Alexander
235–238	Maximin
237–238	Gordian
238	Pupienus
238	Balbinus
238–244	Gordian II
244–249	Philip
249–251	Decius Gaius
251–253	Gallus Gaius
252–253	Aemilian
253–259	Valerian
259–268	Gallien
268–270	Claudius II
270–275	Aurelian
275–276	Tacitus
276–282	Probus
281–283	Carus
284–305	Diocletian
286–305	Maximian
305–306	Constantius I
305–311	Galerius
306–307	Servius Flavius
306–312	Maxentius
311–324	Licinius
311–337	Constantine I
337–340	Constantine II
337–361	Constantius II
337–350	Constans
361–363	Julian
363–364	Jovian
364–375	Valentinian I (Rome)
364–378	Valens (Constantine)
375–383	Gratian (Rome)
375–392	Valentinian II (Rome)
379–395	Theodosius (Constantine)
383–388	Maximus
392–394	Eugenius
395–408	Arcadius (Constantine)
395–423	Honorius (Rome)
408–450	Theodosius II (Constantine)
425–454	Valentinian III (Rome)
450–457	Marcian (Constantine)
455	Petronius Flavius (Rome)
455–457	Avietus (Rome)
457–461	Majorian (Rome)
457–474	Leo I (Constantine)
461–465	Servius (Rome)
467–472	Anthemius (Rome)
472	Olybrius (Rome)
473–474	Glicerius (Rome)
473–475	Julius (Rome)
473–474	Leo II (Constantine)
474–491	Zeno (Constantine)
475–476	Romulus (Rome)

* Overlapping dates are indicative of disputed reigns when two or more individuals claimed office.

Eastern Emperors

474–491	Zeno
491–518	Anastasius
518–527	Justin
527–565	Justinian
565–578	Justin II
578–582	Tiberius
582–602	Mauritius
602–610	Phocius
610–641	Heraclius
641	Constantine III
641	Heracleon
641–668	Constans II
668–685	Constantine IV
685–695	Justinian II
695–698	Leontius
698–705	Tiberius III
705–711	Justinian II*
711–713	Philippicus
713–715	Anastasius II
715–717	Theodosius III
717–741	Leo III
741–775	Constantine V
775–780	Leo IV
780–797	Constantine VI
797–802	Irene
802–811	Niciphorus
811	Stauracius
811–813	Michael I
813–820	Leo V
820–829	Michael II
829–842	Theophilus I
842–867	Michael III
842–866	Bardas
867	Theophilus II
867–886**	Basil
886–912	Leo VI
912–913	Alexander III
913–959	Constantine VII
919–944	Romanus
959–963	Romanus II
963–1025	Basil II
963–969	Nicephorus II
969–976	John I
1025–1028	Constantine VIII
1028–1050	Zoe
1028–1034	Romanus III
1034–1041	Michael IV
1041–1042	Michael V
1042–1054	Constantine IX
1054–1056	Theodora
1056–1057	Michael VI
1057–1059	Isaac I
1059–1067	Constantine X
1067	Andronicus
1067	Constantine XI
1067–1071	Romanus IV
1071–1078	Michael VIII
1078–1081	Nicephorus III
1081–1118	Alexius I
1118–1143	John II
1143–1180	Manuel I
1180–1183	Alexius II
1182–1185	Andronicus I
1185–1195	Isaac II
1195–1203	Alexius III
1203–1204	Isaac II *
1204	Alexius IV
1204	Alexius V

Frankish (Crusader) Emperors

1204–1205	Baldwin I
1205–1216	Henry
1216–1217	Peter of Courtenay
1218–1228	Robert
1228–1261	Baldwin II

Nicaean Emperors

1206–1222	Theodore I
1222–1254	John
1254–1259	Theodore II
1259–1261	John IV
1259–1261	Michael VIII
1261–1282	Michael VIII
1282–1328	Andronicus II
1295–1320	Michael IX
1328–1342	Andronicus III
1342–1347	John V
1347–1354	John VI
1355–1376	John V*
1376–1379	Andronicus IV
1379–1391	John V*
1390	John VII
1391–1425	Manuel II
1425–1448	John VIII
1448–1453	Constantine XIII

* Restored.

** Time overlap due to disputed succession.

Holy Roman Emperors

800–814 Charlemagne
814–840 Louis I
840–855 Lothaire
855–875 Louis II
875–877 Charles II
877–887 Charles III
891–894 Guido
892–899 Lambert and Guido
896–901 Arnalf
901–905 Louis III
905–924 Barangar
924–926 Rudolph
926–945 Hugh
945–950 Lothaire III
952–962 Barangar

German Line

911–918 Conrad I
918–936 Henry I
936–973 Otto I
973–983 Otto II
983–1002 Otto III
1002–1024 Henry II
1024–1039 Conrad II
1039–1056 Henry III
1056–1106 Henry IV
1077–1080* Rudolph
1081–1093 Herman
1093–1101 Conrad
1106–1125 Henry V
1125–1137 Lothaire II
1138–1152 Conrad III
1152–1190 Frederick Barbarossa
1190–1197 Henry VI
1198–1212 Otto IV
1198–1208* Philip II
1212–1250 Frederick II
1246–1247* Henry Rasp
1247–1256 William
1250–1254 Conrad IV
1257–1273 Richard
1273–1291 Rudolph
1292–1298 Adolph I
1298–1308 Albrecht
1308–1313 Henry VII
1314–1347 Louis IV
1325–1330* Frederick
1347–1378 Charles IV
1347–1349* Gunther
1378–1400 Wentzel
1400–1410 Rupert
1410–1437 Sigmund
1410–1411* Job
1438–1439 Albrecht II
1440–1493 Frederick III
1493–1519 Maximilian I
1519–1556 Charles V
1558–1564 Ferdinand I
1564–1576 Maximilian II
1576–1612 Rudolph II
1612–1619 Mathias
1619–1637 Ferdinand II
1637–1657 Ferdinand III
1658–1705 Leopold I
1705–1711 Joseph I
1711–1740 Charles VI
1742–1745 Charles VII
1745–1765 Francis I
1765–1790 Joseph II
1790–1792 Leopold II
1792–1806 Francis II

Roman Popes

?42–?67 Peter
?67–?79 Linus
?79–?90 Anacletus I
?90–?99 Clement I
99–?107 Evaristus
107–116 Alexander I
116–125 Sixtus I
125–136 Telesphorus
136–140 Hyginus
140–154 Pius I
154–165 Anicetus
165–174 Soter
174–189 Eleutherius
189–198 Victor I
198–217 Zephrynus
217–222 Calixtus
222–230 Urban I
230–235 Pontian
235–236 Anterus
236–250 Fabian

* Disputed successions and rivals.

250–253	Cornelius
253–254	Lucius I
254–257	Stephen I
257–258	Sixtus II
259–268	Dionysius
269–274	Felix I
275–283	Eutychian
283–296	Caius
296–304	Marcellinus
308–309	Marcellus I
309–311	Eusebius
311–314	Melchiades
314–335	Sylvester I
336	Marcus
337–352	Julius I
352–366	Liberius
366–384	Damasus I
384–398	Siricius
398–401	Anastasius I
402–417	Innocent I
417–418	Zosimus
418–422	Boniface I
422–432	Celestine I
432–440	Sixtus III
440–461	Leo I
461–468	Hilarius
468–483	Simplicius
483–492	Felix II
492–496	Galasius I
496–498	Anastasius II
498–514	Symmachus
514–523	Hormisdas
523–526	John I
526–530	Felix III
530–532	Boniface II
533–535	John II
535–536	Agapetus I
536–538	Silverius
538–555	Vigilius
556–561	Pelagius I
561–574	John III
575–579	Benedict I
579–590	Pelagius II
590–604	Gregory I
604–606	Sabinianus
607	Boniface III
608–615	Boniface IV
615–618	Deusdedit
619–625	Boniface V
625–638	Honorius I
638–640	Severinus
640–642	John IV
642–649	Theodore I
649–655	Martin I
655–657	Eugene I
657–672	Vitalian
672–676	Adeodatus
676–678	Donus
678–681	Agatho
682–683	Leo II
684–685	Benedict II
685–686	John V
686–687	Conon
687–701	Sergius I
701–705	John VI
705–707	John VII
708	Sisinnius
708–715	Constantine
715–731	Gregory II
731–741	Gregory III
741–752	Zacharias
752	Stephen II
752–757	Stephen III
757–767	Paul I
768–772	Stephen IV
772–795	Adrian I
795–816	Leo III
816–817	Stephen V
817–824	Paschal I
824–827	Eugene II
827	Valentine
827–844	Gregory IV
844–847	Sergius II
847–855	Leo IV
855–858	Benedict III
858–867	Nicholas I
867–872	Adrian II
872–882	John VIII
882–884	Martin II
884–885	Adrian III
885–891	Stephen VI
891–896	Formosus
896	Boniface VI
896–897	Stephen VII
897	Romanus
897	Theodore II
898–900	John IX
900–903	Benedict IV
903	Leo V
903–904	Christopher
904–911	Sergius III
911–913	Anastasius III
913–914	Lando
914–928	John X

928	Leo VI	1198–1216	Innocent III
929–931	Stephen VIII	1216–1227	Honorius III
931–936	John XI	1227–1241	Gregory IX
936–939	Leo VII	1241	Celestine IV
939–942	Stephen IX	1243–1254	Innocent IV
942–946	Martin III	1254–1261	Alexander IV
946–955	Agapetus II	1261–1264	Urban IV
955–963	John XII	1265–1268	Clement IV
963–965	Leo VIII	1268–1276	Gregory X
965	Benedict V	1276	Innocent V
965–972	John XIII	1276	Adrian V
973–974	Benedict VI	1276–1277	John XX
974–983	Benedict VII	1277–1280	Nicholas III
983–984	John XIV	1281–1285	Martin IV
984–985	Boniface VII	1285–1287	Honorius IV
985–996	John XV	1288–1292	Nicholas IV
996–999	Gregory V	1294	Celestine V
999–1003	Sylvester II	1294–1303	Boniface VIII
1003	John XVII	1303–1304	Benedict IX
1003–1009	John XVIII	1305–1314	Clement V
1009–1012	Sergius IV	1316–1334	John XXI
1012–1024	Benedict VIII	1334–1342	Benedict XII
1024–1032	John XIX	1342–1352	Clement VI
1032–1045	Benedict IX	1352–1362	Innocent VI
1045–1046	Gregory VI	1362–1370	Urban V
1046–1047	Clement II	1370–1378	Gregory XI
1048	Damasus II	1378–1389	Urban VI
1049–1054	Leo IX	1389–1404	Boniface IX
1055–1057	Victor II	1404–1406	Innocent VII
1057–1058	Stephen X	1406–1415	Gregory XII
1058–1059	Benedict X	1409–1410	Alexander V
1059–1061	Nicholas II	1410–1415	John XXII
1061–1073	Alexander II	1417–1431	Martin V
1073–1085	Gregory VII	1431–1447	Eugene IV
1087	Victor III	1447–1455	Nicholas V
1088–1099	Urban II	1455–1458	Calixtus III
1099–1118	Paschal II	1458–1464	Pius II
1118–1119	Galasius II	1464–1471	Paul II
1119–1124	Calixtus II	1471–1484	Sixtus IV
1124–1130	Honorius II	1484–1492	Innocent VIII
1130–1143	Innocent II	1492–1503	Alexander VI
1143–1144	Celestine II	1503	Pius III
1144–1145	Lucius II	1503–1513	Julius II
1145–1153	Eugene III	1513–1521	Leo X
1153–1154	Anastasius IV	1522–1523	Adrian VI
1154–1159	Adrian IV	1523–1534	Clement VII
1159–1181	Alexander III	1534–1549	Paul III
1181–1185	Lucius III	1550–1555	Julius III
1185–1187	Urban III	1555	Marcellus II
1187	Gregory VIII	1555–1559	Paul IV
1187–1191	Clement III	1559–1565	Pius IV
1191–1198	Celestine III	1566–1572	Pius V

1572–1585	Gregory XIII
1585–1590	Sixtus V
1590	Urban VII
1590–1591	Gregory XIV
1591	Innocent IX
1592–1605	Clement VIII
1605	Leo IX
1605–1621	Paul V
1621–1623	Gregory XV
1623–1644	Urban VIII
1644–1655	Innocent X
1655–1667	Alexander VII
1667–1669	Clement IX
1670–1676	Clement X
1676–1689	Innocent XI
1689–1691	Alexander VIII
1691–1700	Innocent XII
1700–1721	Clement XI
1721–1724	Innocent XIII
1724–1730	Benedict XIII
1730–1740	Clement XII
1740–1758	Benedict XIV
1758–1769	Clement XIII
1769–1774	Clement XIV
1775–1799	Pius VI
1800–1823	Pius VII
1823–1829	Leo XII
1829–1830	Pius VIII
1831–1846	Gregory XVI
1846–1878	Pius IX
1878–1903	Leo XIII
1903–1914	Pius X
1914–1922	Benedict XV
1922–1939	Pius XI
1939–1958	Pius XII
1959–1963	John XXIII
1963-	Paul VI

English Monarchs

871–899	Alfred
899–924	Edward
924–939	Ethelstan
939–946	Edmund
946–955	Edred
955–959	Edwig
959–975	Edgar
975–978	Edward
978–1016	Fthelred
1016	Edmund
1017–1035	Canute
1035–1040	Harold
1040–1042	Harthacanute
1042–1066	Edward
1066	Harold
1066–1087	William I
1087–1100	William II
1100–1135	Henry I
1135–1154	Stephen
1154–1189	Henry II
1189–1199	Richard I
1199–1216	John
1216–1272	Henry III
1272–1307	Edward I
1307–1327	Edward II
1327–1377	Edward III
1377–1399	Richard II
1399–1413	Henry IV
1413–1422	Henry V
1422–1461	Henry VI
1461–1483	Edward IV
1483	Edward V
1483–1485	Richard III
1485–1509	Henry VII
1509–1547	Henry VIII
1547–1553	Edward VI
1553–1558	Mary
1558–1603	Elizabeth
1603–1625	James I
1625–1649	Charles I
1649–1660	Interregnum
1660–1685	Charles II
1685–1688	James II
1689–1702	William III and Mary
1702–1714	Anne
1714–1727	George I
1727–1760	George II
1760–1820	George III
1820–1830	George IV
1830–1837	William IV
1837–1901	Victoria
1901–1910	Edward VII
1910–1936	George V
1936	Edward VIII
1936–1952	George VI
1952–	Elizabeth II

English Ministries

Robert Walpole, 1721–1742
John Carteret, 1742–1743
Henry Pelham, 1743–1754
Duke of Newcastle, 1754–1756
William Pitt, 1756–1757
William Pitt and the Duke of Newcastle, 1757–1761
Lord Bute, 1761–1763
George Grenville, 1763–1765
Lord Rockingham, 1765–1766
William Pitt, 1766–1768
Duke of Grafton, 1768–1770
Lord North, 1770–1782
Lord Rockingham, 1782
Lord Shelburne, 1782–1783
Charles Fox and Lord North, 1783
William Pitt, (Younger) 1783–1801
Henry Addington, 1801–1804
William Pitt (Younger) 1804–1806
Charles Fox, 1806–1807
Duke of Portland, 1807–1809
Spencer Perceval, 1809–1812
Lord Liverpool, 1812–1827
George Canning, 1827
Lord Goderich, 1827
Duke of Wellington, 1828–1830
Earl Grey, 1830–1834
Lord Melbourne, 1834
Robert Peel, 1834–1835
Lord Melbourne, 1835–1841
Robert Peel, 1841–1846
John Russell, 1846–1852
Lord Derby and Benjamin Disraeli, 1852
Lord Aberdeen, 1852–1855
Lord Palmerston, 1855–1858
Derby and Disraeli, 1858–1859
Palmerston, 1859–1865
Russell, 1865–1866
Derby and Disraeli, 1866–1868
William Gladstone, 1868–1874
Disraeli, 1874–1880
Gladstone, 1880–1885
Lord Salisbury, 1885–1886
Gladstone, 1886
Salisbury, 1886–1892
Gladstone, 1892–1894
Lord Rosebery, 1894–1895
Salisbury, 1895–1902
Arthur Balfour, 1902–1905
Henry Campbell-Bannerman, 1905–1908

Herbert Asquith, 1908–1916
David Lloyd George, 1916–1922
Andrew Bonar Law, 1922–1923
Stanley Baldwin, 1923–1924
Ramsay MacDonald, 1924
Baldwin, 1924–1929
MacDonald, 1929–1931 (Labor); 1931–1935 (National)
Baldwin, 1935–1937
Neville Chamberlain, 1937–1940
Winston Churchill, 1940–1945
Clement Atlee, 1945–1950
Winston Churchill, 1950–1955
Anthony Eden, 1955-1957
Harold Macmillan, 1957-1963
Douglas Home, 1963-1964
Harold Wilson, 1964